MARTIN LUTHER

THE MAN AND THE IMAGE

BY

Herbert David Rix

IRVINGTON PUBLISHERS, INC.
551 FIFTH AVENUE NEW YORK, N.Y. 10017

Library of Congress Cataloging in Publication Data

Rix, Herbert David, 1908-
   Martin Luther: the man and the image.

   Includes index.
   1. Luther, Martin, 1483-1546. 2. Reformation--
Biography. I. Title.
BR325.R65   284.1'092'4 (B)   82-15270
ISBN 0-8290-0554-4   AACR2

Printed in the United States of America

CONTENTS

            ILLUSTRATIONS

FOREWORD

The popular image of Martin Luther, shaped by the demands of patriotic sentiment and religious zeal, bears little resemblance to the character revealed by a thoroughgoing analysis of the historical data. A relatively minor part of the available material on Luther is exploited by most biographers, who concentrate on the period up to his mid forties and virtually ignore the remainder of his life (he died at 62).

The aim of this book is two-fold: to portray Luther's character at successive stages of his career and to account for his psychic development with the aid of concepts from such disciplines as modern psychiatry and theology. Much of this background material appears in the first three chapters, which carry the story of Martin's life to the episode of his stay at the Wartburg castle, where in May 1521, aged 37, he went into hiding to escape the fate of a condemned heretic. Chapters 4 to 7, primarily topical in arrangement, depict Luther in action during the 1520s against whomever or whatever he perceived as a threat to his security, and the last three chapters reveal what he became during the 1530s and 1540s. Readers interested primarily in the portrait of Luther rather than the theological or psychiatric elucidations may prefer, after reading the Introduction, to turn next to one or another of the later chapters. Readers who wish to preserve their faith in the conventional Luther image are advised to close the book at this point.

The principal indebtedness of the student of Luther is to the editors of the Weimar edition of the complete works. The five years or so an interested scholar must spend in familiarizing himself with this immense store of material seem brief in comparison with the hundreds of thousands of hours devoted by the Weimar editors over the past century to making it available. I am happy to acknowledge the courtesy of the librarians of the former Hartford Seminary Foundation and of the Yale University libraries (Sterling, Divinity School and Medical School) in permitting me to use their collections. Also I wish to express my gratitude to Professor Paul Hacker of the University of Muenster for some enlightening conversations and to Emerita Professor J. B. Ross of Vassar College for reading portions of the manuscript and making helpful suggestions. From the enormous secondary literature I should like to single out the study of Luther made by Dr. Paul J. Reiter (see the Introduction) in the 1930s, now somewhat outdated owing to subsequent advances in psychiatry, which inspired my own examination of the Luther record. The translations given here of Luther's utterances and those of various of his contemporaries are largely my responsibility.

Note: As a representative exhibit of present-day Luther cult positions and attitudes, the final chapter of I. D. K. Siggins' *Luther* (New York, 1972) deserves mention. This work contains an extensive bibliography.

CHRONOLOGY

1483   Luther born at Eisleben 10 Nov.; family later moves to Mansfeld

1498   In school at Eisenach; friendship with John Braun

1501   Enters University of Erfurt; A.B. 1502; M.A. 1505

1505   Begins study of law at Erfurt; switches to Augustinian monastery

1506   Makes monastic vows; ordained to priesthood 1507 and says first mass

1508   Teaching and study at Wittenberg; later recalled to Erfurt

1510   In Rome to assist with a problem of his monastic community

1512   Granted doctorate in theology at Wittenberg

1513   Begins career as lecturer on Scripture at Wittenberg

1515   Elected to 3-year term as district vicar of his order

1517   Sends protest on indulgence traffic and copy of 95 Theses to Archbishop of Mainz, who initiates heresy prosecution

1518   Begins writing for public; 15 publications in 1518. At Augsburg to answer heresy charge; Melanchthon arrives in Wittenberg

1519   Debates with John Eck at Leipzig on papal power; publishes innovations on theology of sacraments; 22 publications

1520   Further embroilment with ecclesiastical authority; promulgation of *Exsurge Domine* in Rome is followed by open attack on the Church; psychotic symptoms appear by midsummer; 25 publications

1521   Summoned to Diet of Worms before Charles V; excommunicated for heresy and put under ban of Empire; hides in Wartburg Castle in May; clandestine visit to Wittenberg in Dec.; 24 publications

1522   Returns to Wittenberg early March; first clash with Carlstadt; attacks Henry VIII and the German bishops; German version of N. T. appears in Sept.; 10 publications

1523   Resumes Scripture lectures; initiates translation of O. T. and campaign to ban the mass in Castle Church; aids in 'escape' of nuns from Nimbschen convent; proselytizing letter to Duke of Savoy; 21 publications

1524   Tract against Muentzer; encounters parishioners of Orlamuende; Carlstadt forced into exile; 15 publications

1525   Tracts against Carlstadt (Jan.) and Erasmus (Dec.); views area of Peasants Revolt in April-May; attacks peasants; weds Catherine in June; letters to Henry VIII (Sept.) and Duke George (Dec.); 17 publications

1526   First child — Hans — born 7 June; 12 publications

1527   Answers attack by Henry VIII; long tract against Zwingli; severe depression July to early 1528; remains in Wittenberg during plague epidemic. Daughter Elizabeth born 10 Dec. (dies Aug. 1528)

1528   New tract against Zwingli; visits parishes in Nov.; 8 publications

1529   Tract against Duke George; Catechisms — Large and Small; birth of Magdalene 4 May; to Marburg for conference with Zwingli and Philip of Hesse in Sept.-Oct.; 10 publications

1530   Attacks Wittenberg congregation in New Year's sermon; refuses to visit father in Feb.; to Coburg in April for Diet of Augsburg, returning 13 Oct.; 18 publications

1531   Involved in Zwickau parish dispute, March-Aug.; attacks Augsburg decrees; refuses deathbed visit to mother in May; lectures on Galatians in summer; son Martin born 9 Nov.; 8 publications

1532   For next several years often incapacitated by dizzy spells, headache, attacks of stone, etc.; severe anxiety attack 16 May. During 1532-34 preached only about once a month in church, more often in his residence; for years 1532-1536 published only a dozen rather brief tracts

1533   Reacts to Duke George's charge of 'renegade monk'; son Paul born 28 January; last child Margaret born 17 Dec. 1534

1537   Serious illness at Smalkalden conference of schismatic governments in Feb.-March; persecution of Agricola as 'Antinomian' begins July

1538   George Karg imprisoned at Wittenberg in Jan. for rejecting Luther's theology; harassment of Simon Lemnius in June

1539   Reaction to proposed Council of Trent: "On Councils and Churches"

1540   Bigamy of Philip of Hesse; at Eisenach June-July for conference on bigamy; after return to Wittenberg Sunday sermons virtually cease until 1544, thereafter average 2 a month; Agricola flees Saxony

1541   Attack on Duke of Brunswick in "Against Hans Wurst"

1542   Prepares unconventional will

1543   Antisemitic tracts: "Against the Jews and Their Lies," etc.

1545   Attack on papacy: "Against the Papacy at Rome," publication of anti-papal cartoons; Preface to Latin writings; travels about Saxony in July-Aug.; to Mansfeld in Oct. and Dec.

1546   To Eisleben 23 Jan.; dies there suddenly 18 Feb.

For an exhaustive chronology of Luther's activities, writings, correspondence, etc., the following books, which provided the information for the above chronology, are invaluable:

Georg Buchwald, *Luther-Kalendarium* (Leipzig, 1929)

Gustav Kawerau, *Verzeichnis von Luthers Schriften,* 2nd rev. ed. by Otto Clemen (Leipzig, 1928)

INTRODUCTION

In his *Life and Letters of Martin Luther* Preserved Smith remarked that of the more than 2000 books and a similar number of articles written on Luther by 1910 most "are now useless."[1] To update this statement to the last quarter of the century, only the numbers need be changed. That is, if by 'useful' is meant a treatment of Luther that delineates his actual character and motivations. A number of obstacles have conspired to prevent the realizing of this goal.

First off, there is the enormous mass of Luther's utterances, written and oral, reproduced in the Weimar edition of the complete works, which began publication in 1883 and is still not quite finished. One of the editors of this scholarly compilation, Karl Meissinger, refers to this heritage as a calamity, wishing it could be reduced to a fifth of its bulk, for to complete a meaningful survey of it is the labor of many years.[2] Luther's published writings and scriptural commentaries along with records of his university lectures and sermons fill more than 65 of the large Weimar volumes. In addition there are the numerous volumes of his correspondence, Table Talk and biblical translations. In a given generation, the scholars who accomplish the task specified by Messinger — and no one else is in a position to know much about the real Luther — are greatly outnumbered by authors who beguile an unsuspecting public with their ill-founded opinions about him.

An even more serious difficulty arises from the maldistribution of Luther's literary remains over his lifetime. An indispensable source of information for the study of a character such as Luther is his correspondence. A fair proportion of this has survived, amounting to about 2600 letters. But this number is very heavily weighted toward his later years. For the first decade after he entered a monastery in 1505 at the age of 21, not even ten letters are extant. It is not until 1518, following the notoriety he achieved from the 95 Indulgence

1

Theses, that we begin to have a substantial number of his letters, in all about 90 for that year. And by that time much of the most interesting part of his development was behind him.

During the interval of more than a dozen years from age 21 to 34, this most famous of German writers wrote little for publication, 1518 being the year his writing career effectively began. The principal source of information for the course of Luther's mental development prior to 1518 is found in the records of his university lectures on Scripture, which date from 1513 on. Since none of this material was published until modern times (the very important lecture course on Paul's Epistle to the Romans in 1908), it was not possible for interested scholars to undertake a meaningful analysis of the history of Luther's inner life until well into the 20th century. Luther's recorded reminiscences for the period before 1518 date mainly from the years after 1530 when his personality had undergone a radical change. The unreliability of these reminiscences compounds the difficulty arising from the scantiness of the contemporary record for the period of his major development.

A third factor that has blocked understanding of Luther's character was pointed out by the eminent French historian Lucien Febvre. In a brief but perceptive biography of Luther published in 1927 he observed that a psychology needed for describing Luther's abnormalities was not yet available though it would doubtless be produced in the future.[3] At that very date the key role played by anxiety in disorders like Luther's was becoming recognized. Less than a decade later an important theoretical monograph[4] appeared on the unconscious defense mechanisms, which were thereafter given extensive investigation.[5] With the continuing advances made in the understanding of emotional illness by clinical psychiatrists, formulation of the new psychology forecast by Febvre was under way around mid-century.

The fact of Luther's psychic disorder was discussed privately by his intimates at Wittenberg and also recognized by some of his more discerning contemporaries outside the inner circle. The first important attempt in modern times to deal with his symptoms was a two volume work by a Copenhagen psychiatrist, Dr. Paul J. Reiter, published in 1937-41: *Luther's Environment, Character and Psychosis.*[6] In this study Reiter identified Luther's severe depressive breakdown in 1527 as a major psychotic episode and also diagnosed the manic symptoms of earlier years along with other periods of depression. Reiter's contribution was to provide a professional interpretation of a substantial amount of data from the Luther record in terms of the psychiatric concepts available in the 1930s.

Two of the commercially successful books on Luther published in the U.S.A. in the 1950s (and elsewhere in translation) show an acquaintance with Reiter's work. The earlier of these, a conventional biography by the Rev. Roland H. Bainton,[7] is an attempt to demonstrate the familiar Luther-cult thesis that Luther was a religious genius with a divine commission to restore true religion to a society misled by the erroneous teachings of the decadent church of his day. Bainton's allusions in his opening chapter and elsewhere in his book to the depressions and manic symptoms described by Reiter show him to be completely at sea with this material. Bainton is most reluctant to admit that Luther's psychic disorder was pathological and attributes the condition to a greater than average sensitivity to the baneful religious teachings inflicted on him in childhood. Bainton does recognize that Luther's emotional abnormalities persisted as strong as ever after he escaped from the influence of the teachings, a puzzling matter Bainton is at a loss to account for.

The other book, a psychoanalytic essay by Erik H. Erikson,[8] is on the surface a totally different sort of work from Bainton's. It too was written to demonstrate a thesis: that in his youth Luther suffered an identity crisis. When he began his task Erikson, it appears, was unaware that for the period of interest the Luther record is exceptionally barren and he scanned "thousands of pages of the literature on Luther" fruitlessly seeking evidence for the postulated identity crisis. Instead of making a systematic examination of Luther's works (as Reiter had done) Erikson proceeded on the bold assumption that from a perusal of books about Luther by authors who had failed to understand his psychic constitution he could himself — by virtue of his acknowledged command of psychoanalytical theory — provide a solution of the mystery of Luther's behavior. On the slight foundation he derived from these secondary sources Erikson erected an imposing speculative apparatus, equipping Luther with a variety of crises and the Oedipus complex which is *de rigueur* for these occasions. Being quite unversed in the ways of historical research, he tried to accomplish in one year what a properly qualified scholar could hardly achieve in five, and was baffled by such a key problem as Luther's actual relation to his mother. The basic irresponsibility of this work, which provoked a critique by Bainton, is symbolized in its characterizing Luther on one page as a "colossal crybaby" and on another as possessing a total self-discipline that rarely broke down. Since essentially what Erikson did in *Young Man Luther* was to psychoanalyze the imaginative image propagated by the modern Luther cult, his book evidently belongs with the "more than 2000" referred to by Preserved Smith.

A fourth obstacle hindering an accurate description of Luther's personality is that valid interpretation of the data demands a multidisciplinary approach. The disciplines that must be controlled include those dealing with contemporary cultural, social and political

conditions, with ecclesiastical matters both theological and institu-
tional, with Scripture criticism and exegesis, and with clinically
established descriptions of neurotic and psychotic symptoms and
dynamisms. A narrower approach, no matter how well intentioned,
can result in little more than a retouching of the traits of the
legendary image. A writer such as R.L. Fife in his scholarly study,
The Revolt of Martin Luther,[9] who foregoes a detailed analysis of
Luther's problems with theology and Scripture, problems which lie
at the heart of his inner conflicts, thereby cuts himself off from any
significant understanding of Luther's psyche.

A notable instance of how this inadequacy of background has affected the appreciation of Luther's personality during his monastic
period shows up in the lack of attention to his early preoccupation
with the teachings of the "Imitation of Christ" by Thomas a Kempis
(see Ch. 1). Indeed, prominent Luther scholars have denied he even
knew the work,[10] despite its immense popularity in monastic circles
in the generation preceding his birth and long thereafter. An examination of his earlier academic lectures and sermons, as well as
later productions, shows that Luther took from this little work —
which is itself steeped in biblical themes and language — more
perhaps than from any other book save the Bible itself. The profound transformation in Luther's theological outlook during the
years 1518-20 is mirrored in his step-by-step repudiation of key
teachings of the "Imitation of Christ" at this time, culminating in a
half-regretful reproach to its once admired author in a sermon of the
spring of 1521. (Concurrently there was a similar, little publicized
parting from another former mentor — Augustine.) Allied to this
ignoring of Luther's one-time concern with the most famous piece of
spiritual writing of the later middle ages is the state of confusion regarding Luther's fabled "Tower Experience" (see Ch. 9), for which
dates have been suggested anywhere from 1508 to 1519.

An even more striking instance of the effect of a too narrowly
based approach is seen in the failure of nearly all modern Luther
scholars to deal with the remarkable falsifications in Luther's works.
Beginning about mid-1520 and increasing in volume over the remaining years of his lifetime, there appear in his utterances thousands of
false statements with regard particularly to ecclesiastical teachings,
Scripture and monastic life. A well informed contemporary observer
personally acquainted with Luther, who collected and read his writings as they were published, remarked about this trait in the later
1520s, declaring Luther would stop at no lie (See Ch. 7). When at the
beginning of the 20th century the learned medieval scholar Henry
Denifle rediscovered this unexampled mass of falsehood in the writings of one heralded as a religious paragon, he gave vent to his
outrage by publishing an ill tempered treatise[11] in which the por-

trayal of Luther's character is even farther off the mark than in the standard biographies. But Denifle's reaction was exceptional; the silence most writers on Luther maintain regarding the falsifications implies the absence of a background necessary for evaluating this material.

From recent advances in the understanding of the emotionally disturbed it is now clear that the falsifications for the most part reflect the operation of the unconscious defense mechanisms referred to above and thereby constitute an invaluable key to the interpretation of Luther's psyche. For example, from a patently untrue statement about the gospel according to Matthew he inserted in the first edition of his German N. T. we learn that Luther suffered a serious inner conflict over the contradiction between his *sola fide* doctrine ['by faith alone'] and Scripture (see Ch. 3). This falsification, which has bewildered his commentators, demonstrates his inner turmoil over the contradiction more forcibly than would a candid avowal.

The last of the obstacles in the way of an understanding of Luther to be mentioned here arises from the obscurantist practices of the biographers, who have cooperated in a successful coverup of the real Luther. For the most part they utilize a limited selection of material ranging from his childhood to a point in his early forties (Luther was 41 when he married Catherine von Bora and died at 62) and then taper off rapidly, leaving the last 15 to 20 years nearly blank. For example, the work by Bainton cited above devotes only a half dozen pages of three hundred to the period embracing the entire second half of Luther's professional career. An unofficial but effective censorship is nowadays exercised in Germany, where he is revered as a national hero, to forestall any serious questioning of the popular Luther image. Even a matter of such small intrinsic significance for Luther's character as the story of the posting of the 95 Indulgence Theses on a church door in 1517 is zealously protected. When the fictitious basis of this story was exposed in the 1960s[12] numerous guardians of the image rallied in protest. Academic scholars outside of Germany do not undertake to challenge the image because the enormous investment of time demanded can be spent more profitably on other enterprises.

In the portrait of Luther given here due emphasis is placed on his middle and later years — the most fully documented period of his life. The history of his psychic disorder is presented in some detail for it was this that determined much of his behavior and without it his life story would have been altogether different. The young Luther suffered from a psychoneurosis of which the symptoms became evident during adolescence. A central feature of the neurosis was the experience of terror aroused in him by the belief he was to be eternally damned for his sins by the judgment of a vengeful deity. His theological effort was directed principally to finding an escape from this personal dilemma. How long he might have continued at the neurotic level in the absence of stress from without is problematical. But after about two years of the pressure from the heresy prosecution his neurotic defenses gave way and he developed typical manic-depressive symptoms. About a decade later he began to stabilize in a paranoid condition; the reflection of this paranoid element in his utterances and behavior toward others during the last decade and a half of his life explains why the biographers shy away from the Luther of these years.

Luther's psychic disorder was by no means a merely negative phenomenon though it caused him endless suffering. It is noteworthy that almost everything he wrote for publication was linked − directly or indirectly − to the effect of his emotional disturbance on his experience of religion. As is well known, the heightened sensitivity observed in individuals with a disorder like Luther's who happen to be endowed with a creative talent contributes greatly to their achievement as writers or artists. Likewise the emotional personality associated with the disorder was an important factor in Luther's extraordinary effectiveness as preacher. His *sola fide* doctrine appealed strongly to neurotics with anxieties similar to his, of whom Melanchthon (author of the 'Augsburg Confession') is the best known, and several fellow neurotics formed a supportive circle around him until death. If Luther had enjoyed normal psychic health, then instead of joining a monastic order and becoming involved in religious controversy he would probably have followed the career in law planned for him by his father and made little or no impact on the pages of history.

Chapter 1

The First Decade of Monastic Life

i. An anxiety-ridden youth

Apart from some dates and place names, little is known about Luther's early education. First he attended the village school of Mansfeld, the community to which his parents moved some months after his birth in nearby Eisleben in November 1483. At the age of 13 he was sent to a school in the city of Magdeburg about 50 miles north of his home. The next year he was transferred to another school in the town of Eisenach, which lies 60 miles or more to the southeast of Mansfeld. Here he remained for three years and during this period formed the first of his special attachments with another man to be described below. Since Martin was being prepared to enter college, for which in those days the principal requirement was fluency in Latin – reading, writing and speaking – it would appear he was judged not to be sufficiently adept until the age of 17.

Thereupon he entered the University of Erfurt (1501) and during the ensuing four years he was granted the degrees of Bachelor of Arts and Master of Arts (February 1505). He was now qualified to teach the liberal arts himself, but his father Hans Luther, who thus far had been in charge of planning Martin's career, had destined him for the law instead. Hence when the summer term of the Erfurt law school opened in May, Martin dutifully enrolled in the program of studies that would prepare him to become a lawyer. In taking this step he was not following his own inclination, for the law was perhaps even more unattractive to him than the philosophy he had been forced to struggle with in the liberal arts program. Hans himself had no formal education, but like many an ambitious father so handicapped had dreams of giving to his son what he himself lacked. Of peasant origin, he had left the family farm to seek his fortune in the mining industry. It was to be near the mines that after first settling in Eisleben with his wife Margaret he had presently moved to Mansfeld. There

7

several other children were born of whom six or more lived beyond
infancy, and there Hans advanced to modest affluence and social
position.

After six weeks in law school Martin requested leave to visit his
parental home in Mansfeld, about two days journey (on foot) from
Erfurt. On his return to Erfurt he was overtaken by a thunderstorm when not far from the city, and while terrorized by a very
close lightning discharge (as he later told friends) made a vow to St.
Anne he would become a monk. After announcing this intention to
his associates at the university, he disposed of all his books save
copies of Virgil and Plautus, attended a farewell party a few days
later, and then presented himself for admission to the Erfurt house
of the Augustinian order. It would be desirable to have some contemporary testimony about this drastic change of course, which turned
out to be one of the most serious errors of judgment Martin ever
made. But from what is known about his character one can deduce
with reasonable certainty what happened. While there is no way of
telling how long he had been considering the change, what advice he
took from others and why he selected the Augustinians, we can
nonetheless be sure of his motivation.

He would have planned the move for a period of several months,
for though he was capable of radical changes of outlook he would
first spend a long time coming to a decision. It would appear that out
of respect for his father he would go through the motions of enroll-
ing in the legal curriculum rather than refuse bluntly even to start.
After a trial of some weeks he was in a position to explain he now
knew the law was not for him and he felt impelled to enter the religious life. There must have been a fearful blowup at the family
home when he arrived to report his decision and ask permission to
become a monk. In later years he liked to boast of his stubbornness.
Since Hans was likewise a man of very strong character, there could
be no yielding on either side, and two years afterward when he came
to Erfurt to be present at the celebration of Martin's first mass after
ordination, he seems to have still been reacting to the shock. Martin
had his own way of reacting; it is not improbable that he vowed
never to enter the Mansfeld home again, for there is no indication he
ever went back. As recounted below (Ch. 8), a quarter-century later
he refused deathbed visits to both parents. When death came to
Martin himself during a sojourn in his native land some fifteen years
after his mother's demise, he was staying not in the family home now
in possession of his youngest brother James but at a stranger's house
in Eisleben. As for the story of the thunderstorm and the vow, we
recognize this as a typical Lutherian device for justifying behavior
of which Martin could not be proud, in this instance of flagrant disobedience to his parents. As we shall see, he possessed a remarkable

flair for providing alibis like this. [For an example of the regressed Luther's equivocations about why he became a monk see his letter to Melanchthon of September 9, 1521 and the preface to "Judgment of Monastic Vows" in LW 48, 300-01 and 331-36.] When he appeared before the Augustinian prior some days afterward he would have had to present a much sounder reason for so weighty an undertaking than a vow made in a moment of panic. To complete this part of the narrative, Martin was kept waiting for a period of several weeks for his father's permission, which is said to have been reluctantly granted only after an attack of plague in Mansfeld carried off two of Martin's younger brothers and softened the father's heart.

An explanation of the actual motive which led Martin into the religious life is to be sought in his psychic state at this stage of his career. Since adolescence, as related in a letter dated January 1, 1528 to a friend Gerard Wiskamp, he had been suffering anxiety attacks, followed by periods of depression. Luther provides numerous descriptions of these states, which because of their content he interpreted as 'temptations' (*Anfechtungen* or *tentationes*). In an account written early in 1518 he describes vividly the intense pain he experiences on these occasions:

> I knew a man who declared he himself often endured this suffering, though for very short periods of time. It is so severe and so much like hell that the tongue cannot describe it nor the pen write of it nor one who is without such experience believe in it. It is so great that if it were to continue for a half-hour, nay even the tenth part of an hour, he would perish utterly and his bones be reduced to ashes. At these times God manifests himself in terrible wrath. There is no part of the soul but is filled with the most bitter sorrow, terror, panic, sadness, and these feelings all seem to go on endlessly.[1]

For another account of these states we quote a passage from the "Commentary on the First Twenty-two Psalms" published during the following year (1519), in which Luther comments on the verse: "In death there is no remembrance" (Ps. 6:5):

> What is it like for those who are in death and hell? First, they are cut off from God, and also in a state of eternal blasphemy . . . . They seek a place of refuge and find none. Soon they are overwhelmed by a most burning hatred of God, first wishing there were a different God and then that they themselves did not exist . . . . This enmity and flight from God continue endlessly . . . . These matters are not understood by the carnal, or by any of our inexperienced theologians — as though no one could experience hell because from hell there is no redemption. By such reasoning we may not say Paul experienced the joys of heaven because its bliss

cannot be lost . . . Indeed it is true that in their agony they feel nothing but hell, with no prospect of redemption . . . . What they experience is what takes place in hell; even the hatred and blasphemy of God are about the same.[2]

In both of these passages, though they are presented in the third person because of Luther's comparative reticence at this period, he nevertheless indicates he is speaking from first-hand experience. In each he refers to the experience of Paul ["I knew a man . . ."] related in 2 Cor. 12; at this time Martin has begun to identify strongly with Paul. Also in each he emphasizes that only those with personal experience can describe or understand such states. Later on we shall examine other accounts depicting Luther's awareness of material usually repressed but at times breaking through into his consciousness and exciting these states of terror. At one time or another various of Luther's associates witnessed him during these states, which as anyone knows who has observed such manifestations can reduce a person of ordinarily cheerful mien temporarily into a cringing, pleading caricature of his usual self. Melanchthon reports that Luther once told him the states of terror he experienced in his youth before entering the monastery were similar to those seen by Melanchthon in later years.[3]

It is instructive to observe the increasing frankness of these disclosures in Luther's writings, an indication of the psychic changes taking place in him, especially from 1518 on. At the beginning, his reaction to these experiences would be to try to repress them totally, and that helps account for the absence of disclosure during the early neurotic phase of his disorder. The work in which the first of the two quotations above occurs was one of the last to be written during this phase, that is, before Martin began reacting to the stress of the heresy prosecution that was under way by the summer of 1518. It is significant that in this description Luther avoids a revelation of the content of the anxiety state; such a revelation would be unlikely to occur until the defense mechanism (repression) had lost enough of its effectiveness to permit the undesirable material to intrude more freely into his consciousness. The disclosure in the second quotation, from a work written during the initial period of stress (1519), is introduced not as a confession but only indirectly as a scriptural interpretation.

Two comments may be made on this passage. Coming after the stress of the Augsburg ordeal (see Ch. 2 below), it exceeds in frankness the earlier quotation and now reveals the content of the anxiety states. As for the practice of introducing material from his own experience into an exposition of scriptural tests, this is one of the most pervasive features of Martin's lectures and sermons. It is related to his attempts to find in Scripture an understanding of his psychic problem. It is also related to his desire to identify with the scriptural writer, at first with David, who for Luther is the author of the Psalms, but more especially with Paul. This habit of identifying with a celebrated personality is of course an extremely common trait. But when carried to such extremes as observed in Luther it betokens an immature and insecure personality, being one of the numerous indications of his disorder.

Another source of information about Luther's inner life is to be found in his report of a theological disputation in which he participated at a chapter meeting of his order in Heidelberg during the spring of 1518. This was the period when the Indulgence controversy was beginning to take shape. The following excerpt from the disputation provides more than a hint of the painful experience on which the reported theological conclusion is based:

> What man does not tremble and despair at the thought of death? . . . . Whoever hates death, which is God's will, or at least does not love it, loves God much less than himself, nay *he hates God.* And we are all alike in this.[4]

The way in which Luther abruptly slips in the non-sequitur about hating God is most revealing of his personal problem. The claiming for himself in this deplorable state the fellowship of the entire human race, an early instance of projection, is unusual for him at this date. His extreme fear of death is one of his most prominent character traits. As he remarks elsewhere in the "Commentary on the First Twenty-two Psalms" about the fear of death and the 'temptation' of despair:

> Nothing afflicts us miserable men more frightfully than the terror of death, because as Adam's sons we must all undergo it . . . . Despair is the most grievous of temptations because it provokes a great and eternal hatred of God, blasphemy, cursing, and all the torments of hell, things that are not to be spoken of.[5]

For a direct and completely unabashed revelation of his hatred of God, one may recall the oft quoted remark in the preface to the collected Latin writings of 1545, composed long after his regression: "I hated the righteous God who punishes sinners."

Since by choosing to become a monk Luther appeared willing to add to his already heavy burden the new source of anxiety associated with wilful disobedience to his father (for which he could of course provide an excuse), we conclude that the terror at finding himself in peril of certain damnation because of his 'blasphemous' thoughts was what led him to embrace the monastic way of life as the best means of escaping this fate. An interesting confirmation of this conclusion is provided in the 1531 "Lectures on Galatians," a work which could

well carry the subtitle: "The Confessions of Martin Luther." In a
passage illustrating what goes on within a man who is struggling to
escape from an anxiety attack involving extreme hatred of God, he
represents the man as saying: "If I live longer, I shall amend my life,
or I shall enter the monastery."[6] Inasmuch as this comment is of
most dubious relevance to the verse he is discussing, there is good
reason for believing the passage reflects his own experience.

ii. Difficulties with the monastic way

In view of the intense fear of death and damnation associated with
his psychic disorder, Luther's motive in becoming a monk could be
described as at least to some extent conventional. He was acting on
the conviction originating in the early Christian centuries that the
self-denial of the hermit or monk truly represented the forsaking of
possessions, home and family for which Jesus declared the reward
would be eternal life (Matt. 19:29; Mk. 10:3; Lk. 18:29-30). The violence of Luther's rejection of this scriptural interpretation in later
years after he had also rejected monastic life is no mere case of sour
grapes. Rather it is a pathological reaction to his fear that the aban-
donment of his early ideal would jeopardize his salvation. To the
modern reader it may appear strange that Luther as a young man did
not adopt a simpler (and not uncommon) way out of his predica-
ment by giving up his belief in God, Satan and hell. But this was not
a possible solution for him; all three constituted unremovable
components of his world, however much his view of their theological
content might vary at different stages of his career. They were
integral to his entire outlook, to both his religious faith and his
psychopathology.

In an age when the kind of professional therapy he so badly needed was unheard of, this substitute of a 'religious' solution turned out
at first to be more effective than might have been anticipated. At
least Martin was able to maintain tolerable control of his anxiety for
a decade or more after his entrance into the monastery, and did not
regress into psychosis until after he had replaced the monastic ideal
with what he liked to call evangelical liberty. But basically Luther
was most unsuited for the monastic life, a matter we shall now ex-
plore. For a brief formulation of the monastic ideal we may consult
the twelfth century abbot, Bernard of Clairvaux, one of the most
outstanding figures in Western monasticism and in Luther's day,
judging by the number of editions of his writings, the most widely
read of the Fathers of the Church. Bernard's writings appealed
strongly to the young Luther, who was so captivated by the evident
holiness of this richly endowed personality that he could never forget
Bernard. In the years after 1520 when the recognition of a holiness

such as Bernard's had become hateful to him, he adjusted by replacing his earlier image of the man with a fantasy that constitutes one of his more persistent falsifications.

For Bernard the two-fold aim of the monk is to learn to know himself and to know God.[7] Man is a noble being, even though a sinner, because possessing the gifts of reason and free will, he is created in the image of God. But to realize his magnificent potential he must free himself from the egoism and self-will which have led him away from God and replace them with the charity which is a participation in the life of God. The communal life of the monastery provides an ideal locus for this process of liberation with its opportunities for ascetic self-denial, fraternal charity, humility and prayer. Bernard emphasizes the importance of meditation on Scripture, of imitation of Jesus, who is the perfect image of God, and of the reception of Jesus in the Eucharist as aids in the monk's effort to progress toward a life of union with God. This summary sketch of the monastic ideal, at one time Luther's own goal and later the object of his bitterly hostile vilification, is presented here to help bring out the peculiar problems he faced in trying to meet its challenge.

A major obstacle to Martin's achieving any real success in the monastery was the extremely egocentric character that appears inevitably in those who suffer from a psychic disorder like his. As is well known, one of the most important elements in the formation of a properly integrated personality is the ability to encounter other human beings as persons, to learn from the encounter what is lacking in oneself and, enlightened by this knowledge, to attempt to remedy one's shortcomings. Along with this goes the recognition of the value of the other as a person, a being endowed with the same rights and potential as oneself. For the egocentric personality other people appear not as persons — self-determining beings each with his own aims, capabilities and requirements — but as objects, of interest only insofar as they may either serve his needs or present some sort of threat to his own security. The defect of egocentricity is shared to some extent by all, but in the normal individual it may be reduced or eliminated and, as we have seen, this reduction — the replacement of egoism by the virtue of charity — is one of the prime objects of the monastic discipline. The monastic aim, of course, is not humanistic but religious; in the Christian faith charity or love for others is not merely recommended as desirable but required.

For the pathological egocentric such as Luther — and it must be stressed that he endured this handicap through no fault of his own and that it could be ameliorated if at all only by a therapy not to be discovered until centuries after his death — for such a person this aspect of the monastic ideal was simply inapplicable. He could learn the words that describe the ideal, and as any reader of his Lectures on Romans is aware he describes it quite faithfully, reflecting the teaching of Paul on Christian charity. The fact that there was never any real adaptation of his own person to the ideal would not occasion much comment; this is perhaps the most difficult problem in Christian living and there would be plenty of fellow monks displaying a comparable lack of progress.

A second characteristic of one afflicted with a psychic disorder such as Martin's that would render him essentially unfit for monastic life is an extreme dislike for externally imposed restraints. Since in agreeing to live according to a monastic rule the postulant has to accept a number of potentially onerous restraints of which he would otherwise be free, it is evident that Luther was inviting a special sort of unhappiness when at the age of 22 he promised to live according to the rule of the Augustinian order. The record does not show his reaction to these restraints during the first decade in the convent, but by 1516, when we begin to have some data, it is apparent that this aspect of his profession is a source of grief. From all the noise he made about monastic vows in later years, one is given the impression that the vow of chastity is central to the monastic way, but this is not the fact. The really difficult vow is obedience to a superior because this involves giving up what in a sense constitutes the human person, namely, the power of choice.

In comparison with these two handicaps to the fulfilling of his monastic commitment, the one we shall describe next is far more serious in that it also prevented him from realizing an authentic religious life. In one of his minor treatises Augustine asserts that

> the capacity to have faith like the capacity to have love belongs to man's nature, but to have faith even as to have love belongs to the grace of believers.[8]

In formulating this teaching Augustine had in mind the normal human being; he did not allow for the unfortunate individual who lacks the capacity to love God. Now such an unfortunate was Martin Luther.

He exhibits a variety of responses to his awareness of this condition. In the Lectures on Romans (1515-16) where the subject is discussed more frequently than elsewhere in his works, he expresses the view that in this life only the saints — such as Bernard — are privileged to experience love for God (9:3).[9] Others must wait until death for this grace (4:7), a view he repeats in the "Commentary on the First Twenty-two Psalms" (Ps. 6:2). In accord with his personal experience, at this period he associates love of God with tribulations. Martin's customary silence about a man's awareness of God's love for him is likewise significant in this connection. His own experience is rather of a wrathful God who must be appeased. A somewhat different approach can be found in the disputations where Luther appears as academic theologian. In a 1517 disputation[10] he proposes the argument that man, being a sinner, can not possibly love God. We noted above a thesis of the 1518 Heidelberg disputation in which this position is reenforced with the statement that all men hate God.

To corroborate our conclusion about Luther's unhappy plight, we look ahead to the early 1520s, the period of his regression, and observe the application of the denial mechanism to the scriptural injunction about loving God with one's whole heart and soul (Matt. 22:37). The following passage is taken from a 1523 sermon, in which Luther deals with the 'greatest commandment.' Here we see him engaging in a major falsification of a key scriptural utterance.

> To love God as he is in his majesty is not of this world and God does not ask it of us. Love God in his creatures; he does not want you to love him in his majesty. What need does he have of our love? If I must love him, that means I must give to him. But what can I give him or do for him?[11]

To digress a moment, it is worth remarking that the artistry of this passage, considered as an exercise in rhetoric, is flawless. It beguiles the audience into believing the scriptural text in question means just the opposite of what it says and drives home the falsification with an apparently irrefutable argument, that God doesn't need our love, without, however, going too far and asserting he doesn't need our faith in him or our worship or even our very existence. Despite the unabashed sophistry it is bathed in that atmosphere of pious sincerity that admirers of Luther seem to find irresistible. Theologically speaking, the argument is aimed at the very heart of the Christian faith, or any religion which is God-centered rather than man-centered. It destroys the Christian motive for loving one's neighbor, which is commanded not because the neighbor is in himself lovable but for the 'love of God.' As will be pointed out later on, the denial mechanism served Luther as a principal shield against anxiety subsequent to the psychotic regression of 1520. Our primary interest in the sermon passage at this point is the evidence it provides for the unhappy state he was loath to reveal in his earlier years. His use of the denial mechanism here is interpreted as showing how painful to him was his awareness of the condition.

To summarize, we find that in addition to the ordinary problems a monk encounters in trying to live according to the rule of his order, Luther suffered from the extraordinary handicaps of an extremely egocentric psyche, a characteristic intolerance of external restraints, and an inability to experience a love for God. It is therefore not to be wondered at that his monastic profession ended in shipwreck; the remarkable thing is that he made such a comparative success of it for at least a decade. We shall now consider some facts which at the psychological level made this possible.

iii. The attachment to John Braun and Staupitz

As remarked earlier, we have little contemporary data on Luther's inner life prior to 1513, nor any idea of how extensive was his early correspondence, which would be a principal source of such data. But there is one notable exception, the letter he wrote on March 17, 1509, to John Braun, Franciscan friar and vicar of St. Mary's church in Eisenach, where Martin had lived and attended school for three years (1498-1501) before matriculating at the University of Erfurt. There is also one earlier letter to Braun in April 1507, inviting him to the celebration of Martin's first mass, in which we learn of his attachment to the older man, whom he refers to in another letter at this time as "my most beloved (*amantissimus*) friend." Following his ordination Martin engaged in theological study for a time at Erfurt but in the autumn of the following year (1508) he was sent to teach in the arts faculty of the recently founded Wittenberg University, his assignment being to conduct a course in the Nicomachean Ethics and other works of Aristotle. It was in this environment that he composed the letter in question. This letter has received little attention from Luther's biographers despite its unique witness to his personality during the years before he began his series of lectures on Scripture.[12]

> Brother Martin Luther, Augustinian, wishes you health and the Savior himself, Jesus Christ. Please stop, my master and father, even more loved than revered, stop, I say, wondering . . . why I went away silently and unkown to you; or at least would have gone away, as if there had never been a bond between us, or as if forgetfulness, the source of ingratitude, had blotted out the memory of your kindness from my heart, in short, as if some cold and despotic north wind had extinguished all the warmth of love. It is not so, I did not do this, or rather I did not plan to do this . . .
>
> I went away, I admit, or rather I did not go but left the greater and better part of me still with you, and always will leave it . . .
>
> Though I neither can be nor wish to be equal to you in whatever is good, and though I may have nothing else, I do have a profound affection for you. *I can not even give it to you now, but, I affirm, it was very often given to you in my own way in the past.* There is nothing your generous spirit expects from me (I know) except what is of the spirit, that is, unity in the knowledge of the Lord, one heart and one mind, one faith in the Lord.
>
> Do not wonder that I went away silently, for I left so suddenly my brothers hardly knew of it. I wanted to write you but could

not, I had so little time and leisure. I could only grieve I was forced to go away without greeting you. Now by God's decree or permission I am at Wittenberg. If you want to know how I am, I am quite well, thank God, but *my studies are extremely difficult, philosophy most of all. I would most gladly have exchanged that from the start for theology;* I mean the theology that looks for the meat of the nut, and the kernel of the wheat and the marrow of the bones. But God is God; man is often or rather always mistaken. He is our God, he will rule us in sweetness and forever.

I ask you to accept this letter, which I have written hastily and without plan; and if you can send any messengers to me let me share in your letters. I will try to do the same. Farewell in the beginning and the end, and hold me in mind such as you would wish me. Again farewell.

Brother Martin Luther, Augustinian

Standing out among the ardent avowals of Martin's regard and friendship for Braun, which may perhaps be viewed to some extent as literary embellishments, there is the italicized sentence in which he recalls how he has repeatedly bestowed his love on the older man when they were together. This passage sounds like more than a rhetorical flourish and presumably indicates some sort of affectionate physical contact between Martin and John Braun, initiated by Martin. Before presenting an interpretation of this sentence I should like to consider a parallel expression from a letter Luther wrote to Staupitz October 3, 1519. The friendship with Staupitz is far better documented than the one with Braun, and Staupitz's character and career are very well known. It appears that the friendship developed during this first sojourn of Luther's at Wittenberg and became probably the strongest attachment he ever formed with any human being. In later years when he declared that the very name of monk stank in his nostrils and was likely to evoke from him a string of abusive epithets, he referred almost reverently to Staupitz, who was successively a vicar general in the Augustinian order and abbot of a Benedictine monastery, as that 'worthy man.' The letter is a reply to one he had just received from Staupitz, which is not extant. The reader should recall that Luther is here a man of 36 and is less than a year away from his permanent break with the Church. After a couple of pages of academic and political news, Martin writes:

What do you want to hear about me? You are too much away from me. I have been most sad for you today, as a weaned child for its mother. I beg you, praise the Lord even in me, a sinner. I hate my wretched life, I fear death, I am empty of faith; and am full of other gifts that Christ knows I don't desire except to serve him . . .

Last night I dreamed you were leaving me while I was bitterly weeping and grieving, but you waved to me, telling me to be calm and you would return to me. This has indeed come to pass this very day.[13]

The data provided in these two letters on Luther's relation to Braun and Staupitz (later Melanchthon will be added to the list) can best be interpreted as evidence of a type of relation observed clinically in individuals who manifest marked neurotic and/or psychotic symptoms. It is now generally recognized that such symptoms appear in individuals who during infancy and very early childhood have failed to lay the foundation for a future healthy psyche. The relative importance of environmental as opposed to genetic factors in the development of the disorder is not at present well understood, but for our purposes it is sufficient to remark that with the constitution the child inherits it is unable in the environment it encounters to develop a well integrated psyche. For most infants the mother is the dominant feature of the environment, and the failure of the child to establish a good loving relationship with the mother is regarded as of primary significance in the formation of the psychic disorder. In later (adult) years two of the ways this unsatisfactory child-mother relation manifests itself are that the individual exhibits toward the mother an unloving attitude ranging from indifference to hatred, and tries to find a substitute for the mother relation it needed but failed to find in infancy. [For the concept of the 'maternal substitute' the reader may consult John D. Rosen, *Selected Papers on Direct Psychoanalysis* (New York, 1968).]

These are well established clinical observations and can readily be illustrated from the psychiatric literature; the knowledgeable reader may himself recall examples from well known figures of the past. By way of illustration, John Ruskin, a neurotic in whom the manic-depressive symptoms did not appear until comparatively late, expressed an attitude of indifference to his mother when she was lying in her coffin. As is well known, Ruskin's mother lavished on him, her only child, an extraordinary amount of care and attention from infancy to adulthood, but did not win his love. An example of the other extreme is provided by Mary Lamb, older sister of the essayist Charles Lamb, who during a manic attack in her early thirties killed her mother with a kitchen knife. Luther's avoidance of his mother — so far as is known he saw her only twice, at wedding celebrations, during the last quarter-century of her life — is obviously symptomatic of his disorder.

To illustrate the other symptom mentioned above — the search for a maternal substitute — it is illuminating to consider the case of Jean-Jacques Rousseau, who was cared for during his early years by an aunt, his mother having died at the time of his birth. There is a striking parallelism in the careers of Rousseau and Luther: both men attracted an enthusiastic following by their writings, fell afoul of authority and to escape punishment went into exile, still supported by their admirers; both contracted somewhat irregular unions with penniless household servants (Luther with an ex-nun and Rousseau with a chambermaid) whom they were friendly with but did not love; and both spent their final years in a state of paranoid regression, dying suddenly from a cardio-vascular condition associated with the severe emotional stresses to which they were subject. Their basic ideas were in almost exact contradiction, Rousseau holding that man was naturally good but corrupted by society, while Luther held that man was irretrievably corrupted by original sin so that not even an omnipotent God could restore him to goodness but only choose to overlook his permanently sinful condition. The point of interest in our comparison is not the content of these doctrinaire positions but rather that each man acquired his conviction by reflecting on his experience of neurosis and that likewise for each man the literary development of his idea was carried on as a defense against his anxiety.

As for the selection of a maternal substitute, the fact that Rousseau's was a woman − Mme. de Warens − and Luther's were all male is not particularly significant, for it is observed clinically that the neurotic individual will choose for this role whoever or whatever is available that appears to fulfil his need. For the reader not familiar with the details of Rousseau's biography, it may be stated that at the age of 16 he first encountered Mme. de Warens, a woman 12 years older than himself, who was then living at Annecy on a pension from the King of Sardinia, having been separated from a much older husband some years earlier. According to the account near the beginning of the third book of the *Confessions* he developed his extraordinary attachment for her at once; she inspired in him "peace of heart, calm, serenity, security, assurance," in other words, a most effective relief from his neurotic anxiety. He resided with her much of the time from then until at the age of 29 he left her home to earn his living in Paris. He soon came to call her Maman and speaks of his delight in having a young and pretty mother to caress:

> I say caress literally, for it never occured to her to deny me kisses and the most tender motherly caresses, and I never had any inclination to go beyond this . . . . I experienced neither raptures nor desires when with her; I was in a state of blissful peace, enjoying myself without knowing why. I could have passed my life and even eternity in this way without boredom; but became most unhappy when she was absent from me.[14]

It is this passage from the *Confessions* which I would suggest as a key for interpreting the remark about "showing you my love" in Luther's letter to John Braun. Given the parent-child relation Martin experienced with the Franciscan priest, one would expect fond embraces when the two were together. It was a case of a love-starved child at last finding love. The suspicion that this letter refers to a homosexual relation, which is possibly why Luther biographers have been silent about it, has no solid basis and as will be shown in a later chapter such an aberration would be rather out of character for Martin. It is likely that his own experience in the presence of John Braun, or later with Staupitz or Melanchthon, was something like Rousseau's with Mme. de Warens. In the earlier letter to Braun (April 22, 1507) inviting the Franciscan to be present at the celebration of his first Mass ten days later, he is equally effusive, twice emphasizing the many occasions in the past when he has enjoyed Braun's kindness to him. The way in which Martin must have kept up this relation is indicated by his reference in the 1507 letter to a visit he made to Braun not long before the date of the letter. (The distance from Erfurt to Eisenach is about 35 miles; the letter does not explain Martin's occasion for traveling to Eisenach at that time, shortly before his ordination.) We last hear of Braun in 1515-16, when Luther refers to sending him a copy of a sermon he had delivered at the chapter meeting of the Augustinians at Gotha.

But long before 1515 Braun had been replaced in his role of maternal substitute by John von Staupitz, and the date of Martin's first encounter with Philip Melanchthon was little more than three years in the future. We shall return to a discussion of the Luther-Staupitz relation in a later chapter. At this point it should be remarked that what probably helped more than any other factor to keep Martin in relatively good psychic balance until his mid thirties was the relief he experienced with the men in whom he found a substitute for the defective mother-child relation. Other men doubtless helped him to a lesser degree; in particular, he refers with gratitude to the Augustinian at the convent in Erfurt who acted as novice master at the time Martin began his monastic career. But such individuals could give him only minor assistance; those who played a decisive role were successively Braun, Staupitz and Melanchthon.

As Rousseau tells us explicitly and Luther definitely implies in the fragmentary correspondence that survives, to be really effective in helping the sufferer from neurotic anxiety the maternal substitute must be present physically. It was part of Luther's misfortune to be frequently separated from the men he cultivated for this role and it must have been the permanent separation rather than disenchantment with the person that led him to form attachments with a series of individuals. It is this requirement of actual proximity which helps explain the gradual worsening of Luther's neurotic symptoms after he began lecturing on Scripture in 1513 and also the length of the depression — upwards of six months — he suffered in 1527. In the earlier situation he was deprived of the society of Staupitz and in the later of Melanchthon.

iv. Reaction to philosophy and theology

We shall now return to the letter to John Braun quoted above and direct our attention to the second of the italicized portions, in which Luther speaks of how difficult he finds the study of philosophy. This admission is unique in the Luther record, for once he begins his open attack on the teaching of philosophy in the universities he is inclined to boast of his own superior understanding of it. It will be recalled that Luther had been sent from Erfurt to Wittenberg to lecture on the Nicomachean Ethics of Aristotle, and presumably it is this work that he has in mind in the letter to Braun. It is not surprising that when the term ended Luther was sent back to Erfurt and a note was made in the University records that Luther had 'failed to satisfy the faculty.' (Thus Smith, p. 11; other authors say the reason is unknown.) This is not difficult to explain, for Martin had inherited a mind (as has many another collegian) unsuited for grasping the concepts of philosophy. On the other hand, he had a remarkable memory for words; later on when he is deriding philosophical study by running through some of the terminology it is evident that his ability to recall the terms is markedly superior to his understanding of what they mean.

Apart from his lack of natural aptitude for philosophy, it might be pointed out that the Luther of history was not the intellectual giant celebrated in the Luther legend. His academic record bears this out. Martin entered the University of Erfurt at the rather advanced age of 17 yet was in the lower half of the class that received the bachelor's degree the following year. By way of comparison, Melanchthon, whose precocity was celebrated, entered college at the age of 12, took the bachelor's degree at 14 and the master's degree a few weeks before his seventeenth birthday. John Eck, later to become one of Luther's principal theological opponents, and Justus Jonas both had records similar to Melanchthon's. It is often mentioned that for his master's degree Martin finished second in a class of 17; what is not revealed is that a bright boy in Luther's day could be granted the M.A. at an age below that at which Luther entered college.

Boys could complete their college work at an appreciably earlier age in those times than in ours because of the comparatively limited range of subject matter in the medieval curriculum. In particular, a lad with a superior aptitude for Latin could move through the program quite rapidly. Martin's own comparative retardation may have been due in part to emotional factors which slowed his learning rate. Furthermore, he was not the great language expert he is often represented to be. If his stories in the Table Talk about his school days are to be credited, a knowledge of Latin did not come to him readily. His exceptional verbal fluency was primarily in the use of his native tongue. After 1521 his writings with few exceptions are in German, his use of Latin thereafter being largely confined to academic work and correspondence, in accordance with current practice.

The way Luther stored up his resentment over the years at having been forced by academic requirements to work at a subject which he regarded as worse than a waste of time is nowhere evidenced more vividly than in the 1520 pamphlet addressed to the German nobility, the first of his writings in which he demonstrates his break with the past. Here Aristotle is a 'damned, conceited, wily heathen' sent by God to punish us for our sins.

> His work on Ethics is the most vexatious of all books. It opposes God's grace and Christian virtues outright [subjects about which Aristotle had not been privileged to hear], yet is counted as one of his best works. O, may such books be kept from all Christians! Let no one dare charge me with speaking too strongly or about matters of which I am ignorant. My good friend, I know well what I am talking about; I understand Aristotle as well as you and the likes of you. I have lectured and heard lectures on him with a better appreciation than St. Thomas or Scotus. I say this without boasting and if need be can easily prove it.[15]

Seldom has the backward and disgruntled student been given the opportunity to pour out his wrath on his professors with such abandon. What a difference between the Luther of 1509 and of 1520. It is not his understanding of philosophy that has improved so remarkably in the interim; rather we are here witnessing an uninhibited discharge of pathological hostility against a favorite target. If the reader is puzzled at this display of childish boasting from a supposedly mature man, let it be recalled that psychotic regression, Luther's state when he wrote this pamphlet, can be described as a shift from the adult toward the infantile level.

Martin has another objection to the study of philosophy besides the problem of comprehension; philosophy offers him no relief from anxiety. The consolations of philosophy may be effective for others, as the title of the well known work of Boethius suggests, but not for Luther. Hence his preference for the theology that burrows into the meat of the nut and the marrow of the bone. One could wish Luther had stated his preference more specifically, but it is certain he is rejecting a theology that utilizes the philosophy of Aristotle, or any other philosopher, to help elucidate its concepts. During the next several years Luther was to look into a variety of approaches before he found a 'theology' which he thought would provide a saving bulwark.

After his first teaching assignment at Wittenberg, Martin resumed theological study and teaching at Erfurt, this regime being interrupted for a few months during the winter of 1509-10 when he was sent to Rome as a companion to an older Augustinian on business of the order. The modern traveler is impressed by the ruggedness of one who could hike over the Alps and on through the other mountains of northern Italy in winter, and after a few weeks in Rome, carry out the return journey. The view of all those peaks, ridges and chasms does not appear to have affected Martin's imagination as it did, for example, that of Pieter Breugel, who made the same journey later in the century; what intrigued him especially were the excellent accommodations for the sick in Italian hospitals, particularly in Florence. As an indication of the ever present anxiety there is Martin's eager desire to make a general confession while in Rome, though he had already made one earlier at Erfurt.

It was apparently about the time of his return from Rome that John von Staupitz decided Martin should proceed to the doctorate in theology in order to replace him as professor of biblical theology at Wittenberg. In his later references to the decision, Luther emphasized that he had not himself sought this responsibility, that on the contrary he felt unqualified for it, and that he had accepted it under the compulsion of monastic obedience. He had been granted a degree in Biblical Studies at Wittenberg in March 1509 while teaching in the faculty of arts, and later in the year, after his return to Erfurt, had taken another degree in theology from the University of Erfurt which qualified him to lecture on a standard theological text, the *Sentences* of Peter Lombard. In 1511 Staupitz recalled Luther to Wittenberg and in October of 1512, shortly before his twenty-ninth birthday, Wittenberg granted him the doctorate in biblical theology. The brevity of the period of his doctoral studies, a requirement of ten years or more in preparation for the doctorate being customary in those days, is probably to be explained by the pressing need for the replacement for Staupitz, who doubtless exercised some influence in the award of this "quickie" degree. Apart from that, Wittenberg was an institution without traditions, having come into existence only a decade earlier. And it had already granted the doctorate to others after a short period of residence, e.g., to Andrew Carlstadt (Bodenstein), who presently rose to be dean of the theological faculty.

Given Luther's highly individualistic approach to theology it is questionable whether further exposure to academic courses would have significantly affected his outlook. As Febvre[16] has pointed out, when a man of Luther's temperament opens a book, he sees in it only one idea — his own. A phrase or turn of thought strikes him and he grasps it, adapting it to his own use. During Luther's monastic years, whether as graduate student or faculty member, he was not interested in mastering the thought of the great or lesser theologians of the past as a discipline or specialty but rather looked into them in search of a solution to his personal problem. With regard to learning subject matter presented in his courses, it is to be presumed that in his earlier years as a student he acquired the art of memorizing what he needed for purposes of examination, without making it really his own. The often repeated story of his ability to recite entire pages from the works of the fifteenth century scholastic theologian, Gabriel Biel, a "required" author during Luther's student years, bears this out. It is fairly obvious that the principal effect on Martin of being forced to read the volumes of Biel or similar theologians was to inspire in him a hearty dislike of the whole tribe. In the earliest extant writing by Luther, consisting of marginal notes in books he was reading in the period around 1510, a scholar[17] who recently investigated this material can find no indication that scholastic theology had any influence on Luther's own thinking.

His hatred of philosophy can be better understood in the light of his distaste for the academic theology of his day. Here was a discipline which was reputed to illuminate the most profound questions on the relations of man to God, yet for Martin it not only provided no illumination but rather engendered erroneous doctrine. Since on topics in the area of his disturbance Luther never tolerated any views discordant to his own and habitually expressed harsh judgments on whoever disagreed with him, he could not but react in this fashion. His relation to the most widely respected of the medieval theologians, Thomas Aquinas, illustrates another aspect of this general attitude. Luther had on some occasion looked into the *Summa Theologica* and been badly upset by Thomas' method of presentation. It will be recalled that each of the hundreds of topics discussed in this work is introduced as a question, e.g., "Whether God is merciful," and the discussion begins with one or more objections, for in marked contrast to Luther, he always stated his opponent's case fairly and courteously before presenting his own view and refuting the opposing one. It would appear that in the course of reading one of these discussions Martin had been so shaken by the arguments against a doctrine of the faith advanced by a non-christian opponent of Thomas that, terrified, he closed the volume and never dared open it again. While later on Luther repeatedly refers to Thomas, it is evident that he has no real acquaintance with the teaching of the thirteenth century theologian and even attributes to him positions diametrically opposed to what Thomas actually held.

One of the most striking illustrations of Martin's incapacity to appreciate what did not bear immediately on his own preoccupations is to be found in his reaction to the *Confessions* of St. Augustine. Despite the very great admiration he professed for

Augustine during the period we are now examining, he was able to say some years later of this book, one of the outstanding master-pieces of Western literature, that "it teaches nothing."[18] This re-mark should be interpreted to mean that Luther could find nothing in the *Confessions* that would throw light on his own quest, which unlike Augustine's was not a search for the knowledge of God but rather for a means of escape from the eternal damnation to which he so often felt he was doomed.

v. The defensive programs

Beginning with the year 1513 there is a progressive increase in the documentation on Luther's inner life. Until early 1518, while trying out various approaches to a doctrinal solution of his psychic problem, he enjoyed a good deal of freedom from external stress. What distinguishes these years from the later ones, when he was continually subject to stress from without, is his ability to function with comparatively little dependence on the medically described ego defense mechanisms that begin to multiply in his writings and ser-mons after the middle of 1520.

At this point it is desirable to survey the range of Luther's de-fenses against anxiety. They can be classified under four headings. First, there are the above mentioned ego defenses or defense mech-anisms, such as repression, which predominates during the earlier years, or projection and denial, which form so prominent a feature of his behavior from 1520 on. This topic will be treated at length in a later chapter. Then there is the defensive use of Scripture, which provides material in the form of either 'consoling texts' or expres-sions of religious emotion, especially the Psalms, into which Luther can read his own experience. Related to this is Luther's practice of identifying with scriptural personages, especially St. Paul. Next, there are the more comprehensive approaches to a solution of his problem, approaches with a quasi-theological orientation. These differ from the defensive use of Scripture in their much broader application. It is possible to distinguish three of them, which we here refer to as 'programs.' They are (1) the way of monastic 'works'; (2) the *theo-logia crucis* (theology of the cross); (3) the *sola fide* (by faith alone). To some extent they follow one another chronologically, but there is considerable overlap in the years before 1520. Finally, there are a number of activities deliberately employed in the combat with anxiety such as carousing with boon companions or daydreaming about pretty girls, of which Luther gives a fascinating account in a letter of advice written from Coburg in the summer of 1530 to one of his disciples afflicted with neurotic anxiety. We shall ordinarily refer to these forms of behavior as defensive 'devices' or 'techniques.'

It would appear that Luther made little use of such measures prior to 1519.

The earliest of Martin's defensive programs, which probably dates back to the beginning of his monastic life, is an attempt to free himself from the fear of damnation by the performance of 'good works.' As remarked earlier, it is most likely that Martin entered the monastery to take advantage of the many opportunities he expected to find there for carrying out such a program. It is unknown how early he became dissatisfied with this approach and began to develop another one, which he called the 'theology of the cross.' But as he explains in a letter to a fellow Augustinian, George Spenlein, dated April 8, 1516, he found it difficult to abandon the original program:

> The temptation to presumption burns in many these days, especially in those who strive to be just and good with all their might. Unaware of God's righteousness, which is given us lavishly and freely in Christ, they keep trying to do good of themselves so they may stand in confidence before God as if adorned with their virtues and merits — which is impossible. You were of this opinion or rather error when with us. I was too, and now also fight against the error but have not yet overcome it.[19]

It should be noted that Luther in 1516 presents this program as arising from his own erroneous view. In later years it became one of his most persistent falsifications that this 'way of salvation' represents an official teaching of the Church. Of particular significance is that he does not resort here to the defense of projecting this error on his fellow Christians as he was prone to do in subsequent years. Instead, he accepts responsibility for it, though he could not of course be aware of its association with his psychic disorder. That Luther never succeeded in abandoning the program, no matter how often he jeered at others he judged guilty of holding it, (the 'works-righteous', 'work-saints', etc.) is apparent from the following passage from a sermon delivered to his Wittenberg congregation in the late 1530s:

> How I feel within myself that I would gladly give up all I have, even life and limb, if I could find for once a single work (done by myself) on which I could rely and could present to God, a work he would be bound to honor and for which he would bestow on me his grace and eternal life. I can't bring myself (as I should and must) to complete resignation to Christ without any presumption or reliance on my works or my own merit.[20]

By way of comment on the self-revelation Martin provides in this sermon of 1537, it should be observed that his defensive strategy is inextricably bound up with his anthropomorphic concept of God. No matter how movingly he can speak about the wondrous mercy of

Christ, there is always lurking in the background his unChristian view of God as a vindictive judge who must be 'placated.' From his reminiscences it is apparent he developed this attitude in childhood or youth; it is at the basis of his endlessly repeated experience of hating God and his inability to love God. While Luther expressed a perfectly orthodox view of the Trinity, this was a Christian doctrine well removed from the center of his preoccupations; for him, experientially, the Father and the Son were not only distinct Persons but — much of the time — distinct Beings as well. It is essential to specify 'much of the time,' for Luther's approach to God was emotional, not intellectual, and his emotions fluctuated continually. As he once remarked, 'My mood changes ten times a day.' Later on, when he invokes the explanation of 'two times,' designated as the 'time of grace and of the Law,' there is effectively a different God for each time.

As for his remark about 'complete resignation to Christ,' this phrase is central to an understanding of the term 'faith' as it is used in the N. T.: total dedication of the human person to the divine as revealed in Jesus. Martin's inability to experience faith as presented in Scripture, like his inability to love God, is one of the most disabling consequences of his psychic disorder. It is thus not surprising that for the unattainable faith described in Scripture he would introduce a substitute, which became the basis of the *sola fide* program. His extraordinary attitude toward Jesus, just hinted at in this sermon excerpt, which must be appreciated by those who would understand his personality, will be analyzed later in this study.

Luther's admission after living for nearly two decades in the state of evangelical liberty that he still yearns to get into heaven on his own merits is the point of paramount interest in this self-revelation. Alongside the radical changes that appear in his behavior and outlook during the course of his life, we are even more interested in determining the permanent features of his character such as the one displayed here. A consideration of this trait throws considerable light on the motivation of his celebrated combat with the ecclesiastical structures of his day. The antagonist he was combatting was an indissoluble amalgam of actual officialdom and the projection of his own inner conflicts.

Since our knowledge of the second of Martin's defensive programs, the 'theology of the cross,' derives mainly from the four courses of lectures to which he devoted his first years (1513-18) as professor of sacred Scripture, we shall now briefly review this work. These lectures, which Martin wrote out before delivery, provide our major source of information on his inner life during this five-year period. Only a few dozen letters from these years are extant and he did not start writing for the public until along in 1518. It is worth pointing

out that very few of Luther's contemporaries were acquainted with
the lectures. Apart from a revised version of one of the lecture series
(on the Epistle to the Galatians) which Luther published with
Melanchthon's assistance in 1519 and later, the written texts of the
lectures were not printed until modern times. One of them (on the
Epistle to the Hebrews) was first published — from a student's
notes — as late as 1929.

It was predictable that Luther would begin his career as lecturer
on Scripture with the book that he knew best and which during the
Middle Ages was the one most widely used for both liturgical purposes and private devotional reading, the Psalms. It might be noted
here that until along in the 1520s this was probably the only O. T.
book on which he lectured, and that he continued to compose commentaries on many individual Psalms in later years when in his
lectures he had shifted almost exclusively to the O. T. (There is
extant (WA 4:527-86) a set of student's notes for a lecture series on
Judges, possibly by Luther, delivered apparently to a monastic audience during 1515-17, and containing a spirited defense of monastic
obedience.) Following a two-year (1513-15) series of lectures on the
Psalms, Martin devoted the next course to one of the most weighty
theological writings in the N. T. — Paul's Epistle to the Romans.
Then he lectured on Galatians (1516-17) and after that on Hebrews
(1517-18).

The early lectures on the Psalms (*Dictata super Psalterium*),
though often conventional, bear the marks of Martin's personal
approach, and this feature becomes increasingly prominent with
time. In a letter to his friend at the Electoral court, George Spalatin,
of January 18, 1518 Martin provides an illuminating account of his
method of studying Scripture. The basic principle of the method is
that one cannot grasp the meaning of Scripture by study or 'innate
intelligence'; instead one depends on prayer and divine guidance.
Luther claims to know this from his own experience. For supplementary reading he recommends three of Augustine's writings in the
Pelagian controversy of the early fifth century. It is significant that
instead of suggesting some of Augustine's commentaries on Scripture,
which he had himself made use of, Luther selected these polemical
writings. In them Augustine, in opposition to the Pelagians, who
greatly exaggerated the unaided moral power of man, stresses the
need of divine grace for a human nature weakened by the effects
of original sin. This is an aspect of Augustine's work that had strong
appeal for Luther, preoccupied as he was with the personal problem
outlined above.

Needless to say, the modern Scripture scholar would find it hard
to understand how anyone could take seriously these recommendations for dealing with the problems of scriptural exegesis. What

Martin regarded as divine guidance was merely his own egocentric habit of adapting what he picked up from his reading to his psychic needs. The date of this letter should be noted; in January of 1518 he has now had several years of experience in lecturing on Scripture and is nearing the end of his third lecture course on the epistles of the N. T. It is true that in preparing his lectures Luther consulted a number of widely used commentaries, but as time went on he came to depend less and less on such material, and never allowed it to interfere with anything vital to his interests. In later years the only notable change in his method was to abandon explicitly his use of Augustine and other authors in favor of exclusive dependence on his own opinions.

The program Luther denoted as the 'theology of the cross' may be described as man's humble acceptance of God's will when faced with trials in which everything seems to run counter to his own intention. It involves recognizing both the inevitability and the salutary effect of the suffering the Christian must endure with patience if he would persevere to the end. As I have shown elsewhere[21] this is one of several themes Luther borrowed from the work known as the *Imitatio Christi* ("Imitation of Christ"). The four little treatises that make up this work date from a period well over a half century before Luther's birth. After enjoying very wide circulation in manuscript for several decades, this compilation was first printed about 1472. It was an almost instant best seller; some 80 editions appeared during the remaining years of the fifteenth century. We have no information on when Luther encountered the *Imitatio,* but it seems likely he had read it before leaving Erfurt University and it may well have influenced his decision to enter a monastery. In the *Imitatio* the theme is called the 'road of the cross' (*via crucis*), the name Luther himself used prior to 1518. He writes about it principally in the Lectures on Romans but references to it occur elsewhere in his works of this period.

To look briefly at its subsequent history, it was in a long tract Luther prepared in early 1518 to clarify his position on the Indulgence Theses, the "Explanations" (*Resolutiones*), that he re-named the program 'theology of the cross' (*theologia crucis*). He gave the new name further exposure at a disputation in Heidelberg the last week of April that year. In the disputation, as in the "Explanations," he was attacking the scholastic theologians, and doubtless chose *theologia crucis* to contrast with *theologia scholastica* (scholastic theology). He never produced a tract on the 'theology of the cross,' his comments on it being in the nature of *obiter dicta* in his lectures and sermons. In the famous essay "The Freedom of the Christian" of 1520, Luther's longest exposition of the *sola fide,* the 'theology of the cross' has dropped below the level of a whisper. Thereafter, explicit references to it in his writings are extremely rare. The loss of interest in this theme was a natural consequence of the radical change in his religious outlook just before and during the early 1520s.

In the Lectures on Romans Luther developed a new topic that may be regarded as preparing the way for the *sola fide* (see Ch. 2). He was plagued by his inability to experience love for God, and in consequence his being in a state of sinful disobedience to the greatest commandment of the Law. Since this 'sin' is with him constantly, it can not be reckoned as an 'actual' sin, that is, a specific act of disobedience such as a deliberate violation of one of the Ten Commandments. Therefore it must be associated with original sin. Traditionally, the guilt of original sin is washed away in baptism, but there is a residual effect, a disorder of the senses with respect to the reason and the will, which makes men prone to sin after baptism. For well over a thousand years before Luther's time Christian theologians had denoted this legacy of Adam's sin with the term 'concupiscence.' Augustine, for example, brings out the distinction between sin and concupiscence in one of his works as follows:

> If it is asked, how can this concupiscence of the flesh remain after baptism, through which all sins are forgiven, the answer is that concupiscence of the flesh is remitted in baptism not in such a way it no longer exists, but rather that it is not *imputed* as sin.[22]

Luther had occasion to deal with the term 'impute' when discussing the fourth chapter of Romans, where it appears in a quotation from Psalm 32:

Blest are they whose iniquities are forgiven,
    Whose sins are covered over.
Blest is the man to whom the Lord
    imputes no guilt.

In commenting on this passage Luther introduces a startling misquotation of the sentence of Augustine given above, identifying sin with concupiscence and stating that this 'sin' is not remitted in baptism.[23] Barely five years earlier in a commentary on a theological treatise widely used in medieval universities, the "Sentences" of Peter Lombard, Luther had quoted the same statement of Augustine accurately.[24] His commentary included an exposition of the standard teaching on the relation between original sin and concupiscence. To emphasize his adherence to it he remarked that to claim sinful guilt is associated with concupiscence or that such guilt is *not* remitted in baptism would be to offer "insult to baptism and the grace of God." The fact that in his Lectures on Romans he now himself offers this "insult to baptism and the grace of God" and backs up the 'insult' with a palpable falsification of the text of Augustine makes this one of the more significant passages of the lecture course.

The key word in this section of the lectures is 'impute.' In one grammatical form or another it appears some two dozen times in the pages of comment ostensibly devoted to Romans 4:7. In much of this section Luther emphasizes the goal of having God not impute a man's sins to him, i.e., overlook them. He then makes a transition to righteousness or justification, affirming that one can never be without actual sin as long as he is afflicted with concupiscence. This doctrinal position will generate various progeny − ultimately the doctrine of man's total depravity. At this time it is responsible for the emphasis on what Luther likes to call 'alien' righteousness, that is, a righteousness applied externally, like a plaster, with no real effect on the inner man. The one who lives an upright life is not righteous; the only righteous man is the one who, by acknowledging that he is unrighteous because he can't keep the commandments, has righteousness 'imputed' to him. In the decades to come this word 'impute' was to be received with enthusiasm through much of northern Europe. It inspired a delightful couplet in Samuel Butler's satire on the English Puritans, *Hudibras,* in the later seventeenth century, a couplet which could almost serve as a translation of some of the language to be found in the Lectures on Romans:

> Virtue is impious if 'tis rooted
> In nature only, and not imputed.

Looking ahead to the Luther of later years, we see here a fore-shadowing of what will become commonplace in his behavior by the 1520s, that is, repudiation of positions he had once proclaimed with conviction and tampering with the text of his authorities, whether Church Fathers or Scripture, to help justify his innovations. The reversal of his views on concupiscence between 1510 and 1515 stems from his unhappy experience with the greatest commandment of the Law, as outlined above. The falsification of the text of Augustine may be described as a lapse into a species of wish fulfillment in consequence of severe inner stress; it heralds the preponderant role of unconscious defense mechanisms in his future behavior.

Chapter 2

A Time of Transition 1515 – 1520

i. Interlude with the Mystics

It is not surprising that in the search for a theological solution of his personal problem Luther would be attracted to mystical writers and as with the *Imitatio Christi* look to them for help. The most influential mystical theologian during the middle ages was an anonymous author of the late fifth or early sixth century known as Dionysius or Pseudo-Dionysius the Areopagite. Luther developed an interest in his work and also in the Rhineland mystic John Tauler (1290?-1361), who was a disciple of a fellow Dominican, Meister Eckart. Luther's earliest extant references to Dionysius are to be found in his 1513-15 lectures on the Psalms. His apparent familiarity with Dionysius at this time suggests at least some prior acquaintance. He admires Dionysius' 'negative theology,' that is, the neoplatonic approach to the utter transcendence and incomprehensibility of the Godhead which asserts that all that can be known of God is what he is not.

Thus in his comment on Ps. 18 (17):12, Luther remarks that the blessed Dionysius teaches us to ascend to God by the way of negation because God is hidden and beyond our understanding. Again in Ps. 65 (64):2 – "To you we owe our hymn of praise" – Luther states this verse is to be explained by "ecstatic and negative theology" which praises God in silent admiration of his majesty.

> For as the affirmative way to God is imperfect whether in understanding or speaking, so the negative way is most perfect. Wherefore in Dionysius the word 'Hyper' is often to be found because one must enter into the cloud that is beyond all reasoning. . . . Our own [scholastic] theologians are too audacious when they boldly dispute and make assertions about the divinity. For as I have said, affirmative theology is to negative as milk is to wine. This subject cannot be dealt with by disputation and

32

abundance of words, but in the silent and passive depths of the mind or in a state of rapture and ecstacy. This is what makes the true theologian.[1]

In passing it should be noted that the young Luther, just turned 30, finds a discussion of the divine being to deserve a central role in theology, provided the approach is the neo-platonic negation he praises here in the pseudo-Dionysius and will presently also discover in Tauler. In 1513-14 it is only the disrespectful wrangling about the divine nature in the schools that is objectionable. As he writes a few pages farther on in a comment on Ps. 66:17,

> I hate the opinions of these audacious Thomists and Scotists and others who dispute without fear the holy name of God in which we are baptized and before which heaven, earth and hell tremble.

By 1520 this attitude will shift to an almost exclusive emphasis on the hiddenness of God, with a discussion of the divine attributes ruled out as an unsuitable topic for theology.

Toward the end of 1516 Luther published what is commonly called his first book. It consists of his own brief introduction and the text of a hitherto unprinted manuscript which had somehow come into his hands. This work is a little compendium of leading ideas of the Rhineland mystics Eckart, Tauler and Suso. It describes in traditional fashion the three stages by which the aspirant attains union with God: the purgative, in which he becomes free of sin and sensory desire; the illuminative, reached after he has wholly renounced his own self will, and the unitive, when he experiences the rapture of the mystic vision. This anonymous and nameless treatise, which modern scholarship has succeeded only in identifying as the work of a fourteenth century chaplain of the Teutonic Order (nowadays called the 'Frankforter'), Luther entitled "A Worthy Little Book on Spiritual Things." Somewhat later he discovered a second and more complete manuscript of the same text and printed that also, in 1518, with a new preface in which he announced with characteristic exaggeration that apart from the Bible and St. Augustine he has learned more about God, Christ, man and all things from this book than from any other. For this printing he provided the new title "A German Theology." Before finding either of these manuscripts he had become equally enthusiastic over a collection of Tauler's sermons (Tauler was a popular preacher who so far as is known never produced a book). These sermons he recommended most strongly to his friend Spalatin in a letter of December 1516 and again the following May.

Verbal parallels with passages in Tauler and the Frankforter can be found in Luther's writings during the next few years, but the Rhinelanders exerted no significant influence on Luther. As Strohl aptly puts it,[2] in a detailed analysis of a number of such parallels, Luther was their friend but not their disciple. Much of the essential content of their writings he simply ignored, as indeed was true of his other favorite authors. One of the indications that his enthusiasm for the Rhineland mystics was a temporary infatuation is the comparative rapidity with which they seem to disappear from his consciousness. There is little reference to them, favorable or otherwise, in the record after the mid 1520s. Indeed one has the impression from some of his remarks that in his eyes a principal merit of these books was their being written in German rather than Latin.

With Dionysius the story is somewhat different. Luther's admiration for this author seems to have evaporated by 1520, judging by the unflattering references to him in the "Babylonian Captivity," as well as numerous others even more unflattering on into the 1530s. It is to this period we must turn for first hand documentation on the reason for Luther's disenchantment with the mystic way. In an exposition of Ps. 126 (125): 5-6 written in the years 1532-33 Luther asserts:

> Faith and the life of Christians are not hypocrisy as is that of monks who presume to attain perfection by speculating about the spiritual union, as they call it. From my own experience, I learned that this is a deception. For when I tried this myself in all sincerity, I was never able to experience anything from these speculations. Therefore they are nothing but dangerous fables and hypocrisy.[3]

The caricature of the mystical way presented in this paragraph is a characteristic falsification of the post-1520 Luther who by 1532 is well into the paranoid phase of his disorder. The really interesting feature of this bit of autobiography is its explicit confirmation of Luther's futile attempt to become a mystic, an attempt we could only have surmised from his commentary in the lectures on Romans on the opening verses of Ch. 5: "Being justified by faith, let us have peace with God, through our Lord Jesus Christ. By whom we also have access through faith into this grace wherein we stand." In this comment he speaks reprovingly of would-be mystics "who in the inner darkness would listen to and contemplate the uncreated Word but have not yet had the eyes of their heart justified and purged by the incarnate Word."[4] But granted the need for such purging, who would dare think himself fit for this rapture unless called as Paul was? Therefore, "this rapture cannot be called an access to grace." From this comment it appears Luther had come to believe that a man cannot become a mystic by choice but rather can enjoy this privilege only as a gift of God.

The date of this part of the commentary is early 1516. The inde-cisiveness of Luther's personal doctrinal position at this time may be seen in his other remarks about these opening verses of Rom. 5 quoted above. He directs his attention not to Paul's words about justification by faith but to obtaining peace with God, which to him means a quiet conscience. Then he criticizes two classes of men who in their quest for salvation fall short of the demands here set forth by Paul. The first class includes those who err in trying to approach God by "faith alone" (*sic*!), and in doing so think they can bypass Christ as mediator. The error of the second class arises from their notion that they can be saved by Christ without doing anything or demonstrating their faith. Included in class two are the would-be mystics referred to above who want to experience rapture without being purged or called to this grace.

Later in the spring of 1516 he suggests what might be called a common sense way of dealing with the anxiety aroused by his blas-phemous thoughts. The following passage is part of his comment on Rom. 9:16.

> There would be no sin in a man saying to God in fear and devout humility, 'Why did you make me thus?' Such a one would not be destroyed even if he blasphemed while in a state of severe temptation. For our God is not an impatient and hardhearted God even to the impious. I say this for the consolation of those who are tormented by blasphemous thoughts and in great uneasi-ness. For such blasphemies, being forcibly wrenched from men against their will by the devil, may at times be more pleasing to God than a hallelujah or a song of praise. Indeed the more foul and horrible the blasphemy, the more pleasing to God if the heart feels it to be involuntary, because it was not brought forth willing-ly from the heart. It is a sign that the blasphemy was not willed by the heart and that the heart is innocent of it if the man is thrown into a panic and terrified because of it . . . . Therefore the remedy for such thoughts is not to be troubled about them.[5]

Luther's development of the *sola fide* program may be to some extent a reaction to his failure to experience the rapture of the mystic or to find effective help in his struggle with anxiety from other approaches referred to in the Lectures on Romans. He then fell back on the view that he could experience the relief of a quiet con-science or feel that his sins would not be held against him ('imputed') if he *believed* that he had been granted this boon. He buttressed this implausible hypothesis by recourse to a passage in a sermon by Bernard which refers to the testimony of the Holy Spirit in our hearts that by divine grace our sins are forgiven and that we may be granted eternal life.

In the lectures on Romans this sermon excerpt is quoted at some length (at 8:16-18) and with reasonable fidelity, for at this date (by mid 1516) the *sola fide* program had not yet been seriously undertaken.[6] But when in the Lectures on Hebrews (at 5:1), more than a year later, Luther returns to what must have been a favorite spot in the writings of his favorite medieval saint, fidelity to the source is no longer a desideratum. The rather long passage is now telescoped into two sentences and given the full Lutherian twist:

> You must believe that God can forgive your sins, bestow grace and grant salvation. But that is not enough unless you most firmly believe that it is *you* who have had your sins forgiven, received grace and been granted salvation.[7]

The very different treatment given this passage from Bernard's sermon in the two lecture courses makes it likely that 1517 is the year Luther began constructing the *sola fide* program.

ii. Psychological basis of the *sola fide*

At the annual chapter meeting of the Augustinians at Gotha in May of 1515, Luther delivered a sermon in which he criticized the behavior and attitudes of some of his monastic brethren. He was proud of the sermon and its reception by his fellow monks, and, as we have seen, gave directions for a copy of it to be delivered to his old friend John Braun in Eisenach. At this meeting Luther was elected to a three-year term as district vicar of eleven houses mainly in Saxony and Thuringia. He labored conscientiously at this administrative task, which was added to his work load of teaching and preaching. One of the more interesting items in the extant correspondence from this period shows him instructing the prior of his own former house at Erfurt to keep detailed records of the costs of entertaining guests — usually other monks or friars — so that it would be known how long each one remained and what was spent for his food and drink. On another occasion Martin removes from office — without a hearing — a prior who appears unable to maintain order in his house, giving the man some excellent advice which he himself was to repudiate in a striking fashion a few years later:

> It should console you to recall that it does not suffice for a man merely to be good and pious. There must also be peace and concord with others. Very often what is undertaken with the best intentions turns out to be undesirable and must be rejected so that peace may be preserved.[8]

After ten years in the monastery there are indications that Luther is becoming dissatisfied with his choice of career. As remarked earlier, it was inevitable for him eventually to realize that living according to the monastic rule would not bring effective relief from anxiety, and it is to be presumed that such relief as he experienced came largely from Staupitz and (to a lesser extent) other companions. One of these indications appears in the latter part of the Lectures on Romans, a section composed in the summer of 1516:

> How many monks would most willingly abandon their ceremonies, prayers and rule if the Pope would release them, as he is able to do. Indeed almost all now carry on in their vocation without love and unwillingly. And if any do fulfill it, they do it out of fear, trusting in the most wretched cross of their conscience.[9]

As usual when Luther makes a sweeping generalization about the interior lives of thousands of other people, something about which he could know nothing, we must infer that he is actually describing his own state. A month or so after penning these words, Luther wrote in a letter to a close friend John Lang, Augustinian prior at Erfurt, that he is so busy with his many duties as administrator, lecturer and preacher that "I hardly have any uninterrupted time to say the Hourly Prayers and celebrate [mass]." Luther had time, of course, to do at least some of the things he wanted to do, and in the light of what has just been quoted from the recent lecture it would appear that he found little relish in participating in the communal prayers with his fellow religious or even in saying mass. He would be one of those who fulfilled his responsibility without love and only from a sense of duty.

In this same letter there is a passing reference to the recurrence of his anxiety states ('spiritual temptations'), which Lang would know about through their intimate acquaintance dating from the Erfurt period. In another letter written in the latter part of 1516 to a friend, George Mascov, Luther reveals that his psychic problem is worsening:

> I beseech you to pray to the Lord for me, for I confess to you that every day my life grows more and more like hell, because daily I become worse and more miserable.[10]

It is from the background of his increased psychic distress, with his consoler Staupitz now seldom available in person, that Luther begins replacing the 'theology of the cross' with a new defense, the *sola fide,* which eventually will turn out to be almost its opposite. As usual he proceeded slowly and with deliberation, the new defense only gradually superseding the earlier one and with an extended period of overlap.

One of the earliest expressions of the new program is to be found in

the Lectures on Hebrews, a course Luther began in April 1517 and
continued on into the next spring. He has now been dealing with the
Pauline epistles for two years and is so imbued with Paul's emphasis
on faith that merely encountering the word 'salvation' near the beginning of the second chapter of the epistle sets him off on a lengthy
digression of little relevance to the text [Hebr. 2:3]:

> Faith in Christ cannot possibly become inactive, for it is lively
> and *of itself works* and triumphs, and in this way *good works flow
> spontaneously* from faith. Thus our patience comes from Christ's
> patience, our humility from his humility, and other gifts in the
> same way *if only we firmly believe* that he has done all these
> things *for us.* They err grossly who would begin to expunge their
> sins by good works and acts of penance.[11]

The italicized words on the benefits of 'faith', e.g., the automatic
acquisition of such virtues as patience and humility, may seem more
than a little naive. But we are here in the area of Martin's disturbance, where fantasy easily triumphs over reason and common sense.
Having previously acknowledged that he cannot achieve faith in the
N. T. sense of a total commitment to Jesus, he now devises a substitute, an ersatz faith. All that is to be demanded of Luther's Christian
is to feel confident that Jesus has done all these things for *him.* The
ultimate reward for convincing oneself of this 'truth' is the escape
from damnation. This is put negatively because that is how Luther
views the goal of the Christian; the positive goal − the Beatific Vision
− he has encountered in his reading but it has little meaning for him.

Another aspect of the *sola fide* program not apparent to Luther
it would seem, even in 1518, is that it relieves the Christian of any
responsibility for his salvation − or for his behavior. As will become
increasingly evident, a basic corollary of the *sola fide* doctrine is
that nothing a man *does* in his earthly life has any positive religious
value because his nature is totally and irretrievably corrupt. It is this
feature of the program that will presently lead to a radical shift in
Luther's views on the theology of the sacraments.

The insistence on self reference appears again in Luther's comment
on the opening verse of the fifth chapter of Hebrews:

> It is not enough for a Christian to believe that Christ was ap-
> pointed to suffer for the sake of men unless he also believes that
> *he himself is one of those men.*[12]

In a penetrating study of the development of Luther's ideas during
this period, Paul Hacker calls this attitude "reflexive faith" to distinguish it from ordinary Christian faith.[13] From this time on it
becomes one of the most personal features of Luther's teaching.
Later on he will insist that it is based on Scripture, but it is unrelated

to the passage he is supposed to be commenting on here (or to anything else in Scripture) and in this comment he professes to take his
inspiration from the sermon of Bernard referred to above.

Continuing his commentary on this same verse, Luther applies the
new position to sacramental practise:

> No one receives grace because he is absolved . . . . or communi-
> cated, but because he believes that by being absolved . . . or com-
> municated he will receive grace.

> Their error is great who approach the sacrament of the Euchar-
> ist relying on their having confessed or on their being conscious
> of no mortal sin, or on having prepared themselves by saying
> prayers before. They all eat and drink judgment against them-
> selves, because they are not made worthy or pure by these things;
> instead by this trust in their purity they become even more im-
> pure. But if they believe and trust that grace will be given them in
> the reception, this faith alone will make them pure and worthy.[14]

We comment on this paragraph not as a characteristic distortion of
traditional doctrine but as a revelation of his personal problem,
which made impossible for him a normal sacramental life. Since he
tended to interpret his anxiety attacks, accompanied as they were
with blasphemous feelings about God, as sinful, it was out of the
question for him to attain or persevere in a state of grace in the
ordinary sense of the term and therefore not meaningful. Hence his
serious difficulties with the sacrament of penance. Being unable to
experience love for God, he was in consequence unable to experience
contrition, i.e., sorrow at having offended God. He was aware of this
inability and perturbed by it, and at this period of his life appears
to be swinging around to the view that the fault was not his but
rather in the teaching that sets forth the need for contrition. Furthermore, he is chafing at the requirement of recounting his "sins of
blasphemy" in the confessional. In the dedicatory letter addressed
to Staupitz that introduces the "Explanations of the 95 Theses"
(discussed below) he reviews his discovery under Staupitz' guidance
of the meaning of penitence as a transforming of mind and heart.[15]
He describes his own fruitless attempts to achieve such a transformation and cultivate in himself a love for God. And he goes on to speak
disparagingly of the requirement of "a most laborious confession."

For the present he attempts to reconcile his personal difficulties
and the traditional teaching on the sacrament of penance in a way
described in the tract he wrote during the earlier part of 1518 by
way of explaining the actual position he took on each of the 95
Indulgence Theses. In the section treating Thesis No. 7 he refers to a
man suffering a 'trial' (i.e., himself when beset by anxiety):

> While he continues in this unhappy state of perplexed consci-
> ence he experiences no peace or comfort, unless he resorts to the
> authority of the Church and looks for consolation and relief from
> his sins and miseries in confession . . . . The priest, seeing such
> humility and compunction, . . . will declare him absolved and in
> this way give peace to his conscience. The one who is being
> absolved, if he would enjoy peace of heart, must be most careful
> not to doubt that God has forgiven his sins . . . . Whoever would
> obtain peace in any other way, as for instance by an inner experi-
> ence, . . . wants to have peace in deed, not in faith.[16]

In a later section of the same work treating Thesis 38 the purely egocentric character of Martin's approach is even more pronounced.
After stating that contrition is less important than 'faith' and that
one who believes he is absolved benefits incomparably more than one
who is contrite, he attempts to project his unhappiness at his inability
to feel contrition on his fellow Christians:

> Neglecting this faith, most of us strive only to excite contri-
> tion. We teach men to be confident their sins are forgiven when
> they feel themselves to be perfectly contrite, that is, never to be
> confident but rather to strive to fall into despair . . . .
> This faith is most perfectly exhibited in those who, being af-
> flicted with dread of conscience, feel themselves about to
> despair.[17]

During the next few years Luther issued one statement after another
like a series of semi-annual reports, about his changing attitude on
confession.

At the end of March 1518 Luther delivered the last of the lectures
on Hebrews prior to the Easter recess. These lectures, it appears,
were never resumed, though more than two chapters (of the 13) remained to be discussed. He made comments on individual words
(glosses) as far as the end of the epistle, but the exposition of the
text (*scholia*) stops at 11:8. A week or so later he set out on foot for
a meeting of his order at Heidelberg and was away from Wittenberg
till mid-May. His failure to complete his commentary on Hebrews
is a matter of some interest. He had been working at it a full year, as
long a period as he had allotted to Romans, a work appreciably
longer than Hebrews. (During the earlier course, it is true, he had suffered no distractions comparable to the Indulgence controversy.) It
is doubtless pure coincidence that the commentary breaks off shortly
before reaching a verse which is in unremovable contradiction with
the *sola fide* program: "Strive for the holiness without which no one
can see the Lord" [12:14]. It is also a coincidence that about the
same time Luther would have been lecturing on this verse had he re-

mained in Wittenberg he was telling his brother Augustinians (and some visiting religious) at Heidelberg that the free will is a mere name and can do nothing but commit sin. And to look ahead at another type of singularity, the list of N. T. writings important enough to engage the attention of mature Christians which he issued in 1522 does not include the Epistle to the Hebrews, to the exposition of which he had devoted a year of his life.

Before setting out for Heidelberg Luther published a Latin sermon or tract entitled "On the worthy preparation of the heart for receiving the Eucharist." Commentators on Luther have paid little attention to this tract despite its signal importance for the study of his development. This brief work may be described as his attempt to write in the manner of the *Imitatio Christi;* also it reflects the influence of the new *sola fide* defense currently under development in the Lectures on Hebrews. Indeed it even employs some of the same language about the Eucharist that appears in these lectures. The primary aim of the tract is to advise anyone beset with anxiety and scruples about approaching the altar on how to surmount these and bring himself to communicate despite his fear of doing so. Much of the tract consists of an application of the *sola fide* technique to the special problem Luther himself faced when planning to communicate. Toward the end there appears what is for Luther a most unusual defense. When all else fails to subdue your fears, take refuge in the arms of Mother Church:

> Say boldly to the Lord Jesus: 'Whatever may be my [deficiency], I must obey your Church, which commands me to approach [the altar]. I will come for the sake of obedience if I can present no better reason.' Believe firmly that your reception of the sacrament is not unworthy . . . . Then it cannot happen that the faith of the Church will suffer you to perish, any more than the infant who is baptized and *saved by the merit of another's faith.*[18]

The contradiction between this position and the *sola fide,* which bestows salvation through one's own faith, reveals that as late as April 1518 Luther has not completely committed himself to the new program. More interesting, however, is the psychic state revealed by this defense. Wittingly or not, Luther here proposes the abdication of a supposedly adult status by a denial of personal responsibility and a retreat to the religious condition of a child. For the child's religion is not so much its own as that of the family, and the comparison to the infant Luther makes in this passage is more than a figure of speech. This defense of course reflects the state of emotional stress he is now struggling to cope with, the same kind of stress responsible for the begetting of the *sola fide* defense. The importance of this tract in assessing the development of Luther's psychic disorder in the spring of 1518 can hardly be exaggerated; we see here a definite foreshadowing of the regression — retreat to a juvenile level in the area of his disturbance — that is now little more than two years away. By way of contrast, consider the maturity of judgment reflected in the following passage from the lectures on Romans composed some two years earlier:

> Self-will greatly hinders [our reception of grace]. It brings about dissension with others and makes a man prefer his own way and resist his superiors and those whose words or deeds God wishes to make use of in revealing his will . . . . In the Church God does nothing else than transform this self-will. This transformation is resisted by those who take pleasure in their self-will and disrupt everything, causing schisms and heresies.[19]

iii. At odds with ecclesiastical authority

During the autumn of 1517 Luther had prepared two compositions on the centuries-old ecclesiastical system of indulgences, the famous 95 Theses, which were intentionally expressed in provocative language to promote a lively academic disputation, and a brief tractate on the same subject to present his actual views. The importance of the 95 Theses has been fantastically inflated in the Luther legend, being treated as the primary symbol of Luther's later revolt, and the fabled nailing of a copy of the Theses to the church door in Wittenberg has become one of the most famous non-events in world history.[20] Correspondingly, Luther's repeated assertions that the theses did not all represent his personal views, that some of them were indeed contrary to his views and others dealt with topics about which he was of uncertain opinion have been largely ignored. The little treatise setting forth Luther's actual views is one of the most thoroughly suppressed items in the entire catalog of topics that Luther-cult biographers have not seen fit to disclose to their public.[21] While the text of the 95 Indulgence Theses appeared in vol. 1 of the Weimar edition in 1883, the "Treatise on Indulgences," so embarrassing to Luther partisans, was delayed until 1967 (WBr 12, 2-9) with the editorial comment "hitherto little noticed."

Since the indulgence question is intrinsically so peripheral to Luther's own interests we shall not pursue it in detail. At the end of October 1517 he committed the astonishing error of judgment of sending a copy of the theses to the primate of Germany, the Hohenzollern Cardinal Archbishop of Mainz, whose office forwarded the copy to Rome for its possible heterodox contents. Thus the theses were instrumental in calling to the attention of ecclesiastical authority rather promptly the innovations in doctrine Luther was fathering. But this step speeded up the discovery by perhaps only a matter of months or at most a year or two. Apart from this involvement with officialdom, the unauthorized printing of the theses, in German translation as well as the original Latin, helped greatly to widen the circle of Luther's readers.

In Luther's time heresy-hunting was as popular a sport as 'Communist'-hunting during the McCarthy-Nixon era following World War II. The clerical bureaucracy in Rome reacted promptly to the action taken by the clerical bureaucracy in Mainz and presently Martin found himself summoned to a hearing in Rome. Then a series of politico-legal maneuvers resulted in the commutation of the summons to Rome to a hearing before Cardinal Thomas Cajetan in Augsburg, who was there as a special emissary from Rome during the meeting of the Diet or Reichstag. Luther's prince, Frederick, the Elector of Saxony, was the most important of the numerous sovereigns of the German states, and since he held one of the seven votes for electing the Emperor (the only one of the seven reputed not to be for sale), he and his subjects had to be treated with care. The rather odd way in which Luther's case was handled by Rome during the next two years is explained by the aid the Medici Pope Leo X hoped to obtain from Frederick in preventing the election of the Hapsburg Charles to succeed the aging Emperor Maximilian.

The summons to Augsburg is of considerable interest to the student of Luther's character as providing the first occasion when he had to face possible danger to his person. According to the legend, Luther was a man of unshakable courage, 'Martin the lion-hearted,' a position defended with the greater zeal by many biographers inasmuch as the evidence indicates he was actually nothing of the sort. A letter to Staupitz written September 1, 1518 just before he received notice that he would be required to go only to Augsburg instead of Rome, reveals his inner troubles are more painful than outward dangers:

> Neither the citation [to Rome] nor the unfulfilled threats move me at all. As you know, *I suffer things incomparably worse* which, if I did not sincerely wish to honor the authority of the Church, would force me to regard as vanity these temporal and passing thunderbolts. If I am excommunicated by men, it is you alone I fear to offend, for I am confident your judgment in this affair is correct, trustworthy and from God.[22]

To comply with the official summons, Luther set out on foot for Augsburg, where he arrived in early October. Though he had attempted in his letter to Staupitz to minimize his concern over what might happen to him in Augsburg, as he came nearer his destination severe abdominal pain, induced by his fear of unknown danger, seized him and he finally became so weak that a carriage had to be provided to transport him the last few miles of the journey. As he writes in a letter to Spalatin on October 10, three days later: "I almost collapsed along the way and arrived exhausted, having developed some peculiar and serious stomach trouble. But I have recovered."[23]

The legend-makers have tried to explain away this unheroic display by alleging Martin was exhausted because of weakness arising from monastic austerities, forgetting that not six months earlier he had negotiated the long hike to Heidelberg without collapsing, and while there, like a modern tourist, had climbed the mountain rising up from the city streets not far from the Augustinian monastery to view the castle.[24]

On the later trip to Worms he rode all the way in a wagon provided by the town council and under the protection of the imperial herald, and suffered the same type of symptoms. The monastic austerities were, as we shall see, one of the fantasies Luther invented during his paranoid phase in the 1530s. Anyhow, well before 1518 Luther had stopped taking seriously even ordinary monastic routines.

At Augsburg Luther was to appear before Cardinal Cajetan, a distinguished theologian some fifteen years older than Martin, who, as noted above, remained in the city after the sessions of the Diet to conduct the hearing. Upon Luther's arrival he applied to imperial officials for a safe-conduct and thereby gained several days' rest until the document was drawn up. Conrad Adelman, a canon of the cathedral chapter who had become interested in Luther, wrote to Spalatin that once Luther received the safe-conduct "he appeared with greater courage and confidence before the legate."[25]

Cajetan had been instructed to obtain from Luther a recantation, which would permit a dismissal of the heresy charge. Cajetan himself had no interest in prosecuting the charge and was at first sympathetic to Luther. When the hearing at length began, Cajetan announced two topics on which he asked Luther to acknowledge his error. One of these concerned Luther's rejection of an earlier papal decretal on dispensing to the faithful the treasury of Christ's merits, the other his assertion that in confession the sins of the penitent were forgiven because he believed they were forgiven. Cajetan made no difficulty about the aggressive character of the Indulgence Theses, recognizing that they were merely intended as topics for debate, and these two statements were taken from Luther's published writings. Cajetan's instructions from Rome left the form of the recantation to his discretion but ruled out any discussion with Luther, who instead demanded a discussion that would establish his error before he would recant. Cajetan was actually trying, as he thought, to make matters easy for Luther, and after some stormy sessions running over a period of three days, including additional meetings with Staupitz, who had come down to Augsburg from Salzburg to be with Luther, finally agreed to reduce the matter of the recantation to only the first of the two propositions.

What Cajetan, Staupitz or the other friends of Martin who took part in the sessions could not possibly realize was that the matters proposed for recantation were involved with the *sola fide* defensive program. Any attempt to undermine the program could not fail to arouse in Luther the most stubborn resistance. Since the program was developed by an emotional, non-rational process, although Luther insisted it was derived from Scripture, any fruitful discussion aimed at removing even a part of it was completely out of the question. The utter failure of the Augsburg meeting meant that no reconciliation between Luther and ecclesiastical authority would ever be possible, although negotiations were protracted over a period of another year and a half.

In a letter to Spalatin (October 14) written a few days after the hearings began, Luther manifests his intransigent attitude:

> According to the plan adopted, the articles I must recant and the teaching I must accept are to be prepared by [Cajetan]. . . . But I am busy drawing up an appeal that will get me out of recanting anything at all.[26]

In an earlier letter to Spalatin (August 28) Luther had written:

> *I will never be a heretic.* I can err in a disputation, but *I want to decide nothing.* Yet neither do I want to be captive to the doctrines of men.[27]

It would be difficult to find a more clear cut revelation of Martin's incapacity for self knowledge. That he would always insist on 'deciding' whatever doctrine he pleased, and that he was a helpless captive of the doctrines of a man named Martin Luther were ideas that he could never face up to seriously. His remark about not being a heretic calls to mind the statement of the illustrious mystic Meister Eckart at a tribunal in Cologne nearly two centuries earlier (1326). In the course of defending his writings against the charge of heresy, he declared to his judges: "I can be in error but I cannot be a heretic, for error is a product of the mind and heresy of the will."[28] This statement is admirable for both its terseness and precision, but it does not really apply to Luther. He would doubtless have agreed with it in 1518; in the spring of 1521 he was to write that the way of schism and heresy was the only safe one. Eckart's statement does not hold for a man deprived both of his judgement and his inner freedom by a disorder of the psyche.

At the last session of the hearing on October 14 Cajetan, by now much provoked at Luther's intransigence, told him not to return until he was ready to recant. By this time both Luther and Staupitz had become seriously alarmed over what might ensue and considered the possibility of Martin's seeking refuge in Paris where he would be safe from arrest by Curial officials. Staupitz is said to have tried to borrow funds to finance the journey, and when this attempt failed, himself left Augsburg after releasing Luther from his vow of monastic obedience. As no further word came from the Cardinal, who was still in his quarters writing reports of his unsuccessful mission, Luther finally panicked and arranged with friends to flee unobserved. Augsburg was a walled city whose gates closed at sundown, but during the night Luther was able to make his egress through a small door in the city wall.

A horse and a mounted companion were waiting outside the wall. Luther rode off at a gallop in the darkness, heading north for Nuremberg. Upwards of 20 miles from Augsburg they crossed the Danube at Donauworth but pushed on another ten miles to the village of Monheim. By then both Luther and his horse were exhausted; when he finally stopped and dismounted he was so stiff from the long hours in the saddle that he was unable to stand but fell sprawling in the straw of the stable. For him the ill effects of the ride were temporary but the horse succumbed. Later upon reaching Nuremberg Luther stopped to rest again and seems to have taken occasion to visit the renowned humanist Willibald Pirckheimer. He returned to Wittenberg on the last day of October, just a year after he had sent the 95 Indulgence Theses to the Archbishop of Mainz.

The midnight ride of Luther from Augsburg, fleeing in panic from imaginary pursuers, fittingly symbolizes his fear of a threat to his person. From that time on, he followed two very simple rules, which permitted him to die in bed while a number of his disciples were dying at the stake, even though he lived for 25 years under the ban of the empire. The first rule was: Never go where you might get hurt. And the second: If by mischance you should get into a tight spot, run for cover as fast as you can. While these rules may be described as the dictates of elementary prudence, they have an unheroic ring. In an ordinary man they might even be described as cowardly. But the ordinary man does not suffer from pathological anxiety. Was Luther aware of this unadmirable trait? Very definitely, so much so indeed that he repeatedly makes excuses for it.

Near the end of August, a few weeks before Luther set out for Augsburg, there arrived in Wittenberg a man who was henceforth to play a predominant role in his life. This was the 21-year-old Philip Melanchthon, the recently appointed professor of Greek, so slight in appearance that his new colleagues at first were dubious of the wisdom of the appointment. But a few days later he put to rest these doubts by delivering an inaugural lecture on the reform of the curriculum that demonstrated both the breadth of his learning and his enthusiasm for promoting humanistic studies. Some months before his arrival at Wittenberg he had published a Greek grammar that was to remain in use for generations, and this was only the first of a long list of textbooks that were in later years to win him the title of Preceptor of Germany.

In a letter to Spalatin the last day of August Luther announced his great admiration for the newcomer, saying that from then on Melanchthon was to be his own instructor in Greek. In December, writing to John Reuchlin, the distinguished Hebraist and Philip's great uncle, Luther describes Philip as his dearest and closest friend (*familiarissimus et amicissimus mihi*). On Philip's part the attachment was likewise prompt and profound. Its fervency is attested to in a letter to Spalatin written somewhat later on:

> Nothing more sorrowful could befall me than to be separated from Martin. Therefore on my account as well as for the public welfare . . . try to safeguard the one man I am so bold as to prefer not only to all now living but to all the men of all ages, whether Augustines or Jeromes or Nazianzens.[29]

The early influence of Luther on his younger friend became apparent in the aborting of Melanchthon's earlier plan to edit the works of Aristotle. Philip speedily became imbued with the anti-humanistic, anti-intellectual posture of his older colleague. The year after his arrival in Wittenberg we find him attacking the study of philosophy in general and Aristotle in particular. The positive aspect of Luther's influence manifested itself in the great interest Philip acquired in another 'Greek' author very much favored by Martin, namely, Paul of Tarsus, and particularly his Epistle to the Romans. Because of the disparity of their ages, Philip being almost 17 years Martin's junior, the suggestion that he could replace Staupitz as maternal substitute may appear questionable, though not in conflict with clinical observation. There is evident a mutual bond comparable to the Luther-Staupitz relation in warmth and in the dependence of each man on the other strong enough to survive severe strains later on.

No other incident in Luther's career brought out so fully as the Augsburg affair his very considerable legal talents. Virtually everything issuing from his pen during the period of two months or so after his appearance before Cardinal Cajetan was prepared with a view to escaping the sentence of excommunication that now threatened him. The most substantial of his publications relating to Augsburg, the "Augsburg Proceedings," was a compilation of documents having to do with his transactions with Cajetan. It included a papal breve dated August 23 threatening Luther with imprisonment if he refused to recant. Employing an approach suggestive of the one he was to follow in 1520, he tried to show that this document emanating from the Roman Curia was a forgery. At the time Luther was preparing the "Augsburg Proceedings," Frederick was struggling with the problem posed by a demand from Cajetan to send Luther to Rome or at least into exile. Not caring for either alternative, Frederick forwarded the Cardinal's letter to Luther for suggestions. Luther replied at great length, dwelling on the unfairness of the accusation of heresy since no one had ever proved from Scripture he was in error. He flatters the Elector and plays on his sympathies and his desire for the continued prosperity of Wittenberg University, now threatened by this unjust attack. (This last point was bolstered by a letter to Frederick from the Rector and the faculty, but composed by Luther himself in his own defense.)

The tract entitled "Augsburg Proceedings" is of interest as an early example of Luther's hostile reaction to verbal attacks threatening his defenses. Instead of seeking a way to settle the conflict, he is characteristically sharp, bitter and venomous. He, the completely innocent party, is being wantonly assaulted by a pack of liars seeking only their own glory or profit. It is partly from misinterpretation of such behavior as this, the compulsive reaction of the threatened neurotic, that the legend of Luther's invincible courage has arisen. Also of interest is Luther's publication of the tract in the face of orders from the Elector's court that he maintain silence while the Elector was attempting to negotiate the problem with the Curia. Luther was always very strong on law and order for other people, but in the fashion of similar egocentrics regarded himself as above the law. His compulsive urge to retaliate in print no matter what the consequences stands as one of his most strongly marked and enduring characteristics.

During the period of later November and early December, he again had to face the prospect of leaving Wittenberg. As he reports in a letter to Spalatin of December 9 he had already bade a provisional farewell to the Wittenberg congregation in a sermon. The feeling at court at this time seems to have been that Luther's departure was the only feasible way out for the government of Electoral Saxony. Then there was an abrupt change of policy. This was brought about by a policy change in Rome not occasioned by the heresy prosecution. The Emperor Maximilian being old and in ailing health (he died on January 12, 1519), the problem of the choice of his successor became acute. As remarked earlier, papal policy aimed at preventing the election of Maximilian's grandson, the Hapsburg Charles, because of the potential threat he could pose to the independence of the papacy. It was deemed inexpedient to act against Frederick's professor at a time when it was desired to influence his vote.

For decades the popes had been men motivated primarily to maintain or expand the papacy as an Italian state and also to further their family interests. During Luther's lifetime, the only edifying character to occupy the papal throne was the Dutchman, Adrian VI. (Exception may be taken for Pius III, who succeeded the Borgia Pope, Alexander VI, but died only a few weeks after election.) As the system operated, worldly cardinals elected worldly men as pope, and such popes continued to appoint unsuitable men as cardinals. The system was not broken until the reforming acts of the Council of Trent. (A comparable situation existed in many dioceses in the appointment of bishops, especially in Germany, where the old system persisted on into the 19th century.) The new policy on the Luther problem was to send a German diplomat on the curial staff, Carl Miltitz, to Saxony to find a solution that did not involve banishment. During the next year and a half Luther had various meetings with Miltitz, even one as late as October 1520 after the official proclamation of the papal bull *Exsurge Domine* condemning a number of heretical propositions in his writings and demanding a recantation. The issuance of this document may be taken as an indication of the futility of the Luther-Miltitz discussions. These talks centered around proposals for mutual silence about controversial issues and the appointment of one or more German bishops to examine the issues and make a decision on Luther.

By spring Luther had lost interest in Miltitz and in a letter to him dated May 17 turned down the proposal that he travel to Coblenz for still another session with the envoy. Luther was now working hard to obtain permission from Duke George to debate against John Eck at Leipzig alongside his colleague Carlstadt. Since his Augsburg meeting of the previous October with Cajetan (whom Martin no longer regards as a 'Catholic Christian' because of Cajetan's attempts 'to abolish Christ'), it had become quite clear to him that the office of pope is a mere human institution. It is this discovery that he is now anxious to publicize in the debate that is described below and which he will further expose in a long tract later in the year called "Lutherian Explanation of Proposition 13 on the Power of the Pope."

iv. The debate at Leipzig

The unexpected notoriety and popularity that Luther achieved as a result of the Indulgence affair at first puzzled and distressed him. But eventually he was able to adjust to it and even began playing to the gallery. His native inclination for such activity is reflected in a letter to a friend written when his controversy with John Eck over papal authority was just beginning:

> The more they rave, the more I provoke them. I leave behind
> what they barked at first and follow with something they will
> bark at next.[30]

'They' are the academic (scholastic) theologians. He was participating
in what was to become the first major attempt since the comparatively recent invention of printing to sway public opinion by means of
the press, an avocation for which Luther possessed great natural
talent. At his peak he could turn out copy fast enough to keep
three or four printers busy. As he himself recognized, the quality of
this work was distinctly less impressive than the quantity, but it sold
very well and enriched the printers. Luther took no payment for
himself on the mistaken assumption that the printers, needing to pay
no royalty to the author, would make the price of their wares
cheaper and thereby his message would reach a wider circle of
readers.

While the development of his defenses in his published writings
continued for a time to reflect mainly his private preoccupations,
more and more of his energy was gradually diverted into other
channels, at first in replies to his adversaries and then in an outright
attack on the Church. Thus from 1519 onward Luther's writings, lectures and sermons, hitherto devoted in large part to his search for a
theological solution of his psychic problem, became increasingly
'contaminated' with material representing his personal reaction to
his impact on the society in which he lived. This new experience provided new occasion for attacks of anxiety to which may be
attributed the onset of the psychotic symptoms that appear in 1520.

The effect of the pressure of the heresy proceedings on Luther's
psychic condition is evident in a letter to Staupitz dated February
20, 1519, of which we give two extracts:[31]

> I believe my "Augsburg Proceedings" has reached you, that is,
> the wrath and indignation of Rome. I am being driven and forced
> by God rather than led. I can not remain calm; I wish to be quiet
> and am dragged into the midst of this tumult . . . . I am a man
> exposed to and involved with *socializing, drunkenness, carnal
> temptations, neglect of duty* and other troubles in addition to the
> cares my profession burdens me with.

Attention should be drawn here to Luther's mention of his experience of being driven into action not of his own choosing. During the
next few years he refers rather often to the compulsive behavior
associated with his disorder. It is characteristic that in his aggressive
attacks on the Church or individuals he attributes the source of the
compulsion to God rather than Satan, who on other matters gets

credit for the behavior. Since Luther will soon be starting his 'holy war,' it is natural for him now to select God as the prime mover.

This letter also shows how reticent about certain personal difficulties Luther remains at this time. He is here addressing his most intimate friend, the maternal substitute from whom he has no secrets. A few years hence he will be broadcasting his sexual problems in published writings; now in 1519 he barely mentions them to Staupitz, using only one word — *titillatio.* Early in this same year he became so embarrassed over the unauthorized publication of a sermon on marriage in which he is represented as saying he could not control his sexual urges that in self-defense he published his own version of the sermon (see Ch. 6). Here also we may cite a cryptic confidence to his friend Lang, prior at Erfurt — possibly a new sexual problem he would not trust to the uncertain privacy of correspondence:

> Another and greater trial has been added to these, by all of which the Lord teaches me what man is, which I thought I already knew well enough. You will hear about this personally if you visit me.[32]

With regard to socializing with boon companions or trying to drown his sorrows in alcohol, it may be remarked that these practices later became two of his preferred devices in the battle against anxiety. From the apologetic tone in which Luther mentions them early in 1519 it may be inferred they are recent developments occasioned by increasing anxiety over the threat of excommunication. The apologetic tone may be explained by the fact that these devices represent an abdication of the monastic ideal which Martin has not yet renounced.

The letter makes no mention of what is to become one of his principal defenses and is now in the early stages of formulation: the falsification that the Pope is 'Antichrist.' This is a term found in the Johannine writings, where it denotes one who denies that Jesus is God; it also appears to have apocalyptic connotations. The practice of applying it to the Pope as a supreme insult did not originate with Luther, but rather in anti-papal circles during the later middle ages. At this stage he is not yet committed to making the identification and still honors the Pope as the lawful head of Christendom. Rather he is like the cautious sailor who with fair skies overhead begins to shorten sail because he is concerned about the clouds way off on the horizon. Thus in a letter to his fellow Augustinian Wenzel Link at Nuremberg in the previous December he raises the question of whether the true Antichrist is reigning in the Roman Curia. In a letter to Spalatin a few weeks after the letter to Staupitz he wonders whether the Pope is the veritable Antichrist. Even a year later (February 24, 1520) in another letter to Spalatin describing his reaction to Valla's exposure of the forgery of the Donation of Constantine (recently published by Hutten), he goes only so far as to say he thinks it likely the Pope is Antichrist.[33] This episode is an excellent illustration of how long it could take Martin to bring to maturity his most characteristic attitudes.

His publications in 1519 up until the last months of the year are mainly either a consolidation of earlier work or are related to the debate with John Eck. During this period he was giving the new course of lectures on the Psalms referred to above (Ch. 1), and began to publish it more or less concurrently as *Operationes in Psalmos,* known in English as "Commentary on the First Twenty-two Psalms." It went to press in several batches, roughly the first half in 1519 and the rest in 1520 and early 1521. (The lecture course was ended by the Worms-Wartburg episode.) By 1521 he had in print several hundred pages of material dealing with the first twenty-two Psalms. The lectures he had delivered in 1516-17 on the Epistle to the Galatians appeared in print in revised form during 1519. Perhaps the most interesting of these publications was a reworking of an earlier sermon series on the Lord's Prayer.

A version of these sermons, which were preached during Lent in 1517, was published by a younger disciple of Martin, John Schneider (Agricola), in 1518 from notes he had taken at the time of delivery. Luther's own version, occupying some 50 pages in the Weimar edition, contains rather little material reflecting current developments in his thinking.[34] The *sola fide* program is barely mentioned, figuring briefly in some concluding remarks on the meaning of 'Amen.' Man's free will, denied the previous year at Heidelberg, is still free in this exposition. Not only does Martin here assert that God gives us a free will but he even stresses the need for training and guiding it to conform to the will of God, a conventional point of view that will presently become anathema to him. Likewise he expresses a traditional point of view toward one of the most serious evils of the contemporary ecclesiastical world, the uneducated and untrained clergy. We should regard this as a great scandal, but also as a form of divine punishment for our sinful life. We "make an evil more scandalous when we loathe them and hold them in contempt." The very next year Luther will abandon this point of view and begin his new vocation of "making an evil more scandalous."

The prevailing tone of the exposition of the Lord's Prayer is gloomy and often pessimistic, apparently reflecting Martin's unhappy inner state. To him the meaning of the petition 'Thy kingdom come' is that 'we are still rejected.' Equally disheartening is the meaning of 'Hallowed be thy name.' When we pray this we give testimony that "we defile, blaspheme, dishonor, profane and desecrate God's name. In all Scripture, I don't know any text that more powerfully

and shamefully destroys us than this petition." Here one can see
Luther projecting his guilt feelings aroused by the blasphemous
emotions experienced during the anxiety attacks. The third petition
receives a comparable interpretation:

> It is terrifying to hear ourselves say: 'Thy will be done.' For
> what is more terrible than that God's will is not done and his com-
> mandment is despised, as we ourselves clearly acknowledge in this
> petition![35]

In short, Martin's words about the first three petitions of the prayer
give us an intimate view of his inner life at this period. As might be
expected, man's love for God is nowhere mentioned. In the discussions of the remaining four petitions, one of which will be cited in
a later chapter, Luther continues to emphasize man's unending
sinfulness.

Another revealing composition of the first half of 1519 appeared
as a letter addressed to a community of Franciscan Minorite friars
of Jueterbog. The pastor of the parish of this little village some miles
northeast of Wittenberg and in the same diocese (Brandenburg) was
a recent doctoral student of Luther's named Guenther. The disputation (1517) held prior to the granting of his degree was based on a
set of theses attacking scholastic theology. It is not surprising that
the preaching in the parish church of Jueterbog echoed the new developments in Wittenberg theology. In consequence, during the
first week of May in 1519 two formal complaints were sent from the
convent to the chancery office of the diocese of Brandenburg setting
forth a number of heretical propositions alleged to be drawn from
the preaching in the parish church. Luther naturally was credited
with responsibility for the heterodox material. On May 15 he drafted
a long letter to the brothers of the convent, which begins:

> I have in hand a proclamation which attacks my good name
> foully, and with rash impudence declares certain most true propo-
> sitions of mine to be erroneous . . . . Is this pride and petulance
> your religion and way of observance? Not wishing to return evil
> for evil, I give you this choice: either take back this audacious
> criticism and restore my good name, or I will publish this procla-
> mation of yours with notes exposing your ignorance . . . . Take
> care lest I find you to be heretical . . . . Take either peace or war,
> whichever you wish.[36]

Luther's extreme overreaction to criticism of his theological views
in this letter suggests they have become so thoroughly integrated into
his defenses that he will never give them up.

The year 1519 is highlighted by Luther's participation in a theological disputation at the University of Leipzig in mid-summer. A

noteworthy feature of this event is that it is one of the few occasions when he appeared in public outside Wittenberg before a wider audience than members of his own order or a group assembled to hear a sermon. It is from this occasion that we possess a priceless description of Luther in action written by a competent and sympathetic observer. The Leipzig debate also may serve to introduce two characters who figured largely in his life during the next several years. One of them is his comrade at arms in the debate, Andrew Bodenstein, or Carlstadt, like Luther a professor of theology at Wittenberg; the other is John Eck, professor of theology at the University of Ingolstadt, who had been engaged sporadically in a verbal duel with the Wittenbergers since early in 1518. Eck was soon to become a leading figure in the heresy prosecution and Carlstadt, within a few years, the target of Luther's wrath when he insisted on preferring his own theological opinions to Luther's.

The actual scheduling of the debate and obtaining permission from civil and ecclesiastical authorities to stage it proved to be a tedious affair that Martin was willing to undertake because of his long pent-up desire for this kind of public airing of his ideas. As sovereign of ducal Saxony, Duke George was the ultimate authority at the Leipzig university. The series of letters Luther wrote to him and to Eck, of which about a half dozen are extant along with several of their replies, show his determination to appear in the disputation, which was originally planned to be Eck vs. Carlstadt.

At last toward the end of June the Wittenberg party set out for Leipzig. Carlstadt rode in one wagon along with an enormous load of books to provide citations which his memory was inadequate to retain. In a second wagon were Luther, Melanchthon and Amsdorf. After his severe fright at Augsburg Martin was taking no chances, and had persuaded about two hundred undergraduates to go along as a bodyguard. But finding no need for their services at Leipzig and becoming bored with the endless talking of the principals, they straggled back to Wittenberg while the debating marathon was continuing in full force.

Carlstadt was born to be cast in the role of a comic character. A quarter-century later Luther was to refer to him as Jack Absurdity. Shortly before reaching Leipzig, his wagon lost a wheel and Carlstadt was thrown out on the roadway, half buried in a pile of books and notes, with grievous effects on his subsequent performance since he was unable to restore the notes to order. After some long-winded preliminaries, Carlstadt and Eck tackled one another on the subject of grace and free will. But the real interest for the large crowd of spectators was the contest between Eck and Luther, who replaced Carlstadt after the first few days and argued with Eck, chiefly about the power of the papacy, for the better part of a fortnight.

It was Peter Mosellanus, a well known humanist in the employ of Duke George, who provided us with a sketch of Luther and the other two debaters that is worth quoting in full:[37]

> Martin is of average height, lean of body, and much worn by care and study, so that by looking at him closely one can practically count all his bones. He is still at a manly and vigorous time of life, with a sharp and clear voice. His learning and knowledge of Scripture are commendable, so much so that he has nearly all of it in memory. He has learned Greek and Hebrew well enough to judge the translations. Nor does he lack matter for speaking, having at hand a vast stock of words and ideas. You might perhaps feel a lack of judgment and system in the use of it. In everyday life and manners he is courteous and easy going; he is not at all stoic, not at all arrogant, but at all times he acts the man. In society he is a jovial and agreeable jester, lively and cheerful, everywhere and at all times displaying a happy countenance regardless of what difficulties his opponents may contrive, so that you would hardly believe he could undertake such arduous affairs without the favor of the gods. But most people ascribe to him the fault of being somewhat more imprudent and biting in his response to arguments than is safe for a reformer of the church or seemly for a theologian. I am not sure whether this vice is not shared by all the pedants.
>
> You can observe nearly all these qualities to a lesser degree in Carlstadt, except that he is shorter, his face dark and sunburned, his voice unclear and disagreeable, his memory weaker and his anger more ready. Now Eck is tall of stature with a square and solid body, a strong and distinct German voice . . . . His mouth and eyes, in fact his whole face, are of a type that would certainly make you recognize him as a butcher or Carian soldier rather than a theologian. As for abilities, his memory is remarkable; if his understanding were on a par with it, he would represent nature's perfection. Since his power of understanding is defective, as is his ability to judge, his other gifts count for little.

Eck had observed the heterodox tendencies in Luther's writings long before the debate and utilized them as an opportunity to entice Luther into making statements that would serve to incriminate him. In particular, he tried to identify Luther with the fifteenth century Hussite heresy in Bohemia, the aftermath of which was that Bohemia had been in a state of schism with Rome for a hundred years. At this time Luther was not well acquainted with the details of the affair but had no desire to be linked with the most notorious heretic of recent vintage of Christendom. As Mosellanus points out in the document quoted above, Luther sensed the intent of his adversary and raged like some sort of spirit at being cunningly betrayed on a side issue . . . . He strove above all to clear himself of the suspicion of approving the Bohemian schism. Eck, on the other hand, went all out to impress this view of Martin on everyone, no matter how much Martin himself protested it.[38]

Duke George manifested keen interest in this question and in a private conversation after the debate suggested to Luther he could clear himself of suspicion of Hussite tendencies by publishing a criticism of Hus. So far from accepting this proposal, as we shall see presently, Luther proceeded to take an opposite course.

It had been the plan of the debaters, whose words were recorded by clerks, to obtain a decision on the victor from the Universities of Paris and Erfurt. But one after the other the faculties of these institutions bowed out, leaving Luther to decide for himself he had 'won.' A post-Leipzig letter to Spalatin has this disclosure:

"It is enough for me that the torturer of consciences, the false theology responsible for all I suffered in conscience was overthrown in this disputation."[39] This opinion about the source of his anxiety condition is one of several explanations he offered at one time or another about a problem he could not be expected to understand.

Luther continued to reply to Eck — in print. The tone of his rejoinders is suggested by one of the titles: "Defense of Martin Luther Against the Malignant Indictment of John Eck." In this tract he also continued the feud with the Franciscan community of Jueterbog. In another letter to Spalatin (August 18) he exhibits his hostility to Eck. The practice of excusing himself for slanderous remarks demonstrated in this letter is now well established:

Eck (whom we can now judge and accuse without sin) appears everywhere in the role of a man neither honest nor courteous . . . He is impudent and without shame; there is nothing he is not ready either to defend or abandon for the sake of gaining a little glory for himself. The one thing he wants is by hook or by crook to damage Wittenberg.[40]

With his extreme self-centeredness, Luther is unable to recognize that anyone who differs from him can possibly be inspired by an interest in the truth; his habit of attributing unworthy motives to his opponents is an expression of the pathological hostility that continues until death. The fine words he published in his new commentary on the Psalms evidently do not apply to himself: We must be very careful not to judge or condemn the words . . . of another."[41]

v. The rising tide of Luther's polemics

The months following the Leipzig debate were a time of relative calm for Martin, the last he was to enjoy. Once the new year began he was to become embroiled with a German bishop over a newly published tract on the Eucharist and also with the theological faculties of Louvain and Cologne. His principal publications during this final period of calm consist of the tract on the Eucharist and two others on the sacraments of penance and baptism. These three pieces represent Luther in transition between established Christian teaching and his new gospel. As might be expected the one on penance shows the most advanced state of the transition, while the tract on the Eucharist is still fairly traditional and even emphasizes charity. However, he was to publish another tract on this sacrament the following summer bringing it properly into line with the *sola fide.* The tract on baptism is a curious mixture of *sola fide* and traditional theology with a Lutherian slant; it throws much light on his state of theological ambivalence at this period.

With these three tracts Luther had in effect completed his progress report on this theory of the sacraments for the latter half of 1519. He says something like this in a letter to Spalatin dated December 18. After giving one of the lists of activities he issued from time to time showing how busy he is, he turns to the question of the sacraments:

> As for the other sacraments, neither you nor any other man can hope or look for any sermon on them from me until I am taught by what text I can prove them sacraments. For none of the others is for me a sacrament because there is no sacrament without a divine promise expressly given which exercises faith. It is impossible for us to have any exchange [*negotium* = business] with God except by a word that promises and a faith that receives. At another time you will hear about their invention of those seven sacraments.[42]

There are three points of considerable interest in the quoted paragraph; we shall take them up in the reverse order of their presentation. The last sentence shows not only that Martin has abandoned much of the ecclesiastical teaching on the sacraments but that he is already (December 1519) by his use of the pronoun 'their' erecting a barrier between himself and the Church. The next to the last sentence of the paragraph is an expression of how Luther attempts to turn his highly defective relation to God into a norm for all Christians. As a means of escape from his unhappy plight of periodically being filled with hatred for the angry God of his anxiety attacks, he devised a picture of God as a being who makes promises to a creature whose felicity consists in accepting the gifts offered. By concentrating on what might be called a Santa-Clausizing of the God-man relation he appears to have achieved a measure of success with his problem.

That the success was only partial is apparent from the many disclosures of failure he made in later years, right on to the last sermon preached shortly before his death at Eisleben.

As for the third point, when Luther remarks he will recognize as a sacrament only what is so denoted in Scripture, he is employing the well known *sola scriptura* position, which will be increasingly in evidence from now on. *Sola scriptura,* unlike *sola fide,* is not an integral component of his defensive system. It is perhaps best described as a slogan, for he never attempts to justify it, and his use of it is primarily polemical, in his sallies against the Church or individual opponents. At such times he treats it as a self-evident principle; but when he is advancing a doctrinal position that is unscriptural or antiscriptural, he conveniently shelves the *sola scriptura.* Objectively considered, the *sola scriptura* must be described as the most thoroughly unscrupulous device in his entire polemical armory.

The reason why Luther avoids any attempt to justify the *sola scriptura* is that even his mastery of sophistical argument was inadequate for the task. To show that *sola scriptura* is a valid theological principle he would have had to produce from Scripture 'clear texts' establishing the following points:

1. Scripture is the sole source of Christian doctrine.
2. Scripture consists of the following writings . . . .
3. The only valid text of these writings is . . . .
4. These writings must be interpreted according to the following rules . . . .
5. Anyone who can read the valid text or a translation of it approved by (Martin Luther?) is authorized to interpret Scripture, no further education being required.

The interested reader may fill in the blanks or extend the list, but we shall break it off here to ask how Luther succeeded in making plausible a position so utterly fallacious. He did it by always presenting the *sola scriptura* slogan as a self-evident principle and by taking advantage of the almost universal respect for the Bible as the revealed word of God prevailing among his contemporaries. If we were to ask whether he was himself intelligent enough to see that the *sola scriptura* was sheer hocus-pocus, we would have to reply: Possibly not. But this is not an appropriate question to ask of a man with so unlimited a capacity for self-deception as Luther. He desperately needed something like the *sola scriptura* to maintain his position and that is why it was 'true' for him. As it had only a polemical validity, he could abandon it on any occasion without embarrassment because at such times he needed something else. For Luther the real test of the truth of a position in the area of his disturbance was whether it contributed to his psychic requirements of the moment or the foreseeable future.

The tract on the Eucharist soon got him into trouble with local ecclesiastical authority — the bishop of Meissen in Ducal Saxony. In January 1520 the bishop had placards posted debarring the tract from his diocese. What offended him in Luther's tract was the recommendation that a future council restore the practice of the laity receiving the Eucharist in both kinds. This topic had become so completely identified with the Bohemian schism that to recommend 'the cup for the laity' was likely to arouse the suspicion the advocate was at least a Hussite fellow-traveler. Luther was both surprised and outraged to find his doctrinal pronouncements criticized in an edict "blasphemous and more furious against Christ's gospel than any heresy." In addition to writing letters to various dignitaries protesting the action of the bishop of Meissen — "that silly carnival mask" — he published three pamphlets of varying degrees of acerbity on the question. This episode may be regarded as the first of a series of stresses he experienced during early 1520.

The severity of his reaction to it can be gauged by comments such as the following from a letter to Spalatin written in mid-February justifying the violence of his reply to the bishop's action and incidentally calling attention to his compulsive behavior:

> I have read . . . nothing more poisonous, pestilent, spiteful or mendacious written against not me but God's word . . . . I cannot fear this precipitate and ignorant hostility. God so drives me on. Let him see to it who acts through me, for I am certain none of these things have been sought or requested by me, but they were all wrenched from me by an alien passion.[43]

While still upset by his controversy with the bishop of Meissen Luther experienced another shock as a result of reading a Hussite tract, *De Ecclesia* (On the Church), he had received from Bohemia the preceding autumn and been too occupied to examine. Previously he had tended to regard any heretic with pious horror; now all this was changed when he discovered a kinship between some of his views and those of Hus, a kinship that John Eck had failed to get Luther to admit earlier because Luther knew so little about Hus. With characteristically immoderate language he wrote to Spalatin:

> I have unsuspectingly taught and held all the positions of John Hus, as has John Staupitz. In short we are all in our ignorance Hussites. Even Paul and Augustine are Hussites to the letter. What a marvelous outcome — and without a Bohemian guide or teacher. I am so amazed I don't know what to think, seeing the terrible judgments of God against men — that the clearest gospel truth was publicly burned more than a hundred years ago, and held as damnable.[44]

For the past two years Luther had been looking for arguments to disprove the supremacy of the Pope in order to take the sting out of the sentence of excommunication he had been anticipating since the furor over the Indulgence Theses began. The way he saw it, if one could show papal supremacy to be a merely human convention rather than of divine origin, then papal excommunication would not be a threat to his salvation. He had other 'comforting' arguments besides this, which he had aired in sermons on the 'Ban' in 1518 and again in early 1520, but the anti-papal argument would be the real clincher. This argument had been the principal topic in his debate with Eck and it was this which he now recognized in Hus, who in Luther's book was thereby elevated from the status of heretic to that of saint. On the heels of this recognition, Luther read a recently published version of the well known fifteenth century treatise by Laurentius Valla exposing the eighth century forgery known as the Donation of Constantine. According to this forged document the Roman emperor Constantine (fourth century) following his acceptance of Christianity had given the Pope dominion over a large chunk of Italy, and during the later middle ages the document was cited in support of papal claims to temporal power. This discovery was not exactly relevant to Martin's need for showing the Pope's claim to spiritual supremacy was spurious. His reaction is contained in another letter to Spalatin:

> I have in hand . . . Laurentius Valla's exposure of the 'Donation of Constantine.' Good God, what darkness and iniquity in Rome, and how one marvels at God's judgment over what not only endured for so many centuries but even prevailed and became part of canon law. Lest nothing might be lacking in this most unnatural monstrosity, these vile, stupid, shameless lies practically achieved the status of articles of faith. I am in such anguish I hardly doubt the Pope to be the veritable Antichrist which in the popular view the world awaits, because of the resemblance in the way he lives, behaves, speaks and makes laws.[45]

It should be noted that Luther does not quite assert the claim to temporal power is an article of faith. But presently when the symptoms of his disorder have become somewhat more severe, he will no longer boggle at such falsifications, which become an important constituent of his polemics. In this same letter he refers to an altercation between Wittenberg students and townspeople that prompted him to sermonize on the problem. This event was doubtless more than a little disturbing to him — he calls it an "affair of the devil" — because a larger scale student riot the following July shook him up dreadfully (see Ch. 3).

The final incident to be mentioned as subjecting him to unwonted stress in early 1520 was the publication during February of condemnations of some of his writings by the theological faculties of Louvain and Cologne. To these condemnations was prefaced a letter by Adrian of Utrecht, formerly tutor to the future emperor Charles, now Cardinal Bishop of Tortosa (Spain) and two years hence to be elected as the last non-Italian Pope (until 1978) and the first Pope from northern Europe. He was neither an academic type nor a politician, but a straightforward, conscientious churchman. His evaluation of Luther's doctrines must have been a real crusher to the Wittenberg professor, hypersensitive to any criticism of 'my theology':

> I have seen the errors taken from various writings and tracts of Luther, the teacher of sacred theology, and sent me. They are clearly such crude and palpable heresies that not even a beginning student of theology should have fallen into them. And yet he declares himself ready to undergo fire and death in their support.[46]

At this point we interject Luther's response to an acquaintance in his home town of Mansfeld, who had belatedly sent him a copy of the Louvain-Cologne condemnation. It brings out the detached attitude Martin exhibits toward his family, whom so far as the records show he had not visited for going on fifteen years:

> Greet in my name Pastor John, John Reinick and William, also my flesh and blood. The men of Leipzig and Meissen continue to caw among themselves without stopping and to no purpose. I hear my sister Barbara has died; may she rest in peace, Amen. We shall all follow her. Farewell and pray for me to the Lord.[47]

A revealing indication of Luther's inner state at this time (early 1520) is found in an open letter he wrote to a dissident group in Strasbourg nearly five years later (December 1524). The letter is devoted especially to the question of the Real Presence in the Eucharist, a belief that in the 1520s was being abandoned widely in German-speaking lands. In the letter Luther remarks:

> I confess that if Dr. Carlstadt or anyone else had been able to show me five years ago there is nothing in the sacrament but bread and wine he would have done me a great service. I then suffered most severe temptation (*Anfechtung*) and wrestled and strained, so ardently did I desire to extricate myself. For I saw quite well that so armed I could strike a mighty blow against the papacy.[48]

He adds that the Real Presence was too strongly inculcated in Scripture for him to go along with Carlstadt or others writing against the traditional belief. Knowing his way with Scripture we are unimpressed with this explanation; for Luther, Scripture was like a violin in the hands of a virtuoso who could draw from it whatever music he desired. As is evident from a number of statements he made in this period the reception of the Eucharist had become for him a useful device for allaying anxiety. Of interest here in the above quotation is its testimony that during the winter of 1519-20 Luther was contemplating an attack on Rome and that to make it a success he was strongly tempted to exploit a complete denial of the Real Presence in the Eucharist.

It should be recognized that at this time Luther had no plan for the formation of the visible schismatic church of Electoral Saxony that came into being during the 1520s. Having convinced himself the 'true church' was invisible and the visible fifteen-hundred-year-old church was a creature of Satan because of its being a mortal threat to him, he was free to unleash against it the unbounded hostility manifested in his utterances after mid-1520. In subsequent years with more and more of the German states joining the schism, his attitude shifted again. The church regained its property of visibility for him, and by the later 1530s these schismatic institutions — provided they accepted his doctrine, i.e., the 'pure Gospel' — became the 'true church.' The end of the false 'papal church' he periodically predicted to be just around the corner.

It is a matter of some interest to establish the approximate date of the anxiety attack during which Luther considered an all-out attack on the papacy. We must regard his ordinary state as one of emotional malaise punctuated by the occasional devastating experiences described in the "Explanations." A suggestion of what appears to be his typical state can be found in the "Sermon on the New Testament, i.e., the Holy Mass" written in late spring of 1520: "What greater trial is there than the sin and bad conscience that always fears God's anger and never has rest?"[49] There is no evidence on how frequently the anxiety attacks occurred, but Martin had to be continually on his guard to try to ward them off. It does not appear from the record that he suffered this attack during January or February. In March there is a gap in his correspondence between the 2nd and the 19th. In a letter to Spalatin on the latter date occurs the earliest reference to the Louvain-Cologne condemnation published during February: "I am sending you [the condemnation] by the asses of Louvain and Cologne, whom I am now answering in print."[50] Also in this letter Luther praises strongly the tract *De Ecclesia* ("On the Church") by Hus sent him earlier from Prague and reports that he is having an edition of 2000 copies printed in Hagenau. Since this tract had been condemned as heretical by the Council of Constance in 1415, Luther is in effect repudiating the oath he made when granted the doctorate some years earlier to uphold the teaching of the Church.

This letter tells us that Luther must have received a copy of the Louvain-Cologne document by early March and had his reply to it in press before the 19th. It is reasonable to conjecture that this condemnation of his teaching was the ultimate stress preceding the anxiety attack, which would thus have occurred by the middle of that month. The dissemination of the Hussite tract, hitherto little known in Germany, might be regarded as the first overt act in his attack on the papacy. An indication that during the latter part of March Luther is still experiencing after effects of the acute anxiety state can be found in a letter to Spalatin of March 26:

> I thank the Lord who has *filled my mind with other matters* lest I should read carefully the Cardinal of Tortosa [Adrian of Utrecht], who writes most impiously . . . . This is so horrible a portent I could not let it pass *if my mind were present.*[51]

In his "Response" to the faculties of Louvain and Cologne Martin did not refer to Adrian's preface (quoted in part above), which we may presume inflicted a greater psychic blow than did the detailed critique. The repeated reference in the letter to Spalatin to his current mental distress associated with Adrian's blunt criticism is expressed in the cryptic style he still employs when alluding to conscious effects of the psychic disorder. What he appears to be implying is that he has been fairly successful in repressing the emotions aroused by Adrian's preface, but as we know from the account in the 1524 document, he first went through a most distressing experience.

During approximately the same period when he was working on the "Response" Luther also issued another of his semi-annual pronouncements on the sacrament of penance, "Discussion of Confession" (*Confitendi Ratio*). This tract, which reflects his increasing hostility to ecclesiastical authority, is largely an expression of his personal difficulties with confession. What appears to be a veiled account of the sexual problems he is now experiencing is given in a section on secret sins of the heart. He aserts that by these secret sins he does not mean lustful thoughts about girls or women, which the devil arouses and which may plague one for a long time, a whole day or even a week. Those who would live piously are continually harassed by such passions. Even the intention to avoid them is impossible, vain and deceitful. Only the Decalogue need be considered and not even all of that. Skip the last two commandments and thereby escape the nuisance of wondering if your day-long or week-long desires for a woman are sinful. It is enough to confess those sins against the first eight that you remember distinctly and which are especially bothering you at the time of confession.

Following this tract Luther produced a lengthy discussion of the Ten Commandments, called "On Good Works." He began this composition in response to a request by Spalatin and in a letter to his friend dated March 25 expressed the feeling that this would be his most distinguished publication yet. By now Luther appears to relish his vocation as writer (along with preaching) and 1520 turned out to be the year of his peak production. If one notes a certain discrepancy between the title of the present piece and its subject, this is a matter that will become increasingly prominent in his writings. It is apparant that when writing this tract he had rebounded from the after effects of his most recent anxiety attack and was enjoying good spirits again. He is successful in communicating the enthusiasm he feels for 'faith.' At the moment he experiences no threat to his defensive system and the tract is relatively free of the hostility which within a few months will mark his writings.

A point of resemblance between "On Good Works" and its immediate predecessor on confession is the sloughing off of the last two commandments. He manages to obtain a polemical advantage from his shortened version of the Decalogue. For example, one of the 'works' required by the second commandment is "to oppose all false, seductive, erroneous, heretical doctrine [i.e., teaching contrary to Luther's], all abuse of clerical authority . . . . It must be that among the clergy the greater part preach false doctrine and abuse their spiritual power."[52]   Luther can be seen here warming up for the "Address to the Christian Nobility" and establishing his divine mandate for the task. Also in his discussion of the first two commandments he contrives an argument against a most painful bete noire: the law of loving God and of loving one's neighbor for the love of God, which the gospels call the greatest commandments. Luther artfully uses a scriptural reference to repudiate Scripture, asserting that the tax collector (contrasted with the Pharisee) "calls upon God in his sins, praises him and fulfills the two greatest commandments, faith and the honoring of God."

In a letter dated April 27 Luther states that to his "Sermon on the Body and Blood of Christ" of the previous November "will be added yet another one by me on the use of the mass."[53] This is our earliest reference to the tract entitled "Sermon on the N. T., i.e., the Holy Mass." In its approach it belongs with the preceding tract on good works where in one paragraph Luther refers ten times to the mass as a 'testament,' never as a sacrifice. Such emphasis on so important a doctrinal innovation along with the remark in the letter indicates that he had planned the new tract by some time in April and probably completed it by June. It is only a third as long as "On Good Works," and as that work is preliminary to the "Address," so the tract on the mass is a forerunner of the "Babylonian Captivity." Indeed the first and major part of the "Captivity" is essentially a rehash of the earlier tract to which is added an open attack on the doctrine of the transformation of the bread and wine into the body and blood of Christ. The rejection of this central act of the mass makes its first appearance in the "Sermon on the New Testament."

The word 'Testament' in the title of this tract represents a falsification somewhat reminiscent of the one we noted above at the end of Chap. 1 regarding the (non)-imputation of sin. Here the intent is to eliminate the scriptural term 'covenant,' as it appears, for example, in Luke's account of the Last Supper: "This cup is the new covenant in my blood." To receive a benefit from a covenant, the beneficiary must meet the conditions imposed by the one who makes the covenant. A testament on the other hand provides a free gift with no strings attached. Six years earlier in his lecture course on the Psalms Luther had demonstrated his linguistic sophistication on this question by discussing the Hebrew, Greek, and Latin terms involved.[54] At that time the term 'covenant' was quite acceptable to him. By 1520 the idea that he could not become righteous or be saved unless he fulfilled requirements had become intolerable to Luther. To obtain relief from this nightmare he had devised the *sola fide* program, and in his "Sermon on the New Testament" in the spring of 1520 we observe him adjusting the doctrine of the Eucharist to harmonize with the program. (Later in his translation of the N. T. he employs the Latin loan word 'Testament' − instead of the German *Bund* (= covenant) − in the key passage on the Last Supper in Luke (quoted above) and in 1 Corinthians [11:25] to help propagate the new doctrine.)

In this final statement of his personal teaching prior to his regression Luther inadvertently reveals the emotional problem which impelled him to develop it. While arguing against the sacrificial character of the mass, he remarks with little relevance: "They have been afraid and taught us to be afraid, where there is no fear."[55] Luther is here projecting his pathological fear of the overwhelming divine presence in the consecrated species on the altar. We hear about this severe emotional reaction from a variety of sources, among the more explicit being the account of his terror when saying his first mass. Another such story recounts a comparable seizure he experienced during a Corpus Christi procession of the Blessed Sacrament in 1515 when with Staupitz. In subsequent chapters we shall observe the continuing effect of Luther's abnormal fear of the Real Presence in the Eucharist on his doctrinal pronouncements.

Chapter 3

Regression And Its First Fruits

i. Report of a visitor to Wittenberg

In July of 1520 the record shows that Luther underwent the psychic change known as psychotic regression. Henceforth there is a new Luther, not completely different from the earlier one but different enough to make it desirable to interrupt the chronological account long enough to survey the new traits. The aggressively hostile character observable by mid 1520 persists substantially unchanged for seven years. There is then a half year or more of depression during which the hostility diminishes. By the end of the decade, along with the hostility, persecutory and grandiose delusions whose origin is observable during the 1520s come to play a prominent role. In the present chapter we are concerned primarily with the portrait of the 1520s.

We begin with a description of Luther provided by a visitor to Wittenberg in the summer of 1523, then describe Luther's psychotic symptoms and the defenses against anxiety characteristic of this period of his career before giving an account of the process of his regression. In early August of 1523, less than a year and a half after Luther returned to Wittenberg from his hideout at the Wartburg, a Polish envoy named John Dantiscus arrived in Leipzig on a diplomatic mission. Finding that Duke George was then away at Nuremberg, Dantiscus took advantage of his absence to make a side trip to visit Wittenberg for a look at the famous occupant of the Black Monastery. His description of Luther is part of a report dated August 8 to his superior, the Bishop of Posen. Only a small part of this document has previously been published in English. Dantiscus had been in correspondence with Melanchthon, who arranged the visit with Luther described here:[1]

> It is not possible to write at length about everything I saw there. I found young men most learned in Hebrew, Greek and

Latin, especially Philip Melanchthon, who is foremost among all those who are well grounded in literature and learning. This most courteous and earnest young man of 26 was with me for the three days I spent there. It was to him I explained my purpose concerning Luther on this occasion. According to common opinion, whoever has not seen the Pope at Rome or Luther at Wittenberg has seen nothing. Consequently, I wished to see and talk with him, and that there might be nothing suspect about the meeting I had no other business with him than to greet him and say farewell.

It is not easy for just anyone to approach him; however, he made no difficulty about receiving me and I went to him with Melanchthon at the end of his dinner to which he invited various brothers of his order. (The brothers were possibly members of the Order of Teutonic Knights who had left their chapter house in Ducal Saxony and like the nine nuns from Nimbschen found temporary quarters in the Black Monastery.) They were recognizable as brothers because they wore a white tunic of military cut, but in the way they wore their hair they did not differ from peasants. He stood up, gave me a sort of handshake and assigned me a place to sit. We sat down and remained for a period of about four hours on into the night, speaking of various matters. I found him to be alert, learned and eloquent, but nothing less than abusive, arrogant and spiteful toward the Pope, the Emperor and certain other sovereigns. If I were to give an account of all these things, this day would not suffice, and since the messenger [letter bearer] is ready and waiting I will bring together many things in brief form.

Luther's appearance is as described in books. He has piercing eyes with a startling glitter as is sometimes observed in those who are possessed. The king of Dacia has a similar appearance and I believe they were both born under the same constellation. In speech he is violent and much given to mockery. His dress cannot be distinguished from that worn at court; it is said that in the house where he lives, which was formerly a monastery, he wears the habit of his order. While sitting with him we did not merely converse but also drank wine and beer with much merriment, as is the custom there. He appeared to be in everything a good companion, or as the Germans say: *Eine gutt Geselle.* As for holiness of life, which many among us credit him with, he differs in no way from the rest of us. One can easily observe in him contempt for others and a great sense of vainglory. In abusiveness, railing and jeering he appears obviously licentious. What he is in other respects is clearly depicted in his books. He does a great deal of reading and writing; at that time he was translating the books of Moses from Hebrew into Latin, utilizing Melanchthon's help extensively. That young man was, among the educated Germans, the one I most admired. He disagrees with Luther in some matters, now and then before the whole company, and I very much wish he would do so more often.

It is evident that Dantiscus was rather let down by the contrast between the Luther he encountered in Wittenberg and what he had been led to expect. Melanchthon impressed him as a much more admirable person than Luther. Two features in particular indicate that Luther is here in a manic state: the jovial yet abusive torrent of words that flows from his tongue and the unpleasant glint in his eyes such as is observed in 'those who are possessed.' In that remote age when psychotics commonly mingled with the general population, the ordinary adult was likely to be acquainted with this unmistakable mark of the manic individual. There is previous testimony about the manic glint in Luther's eyes, in particular the account of the Swiss student Kessler in March 1522 (see Ch. 4). By way of illustration I describe in a note at the end of this section a personal encounter with a manic individual similar to the experience of Dantiscus.

We now present an interpretation of the psychotic symptoms Luther manifested during the 1520s (and later). They are characteristic of an individual who after struggling for some years to cope with neurotic anxiety is forced to retreat from the adult level he has hitherto precariously maintained. As remarked in a recent text on psychopathology the psychotic individual must try to meet the challenges of an adult world with a psychic organization that is beset with "infantile impulses, fantasies, conflicts and fears." Even though he may appear to be performing as an adult, his behavior reflects the unsolved problems of his early years, and it is this recurring infantilism that lies at the heart of the psychosis.[2]

The first post-neurotic state may be depression or it may be one called manic or hypomanic (i.e., mildly manic). The actual transformation of an individual from a neurotic to a (hypo)manic state is not always a very striking one. It may be that the individual retires at night showing somewhat more obvious anxiety than usual and rises the next morning with a personality different from the day before. The change may be so slight that it is apparent only to his intimates in the form of greater than ordinary talkativeness and motor activity, accompanied by irritability or a euphoric, exalted mood. On the other hand it may be profound, turning a previously quiet character into a maniacal killer; and it may be anything between these extremes. Similarly, the transition to a state of depression may be marked only by a moderate reduction of activity and general alertness; it also may result in a state of complete apathy. Other symptoms of depression include loss of appetite and insomnia.

In a later chapter we present an eyewitness account of Luther going very dramatically into depression. Some individuals manifest only one type of symptom, others alternate between the two; hence the term manic-depressive psychosis. The aggressive hostility toward others often observed in manic individuals appears to be directed against the person himself when in depression.

The range and the nature of the feelings the individual may experience in these states are suggested in the account of his emotional swings that Rousseau presents in Bk. I of the *Confessions*:

> I have very ardent feelings and when I am in their grip, nothing can equal my impulsiveness. I know neither caution, respect for others, fear, nor propriety; I am impudent, fierce, cynical, fearless. Neither shame nor danger can restrain me; in comparison with the one thing I am pursuing the entire universe means nothing to me.
>
> When my calm is restored I feel nothing but lassitude and timidity. Everything startles and repels me. A fly buzzing past frightens me; I am so sluggish that the need to say a word or move about I find repulsive. Fear and shame reduce me to such a state that I would like to hide from the gaze of all the world. If I must act I don't know what to do; if I must speak I don't know what to say; if anyone looks at me I am quite put out of countenance.[3]

Luther's own reaction to depression, given in a large number of the letters he wrote during the second half of 1527, will be dealt with in a later chapter. After nearly four months in depression he begs Melanchthon to pray for him, "a miserable and despised worm, vexed with a spirit of sadness .... As Christ's sick man I barely stay alive, let alone do or write anything." There is much less in the record about Luther's reaction to the manic symptoms; typically, he emphasizes the compulsive, involuntary aspect, as in this letter to a friend (early 1521):

> I am pressed down by many evils and kept from the sacred things; my life is a cross .... I am not master of myself and am carried along by I know not what spirit but I am not conscious of wishing evil to anyone. (to Conrad Pellikan, WBr 2, 273-74)

A somewhat similar account appears in a letter to Hausmann written little more than two months before the visit of Dantiscus: "I am well enough in body but so distracted by external affairs that the spirit is almost extinguished and I seldom attend to it. Pray for me that I may not end as flesh."

The duration of the symptoms can vary as much among individuals as does the severity of the symptoms. In the absence of therapy, and particularly if the external pressures that helped bring on the attack are not removed, the symptoms may be prolonged into a period of months or even years; on the other hand, especially in a favorable environment, they may be remitted within a matter of days or a few weeks. The individual then returns to what has been called a neo-neurotic state, with the possibility of a later recurrence of the psychotic symptoms. According to the diagnosis made by Dr. Reiter, Luther manifested manic or hypomanic symptoms during much of the 1520s.

This diagnosis has been rejected or ignored by virtually all the writers who have subsequently dealt with Luther as either biographers or theological specialists. The reason commonly given for the rejection is that Luther's work output in the 1520s is incompatible with the diagnosis. To show that this contention is uninformed and spurious, one might cite the medical literature, from which it can be learned that during and after a psychotic attack the patient is likely to retain and be able to exercise competently skills acquired previously. But since the ordinary reader may lack ready access to this literature, I will mention instead the example of various well known authors whose achievements invalidate the contention.

Ezra Pound, widely regarded as the most distinguished American poet of the twentieth century, fell afoul of the law (as Luther did) for attacking public authority in the early 1940s. At the time, Pound was in Italy; in 1945 he was captured by the American armed forces, returned to the United States as a prisoner guilty of treason, diagnosed as an incurable paranoid by a team of American psychiatrists and incarcerated in a government mental hospital. Prior to and during the period of his imprisonment he continued to write distinguished verse. Another highly gifted American poet, Theodore Roethke (1908-63), who from the age of 27 till his death at 55 sporadically suffered manic attacks requiring hospitalization, produced a most respectable body of verse, winning a number of literary awards including the Pulitzer Prize for poetry. He continued to write while in hospital as well as after release and in addition had a most distinguished teaching career. In brief, his accomplishment was far superior to that of the vast majority of his academic contemporaries who enjoyed normal psychic health.

For a third example, we may consider the story of Virginia Woolf, who suffered severe attacks of depression from her early thirties until her successful suicide atttempt in 1941 at the age of 59. Virtually her entire literary output, one of the most considerable among British writers of distinction in the twentieth century, occurred subsequent to her first psychotic attack. I have selected writers to illustrate a fact well known to psychiatry, a fact of which the Lutherian authors appear to be unaware, but illustrations could have been chosen from other fields. Here I will mention only the painter,

Vincent Van Gogh, who produced a large output of distinguished work between the time when his psychotic symptoms first appeared until his death by suicide at the age of 37. On the subject of suicide, it is apparent from his numerous references to it that Luther was restrained from taking his own life during the 1520s mainly by his conviction that he would thereby ensure the damnation he was at such pains to escape.

Among the manic symptoms apparent in Luther's writings, mention may be made of the mood of exaltation that is manifest in the tract called the "Freedom of the Christian," especially in the prefatory letter to Leo X. The manic exaltation is even more striking in his letter to Elector Frederick of February 22, 1522 when he was leaving the Wartburg to return to Wittenberg. The letter begins: "Grace and joy from God the Father on the acquisition of a new relic." The ecclesiastical historian Harnack, for instance, without knowing the cause of the exaltation, remarks that this letter is almost unique in history. Reiter calls attention especially to the manic traits prominent in the tract entitled "Answer to the Hyperchristian, Hyperspiritual, and Hyperlearned Book by Goat Emser in Leipzig" of March 1521. One can account for the manic exaltation in these latter two documents from the fact that on each occasion Luther's anxiety was increased beyond the usual level by the threat of danger to his person, the tract against Emser being written when he was contemplating his trip to Worms in the spring of 1521, and the letter to Frederick when he was leaving the safety of the Wartburg a year later.

At present there does not seem to be any established way of writing for the general public about psychotic characters whose careers are of sufficient intrinsic interest to warrant such treatment. In this study of Luther, emphasis is placed on his defensive manoeuvres because these furnish us with perhaps the most useful and revealing guide to an understanding of his personality. Since our aim is to provide a picture of the Luther of history rather than to present a psychiatric case study, we are not as much concerned with the specifically psychotic symptoms as was Reiter. Nevertheless, they must be included if the picture is to be authentic. In fact, the symptoms themselves — moods, attitudes, behavior patterns, etc. — constitute a form, albeit not very successful, of a defense against anxiety. According to this interpretation, the individual with manic or depressive symptoms has carried out a partial retreat from reality in an attempt to control his anxiety. Outside the area of his disturbance he may remain in good contact with the real world, and it is believed the manic or depressive symptoms play a role in helping him maintain this curtailed contact, which is preferable to the complete break — regression all the way to an infantile level that otherwise threatens him. But the anxiety remains.

It is often remarked that the analysis of psychotic symptoms from written records alone without the opportunity to question the patient may cast doubt on the validity of the interpretation. This observation may be true in general but Luther is an evident exception. For apart from the unmistakable descriptions of his symptoms recorded by his associates, we have an enormous mass of data spread over a period of three to four decades. In some respects the student of Luther's disorder is more favorably situated than the clinical psychiatrist working with a patient brought to him for treatment. For with Luther it is possible to observe the development of the disorder over a period of years — before, during and after the formation of the psychotic symptoms. The clinical psychiatrist, on the other hand, does not see his patient until after the symptoms have been formed, and he must try to deduce or infer the underlying causes by questioning a disturbed individual with whom it is often difficult if not impossible to make adequate contact. And a clinical psychiatrist will seldom encounter a patient with the ability and the desire to communicate such as Luther had. Neither is he likely to encounter one who has devoted the inventiveness and energy of genius to devising defences. Apart from these considerations, it is not our task to burrow into a patient's early childhood in an attempt to expose the roots of the disorder so that effective therapy may be practiced. Our task is the much less demanding one of identifying the disorder and utilizing its manifestations to describe an individual of adult years.

— — — — — — — — —

Note: Many years ago when I visited a new neighbor to make his acquaintance, he asked me to accompany him on an errand to a nearby community. As it would have been ungracious to refuse, I rode along in his car. Two things in his appearance struck me: he was extremely jovial and talkative, and there was a peculiar glint in his eyes I had never before observed in anyone. Being unacquainted with psychiatry, I was little concerned over these manifestations. My new friend talked almost continuously to me and to the person he had driven out to see. We returned home without incident. Presently he vanished from the neighborhood and I learned he was hospitalized for psychiatric treatment. After his discharge some time later, the glint was gone from his eyes and the flow of talk had dried up. Subsequently he told me about his feelings when in depression but never alluded to the manic states. Of interest is the fact that the manic symptoms did not interfere with his driving a car or transacting business with a client.

ii. Defense mechanisms, conscious devices and delusions

According to current psychiatric theory, the negation involved in the ego defense mechanism known as 'denial' is carried out unconsciously in an attempt to deal with an intolerable emotional conflict. Because of the frequency with which it appears in his utterances, written or spoken, denial may be described as Luther's principal defense mechanism from 1520 to his death in 1546. In this section we shall first present a simple example of denial and then discuss problems of interpretation for other examples. During his stay at the Wartburg, as described below, Martin began to translate the New Testament into German, and with the help of associates published the translation about six months after his return to Wittenberg. Following a not uncommon practice he composed prefaces to the whole work and to a number of the individual books. In the general preface he proclaims we must get rid of the notion that in the N. T. there are four gospels, for there is only one gospel, and indeed the N. T. is only one book. After expatiating at some length on what the word gospel really means, he proceeds to cast a little more light on this remarkable proclamation. Even though the N. T. is just one book, some of the books of which it is composed are far more important than others. For instance, with regard to the four gospels, only one is really significant, the gospel of John. The reason for this is that John records a great deal of Christ's preaching but not much about his works, whereas Matthew, Mark and Luke have recounted many of his works but few of his words.[4] Now since Christ's works "are of no help to me," it follows that these three (the Synoptic gospels) are not really worth one's time. You can learn all you need for your salvation from John, Paul — Romans, Galatians and Ephesians — and the first epistle of Peter. (Since Luther ruled out any eucharistic reference in John, he was here repeating his earlier stand in the "Freedom of the Christian" that the Eucharist is not essential.)

In this remarkable description of the N. T. writings by the man who first revealed their true meaning to the world, attention should be called to the statement that the gospel according to Matthew records only a few of Jesus' words. Actually, of course, the first gospel is the most extensive collection of "Christ's words" (as the term was used in Luther's day) in the entire N. T. In the early Church, in particular, this gospel was the favorite part of Scripture for catechetical instruction because its author had deliberately set out to record as much of the teaching of Jesus as he could assemble. In short, Luther's statement in the preface is one of his most astonishing fabrications. For one unacquainted with modern psychiatry, only two interpretations can be put on it: either it comes from a writer grossly ignorant of the contents of the N. T., or it is a deliberate lie. Since Martin has been working diligently on the translation during the past year, he can hardly be so badly informed; therefore it must be a lie. But why would he of all people concoct such a childish and pointless falsehood?

It is not difficult to discover the intolerable emotional conflict Luther is here trying to evade. For some time it had been apparent to him that much of the N. T. is in stark, unremovable contradiction with the foundation of his defensive system, the *sola fide* program. It is impossible to square this program with the teachings of Jesus recorded in the Synoptic gospels. (It is not possible to square it with the gospel according to John either, but in this gospel the contradictions with the *sola fide* are somewhat less obvious than in the Synoptics and by adroit manipulation Martin could learn to live with them. Also for him the fourth gospel contained more 'consoling texts' than the others.) One of the ironies of this situation is that during the early stages of the *sola fide* formulation Luther used texts from the Synoptics rather than from John to bolster his arguments, in part because his favorite noun 'faith' [Gr. *pistis*] is not to be found in the fourth gospel. But this is early days, only 1522, and after further regression from reality Luther will be able to face the gospel according to Matthew again, and even deliver a sermon series on the part known as the Sermon on the Mount.

We consider next a type of denial in which Luther goes beyond straightforward negation and invents a substitute 'fact.' In the follow-up to his brief tract called "On Avoiding the Doctrines of Men" (a title which reveals his superb gift for unconscious humor) he confronts a famous saying of Augustine: "I would not believe the gospel if the authority of the Catholic Church had not impelled me to." Since long before he wrote this tract (1522) Luther had rejected ecclesiastical authority in favor of his own interpretation of Scripture, the sentence from Augustine was a real challenge. He denied that Augustine could have written this because "it conflicts with his other writings" (no other writings cited). Then Luther composed an extended substitute quotation so phrased he could accept it himself and declared this to be what Augustine wrote.

Another such falsification involves what is here called the 'Bernard fantasy.' As noted earlier, Martin admired Bernard perhaps more than any other figure in the Christian past. In his first blast of hostility against monastic life in 1521 he had to exempt Bernard, founder of some 160 monasteries and one of the strongest advocates of the monastic ideal in history. Also in later years when he had consigned most of the Christians of the first fourteen centuries to perdition for not holding the Lutherian gospel, Bernard had to be saved. The basis of the Bernard fantasy was a phrase lifted out of a sermon Bernard wrote fifteen years or so before his death in which he la-

mented he had wasted time by not devoting every moment of his life
to the service and love of God. To exemplify what Bernard himself
means by 'wasting time' we note this sermon excerpt:

> Conversations provide an enjoyable way to pass the time. To
> pass the time! To lose an hour! Indeed that hour that the mercy
> of God gives you to do penance, to obtain forgiveness, to acquire
> grace, to merit the glory of the promised hereafter.[5]

In its first appearance in 1521 the fantasy goes as follows:

> One day when sick unto death he made this confession: 'I have
> lost my time, for I have lived as a son of perdition; but one thing
> consoles me, that you will not despise a contrite and humble
> heart.' . . . . These are the words of a really Christian heart that
> puts all its trust in Christ and despairs absolutely of his works. He
> does not glorify himself for the vows of poverty, obedience,
> chastity; instead he speaks about a lost lifetime. By this faith he
> was saved and justified with all the saints.[6]

After many repetitions over the years the fantasy takes this form
in a 1538 sermon which distorts an anecdote from the "Golden
Legend."

> St. Bernard had lived as an admirable monk . . . But when death
> approached he said: 'Oh! I have lived evilly but, heavenly Father,
> you gave me your Son, who has a two-fold right to the kingdom of
> heaven' . . . . Thus he abandoned the monastic order, cowl and
> rule for Christ . . . And so Bernard was saved.[7]

What Luther is concerned to negate here is that Bernard, whom he
regards as the most holy person he had ever encountered, was also
the foremost proponent of the monastic ideal, from which he himself
had fallen away. The painful experience Luther seeks to escape by
use of the denial mechanism involves the awareness that his defection
from the monastic ideal cuts him off from association with the
person who represents true holiness, once Martin's own goal.

For another example of this type of invention we turn to a writer
Luther habitually treats with disdain, Thomas Aquinas. In an early
fifth century compilation called "Lives of the Fathers" (*Vitae
Patrum*) celebrating the early history of the monks of the desert,
there is recorded a pious notion current in the fourth century that
taking the monastic vows was comparable in its spiritual effect on
the new monk to a second baptism. Once he had renounced the
monastic ideal, Luther seized upon this opinion as a particularly
heinous abomination of the 'papal Church' and assigned its authorship to Aquinas. Here is an early version of the fiction (1523):

> They devise certain states in which one becomes blessed, as
> Thomas the monk-preacher has written. If someone enters religion,

it is as if he had just been baptized. And thus he promises forgiveness and remission of sins by means of one's own works. That is
the blasphemy that must be understood here.[8]

A decade later (1533) after many repetitions the account has developed more lurid colors and shows contamination from the Bernard
fantasy:

This scandalous, impious doctrine of a monastic baptism perjured, faithless and apostate — they hold primarily from St. Thomas.
But at the end of his life he fell into despair and had to say to the
devil: "I believe all that is to be found in that book [the Bible]."
It is from him that this teaching has passed into all the orders, into
all the convents, into the hearts of all the monks, by him that all
through their life so many tender consciences have had to endure a
long martyrdom and finally, in despair, have plunged into the
abyss of hell. That is why with my experience as a monk, as one
who formerly tried so earnestly to be a true monk, I can well call
the state of monkery a devilish and poisoned cake covered with
sugar.[9]

Here it may be that in addition to grief over abjuring his vows,
Luther is also trying to blot out his pain at being excommunicated,
the specific means chosen being his favorite ploy of inventing doctrines contrary to the Christian revelation and saddling them on the
Church. This motive is obvious in some of his cruder falsifications,
such as the assertion that the Pope denies the immortality of the soul,
or that the Pope calls Mary a harlot because as a virgin she gave birth
to a son. It is unknown whether Luther first learned of the 'monastic
baptism' from the "Lives of the Fathers," a work which he disparages
in the Table Talk as most inimical to the *sola fide*. But he would have
encountered it in the writings of Bernard, who was much interested
in the idea (see Ch. 8). After the repudiation of his monastic vows
Luther had to transfer the onus of the monastic baptism from
Bernard to another prominent figure. Thomas was chosen, presumably for his status as a doctrinal authority, and also for frightening
the young Luther with his matter-of-fact presentations of non-
Christian positions in the *Summa Theologica*. It is interesting to note
that Thomas does in fact make a comment about this ancient concept, developed eight or nine centuries before his lifetime. He mentions it in the *Summa* at the tail end of an answer to an objection in
a discussion of monastic vows:

It is stated in the *Vitae Patrum* that those who enter the religious life receive the same grace as those who become baptized.
If, however, they are not thereby completely absolved from the
guilt of sin, at least their entrance into the life of religion is of
more benefit to them than making a pilgrimage to the Holy Land.

(II-IIae, Q. 189, a. 3)

If Martin had chanced to read this rather wry comment in his pre-psychotic days, he doubtless would have greatly enjoyed it.

To close this introduction to Luther's use of the denial mechanism I will cite what is perhaps the oddest instance of it in his collected works. For here the target is not one of his enemies but the young Luther. In a Table Talk item referring to his early writings (cut-off date not specified) he says: "When I wrote those I was not very sincere." (#3572a.)

At the present time over a score of ego defense mechanisms are described in the psychiatric literature. In the Luther record the denial mechanism appears with the greatest frequency; projection is also quite common. As pointed out by Norman Cameron, the mechanisms of denial and projection are especially prominent in the productions of paranoid individuals. A number of examples of Luther's use of the projection mechanism are noted elsewhere in this study.

During the 1520s what might be called a process of despiritualization took place in Luther, accompanying the development of the psychotic symptoms. This process can be seen quite clearly in the changes in his deliberate attempts to control the anxiety which constitutes the central problem of his life. Consider the following group of quotations. The first one, dating from the spring of 1520, reflects the earlier Luther:

> This despair and unrest of conscience is nothing else than a failure of faith, the most severe illness a man can have in body and soul and of which he cannot be healed at once or with dispatch. Therefore it is profitable and necessary that the more uneasy a man's conscience is the more he should go to the sacrament or hear mass . . . . In this way his heart will become sweet toward God and acquire a consoling trust in him.[10]

Two years later, during the summer after his departure from the Wartburg, in a series of sermons on the first epistle of Peter, there is a different interpretation of the cause of the anxiety and a somewhat different remedy:

> If the devil comes and would force you to be despondent on account of your sin, just grasp the word of God, which promises forgiveness of sin, and trust in that. Then the devil will soon leave off.[11]

The Wartburg experience has established Satan as a permanent and dominant feature of Luther's fantasy life and the primary source of his ever-recurring anxiety, replacing the infirmity of faith of earlier years. The Eucharist and the mass as remedy have lost their preferred

role following his expulsion from the Church and been replaced by
the word of God.

The following passage from the famous letter to Jerome Weller[12]
written from the Coburg fortress in the summer of 1530 shows the
profound change of attitude that had developed in Luther during
this decade. Weller, aged 31, at the time an inmate of Luther's Wittenberg home, was a fellow sufferer from anxiety, and Luther in
advising him how to cope with it reveals the devices he himself has
substituted for the Eucharist, the mass and the word of God.

> You should rejoice over this temptation of the devil (anxiety
> state) because it is a certain sign that you have a gracious and
> merciful God. You say that the trial is greater than you can bear
> and you fear that if you can't overcome and suppress it you will
> fall into despair and blasphemy. I know this trick of Satan; if he
> can't triumph in the first assault, he strives hard to weaken and
> tire out his victim until the latter gives up and acknowledges he is
> conquered. Therefore as often as you are beset by this trial, take
> care that you do not begin to dispute with Satan or let yourself
> be attracted by these deadly thoughts. For this is nothing else than
> yielding to the devil and surrendering. But strive to despise to your
> utmost these thoughts the devil excites in you. In this kind of trial
> and warfare, contempt is the most effective and easiest way to
> conquer the devil. See that you ridicule your adversary, and also
> try to talk with someone. By all means avoid being alone, for the
> devil will particularly lie in ambush to overcome you when you are
> by yourself. This devil is to be conquered by ridiculing and despis-
> ing, not by resisting and disputing. Therefore you will confuse him
> by joking and playing with my wife and others and thus you will
> escape those devilish thoughts and help your spirits, my Jerome.

At this point Martin breaks off the counseling to reminisce about
his own trials in the early days in the monastery and how it was
Staupitz who told him God was making him undergo this 'temptation' as an indispensable preparation for his future career. He might
also have pointed out that the technique of repelling Satan by
mockery and derision he had likewise learned in his early years, not
from Staupitz but from the pages of the *Imitatio Christi* (IV, 10).
After a paragraph of reminiscences, Martin returns to the counseling,
but what he writes next is quite original − pure Luther:

> Whenever the devil torments you with these thoughts, get into
> the company of men, drink deeply, tell jokes, talk nonsense or do
> something else that's merry. Sometimes in order to give the devil
> no opening to trouble our conscience about trifles, we have to
> drink deeply, jest, talk nonsense or even commit a sin in hatred
> and contempt of him. Otherwise we may be overcome if we are at

too great pains to avoid sin. If then the devil should say to you: 'Don't drink,' you reply to him: 'I will drink all the more because you tell me not to'; and so I drink freely. You must always do the opposite of what Satan commands. Why else do you think I drink such strong wine, talk so freely, jest so often, except to mock and annoy the devil, who has mocked and annoyed me. I wish I could contrive some spectacular sin to spite the devil so that he could realize that I wouldn't acknowledge it or even be aware of any sin. We should remove the whole Decalogue from our sight and our mind, we whom the devil tries to harass in this way. And if the devil should throw up to us our sins, saying our guilt is deserving of death and hell, we must say to him: 'I acknowledge that I am deserving of death and hell, but so what? Will you then damn me eternally? Not at all; for I know someone who suffered for me and made satisfaction for me and is called Jesus Christ, the Son of God. Where he remains, I will remain also.'

If this amoral advice about the Decalogue may seem incongruous coming from the author of the Catechism (see Ch. 7), Luther is ready with an alibi. He utilizes the device not specified here known as the 'two times': the 'time of the Law' and the 'time of Grace.' Luther advocates the abolition of the Ten Commandments only during the 'time of the Law'; upon emerging from the shadow of this ordeal, he reinstates them.

The Table Talk item No. 141, dated a year and a half after the letter to Jerome Weller, may be cited as the Table Talk counterpart to it. Luther is here more interested in reminiscing about his encounters with Satan than describing his defenses, but the defenses are not slighted and additional devices are revealed. For example, Luther recounts how, after drinking heavily and gorging himself at table he manages to fall asleep.

But when I awake, the devil soon comes and argues with me until I say to him: 'Lick my ass!' God is not angered if you say that. For Satan harasses us mainly by this disputing.

Also in No. 141 Martin mentions another of the devices whereby he tries to divert his attention from the blasphemous thoughts excited in him by Satan — by contemplating mental images of pretty girls. Since he was on very friendly terms with the Wittenberg painter, Lucas Cranach, and must have visited the studio now and then, one wonders if Luther's images of pretty girls were inspired by the Cranach pin-ups of Eve and Venus.

That the devices described in the Coburg letter, especially the practice of drinking and carousing with boon companions, are long established habits is evident from the 1523 narrative quoted above from Dantiscus. Alongside the heavy drinking of his fellow Germans, about which Luther often complains as the national vice, it seems likely that his own drinking was not considered exceptional. As for the carousing and unseemly jesting, Melanchthon in the early 1520s can be heard to deplore Luther's buffoonery. As late as 1525 he is hoping that the marriage with Catherine may at last result in a life style more in keeping with Luther's social and academic position. Melanchthon's own anxiety problem was evidently much less severe than Luther's and there is no indication that he employed any of the distinctively Lutherian devices in trying to handle it.

Luther's writings during the 1520s provide abundant evidence of the development of delusions, i.e., fixed beliefs held despite their evident contradiction of reality. In the psychotic they typically result from the projection of inner states. Their defensive character is obvious in that they provide an acceptable substitute for the painful reality they contradict. For the paranoid personality delusions of persecution are the most common type; more severely disturbed individuals may also develop grandiose delusions. The delusions of the paranoid have a stable, systematic character; they become thoroughly integrated in the disordered psyche. Luther's systematic persecutory delusions develop first, being rather well stabilized by the end of 1525. While delusions of grandeur appear by 1522, at this period they are associated with the manic phase of the disorder and shift with changes in the environment. They do not appear to reach the stable paranoid form until after his sojourn at Coburg in 1530.

The formation of persecutory delusions is favored by the suspicious nature of the paranoid personality. His tendency to react aggressively to what he feels as hostile action on the part of others may be fostered by the memory of brutal treatment received in childhood. We have noted this type of aggression in Luther when reacting to the criticism of his teaching by the Franciscans of Jueterbog in 1519. The preceding year he had reacted similarly to a judgment of his views by John Eck. As remarked elsewhere, Luther was far more sensitive to criticism of 'my theology' than to personal attacks because such criticism was a threat to his defenses. It is thus understandable that he so often speaks of his 'enemies,' and can develop the notion of a conspiracy against him.

An example of this delusional pattern may be cited from the "Defense and Illustration of All the Articles," begun in late 1520. In the introduction he asserts "my enemies have dragged me into the open through cunning and force to win glory and honor at my expense." Here the phrase "dragged me into the open" replaces the fact that he has eagerly taken the initiative and published numerous writings either gratuitously setting forth his heterodox opinions or attacking his opponents. This tract is his fifth rejoinder to the Bull *Exsurge Domine,* which deals almost entirely with writings that appeared prior to his peak publishing year of 1520. The other phrases "by cunning and force" and "to win honor and glory at my expense" are typical examples of delusions engendered by paranoid suspicion. As pointed out by Norman Cameron, the paranoid is quite unaware of his own "hostile, contemptuous, critical and accusing attitudes," his lack of awareness resulting from the "denial and projection which opeate at wholly unconscious levels . . . . He is forever questioning other people's motivation; but he is incapable of questioning his own."[13]

At first Luther's enemies are confined to members of the 'papal Church' who object to the dissemination of his heterodox views. Soon the number will be expanded to include his colleague Andrew Carlstadt and the free-lance agitator Thomas Muentzer, along with the ill-defined group of 'fanatics.' To be added to these are the 'lords and peasants'; in late 1525 Martin refuses to attend the wedding of his intimate friend and benefactor George Spalatin because of the 'conspiracy' to seize and murder him if he ventures outside of Wittenberg. Among his persecutory delusions — as indicated for example in a Table Talk item of the later years (#5370) — was the fear that frequent attempts were being made to poison him.

To illustrate an early stage of the gradiose delusions we again cite the preface to the "Defense of All the Articles." Luther is here discussing the justification for his rebellion:

> Who knows whether God has not called me and raised me up [to teach the world]. They [my adversaries] should fear that it is God they are despising in me. Don't we read that God commonly raised up only one prophet at a time in the Old Testament?[14]

Then Martin lists his forerunners, Moses, Elias, Eliseus, Isaiah, Hosea, Jeremiah, Ezekiel, who resembled him also in being of lowly origin. He next compares himself to three Fathers of the western church, Ambrose, Jerome and Augustine. Falsifying the fact that they were contemporaries, Ambrose having played a leading role in the conversion of Augustine, he asserts that they like the O. T. prophets preached 'alone.' The comparison with Augustine is particularly droll since the latter was one of the most vocal defenders of the authority of general councils and the primacy of the See of Rome which this latest in the series of prophets was now busily attacking.

We turn now to a tract written about a year and a half later, mid 1522, "Against the Spiritual Estate of the Pope and the Bishops Falsely So Called." At this time Luther is still smarting over the loss of his clerical status from the excommunication of the preceding year and requires a new way of validating his claim to speak with authority on matters of doctrine and discipline. The device of the 'priesthood of the believer,' putting all Christians on the same level, is quite unacceptable for this purpose; it was useful in mid-1520 in attacking the status quo, but now Martin has escaped into the state of evangelical liberty, and the notion that any other spokesman for the Christian religion could really be equal to him is simply preposterous. The grandiose delusion displayed in this tract has a twofold aspect: the source of his 'call' to preach and the assurance of the infallibility of his teaching.

For the first aspect, he asserts he is now an 'ecclesiastic'[15] by the grace of God. What is more, he is also an 'evangelist,' being so regarded by Christ, who is the source of both his title and his teaching. Having so handily regained his status as an official preacher, he has no problem about similarly providing a guarantee of the absolute reliability of what he preaches:

> No man nor even an angel may judge my teaching. Because I am certain of it, I will be the judge of both you and the angels (as St. Paul teaches [1 Cor. 6]). Whoever rejects my teaching cannot be saved, for it is God's and not mine. Likewise my judgment is God's and not mine.[16]

As matters later turned out, the question of how a preacher could claim the authority to preach when separated from an authoritative church was not quite so simple as it appeared in this proclamation. In 1522 a controversy over the selection of a pastor developed between a congregation in a small Saxon town called Leisnig and the abbot of a neighboring monastery who had been invested with this responsibility. Early in 1523 Luther published a short tract with a long title setting forth his solution of the problem.[17] Naturally he sided with the congregation and declared that any congregation had the right not only to choose their own pastor but even decide matters of doctrine. (He assumed that all such decisions would be congenial to him.) But, apparently swayed by his current grandiose delusion, he chose to provide an alternative channel — if a preacher felt suitably inspired and there was need for his services, he could go ahead without a specific call from others. Both these decisions were to become a source of grief for him in the future. Some of the religious enthusiasts he dubbed 'fanatics' set up as preachers on their own and he was compelled to take up his pen against them:

> Why do you leave the church where you were baptized and taught and received communion? . . . . Who gave you authority to bring discord and schism to this parish? Who ordered you to hold your pastor in contempt?[18]

Perhaps the reader needs to be reminded that this is Luther asking the questions, not having them thrown at him. The chickens have indeed come home to roost.

In the fixed grandiose delusions of Luther's later years he sees himself somewhat more in the role of great theologian than prophet. There have been too many prophets in Germany since 1520 to let him feel altogether comfortable in this capacity. Furthermore as theologian he has a warranty that no mere prophet can boast of: his doctorate in theology:

> I wouldn't take all the wealth of the world for my Doctor's degree. For in the end I would certainly lose heart and despair . . . if I, like a sneak, embarked on these great and difficult matters without being called and commissioned.[19]

As many be surmised the preachers ('sneaks') Luther is here attacking do not enjoy the prestige of academic degrees. For a representative expression of the mature Luther's grandiosity, consider the following utterance of 1538:

> The papists say: 'Your doctrine is new and our ancestors knew nothing about it; therefore, if it is true, it must be that they are all damned.' Well, what does it matter to us what judgment was made against those who have already departed from this world? Today we preach the word of God; one must only listen and accept it without discussion. We shouldn't be like those who are always asking questions and demand of God why he has revealed pure doctrine to the present age but not to former times.[20]

iii. The process of withdrawal

Luther's attitude of estrangement from the Church during the spring of 1520 was not really acceptable to his conscious self, and he appears to have suppressed it — and the accompanying hostility — at least well into the month of May. His condition may be described as one of unstable equilibrium with greatly weakened ability to weather new shocks from without. An indication of his awareness of his emotional instability at this time is provided in a letter written in June to a theological opponent:

> Watch out you don't drive my outraged patience into a fury. I am a man like you, except that you secretly bite at your leisure and quietly while I, much occupied, am attacked by the teeth of all and asked to be moderate, one man torn to pieces by so many immoderate wolves. The world presses me down and devours me. God! how I am accused . . . . I write this that you may know I choose peace and concord, but if that is not possible, let the Lord's will be done.[21]

What seems to have been the decisive blow that toppled him from this state came from his reading of an abbreviated version (*Epitome*) of a long polemical tract prepared by an Italian Dominican, Sylvester Prierias. The *Epitome*, published at Perugia late in 1519, apparently came to Luther's attention by the beginning of the following June.

Prierias, a man more than 25 years older than Luther, after a distinguished academic career at the University of Bologna, had been called to Rome in 1511 by Julius II and four years later given the position of Master of the Sacred Palace on the recommendation of Cardinal Cajetan. He represented the school of theological writers defending extreme claims for papal authority in the Church in reaction to the advocates of the superiority of the general council, in a controversy dating from the Council of Constance a hundred years before. Luther had previously crossed swords with Prierias in 1518, so that this new critique meant a reopening of old wounds. In assessing the effect on Luther of a criticism of what he called 'my theology,' one must always remember that such criticism disturbed him far more strongly than a bitter personal attack would disturb anyone with a normal psyche, because he experienced the criticism as a threat to his very being. Personal abuse, on the other hand, seemed to affect him but little, and he often remarked he could bear it. This rather peculiar, almost inverted type of sensitivity helps excuse the venomous personal attacks he directs against his opponents. He was probably not fully aware how grievously some of his victims were wounded by these expressions of his pathological hostility. His reaction to the criticism of Prierias appears in a letter of June 7:
"Sylvester Prierias has vomited up something that smells so blasphemous that just to read it almost kills me."[22] About the same time Luther sent to Spalatin a copy of the *Epitome* with instructions to

send it back at once; it will soon be printed in praise and glory of all enemies of the truth, with my notes. I think they at Rome have all become mad, foolish, raging, senseless, fools, stocks and devils of hell. See now what may be expected from Rome, which permits this infernal stuff to go out against the Church.[23]

In this same letter to Spalatin occurs an announcement of what was to be the first section of the "Address to the Christian Nobility":

I have a mind to print a broadside to Charles and the whole German nobility against the tyranny and wickedness of the Roman Curia.

He lost no time in issuing the response to Prierias. A week after the letter to Spalatin just quoted, a second letter to Spalatin indicated "Sylvester's Insanity" was in press, and two weeks later it was in print. At the same time Martin had ready another polemical work against a Franciscan at Leipzig, Augustine Alveld, whose most recent

tract against Luther's disparagement of papal authority dated from
only mid-May. Luther had at first affected to be little concerned
about Alveld's pamphlet because of its low intellectual quality and
decided to answer it only because, being written in German, it might
"poison poor laymen." The anti-Alveld tract is remarkable chiefly
as an example of Luther's facility at heaping up sophistical arguments. It represents one of the complete turnabouts in policy which
are so common in Luther during these years of rapid change. As recently as the end of June of the previous year in the "Sermon on the
Ban" he had preached the virtue of accepting an excommunication,
particularly an unjust one, as something calculated to render the
injured one acceptable to God. The purpose of the tract against
Alveld is to demonstrate the papacy is an evil invention of evil men
and has no right or power to excommunicate anyone. Luther goes so
far as to assert that almost all the popes from the very beginning have
sought only their "own profit and glory." In the paragraph following
this characteristic slander he warns his audience about "poisonous
tongues," a form of unconscious humor that is one of the rewards of
reading Luther from this time on. He manages to maintain his poise
throughout most of the tract, but toward the end, after piously accepting the papacy as a merited punishment inflicted on Christians
by divine providence, suddenly breaks off to address the Pope in the
words: "That is the way you act, you scarlet whore of Babylon."

The "Response" to Prierias, unlike the reply to Alveld, is not a
sophistical argument against papal authority. Instead it is a reprint of
Prierias' *Epitome* decorated with marginal wisecracks by Luther and
provided with highly emotional foreword and afterword. In the
foreword we learn the reason for this mode of rebuttal: the *Epitome*
is such a sheer horror it provides its own refutation:

> It is so filled with blasphemies from start to finish that I believe
> it was brought forth in the midst of hell by Satan himself . . . .
> Therefore, read it and lament over the fall of the Roman Church
> from glory; he [Prierias] has not only conceived these heretical,
> blasphemous, satanic, hellish poisons but also propagated them
> throughout the world.[24]

Prierias is a greater heretic than Arius, Manicheus, Pelagius, and
all the rest. If the Pope and cardinals do not repudiate him, then
Luther will be forced to break with them.

> Blessed be Greece, blessed be Bohemia, blessed be all who have
> separated from her [the Roman Church] and gone out from the
> midst of this Babylon; and damned be all those who commune
> with her. Her former faith is extinguished, the Gospel is proscribed,
> Christ is in exile. Only one hope remained, the authority of sacred
> Scripture and at least a proper belief in it, if no understanding. But

now Satan has conquered that also.

Thus Luther predicts that he will go into schism if his conditions are not met and — by anticipation — bids farewell in a grand rhetorical flourish laced with scriptural allusions:

> Now farewell, unhappy, lost and blasphemous Rome; as you have deserved, the wrath of God has at last come upon you. Despite so many prayers offered for you, daily you have become worse. We would have healed Babylon, but she is not healed; therefore we leave her to become the dwelling place of dragons, evil spirits, goblins, witches, and may her name likewise become an eternal confusion, filled up as she is with idols of greed, traitors, apostates, beasts, lechers, robbers, simoners and an infinity of other monsters.

After this impassioned exordium, Luther lets his reader begin on the pages of Prierias but with ample guidance from his own pen in a running commentary. When the text of the *Epitome* is finished, there follows a peroration bedaubed with rhetoric even gaudier than in the introduction. In the opening sentence we hear about "Roman Nimrods, Ishmaelites, bloodsuckers, sybarites, sodomites, and Antichrists seducing the whole world (as Peter foretold) with their feigned words."[25] Luther then proceeds to steal his own thunder from the still unwritten "Address":

> It appears to me that if the fury of the Romanists continues like this, there is no other remedy than for the Emperor, kings and princes to come to a decision and, girded with force of arms, attack these plagues of the earth not with words but with steel . . . . If we punish thieves with the gallows, robbers with the sword, heretics with fire, why should we not use all our weapons against these teachers of perdition, these cardinals, these popes and the entire dregs of this Roman Sodom that has been endlessly corrupting the Church of God, and wash our hands in their blood, so that we may free ourselves from the conflagration that threatens to overwhelm us.

After a few more paragraphs quoting Scripture against the Pope, in the course of which he introduces the term 'papists,' Martin winds up his epilogue to the *Epitome* with a rousing period:

> If the princes, bishops and the rest of the faithful do not admonish, arraign and accuse the erring Pope with regard to his crimes, and treat him as a heathen, they are all blasphemers of the way of truth, and deniers of Christ, and will with the Pope be damned eternally. I have spoken.

The Prierias affair of June 1520 represents the culmination of a development in Luther that began two and a half years earlier in his troubled reaction to the furor resulting from the publication of the Indulgence Theses. Psychologically or medically speaking it marks the onset of psychotic regression. The hostility consequent upon the disorder now definitely focuses on the figure of the Pope, not as a specific person, e.g., the current Medici Pope Leo X, but a fantasy without distinct individual identity. The hostility has of course many other targets: Luther's anthropomorphic God during the anxiety attacks, Satan at any time, Moses as symbol of the Decalogue, anyone who dares disagree with 'my theology,' and in later years the Jews. But the Pope is the target of choice, and we shall see this hostility rising to its peak expression during the final year of his life in the scatalogical cartoons commissioned by Luther from Cranach's workshop and elucidated by appropriate comments in Dr. Martin Luther's best doggerel style as well as in his pamphlet "The Papacy at Rome Founded by the Devil."

If one asks why the Pope and not Satan (who anyhow ranks as a very strong second) the explanation is that for Luther the papacy symbolizes the power that excommunicates him as a heretic and therefore constitutes a menacing threat of eternal damnation, the very heart of his intrapsychic conflict. Hence the endless vilifications of the papacy that pour from his tongue and his pen from now till his death in a torrent that crosses the seas and bears fruit in such a fantasy as the 'Giant Pope' of the dissenting preacher John Bunyan a century and a half later. This vilification of the papacy, presently extended to all former co-religionists who refuse to accept his views, and the accompanying falsifications, are typically delivered in a highly emotional tone at times verging on the hysterical. The falsifications, which we have previously identified with the denial defense mechanism, likewise increase in volume in Luther's writings and discourses from this time onward. In fact, *in the area of his disturbance,* he is no longer able to present official ecclesiastical teaching objectively or correctly but habitually falsifies it.

The appearance of this mass of abusive material and mendacious fantasy in Luther's writings is one of the clearest indicators of his regression — from an adult toward an infantile level. In today's society an individual with these symptoms would be receiving psychiatric help, either on his own initiative or that of his family or associates, and would be removed so far as possible from situations presenting undue stress. Luther did receive some (non-medical) help from his association with Melanchthon — as he formerly received it from Staupitz — but the major stress on him, that is, the heresy proceedings, continued to increase in intensity until the excommunication, and thereafter new stresses appeared. It is thus not surprising that his psychotic symptoms persisted and increased in intensity till death.

It was pointed out earlier that an individual in whom these symptoms appear may continue to exercise skills learned previously. The skills Luther acquired during his school and college days included the art of composing sentences remarkable for vigor of diction and imagery, and embellished with the dozens of rhetorical patterns or figures taught by the medieval rhetoricians, and also the art of public disputation, that is, the ability to invent arguments calculated to triumph over an opponent without regard to their truth value. These skills he retained till death, along with a certain histrionic power of conveying his emotion of the moment. There is, on the other hand, a decline in Luther's power to organize material coherently, but this was never one of his strong points anyway.

The most obvious change in his writings in this new phase is that the defensive elements − previously apparent − now dominate. In the numerous writings he produced during the second half of 1520 there is little that is not largely defensive in either purpose or content. It is notorious that he never presented a systematic account of 'my theology.' One reason for this deficiency is that the material so designated is not a theology but an assembly of defensive contrivances clothed in theological terminology. The defensive nature of his output in turn accounts for the fundamental self-contradictions for which Luther is famous: at one time or another he may be found on either side of almost any doctrinal question one cares to name.

It is not a coincidence that so much of Luther's literary output consists of commentaries on the writings of others, a form which minimized the problem of devising his own structure. But even the commentaries are not remarkable examples of composition, as Luther himself realized. Note the criticism he directed at his second commentary on the Psalms [*Operationes in Psalmos*] published during the years 1519-21:

> My psaltery disgusts me, not so much for the sense, which I think is correct, as for its verbosity, confusion and chaotic arrangement.[26]

Early in July Luther received another shock in the form of a letter sent to the Elector Frederick from Cardinal Riario requesting that Luther be forced to recant or turned over to ecclesiastical authority. The letter was shown to Luther with a request for suggestions about how it should be answered. His reply, given in a letter to Spalatin dated July 9, shows a Luther we seldom see at this period:

> I read the Roman letter in silence and great pain, seeing so much stupidity and impiety in the leaders of the Church . . . My published books testify to how often I confess and complain that *I came into this affair not by my wish but was pulled in by force.*

Thereafter I offered peace and silence many times. Where don't *I request and seek to extort better information?* Thus far I have been minded to be silent if permitted, that is, if they also would restrain themselves.

It is known to all that *Eck had no other reason for dragging me into the papal question* than to ridicule and trample on me, my name, all my writings and our university. Now when they see the man was stopped by divine power, they charge me with insane ambition. Why should I, a wretch, strive for glory, I who ask nothing but privacy and seclusion, *to be ignored by the public?* Whoever wants it may have my position. Let him who wishes burn my writings. I ask, what more shall I do?

But I also say this: if I am not permitted to free myself from the office of teaching and the ministry of the word, I will be free in the performance of the ministry. Burdened with so many sins, I will not add the unpardonable one that, placed in the ministry, I fail in it and be found guilty of impious silence . . . *Let Sylvester, Eck, Cajetan and the others be punished,* those *who for their own glory and without any reason began this tragedy* for the Church of Rome. *I am innocent.* What I did and do I am forced to do, *always ready to be silent* if only they do not require the gospel truth to be silent . . .

If I can not obtain this, let them deprive me of my ministry and *allow me to live and die in a desert corner.* Wretch that I am, I am forced to teach and suffer evil at the same time for it, while others are free to teach and are honored for it.[27]

It is difficult to recognize in this letter by a man with most of the fight gone out of him the author of the reply to Prierias quoted above – or the author of a second letter to Spalatin, to be quoted presently, dated the following day, July 10. It would appear that Luther is here emerging from a state of depression. That he was in depression at least once that year is suggested by a Table Talk item where he refers to a time in 1520 "when I was writing so much" and for a whole week "I could neither eat nor drink nor sleep." These are typical symptoms of depression and the week in question may have occurred after Luther began work on the "Address to the Christian Nobility" in mid-June. Tardiness in the completion of the "Address" and certain anomalies in its structure may be explained by its composition being temporarily interrupted.

To point up how freely Luther is now using the denial defense, I have italicized several examples of it in the letter just quoted. The 'affair' was started by his unwisely sending a copy of the Indulgence Theses to the Archbishop of Mainz. The disputation with Eck took place only because of Luther's strenuous efforts to arrange it. The

same explanation applies to the third example (in the third paragraph) so far as Eck is concerned, and Cajetan was merely carrying
out an unwelcome assignment from the Curia. The "I am innocent"
is a curious echo of what a few years previously Luther called the defense of recalcitrant heretics. The statement about the desire of this
compulsive talker to keep silence is the most preposterous of all, and
so far from being ready to retire to a desert corner, he is in the midst
of writing a pamphlet in the vernacular to set the whole church in
Germany in disarray, and planning a second one — "The Babylonian
Captivity of the Church" — in which he exclaims:

> While my opponents are congratulating themselves about tri-
> umphing over one of my so-called heresies, I will be busy con-
> cocting a new one.

After sending the letter to Spalatin quoted above, Luther continued to stew over the letter from Cardinal Riario, and the following
day (July 10) wrote again to Spalatin. Now his spirit of defiance
toward the papacy is again aroused, and, quoting a phrase from a
recent satirical pamphlet by Ulrich von Hutten, he says:

> For me the die is cast; I hold the Roman fury in contempt
> . . . . and *I will never be reconciled* or communicate with them.

This position is in such complete contradiction with the morality
he had until recently preached as to call for comment. In an earlier
chapter we referred to one of Martin's more vigorous compositions,
the "Exposition of the Lord's Prayer for Simple Laymen." Concerning the petition: "Forgive us our trespasses as we forgive those who
trespass against us" he says that this

> is the mightiest letter of indulgence which ever came upon earth,
> and which moreover is not sold for money but is freely given to
> everybody . . . . But if you do not forgive, neither will my Father
> forgive you.[28]

He then goes on to describe two human types who by their conduct
deprive themselves of this 'indulgence.' Those of the first type say
of their neighbor:

> I cannot and never will forgive him for that; *I will never be
> reconciled with him.* These carry a beam, aye, many beams in their
> eyes and do not see them.

When Luther published these forthright words in 1519 he could have
had no notion withat within a year and a half he would enroll himself as a life member in his class one.

It is not necessary to conjecture what he did to accommodate
to this unhappy plight. He reduced the standards from a Christian
to what might be called a Lutherian level. In all his subsequent

comments on this petition of the Lord's Prayer he hedged in some way on this matter of how divine forgiveness is granted only to those who forgive their fellow men. In this way he dodged the contradiction between the prayer and the *sola fide* program. He made other adjustments also. In a letter to his friend John Lang dated August 18 he absolved himself for his violent attack on the papacy in the "Address" with his personal version of the slogan that the end justifies the means:

> I am convinced that the papacy is the true and genuine seat of Antichrist and I think anything we do against its deception and wickedness for the salvation of souls is permitted.[29]

This subterfuge may conveniently be labeled the 'Lutherine privilege.' He gave it rather little publicity, but for the rest of his life there is no feature of his polemical system to which he adhered with greater fidelity, allowing for occasional modifications to adapt it to changed circumstances. In October he contrived a similar device for 'satisfying his conscience' in a reply to a criticism of Eck about the dubious ethics of the "Address":

> We are concerned not with conduct but with doctrine. Doctrine can remain quite sound in a man even though his conduct be evil. Evil doctrine is a thousand times more harmful than evil conduct.[30]

These two statements relating to the "Address", along with the refusal ever to be reconciled with the members of the 'papal church,' reveal that Luther has given up his long struggle to conduct his life according to Christian standards. The formation of such an attitude would of course be quite out of character for the Luther of earlier years and serves to corroborate the conclusion that his regression occurred during the summer of 1520. However, the development of this earmark of the regressed Luther is hardly surprising in a psyche that could produce the *sola fide* defense, with its implicit minimizing of responsibility for one's conduct. An early indication of this tendency is Luther's failure in the lectures on the Psalms in 1513-14 to comment on a passage that must have caused him no little anguish: that God in his judgment will render to everyone according to his deeds (Ps. 62:13). Paul quotes this verse in his epistle to the Romans (2:6); in 1515 when Luther encountered it there for the second time in his early lectures he was again silent about a scriptural injunction so inimical to the *sola fide.*

iv. Launching of the attack on the Church

The papal bull, *Exsurge Domine,* which bade Luther recant

within sixty days the 41 condemned propositions selected from his
publications (mainly those of 1518) was completed at Rome in mid
June. It was then already well out of date, for Luther had proceeded
much farther along the paths of heterodoxy in his writings of the
preceding half year. Also he had by then started composing the
violent attack on the papacy known as the "Address to the Christian
Nobility of the German Nation." Owing to the slowness of communi-
cations, Luther apparently did not see the text of the bull until October, two months after an edition of 4000 copies of the "Address"
had gone on sale, and indeed after he had expanded the text for a
second printing. To review briefly the contents of the "Address,"
somewhat more than three-fourths of it is devoted to complaints
about the Pope and cardinals and administrative abuses in their
offices — complaints that had been sounded frequently in Germany
for many years — and about ecclesiastical laws dealing with fasting,
abstinence, holy day observances and marriage. As a remedy, what
Luther demands in effect without saying so explicitly is that the Germans break off relations with Rome and set up a schismatic church
like the one that came into being in Electoral Saxony upon the death
of Frederick five years later. Luther concludes this part of the tract
by calling upon God to destroy the papacy and cast it into hell, in
the same vein we noted in the "Response" to Prierias in June. The
tone is markedly negative throughout, since the burden of the "Address" is essentially: "Get rid of all these things in the Church that I
find offensive."

Having in effect invited his countrymen to go into schism, he
then calls for an end of the Bohemian schism, or more precisely a
union between the Bohemian schismatics and the Germans. His next
topic deals with the universities: they should throw out most of the
existing curriculum and concentrate mainly on teaching Scripture.
Here occurs the personal reference quoted earlier about Aristotle,
that 'damned, conceited, rascally heathen'. Luther seems to forget
he is supposed to be haranguing the Emperor and the German
princes and knights, few of whom would know about Aristotle. His
sudden shift to the second person singular and the truculent tone —
"My good friend, I understand Aristotle as well as you or the likes of
you" — suggests that he is re-enacting a scene with the academic
superior who in 1509 ordered him recalled from Wittenberg to Erfurt.

An equally revealing personal matter surfaced in an earlier section
(15) in which he condemns a rule governing the confession of certain
secret mortal sins in convents, whereby the power of absolution is
reserved to the abbot or bishop. This rule 'forces' the monk to receive communion with unforgiven sin on his conscience because he
can't stomach the telling of it to the designated confessor. The over-
powering emotion with which Luther apostrophizes the authors of

the rule: "O blind shepherds! O mad prelates! O ravening wolves!" is good evidence he is here airing a problem of his own. Still another personal problem crops up in the section on the Bohemian schism. Recalling the fate of John Hus, Luther asserts that God himself commands that a safe-conduct be honored (no scriptural reference provided), even if the world should fall. He is evidently concerned about the possibility of future trips outside of Electoral Saxony, such as the journey to Worms the following spring.

From matters ecclesiastical and academic, Luther abruptly turns his attention to some details of secular life that offend him and calls upon his fellow Germans to spend less money on dress, cut down the wasteful spice trade, stop buying annuities as a form of speculation, eat and drink less, abolish houses of prostitution, and avoid making the vow of chastity before the age of 30. (Elsewhere he raises this limit to 60 or so.) Also in this, the final section of the "Address," in one of his wilder hyperboles he complains that today every man wants to enter the priesthood or a monastery instead of getting a job to support himself. In concluding he threatens his enemies with another polemical tract (the "Babylonian Captivity"):

> Up to now I have many times offered peace to my adversaries but I see that God has compelled me to open my mouth wider and wider and give these idle ones something to speak, bark, shout and write about. Well, I know another little song about Rome and about them. If they want to hear it, I will sing that one too and pitch the notes up high. Do you understand, dear Rome, what I mean?[31]

Anyone acquainted with the productions of patients in a manic state will find this passage to have a not unfamiliar ring.

A critical examination of the "Address" suggests that it was an occasional composition provoked primarily by the *Epitome* of Prierias. As a fitting response to the Prierias tract, which exalted papal authority, it develops a fundamental attack on the office of the Pope. Having proceeded thus far, Luther apparently found this to be an opportune occasion to discharge some of his other favorite gripes such as those against clerical celibacy and houses of prostitution, which are treated toward the end although he has already fulminated against celibacy back toward the middle of the tract. This explanation accounts for the notable lack of unity in the work (only a minor part of it is actually directed to the German ruling classes) and the amateurish repetitions. It is well known that Luther's pamphlet was to no small extent inspired by the recent satires of Ulrich von Hutten on the papacy, and the introductory ploy on the 'three walls' which protect the 'Romanists' was lifted from a letter Luther had received from his friend Wolfgang Capito late in 1518. This borrowing is an excellent illustration of how Luther could store in his memory for an extended period an idea or phrase encountered in his reading and bring it out later in his own distinctive style. It is probable that the structural faults of the "Address" are also in part attributable to Luther's disturbed emotional state during this time, of which more will be said presently.

Even he must have felt the inconsistency of addressing this complaint to the 'Christian nobility' because he had very small respect for these gentry and not many months earlier had inserted an abusive attack on them in one of his publications. Similar attacks came from his pen not infrequently for the rest of his life. In his low opinion of the German princes, who nevertheless listened to his call and set up their own territorial churches during the next few decades, Luther is seconded by a modern historian who describes them as one of the most worthless groups of individuals that ever decided the fate of their subjects.[32] Luther's indirect acknowledgement of his duplicity appears in the apologetic note he added to the conclusion of the second printing of the "Address," saying in effect that while the temporal rulers of Germany were bad the spiritual rulers − who were recruited from the same class − were a whole lot worse.

During the period of the production of the "Address" one of the perennial town-and-gown altercations that enlivened academic routine broke out in Wittenberg. It is of interest because of Luther's immoderate reaction to the possibility of physical violence to himself. In a letter to Spalatin of July 14 he describes his fury at seeing the university president take the part of the students in a way that might have led to "murder and bloodshed" and requests Spalatin to persuade the Elector to censure him severely. The following Sunday Luther preached against the students in his sermon, provoking the reaction described in his next letter to Spalatin (July 17):

> Good God, what hostility I aroused. They cried out I was siding with the council and revealed the thoughts of their hearts, whereby it could be learned who had truly listened to our theology and who falsely . . . . I can readily see Satan, who when he saw nothing accomplished at Rome or abroad, found this evil that he might harm us badly here.[33]

This 'law and order' message comes from one who is at the very moment inciting his fellow citizens to overthrow by violence the ancient system of ecclesiastical law that he as a priest and 'sworn doctor' is pledged to uphold. This strange mixture of innate conservatism and revolutionary spirit exhibits the psychic disarray into which Luther has now fallen. As we read on in the letter we observe also the abject fear of violence to his person that contrasts so markedly with the courage bestowed on him by the legend makers:

"For this reason I am most fearful and alarmed. Each of the last three years I have encountered great dangers: first at Augsburg, second at Leipzig and now at Wittenberg." How little Luther understands himself is revealed by his remarks on the offer of protection from Sylvester von Schaumberg and Francis von Sickingen and their warriors. This offer "made me secure from the fear of men," a consolation he repeats in another letter to Spalatin a month later: "I can now be safe in the midst of Germany." He was indeed safe from molestation by papal authority but the fear of men bedeviled him till death.

Further indications of his disturbed state at this time of crisis appear in other correspondence that summer. On July 29 he writes to Lang,"I am overwhelmed with men and affairs and conversation." On August 24 concerning the draft of a legal plea to the Emperor he has sent to Spalatin for revision, he states that when writing it he was "pressured by I don't know what burdens of soul."

Some half-dozen years before the period we are now considering, when the *theologia crucis* held the center of the stage and the *sola fide* was still well over the horizon, Luther made the following comment in his lectures on the Psalms:

> Heretics must be described as those who especially wish evil to the Church. For they ascribe to her the falseness and impurity of wicked and evil Christians, and from this small amount of evil they conclude all to be evil . . . . They alone wish to be considered good and the Church reputed bad. For they can't appear to advantage unless they depict the Church as evil, false and untruthful.[34]

The pamphlet called the "Babylonian Captivity of the Church," which Luther was assembling during September of 1520 and had in print by October 6, he referred to with the musical term 'prelude.' The work may be taken as the prelude to the endless verbal abuse, such as was described in the passage just quoted, that he heaped upon the Church from then till his death. The "Captivity" is his longest composition of that most prolific of all years, half again as long as the "Address," but it is by no means the most original. In fact it is to a large extent a compilation of material from previous writings. The underlying reason for this is that by mid-1520 Martin had intellectually shot his bolt, so that much of the material he fed to the printing presses over the next quarter-century is made up of sterile attacks on the Church and frantic attempts to put down the swarm of heterodox preachers and pamphleteers who much to his dismay sprang up in the wake of his own revolt.

The psychic distress described above manifests itself in various ways in the "Captivity." The Wittenberg colleague to whom the tract is dedicated is referred to by an erroneous name and Luther forgot to terminate the Dedicatory Epistle, becoming involved instead in a verbose and pointless discussion of the 'cup for the laity.' Early in the tract he asserts there are just three true sacraments, but later on the number shrinks to two. Since between a third and a half of the tract is devoted to matters that offend him in the mass and the Eucharist, it would appear this work represents the 'mighty blow' he planned during the anxiety attack of the preceding winter.

We shall now examine one of these matters in detail because it provides insights important for an understanding of Luther. The doctrine commonly designated by the term 'transubstantiation' Luther, in one of his characteristic falsifications, ascribes to the 'Thomistic church.' It is an ancient teaching that in the mass the bread and wine are transformed into the body and blood of Christ. As with other teachings, this was not formulated in precise theological language until questioned by a dialectician, Berengarius of Tours, about the year 1050. To resolve the controversy, recourse was had to the philosophical concept 'substance,' i.e., an object, not necessarily material, capable of independent existence. It contrasts with 'accident,' or property of a 'substance.' Thus wine is a 'substance,' its redness an 'accident.' These terms permit the precise formulation, named 'transubstantiation,' that at the consecration in the mass the 'substances' bread and wine are unequivocally changed into the 'substances' Christ's body and blood, while the 'accidents' (appearances to the senses) remain as before. This statement represents a mystery which is held in faith, not grasped by reason. Berengarius, to avoid condemnation for heresy, ultimately accepted this formulation.[35]

In rejecting this eucharistic doctrine in the "Babylonian Captivity," Luther fabricated the story that Aquinas (two centuries after Berengarius) replaced the '1200 year old' doctrine with a new one inspired by Aristotle. Thereby, at the outset of a career of prevarication unique in ecclesiastical history, he set for himself a standard of mendacity that he subsequently often equalled but rarely surpassed. Displaying his contempt for the teaching authority of the Church, he adopted as his own a position defended by the 14th century British eccentric Wyclif (and similar to that of Berengarius) that had been condemned by the Council of Constance.

Luther's concluding remarks on the mass in this tract tell us much about one of the motives underlying his peculiar attitude toward it. "The mass was provided only for those who have a sad, afflicted, alarmed, confused and wavering conscience. It is only they who communicate worthily."[36] Few sentences in his works reveal so graphically as this one, in its utter egocentricity, the extreme pathos of his situation. From this time forth he often gives voice to the delusion that the Eucharist is intended only for the emotionally sick like himself.

v. Reaction to the bull of excommunication

It is instructive to examine the list of Luther's writings during the last quarter of 1520 following the execution of the long-planned attack in the "Babylonian Captivity." All of them relate to his impending excommunication. Since Luther commonly wrote about what was foremost in his mind at the time of composition, there is no question what his concern was during this period. The printing of the more lengthy items 6 and 8 in the list given below, though not completed until the early months of 1521, was begun in December. Latin writings are so identified; starred items are available in English translation.

1. On the New Bull and Lies of Eck
2. Against the Accursed Bull of Antichrist (first 6 articles; Latin)
3. Against the Bull of Antichrist (first 12 articles)
*4a. Letter to Leo X (Latin)
  b. On Christian Liberty (Latin)
  c. Letter to Leo X
  d. Freedom of the Christian
5. Renewed Appeal of Dr. Martin Luther for a Council (Latin and German texts)
6. Assertion of All the Articles Condemned in the Bull (Latin)
*7. Why the Books of the Pope and His Disciples were Burned
*8. Defense and Explanation of All the Articles Unjustly Condemned in the Bull

Items 2, 3 and 6, justifying respectively the first 6, the first 12 and then all 41 of the articles condemned by *Exsurge Domine,* give the impression of a man approaching a goal by a series of successive approximations. Item 8, a German version of item 6, covers the same ground as its predecessor but omits certain material Luther judged inappropriate for tender consciences. Item 5 gives additional evidence that Luther possessed a real talent for legal maneuvers. Item 7 is a verbalization of Luther's tit-for-tat in the popular outdoor pastime of book burning.

John Eck, Luther's antagonist in the Leipzig debate, was assigned the task of officially proclaiming the papal bull in what might be called roughly the eastern half of the German lands. This document condemned 41 propositions drawn from Luther's writings and threatened him — and his supporters — with excommunication within 60 days of the posting of the document if no recantation was forthcoming. It was issued at Rome in June, but Eck did not begin distributing it in Germany till the latter half of September. Late in August at a chapter meeting of the Augustinians in Eisleben, von Staupitz resigned as vicar general and Wenzel Link, formerly prior at Wittenberg, was elected to replace him. At the instigation of the envoy Miltitz, Staupitz and Link called on Luther at Wittenberg to ask that he write a letter to Leo X aimed at reconciling his differences with Rome. Luther appeared to be agreeable but failed to write the letter, possibly because he was then busy with the "Babylonian Captivity," which issued from the press just a month later, October 6. As we have already seen, this tract could have no other result than to make the breach permanent. The occasion of Staupitz' visit (September 6) proved to be his final meeting with Martin, for he then returned to his haven at Salzburg and presently became abbot of the Benedictine monastery there. (He appears to have been regarded as the most distinguished abbot in the history of the Salzburg chapter, as indicated by the prominence of his memorial in the sacristy of the abbey church.)

The exact chronology of Luther's writings listed above is rather obscure. The first one, "On the New Bull and Lies of Eck," inspired by Eck's recent pamphlet replying to Luther's slurs on the Council of Constance, was apparently written before Luther actually saw a copy of *Exsurge Domine.* In it he adopted a posture in regard to the bull that he maintained for the next several weeks, that the bull purporting to be brought from Rome by Eck was only a forgery. In his pamphlet Eck had charged Luther with the sin of pride in elevating himself above the Fathers and councils. Luther's response — that evil conduct in a Christian teacher is a rather trifling matter in comparison with his doctrine — was quoted earlier. After this enunciation of what was to become a favorite alibi, there comes a mingling of the *sola scriptura* with his identification with Paul:

> Where I have a clear text, I will raise it up above all the angels, as Paul does in Galatians 1,8. It doesn't bother me and St. Paul if for that reason this lying mouth [Eck], an enemy of the truth, calls us both heretics.[37]

This tract attacking Eck appeared about mid-October, but earlier in the month Luther had finally seen a copy of *Exsurge Domine;* this is his reaction, in a letter to Spalatin dated October 11:

> That Roman bull brought by Eck has finally arrived . . . I despise it and *now assail it as impious and false and in all ways Eckian.* You can see in it Christ himself condemned but nothing bearing on the case, calling me not to be heard but to recant. Thus you can know they are full of wrath, blindness and insanity, seeing and understanding nothing. *I shall continue to act as if it were a*

*fictitious and fabricated bull, suppressing the Pope's name, though
I believe it to be truly their very own* . . . I suspect it will acquire
authority if we show too much care and solicitude for it, but if
ignored it will make little impression.[38]

The first italicized passage in the letter refers to a tract now being
composed (in Latin) entitled "Against the Accursed Bull of Antichrist" (item 2 in the list above). Anyone who has been misled by
the Luther-cult writers into viewing Luther as a model of candor
should become aware that the program of deceit announced in the
second italicized passage represents standard operating procedure
for the Luther of 1520-1546. To determine when the deceit is conscious and when it signals the action of an unconscious defense
mechanism is not always possible. On this occasion it is obviously
conscious. Ignoring his own suggestion in the closing remark, Luther
was now embarked on a course of action calculated to keep the bull
very much in the foreground of public attention rather than let it
quiet down.

At some period in October Luther also composed in German an
attack on the bull (item 3 in the list). Precise information on the date
of composition is not available. From a letter of November 4 to
Spalatin we know the Latin tract was already in print at that date
and the German one was being printed. It is instructive to compare
the two tracts for the light thrown on Luther's attitudes toward his
prospective audience and his habits of composition. In both tracts
Luther sticks to his program of making believe he regards the bull as
a (possible) forgery. But he can't refrain altogether from mentioning
the name of Leo. In the Latin tract, addressed formally to the
'Christian Reader,' after several pages devoted to the art of name-
calling at which he was a master, he suddenly shifts gears and cries
out:

You, therefore, Leo X, you Lord Cardinals of Rome, and whoever else you are in Rome, I call you to account and say to you
openly: 'If this bull was issued in your name and with your
knowledge, and if you admit it is yours, then I will use my
authority by which through God's mercy in baptism I was made a
child of God and coheir with Christ, founded upon a firm rock
which the gates of neither hell, heaven nor earth can frighten. And
I will state, advise and admonish you in the Lord that you have a
change of heart and do away with these devilish blasphemies and
these unspeakably audacious impieties now. And do it fast.[39]

And so Luther rolls on through a highly rhetorical expression of
his manic grandiosity, threatening to denounce Leo as the chief
enemy of Christ, ignore his censures, and destroy the bull and all the
decretals, i.e., the canon law (see item 7 above). The corresponding

threat in the German version, which is pitched on a lower tone rhe-
torically than the Latin, is more in keeping with the approach followed in the "Address to the Christian Nobility":

> It would be no surprise if the princes, nobles and laity banged
> the Pope, bishops, priests and monks over the head and drove
> them out of the land . . . . I hope it is perfectly clear that not Dr.
> Luther but the Pope himself, together with the bishops, priests
> and monks will be immeshed in their own misfortune as a result
> of this blasphemous outrage of a bull, and the laity will be glad to
> load it on their necks.[40]

In his polemical tracts Luther has a trick of playing with a word or
phrase that strikes his fancy, repeating it over and over. In the Latin
tract the word is 'Antichrist.' Being forbidden by his self-imposed
ground rule from naming Leo X as the author, he finds Antichrist to
provide a welcome alternative to Eck, who after being designated
as the putative author three or four times at the very beginning is
thereafter largely forgotten. Antichrist as author is named a score or
more of times throughout the tract, thereby satisfying Luther's
urge to belabor the Pope while professing to be undecided on the
question of authorship. In the German tract, on the other hand,
where the public relations problem is somewhat different, Luther
starts off with 'papal power' as the dirty word. Then he gives 'outrage' (*Frevel*) or 'papal outrage' quite a play, but finally relapses into
the favorite epithet Antichrist.

As a rule when Luther prepares a German version of a Latin tract
he does not merely translate, but definitely pitches the vernacular
composition to a (relatively) uneducated audience. Sometimes the
reason for the shift is unclear. For example, in the Latin tract he
ridicules the bull by suggesting that it was written "by ungodly and
insensate papists during a nocturnal feast in the company of whores,
or during the raging dog days." In the German version this is
softened to: "I suspect the bull was written during an evening drinking party or in the dog days." In later years he shows a fondness for
using the German equivalent of 'whore' as a term of opprobrium;
perhaps in 1520 he still feels such language rather indelicate for a
religious prophet.

Recurring to the letter to Spalatin quoted above, we note that in
it Luther mentions he is about to leave for a meeting with Miltitz
at a place some miles out of Wittenberg. The next day, October 12,
right after the colloquy, he notifies Spalatin in another letter that he
has accepted Miltitz' renewed request to write a conciliatory letter to
Leo X. Also he will append to the letter a brief account of his pre-
dicament, showing that it was entirely Eck's fault and exonerating
the Pope. To avoid any reference to the infamous bull, Luther would

date the letter back to September 6, well before the bull was proclaimed in his part of Germany. The result of this rather odd arrangement was the famous letter to Leo and the even more famous essay "Freedom of the Christian," each item being prepared in both Latin and German versions. This essay has been widely hailed as an extraordinary expression of Christian spirituality, and indeed it may well appear so to anyone unacquainted with the medieval literature of piety or even with the "Imitation of Christ," and who reads it out of context and uncritically. The work is certainly filled with noble sentiments, but then so also, for example, are the published platforms of our major political parties that appear regularly in the years divisible by four.

The prefatory letter to Leo is not quite so noble in either tone or content. In fact, it contains some choice examples, particularly in regard to John Eck, of that type of utterance that qualifies Luther for the title of Master of the Denial Mechanism, to borrow an expression from the art historians. Additional evidence of Luther's psychic disarray at this time can be found in the childish self-contradictions. For example, after asserting that he is interested in attacking nothing but ungodly doctrine and will quarrel with no one about his morals, Luther at once proceeds to excoriate the members of the Roman Curia for their immoral lives. In another place, Leo, he says, can by a mere word silence all parties to the controversy (including Luther, it appears) and restore peace. In the next paragraph Luther belittles Leo's actual power; Leo should not listen to the flatterers who grossly exaggerate his power, but instead recall that he is only a servant of servants. The most engaging paragraph of this conciliatory epistle begins with the voluntary prostration of its author at Leo's feet, from which position he proclaims that he will never recant any of his teaching and will make more noise than ever if again pressed to recant.

To turn now to the essay called the "Freedom of the Christian" (German) or "On Christian Liberty" (Latin) which Luther introduces at the end of his falsely dated letter to Leo, it should be noted that it was written in the latter part of October, at a time when he had completed "Against the Accursed Bull of Antichrist." In large measure the work is an exposition of the *sola fide* defensive program. It is basically a summary of topics Luther had been mulling over during the past several years beginning with the Lectures on Romans. What is new in it is the association of what he calls "Christian liberty" with the *sola fide*. The deliberate use of the word 'liberty' or 'freedom' in the title of a work dealing essentially with a different subject, namely, Lutheran 'faith,' is a favorite technique of the Lutherian propaganda. His choice of this title, together with his repeated linking of the word 'freedom' with the *sola fide* in the tract, indicates the intention of cashing in on the universal appeal of this word.

Luther makes very effective use of the call to freedom in the tract. His followers are to regard themselves as kings and priests and lords of everything. But they do not abuse this freedom. They freely and willingly serve their neighbors and submit their will to their neighbor in the freedom of their neighborly love. A month or two after writing this hymn to freedom, Luther is again at work attacking the bull in another Latin tract, "Assertion of All the Articles." In his response to the condemnation of article 36 (taken from the 1518 Heidelberg disputation) in which he denies human freedom, he strengthens his previous denial of the freedom of the will, asserting "It is not in the power of man to choose to do good or evil."[41] In view of this gross contradiction of a central theme of the essay on freedom, one might regard that work as a piece of unscrupulous propaganda designed to sell the *sola fide* program. This problem will receive attention in later chapters.

A remarkable feature of the "Freedom of the Christian" is the almost complete absence in it of the discharge of pathological hostility. There are complaints about the tyranny of the clergy and their suppression of 'liberty' but these are trivial in comparison with what appears in the other compositions from Luther's pen in the second half of 1520, including the letter to Leo X. This suggests that at least at times Luther could control the expression of hostility, that is, when it was to his advantage to do so. To exhibit such unchristian attitudes in an essay promoting Christian faith and love might arouse suspicions of the sincerity of the author.

The greatest weakness of the essay as an account of spiritual life is the absence of any concrete suggestions of how such a life is achieved in practice. Instead the reader is confronted with the bizarre proclamation that the virtues themselves — naively personified — are the real actors on the stage of Christian living and the implication that one who enjoys the gifts of faith, love and freedom is himself a mere passive spectator of their activities.

> Since I am saved by faith alone, I need only faith exercising its power of liberty.
>
> Our faith and love, being still imperfect, must be increased of themselves.
>
> Freedom makes our hearts free from sin, the law and the commandments.

Luther assures us that good works don't make a good man, but rather a good man does good works. He appears unable to rise above this tautology to tackle the important question, How does a man become good?

The nobility of the sentiments in "The Freedom of the Christian" derives in large part from Luther's use of scriptural language. To penetrate below the surface of this masterpiece of dissimulation one must ask what the scriptural language means to Luther. For example, who is the Lutherian 'neighbor'? He is not the neighbor of the parable of the Good Samaritan, but rather one who embraces the gospel according to Luther. At the moment Luther was publishing the noble sentiment about living 'in his neighbor in love' he was striving — successfully — to get a faculty colleague, the professor of Hebrew, fired for daring to criticize the *sola fide* program. Adrian, no neighbor but an "enemy," is "now useless and must soon be dismissed" (Luther to Spalatin, November 4, 1520). With regard to appropriate treatment for another theological opponent, Jerome Emser of Leipzig, (see below) Luther makes a revealing remark in a letter to his friend Amsdorf, a canon of the chapter of All Saints in Wittenberg.[42] Amsdorf is instructed to write against Emser in a contemptuous tone and in particular not to regard him even as a human being. As if to underline this unevangelical dichotomy in the Lutherian ethic, in a letter to Erasmus of 1524 (another aspect of which is discussed in Ch. 7 below) Luther asserts that those who have accepted his gospel must be treated like human beings and their offenses forgiven. His favorite stratagem for forgiving his own unloving behavior to non-neighbors was to style his hatred of them as 'holy.' Naturally material like this, however commonplace in his utterances, was carefully excluded from "The Freedom of the Christian."

vi. The Worms confrontation and the Wartburg hideout

The papal bull *Exsurge Domine* of June 1520 condemned a number of propositions drawn from Luther's writings and bade him recant. A second bull of January 1521 declared him officially excommunicated and requested enforcement of the edict by civil and ecclesiastical authority. The unresponsive attitude to these documents by the governments of many German states and cities revealed the enormous difference between the supreme power of the Pope as described by the theoreticians and the negligible authority he possessed in practice in any part of Europe where he was not supported by the local government. Frederick, the Elector of Saxony, ignoring the directive from Rome, decided to continue the political game initiated a few years earlier by Leo himself. Appealing to the principle that no German could be condemned without a trial, he decided to have his subject Dr. Martin Luther appear before the meeting of the Reichstag at Worms in the spring of 1521. This stratagem permitted Frederick to continue to act as Luther's protector without appearing too brazenly to defy papal authority.

The significance of this episode, little more than a political charade, has been considerably exaggerated by Luther biographers as the culmination of a heroic career. To a large extent it was a rerun of the Augsburg scenario of two and a half years earlier, but now with a much larger cast. Also there had been a radical change in the character of the leading man. At Augsburg he had regarded himself as a loyal, if misunderstood, member of the Church; now he acknowledges his permanent enmity and seeks to persuade his associates to take the same course. Consider this letter to his friend Nicholas Hausmann written within two weeks of the day he set out for Worms:

> What I see when I look at the Church is a horror. I am more and more persuaded that unless one fights against the statutes and commandments of the Pope and bishops with all his force through life and death he cannot be saved . . . The Pope and his followers are enemies of Christ . . . You know what a great outcry is made today that schism and heresy are a crime and a boundless evil. But what can we do? There is no other means of safety in this age of perdition . . . Unless you fight against the Pope and the bishops and oppose their statutes, you will be the enemy of Christ.[43]

Luther was much averse to regarding himself as a heretic or even admitting he had gone into schism; this letter seems to be his most explicit recognition of his new status. In subsequent chapters we shall observe what happened to the 'right to heresy and schism' when with the support of the Saxon government he set up his own orthodoxy.

In the Augsburg affair he had neglected to apply for an imperial safe-conduct until after arrival in the city; but for Worms the safe-conduct is uppermost in his mind. In January he received a letter from the Elector instructing him to appear at the Diet. In his reply, he twice asks for the safe-conduct:

> In all submissiveness I beg your Grace to intercede with his Imperial Majesty for his humble servant that I may have sufficient safeguard and a free safe-conduct *against all violence, about which I must be especially careful* . . .
> Then I am ready in humble obedience, *if I am granted sufficient safeguard and a free safe-conduct,* to travel to and back from Worms.[44]

In the second of these two sentences Luther demonstrates his basic insubordination to civil authority where his own personal interest is involved, since he makes granting of the safe conduct a condition for obeying an order from his sovereign. Especially interesting are the italicized words in the first sentence; next to the prospect of eternal damnation, what he feared more than anything else was the possibility of violence to his person. The many recorded remarks about his cowardliness, concerning which he was extremely sensitive, range from frank admission as in the above letter, to boastful denial of it. But for anyone forced to endure such high levels of anxiety as Luther, even ordinary courage would be too much to expect.

His feverish literary activity continued unabated from the previous year. Before completing his fourth (and longest) response to the bull *Exsurge Domine* he became embroiled in controversy with Jerome Emser, then secretary and court chaplain to Duke George. Luther's extremely disturbed state during February and March while awaiting the safe-conduct for the journey to Worms is revealed in the longest of the anti-Emser pamphlets: "Answer to the Hyperchristian, Hyper-spiritual and Hyperlearned Book by Goat Emser in Leipzig – including some Thoughts regarding His Companion, the Fool Murner." As might be inferred from the title, the principal ingredient of the "Answer to Emser" is personal abuse; however, there are in addition some significant sidelights on Luther's character.

The persecutory delusions which presently are to be numbered among the more prominent symptoms of his disorder have already begun to form. He is beset by enemies: "I stand surrounded by them as in the middle of a ring, one against many."[45] This despite the able support of Melanchthon and other associates at Wittenberg, the protection granted him by Frederick, the most powerful of the German princes, with his good friend Spalatin as Frederick's secretary to handle details, the offer of assistance from the German knight von Sickingen, his numerous and enthusiastic supporters in Nuremberg, Augsburg and elsewhere in Germany.

Luther's self-image in the pamphlet contrasts with the one he reveals in the letter of March 22 quoted above: "I am truly a devout Christian; without any grounds for it, he [Emser] called me a heretic."[46] Luther here appears to resort to the defense mechanism known as 'isolation' to blot out his painful awareness of the official excommunication for heresy expressed in a document which provided quite a number of reasons. One of the more interesting instances of the denial mechanism in the tract occurs in the following passage:

> You scream and lie against me with all your might that I slanderously attack and dishonor the head of the Church, the Pope and the priesthood. I have never done this. For I have taught that the power of the Turk . . . . and other unjust powers be endured and respected.[47]

At times he seems to lose control; indeed this tract was cited by Reiter as one of the clearer indications of Luther's manic symptoms during this period:

/ How often must I scream at you rude, unlearned papists before
you show me some Scripture just once? Scripture! Scripture!
Scripture! Can't you hear, you deaf goat and crude ass? Hey, goat,
get mad and butt me once. But don't back away so far you'll wear
yourself out.[48]

The passage to be quoted next reveals better than anything else in
the tract the tortured state of Luther's psyche. He wants to avoid excommunication but he wants it officially acknowledged that no legis-
lation can be binding under pain of sin. He hopes thereby to be
relieved of the dreadful burden of anxiety which at this period he
believes to have been caused especially by the laws regarding reception of the sacraments of penance and the Eucharist, together with
the regulations governing him as priest and religious. As we have
seen, for two years prior to mid 1520 he devoted incredible ingenuity
to revamping these sacraments to suit his psychic requirements.

Say to your idol the Pope that he can make as many laws over
me as he chooses; I will obey them all. But tell him also he has no
right to do this and I am under no obligation to him but willingly
suffer his injustice, as Christ teaches. I will no longer work against
the Pope; let all things be evil . . . .
When the Pope presses the whole world as if it were his right, he
ensnares countless souls and leads them into hell . . . . *Whoever
believes the Pope has the right and power to make laws at once
thinks he must observe them as necessary and good . . . . He does
this unwillingly* and would prefer — but can't manage — to become
free of the laws. And *thus he is smothered by sins.* For whoever
*does unwillingly what he must do or believes he must do commits
sin in his heart.* And therefore the innumerable laws of the Pope
are like a cord for strangling souls . . . . Only a few — or none at
all — escape him unless they die in the cradle.[49]

This passage read in the light of Luther's psychic development over
the years 1518-21 illuminates the motivation underlying his behavior
during this critical period of his career. The italicized words represent his interpretation of what constitutes his 'sins' at this time.
This pathological attitude toward ecclesiastical law stands as a
counterpart to the *sola fide* defense.

Luther's unusual willingness to become reconciled with the Pope
and obey his laws is very shortlived. In the next paragraph he goes on
in a more familiar vein:

All men hate the papacy except the ones who benefit from it;
and therefore it is properly called an abomination. Thus the
Pope has taken the whole world prisoner with false consciences
and superstition. One must sin without recompense and without

letup, and perish. Woe to you, you horrible abomination! Come, Lord Jesus Christ, and deliver us from the Antichrist! Shove his throne into the abyss of hell, as he has merited, so that sin and death may come to an end. Amen.[50]

On April 2, a few days after the printed version of the "Answer to Emser" was off the press, Luther climbed aboard a wagon provided for his convenience by the Wittenberg town council, and accompanied by three associates set out for Worms. The journey was a triumphal progress. The imperial herald, sent by the Emperor as part of the guaranteed protection, was himself a Luther enthusiast and conducted his hero with appropriate ceremony. In Erfurt Luther was given a royal reception and invited to preach a sermon. There his party was joined by Justus Jonas, an academic trained in canon law, who later transferred to Wittenberg and became a permanent member of Luther's inner circle, ultimately delivering a eulogy at Luther's funeral a quarter-century later.

Despite all this attention and his obvious freedom from danger, Luther was a badly frightened man as he rode along to Worms. At his initial appearance before the Emperor and the assembled dignitaries, when asked if he was willing to recant the errors contained in a collection of his 'little books' assembled for the occasion, he lost his composure and requested time for reflection. This being granted, he retired to his quarters for twenty-four hours and prepared a speech. At his second appearance before the Diet he had regained confidence and explained at length that it would be against his conscience to recant anything. This stance has been interpreted as an act of unexampled heroism by writers ignorant of the nature of Luther's inner problem. Any meaningful recantation was unthinkable because it would mean abandoning the *sola fide* defense and he had been expressing his determination to recant none of his views since the Augsburg confrontation two and a half years earlier. Apart from that he still had the guarantee of a safe return journey to Wittenberg and the promise of continued protection thereafter from the Elector of Saxony.

An episode of no little interest during his last day at Worms, after several fruitless attempts by various ecclesiastics to find some common ground for discussion, was the lecture addressed to him by the secretary of the archbishop of Trier. Perhaps for the first (and last) time Luther had the opportunity to listen to a fairly precise description of how his activities as author during the past year or two appeared to a knowledgeable and orthodox churchman. He appears to have endured this ordeal without flinching.

When Luther left Worms on April 26, escorted again by the friendly imperial herald, he was as before provided with a safe-conduct, good for 21 days. On April 28 he stopped at a small town near

Frankfort and composed a long letter to the Emperor, justifying his actions at the Diet. He also expressed his gratitude for the protection granted to him:

> I most humbly thank your Sacred Majesty because you so scrupulously maintained the safe-conduct to Worms and promised to maintain it until I arrive at my secure abode.[51]

The safe-conduct for the return journey stipulated that Luther was not to preach or write before his arrival at Wittenberg. Nevertheless, after dismissing the imperial herald, whose presence would have been an intolerable embarrassment and whose protection was entirely superfluous, Luther gave three sermons en route. What is more, we presently find him complaining that 'they' violated 'my safe-conduct.' Knowing Luther to be psychotic, one does not regard him as either dishonorable or a liar for such behavior. Since he lacked moral freedom, he was quite unable to resist invitations to preach, and the subsequent falsifications should be interpreted not as lies but as instances of the denial mechanism motivated by his shame at breaking his word.

In accordance with the arrangement for Luther to hide in the Elector's castle, the Wartburg, on a hill overlooking Eisenach, he was intercepted on the journey by a group of horsemen, who faked a kidnapping and rode off by a circuitous route to their destination. This permitted Luther's traveling companion, a fellow Augustinian not in on the plot, to report the 'abduction' in good faith. By this strategem, Luther, an outlaw by imperial edict, was safe from molestation, and the Elector avoided the obloquy of being in open defiance of the law until the following year.

At the Wartburg Martin for the first time in many years enjoyed an abundance of leisure. Along with completing a few works begun earlier, he devoted his ten months in the castle mainly to preparing some polemical tracts and a first draft of the German translation of the New Testament. There were only two interruptions of any consequence, one in early July when he exhibited symptoms of depression for upwards of a week, and the other – of comparable duration – in December when he made a clandestine visit to Wittenberg. The writings of the Wartburg period, largely devoted to propaganda against the Church and monastic life, betray the deteriorating intellectual quality characteristic of the psychotic phase of Luther's disorder, being diffuse, repetitious and of rather haphazard structure. While not of much intrinsic interest they are useful to students of Luther's personality, and together with the extant correspondence, totalling about 40 letters, provide a good picture of Luther during his stay – early May of 1521 to the following March – at the Wartburg.

As pointed out earlier, Luther's extreme fear for his personal safety induced by the summons to Worms had manifested itself in a severe gastro-intestinal attack en route to the city, like the corresponding symptoms experienced on his trip to Augsburg in 1518. By his own testimony, this new attack was much worse than the earlier one. Also this time the fear persisted, for he was now an outlaw under sentence of death. To make matters worse he had to live in solitude, a state most inimical to one with his special psychic needs. A year earlier, the uncontrollable anxiety engendered by the threat of excommunication had driven him into psychotic regression. The additional psychic burden presented by the sojourn in the castle brought on a severe and painful attack of constipation. Despite the medication provided him, the condition continued for five months — until October — by which time he had presumably come to feel that he was safe in the castle.

A constantly recurring theme in the letters from the Wartburg is the need of keeping his whereabouts secret. Since he is ashamed of his evident fearfulness, he frequently resorts to the denial mechanism, asserting that he is hiding only at the insistence of his friends and that he would much prefer open confrontation with his enemies. A defensive reference to his fear and an account of the constipation appear in one of the earliest letters (to Melanchthon) on May 12:

> I was afraid that I might seem to be deserting the battlefield, but there was no way I could resist those who wanted and advised me [to come here]. But I should like nothing better than to grasp my enemies in their fury by the bare throat . . . .
>
> The Lord has afflicted me most painfully in the posterior. My stools are so hard that to expel them I must exert great force, even to the point of breaking out in a sweat. The longer I delay, the harder they become. Yesterday I excreted for the first time in four days; as a result I spent a sleepless night and am still uncomfortable. I beg you to pray for me.[52]

On the same day to his friend Agricola of Eisleben: "An extraordinary captive, I sit here both willing and unwilling; willing because the Lord wishes it, unwilling because I would want to stand up publicly for the word, but I am not worthy of this yet."[53] The alibi that he is unworthy of martyrdom becomes a favorite from this time on. The fear and the constipation are linked in a letter of mid July to Spalatin, who has been sending him laxatives. Martin has become alarmed by a rumor of the betrayal of his secret hideout.

> We are still bravely (sic!) concealing it, though I am indignant that our loyal and successful endeavors have been so easily frustrated . . . . If my malady does not improve, I will seek medical help in Erfurt.[54]

The fear of discovery is also reflected in the letter to Amsdorf cited at the end of the preceding section. Writing in mid July from the Wartburg, Luther says the rumor that he is staying at the Wartburg is untrue. This letter creates a serious problem for the image of a fearless and veracious reformer because it also shows Luther's indifference toward one of the most serious abuses in the ecclesiastical system of his day: the holding of multiple benefices. In the letter Luther congratulates Amsdorf, who derived his financial support from his position as canon at the castle church in Wittenberg, on having been granted another benefice in a remote parish where he would perform no pastoral service but merely collect the income.

To throw his enemies off the scent Luther faked a letter (which has survived) to Spalatin suggesting that he is staying secretly with some friars in Bohemia. This letter he sent to Spalatin with instructions to lose it with "studied carelessness" so that it "will fall into the hands of our enemies." In September he sent Spalatin a newly completed manuscript with a request to have it copied by a court secretary and returned to him because "my handwriting must be kept secret."

What is doubtless the most famous of all the messages from the Wartburg, in a letter to Melanchthon of August 1, brings out superbly the 'enthusiasm' of Luther during this period:

> Be a sinner and sin bravely, but believe and rejoice more strongly in Christ, who is the conqueror of sin, death and the world. We must sin as long as we are here, for this life is not the abiding place of righteousness . . . . Our sin will not pluck us away from the lamb of God even if we commit fornication or murder thousands and thousands of times in one day . . . . Pray stoutly and be a mighty sinner.[55]

In such a state of exaltation who needs the *sola scriptura*?

Chapter 4

Luther As Proselytizer

i. The voice from the Wartburg

Of the several tracts Luther produced during his stay at the Wartburg, the best known is the "Judgment of Monastic Vows," composed in autumn after the psychosomatic symptoms had been alleviated. (The "Judgment" is discussed in Ch. 6.) During his first month of residence at the castle he dealt with what may be presumed was uppermost in his mind upon arrival in a tract called "On Confession, Whether the Pope Has the Power to Require It." Like other Wartburg tracts, "On Confession" is basically a defensive production aiming to justify Luther's new status consequent on the official excommunication. In contrast to the earlier tracts on confession (1518-20) this one is concerned less with Luther's personal difficulties than with trying to show ecclesiastical authority has no right to require anything.

A basic theme of "On Confession" is that whatever ordinance emanates from Rome or a local bishop is merely 'doctrines of men' and must be rejected by all faithful Christians. The tract opens with a selection of scriptural texts, each provided with an appropriate comment designed to show the wickedness of the doctrines of men. Interspersed in this material are stirring apostrophes such as "O Pope, O Bishops, O Monks, O Priests, etc.," or "O you greatest of all whoremasters." After the reader has been emotionally aroused by this extended exordium, Luther switches into his main argument, which is based principally on two texts from the gospel of Matthew and one from the gospel of John. These passages were an endless source of grief for Luther; he returns to them repeatedly during the 1520s and later. I quote here the three texts, and after some elucidation present his rather remarkable exegesis of them.

The first one consists of a promise addressed by Jesus to Peter at Caesarea Philippi, following Peter's confession of faith:

> I will give to you the keys of the Kingdom of heaven. Whatever
> you bind on earth will have been bound in heaven, and whatever
> you release on earth will have been so released in heaven [16:19].

The second text appears in the course of some private instruction
given by Jesus to his disciples:

> Whatever you bind on earth will have been bound in heaven and
> whatever you release on earth will have been released in heaven
> [18:18].

The 'keys' referred to in the first of these texts from Matthew are
a symbol of leadership and authority, the O. T. background for this
symbol being found in Isaiah 22:22. Modern exegetes[1] point out
that in rabbinical Judaism the words *bind* and *release*, for which
there is no O. T. analogue, mean, respectively, to impose and to
remove an obligation. Concerning the authority of the community
indicated in this passage another recent exegete[2] comments that
commitment in faith to Jesus involved the obligation to submit to
the community's rule and to remain in its fellowship; also that
Peter's role as steward was to exercise administrative authority, as
was true of the O. T. chamberlain who held the 'keys.'

The third text in Luther's argument is from a post-resurrectional
appearance of Jesus to the Eleven [John 20:23] :

> If you forgive men's sins, their sins are forgiven; if you hold
> them fast, they are held fast.

Comparing these three texts we note that only the third one mentions forgiveness of sins and only in the first one, directed specifically to Peter, is the authority symbolized by the bestowal of the
'keys' in question. In none of the texts is Jesus represented as speaking to a wider audience than the little band of disciples. We now
observe the completely arbitrary fashion in which Luther disposes of
them. He starts with the second text (Matt. 18:18):

> Here Christ gives the keys to the whole community and not to
> St. Peter. And here also belongs the text of Matt. 16:19 when he
> gave St. Peter the keys instead of the whole community. But in
> the 18th chapter the Lord himself provides a gloss on the passage
> in Ch. 16 about giving the keys to Peter. They are given to all
> Christians, not to the person of St. Peter. And here also belongs
> the corresponding text from John 20:23.
>
> Three texts with one meaning, whereby Christ has arranged for
> the Christian community to punish sin so that the Pope's law
> may be of no need or profit.[3]

The reader should be aware that quite often Luther insists on a
painfully literal rendition of scriptural texts. Here he goes to the

other extreme — or beyond it — winding up this exegetical absurdity
with his rejection of the 'Pope's commandment', which his imperious
psychic needs force him to deny. The symbol of the keys tends to
excite one of his most severe inner conflicts, a conflict that involves
his long standing fear of damnation now greatly exacerbated by the
sentence of excommunication imposed by the community empowered
to bind and release. The symbol cannot be disposed of as a despicable papal fraud since it stands unequivocally in Scripture in a speech
uttered by the Savior himself. (It may be recalled that at this date
(May 1521) Luther has not yet downgraded the gospel of Matthew
as unimportant for salvation.) The keys symbol recurs frequently in
his writings; at the end of the decade he will compose an entire tract
on the subject, and it figures prominently in his last major composition of 1545, "Against the Papacy at Rome, Founded by the Devil."
At times when quoting the text containing the keys symbol he introduces the word *sins* as the object of *bind* and *loose* in one of his characteristic falsifications. In the 1521 tract he rarely shows any awareness that the keys symbolize ecclesiastical authority — naturally,
since the entire aim of his propaganda effort is to deny that ecclesiastical authority can set up binding standards for the faithful. Here
is one of his more picturesque fantasies:

> The keys have to do with sins, not with hearts or consciences.
> It is not hearts or consciences that are locked or unlocked, but
> Heaven. They are not called heart-keys or conscience-keys but
> heaven-keys . . . . Christ did not say to Peter, "I will give you the
> keys of hearts or consciences"; no, such keys he keeps himself till
> the last day.[4]

His insistence on the individual's right to keep his 'secret sins' to
himself here becomes almost obsessional. At one point he asserts:

> There is no authority in the Church to bind or loose secret
> sins; this is a matter of the individual's choice.

To illustrate further the pervasive irrationality of this tract,
consider the following passage, a sort of imaginary dialogue between
himself and a priest:

> Pardon is tied to confession and pardon must follow and be
> governed by confession. If I confess in private, you must forgive
> in private. If I confess in public, you must absolve in public. My
> confession is at my discretion, not yours. Therefore, absolution is
> my right, not yours. I have the right and freedom to demand it;
> you do not have the right to refuse it, but the obligation and
> necessity to give it.[5]

An interesting feature of this 1521 tract on confession is the
sturdy defense of the freedom of the will that keeps cropping up

throughout it. In ringing tones Luther denounces the Pope for trying
to force Christians to do what God has left up to their own free
choice:

> In confession let us be free, free, willing and ready. If we can't
> do that, at least let us forget about commands and compulsion.[6]

It may be recalled that hardly six months before this Luther had
published an equally ringing denunciation of free will in his "Assertion of All the Articles." In rebuttal of the papal condemnation of
his earlier attack on the free will, he had written:

> Freedom of choice is but a meaningless label . . . . All things
> happen by absolute necessity, as Wyclif rightly taught, in an article
> condemned by the Council of Constance . . . .
>
> On other articles such as the papacy, councils, indulgences and
> other needless trifles, one can put up with the levity and folly
> of the Pope and his crowd. But with regard to this article, *which is
> the best and most important part of my doctrine,* one must weep
> and lament at the insanity of these wretches.[7]

Is this great exemplar of authentic religion really double-tongued,
a dissembler who works both sides of the street? or like some of his
British progeny in the following century so wittily described by
Samuel Butler?

> Free will they one way disavow
> Another, nothing else allow.
> All piety consists therein
> In them, in other men all sin.

It is possible in a sense to exonerate Luther from the charge of
duplicity. For at least up to 1521, he had denied the freedom of the
will only in his Latin writings. In German he remained its strongest
supporter, especially when there was a chance thereby to score a
point against the Pope. And to lapse into a style of reasoning often
embraced by Martin, this kind of behavior should not be called
'double-tongued' but rather 'using two tongues.' To this delightfully
personal bi-lingual approach to the topic of human liberty we shall
return later.

In the tract "On Confession" Martin had adverted briefly to the
parable of the Ten Lepers cleansed by Jesus upon "showing themselves to the priests." Since the parable was traditonally interpreted
as symbolizing the absolution of the penitent upon confession to the
priest, Luther felt obliged to remonstrate. Here he puts on his strict-
constructionist hat, exclaiming:

> Why do you force us to confess with this saying which has no
> word on confession, no word on sins — and to O. T. priests when

the keys are given only in the N. T.?[8]

Later in the summer Martin penned a lengthy tract devoted solely to demolishing the traditional interpretation. He starts off asserting that to validate an interpretation of the parable as representing confession of sins "there must be clearly expressed words for confession and sin," which are lacking here. After a tedious discussion of how parables are to be interpreted, he proceeds to stand on its head the principle with which he started the tract. For, following a suggestion of Augustine, he decides the leprosy of the parable stands for heresy. Having found this attractive alternative, he develops it at length, and indulging in the typical medieval fondness for allegorizing, goes on to say the number of the lepers stands for the Ten Commandments. Perhaps the high point of the tract is an academic discussion on the meaning of 'heretic,' which is worth quoting as one of the choicest bits of unconscious humor in his writings. He cites a passage from a Pauline epistle [Titus 3:10] where the word heretic appears and says it is from a Greek verb meaning *choose* or *separate*.

> It has come to pass in Christendom that all are called *haeretici* who have departed from the unity and common way of the Christian faith and practice and believe in their own separate fashion and have chosen their own way. The two words *catholicus* and *haereticus* contend with each other. *Catholicus* means the one who is with the multitude and stands in union with the entire community in faith and spirit, as St. Paul says to the Ephesians 'one baptism, one faith, one Lord, one Spirit.' But *haereticus* is one who has invented his own way and faction. Thus *haereticus* is properly a do-it-my-way in religion, an eccentric who points to an improved way and has chosen for himself a road to heaven along which Christians in general do not travel.[9]

ii. Return to Wittenberg

When Martin made his secret visit to Wittenberg at the beginning of December to learn if it would be a safe refuge in the future, he seems to have found nothing to alarm him. He was sufficiently relaxed to sit for a portrait in his disguise as a knight. One accomplishment of the trip was a decision for the Wittenbergers to undertake a German translation of the Bible, doing the N. T. first. Who originated the plan is unknown; it was evidently not Luther's own idea and may well have been proposed by Spalatin as a measure to divert Luther from composing the scurrilous pamphlets he had been sending Spalatin from the Wartburg. Writing to Lang on December 18 after his return to the castle, Luther speaks of the translation as "requested by friends." Since Luther was not competent in Greek he planned to work from a Latin version to be supplied by Melanchthon. On December 5 Luther asked Spalatin to be sure to send along the "Latin Bible" to him from Melanchthon when ready. (All Luther's mail at this period was channeled through Spalatin at the Elector's court to help guard the secret of his whereabouts.) We have previously noted the use of a Latin intermediary made with Melanchthon's help in the translation of the O. T. In mid-January Luther complains to Spalatin that he has still not received Melanchthon's Latin text. It is likely that in the interim he had been translating from the Latin Vulgate, which he virtually knew by heart.

A few weeks after the return to the Wartburg Luther had a better appreciation of the magnitude of the task. He writes Amsdorf, at whose residence he had stayed during the secret visit to Wittenberg:

> I am translating the Bible, although I have undertaken a task beyond my powers. I see now what it is to translate . . . . Indeed I will be unable to touch the O. T. except with the help of all of you. If it could be managed for me to have a secret room with any one of you, I would come soon and with your assistance translate the whole work . . . . What I prefer is not to hide all the time, since that's impossible, but to have it known I would like to stay in hiding.[10]

We learn from another letter to Spalatin dated at the end of March that he had completed a draft of the N. T. translation at the Wartburg and was now working with Melanchthon on a revision. Since even with the expert help the original draft required nearly twice as long to revise as to prepare, one wonders about its quality.

In December Luther had indicated his intention to remain at the Wartburg until Easter (which in 1522 fell on April 20), apart from occasional visits with Melanchthon for help with the translation. But events forced him to advance the date of his return to early March when the effect of his 18-month propaganda campaign produced results he had been unable to foresee. On his journey to Wittenberg in December he thought he detected signs of mild unrest and these observations led him to write a rather curious tract entitled "A Sincere Admonition to All Christians to Guard against Insurrection and Rebellion." It is marked especially by the lack of judgment that characterizes psychotic regression. Near the beginning Luther assures the reader there is no danger whatever of an insurrection, a view which makes the whole tract sound pointless. He then urges his readers to attempt to frighten the clergy as much as possible by threatening them with violence, while stopping short of actual bloodshed. Only the princes have the right and duty to take the sword against them. He further instructs his followers to imitate his example of reviling the Pope and his adherents, to pray against them,

to withold contributions to the Church, and in general to treat all
such people as heathens. This little tract provides an excellent picture of the Luther of this era just before there is any serious competition from other innovators in religion who like him claim to be
guided solely by the 'spirit,' and before his fear of real civil uproar
forced him to adopt a more restrained propaganda line. Also it
displays his naive conviction that he speaks with the voice of God
and that all who imitate him will do likewise, that he can incite his.
followers to action designed to disrupt the social fabric of Saxony
and yet avoid the physical violence that inevitably follows in those
not inhibited like himself by a horror of actual violence.

Just at the end of 1521 there appeared in Wittenberg three men
from Zwickau of the type Luther was presently to dub 'fanatics.'
Zwickau was a fairly large and prosperous town south of Leipzig in
which there was a good deal of social unrest among unemployed
weavers who had lost their jobs in the economic upheaval arising
from the discovery and exploitation of silver mines in the area some
decades earlier. Also Zwickau in the later fifteenth century had been
the scene of a number of executions for heresy and various heterodox groups could still be found among the economically deprived.
After a good deal of unrest and conflict in Zwickau in 1520-21, only
partly engendered by Luther's inflammatory propaganda, the town
council took a hard line against the chief agitators and ordered them
out of town. One of these, Nicholas Storch, an unemployed weaver
with oratorical powers, was the leader of the three who drifted into
Wittenberg just after Christmas looking for another field of operation.

Storch and his companions preached a medley of doctrines designed to appeal to the poor and uneducated, savoring of anarchy,
elimination of private property and millenarianism. They claimed to
be directly inspired by the 'spirit' and to hold converse with God.
Mark Stubner, another member of the group, was so eloquent that he
managed to impress Melanchthon with the view his inspiration might
be genuine. Before the arrival of the Zwickau trio, the religious status
quo at Wittenberg had already suffered disruption and they could
but add to the existing turmoil. Early in the summer, Carlstadt had
preceded Luther in an attack on clerical celibacy. He himself was not
a pastor, but was in orders like many of the academics of the time
and enjoyed the income from a parish in south Germany
(Orlamuende) with a curate to perform the duties. Presently he renounced the celibate life for good, taking as a bride a 15-year old
girl, himself then being 41; also he came out strongly for communion
in both kinds and denied the Real Presence in the Eucharist.

Another local agitator was a young Augustinian, Gabriel Zwilling.
We first hear of this character in 1517, when Luther sent him away
from Wittenberg after five years of training to the Erfurt house,

with the remark that he had not yet learned the rules and customs of the Order and the hope that Erfurt could do something with him. While it was customary in such transfers to have a replacement, Luther said none was needed for Gabriel. One gathers he was mentally negligible and would not be missed. Later he was returned to Wittenberg, Erfurt presumably having tired of him. But if not very bright, he could make noises, and is said to have taken a leading role in the departure of 15 or 20 members from the Wittenberg house in November of 1521. Among the disorders he promoted in collaboration with Carlstadt was the destruction of images and paintings in the churches of Wittenberg and surrounding villages. Luther provides a revealing glimpse of this *enfant terrible* in a letter to Gabriel in April of 1522 when trying to get him accepted in a vacant Saxon pastorate:

> Above all, take care that you are moderate and wear the garb of a priest. Put away that broad-brimmed headgear on account of the weak, and remember you are sent to those who must be fed with milk and set free from papal snares.[11]

Conditions finally reached such a point that Melanchthon requested the Elector to bring Martin home to restore order. When Frederick temporized, as was his habit, the town council made a direct appeal to Luther to return. Martin's response to this was a letter to the Elector dated about February 24 which is of interest as showing him in the exalted mood often observed in those with manic symptoms. This state was presumably induced by his fear at finally leaving the hideout, a fear which he refers to in a second letter to Frederick a few days later. The first letter is quoted below in full; it may be noted that in his excitement Luther forgets to state the subject of discussion. Despite his hurry he delays starting for about a week.

> Grace and happiness from God the Father on your new relic! I write this greeting, most gracious Lord, instead of the usual salutation. For a long time now Your Grace has been searching out relics in many countries, but now God has heard Your Grace's petition and sent without any charge or effort a whole cross with nails, spears and scourges. Once more I say: grace and joy from God for the new relic! Let Your Grace not be at all terrified; yes, stretch out your arms in confidence and let the nails go in deep; yes, give thanks and be joyful! For it must and will be thus to them who would have God's word. Hence, not only Annas and Caiphas will rage, but also Judas will be among the Apostles and Satan among God's children. May your Grace be judicious and wise, and judge not according to reason and the appearance of things. Do not be alarmed; what Satan wants has not yet happened.
>
> Let Your Grace rely on me even though I am a bit of a fool; I

know these tricks of Satan and others like them. Therefore I don't fear him at all and that hurts him. All this is just the beginning. Let the world cry out and judge; let those fall away who so choose, even St. Peter and the Apostles! They will come back on the third day when Christ has risen again. There must be fulfilled in us: "We act with patient endurance amid riots." (2 Cor. 6:4)

May Your Grace be well disposed to me; I am in such a hurry the pen must run; I have no more time and will myself soon be there if God wills. May Your Grace take no heed of me.[12]

Upon receiving this missive, and doubtless startled by its incoherent enthusiasm, Frederick at once dispatched a messenger to the Wartburg, bidding Luther stay where he was. But Martin was now too excited to obey and set off for Wittenberg. His first objective was Borna, where he was to be provided with an official escort for traversing the territory of Duke George. There is an interesting record of his encounter at an inn at Jena, midway between the Wartburg and Borna, with a Swiss student named Kessler and a companion on their way to Wittenberg. It is from Kessler's account, who saw Luther in disguise as a knight, that we learn of the manic glint in his eyes at this time. As expected this indication of the disorder appears when Luther is in the exalted mood as well as in his more customary mood of bitter hostility (as reported by Dantiscus).

On March 5 Luther reached Borna, and broke his journey long enough at the residence of his escort to write a second letter to Frederick. This was four or five times as long as the one quoted above, relatively coherent, but in much the same exalted tone. Luther is here identifying with St. Paul. He declares, echoing Gal. 1:12, that "I have the gospel not from men but from heaven only, through our Lord Jesus Christ."[13] He is now even on a par with Jesus Christ — "my Lord and I can endure for quite a while that Duke George calls my Lord Christ a man of straw." Luther then goes on to say he did not hide from cowardice, and that he is prepared for martyrdom should the Emperor send soldiers to capture him.

In order to clear himself with the Imperial government, Frederick directed Luther shortly after his arrival at Wittenberg to write a letter explaining his reasons for returning there, and making clear he was there in violation of Frederick's orders. In the course of this letter, which continues the tone of the two previous ones, Luther discloses another recent revelation coming to him from on high. "Not only spiritual but also worldly authority must yield to the gospel, be it voluntarily or not." There are several reasons for his return: (1) that the congregation begged him to come back; (2) Satan has entered his fold; and (3) there may be a rebellion in Germany. But the one sufficient reason is that the gospel needs him and "therefore nothing merely human matters at all to me."[14]

Luther had arrived in Wittenberg on a Thursday evening, and it may be presumed he didn't delay long in going to work on Carlstadt and Zwilling. He shaved off his beard, cut his hair, dressed himself up in the habit of an Augustinian friar and on Sunday ascended the pulpit, from which he held forth daily until the following Sunday (March 16). We shall comment later on the inner state of a man who, shortly after publishing the defamatory "Judgment of Monastic Vows," could stand before a congregation in a church pulpit wearing monastic garb and preaching on Christian morality. Adapting his message to the demands of the moment, in the first sermon he preached a traditional, pre-Lutherian gospel:

> God wants us to imitate him and do things, not merely listen and repeat words, but keep his word; and this comes about from a faith which owes its power to love. For faith without love is not enough; indeed it is not faith, but only a pretense of faith.[15]

The epistle of James is still held in honor, and will not officially become an epistle of straw till summer.

By Friday, sensing that he had his audience with him, he could shift back into his own gospel, belittling 'outward works,' for "Christianity is not based on them but on faith alone, which is bound by no outward works." These sermons were taken down by members of his circle, and the presence in the text of contradictions like this is a guarantee that the transcription is authentic Luther.

Recalling Martin's fondness for repeating certain phrases picked up in his reading, we note at this period a tremendous flair for 'faith and love.' It is forever showing up in the preaching and the correspondence. For example, in a letter dated in mid-June, it occurs eight times in the first two paragraphs. One should realize that the 'love' was reserved for those who exhibited theological harmony with Luther. The 'Satan' who had broken into the Wittenberg fold during Luther's absence was of course Carlstadt and he was accorded different treatment. Zwilling was not a problem, having rapidly succumbed to the charismatic personality. As Luther remarks in a letter to Link three days after the last sermon of the series:

> Carlstadt and Gabriel were the authors of these monstrosities. Gabriel has indeed acknowledged his [error] and changed into a different man; what the other will become or do, I don't know. It is certain he will be barred from the pulpit, which he boldly took over.[16]

But even before this Luther had disclosed the iron hand behind the smooth talk of 'love'; writing to Spalatin on March 13 in the midst of the sermon series, he asks Spalatin's prayers to help tread upon that Satan who set himself up in Wittenberg against the gospel in the name of the gospel . . . *It will be difficult for Carlstadt to give up his views,* but Christ will force him to if he doesn't yield willingly. For we are lords of life and death who believe in the Lord of life and death.[17]

The reader should have no trouble making the proper identifications indicated in this letter. Needless to say, Carlstadt would not yield of his own accord. We hear of this the following month in a letter to Spalatin:

Today I asked Carlstadt privately not to print anything against me; otherwise I would be forced, though unwillingly, to lock horns with him . . . It is certain that, to escape scandal, I won't put up with what he has written.[18]

There was no scandal. As Smith notes, Carlstadt's written defense of his doctrine was confiscated by the university officials and the sections already in print were publicly burned in Wittenberg. This was evidently another triumph for the Word.

The duration of Luther's mood of exaltation, in evidence since late February, is unknown. But before the end of March he seems to have reverted to his more customary state of discharging hostility. Here is an indication from a letter to John Lang dated March 28:

Either the power of the word is still hidden in all of us or is too slight, which I greatly marvel at. For we are the same as before: hard, senseless, impatient, rash, drunken, lascivious, contentious; in short, charity, that symbol and mark of the Christian, never appears . . . .

I see many of our monks are getting out for no other reasons than they entered, namely, for the sake of the belly and carnal liberty. Through them Satan will raise a great stink against the good odor of our word. But what shall we do? They are lazy and seek their own advantage, so that it is better for them to sin and die out of the cowl than in it.[19]

If this seems odd coming from the author of that venomous attack on the monastic ideal, the "Judgment of Monastic Vows," it is less odd than Luther's continuing to wear the Augustinian habit. He seems to have put it on at first (March 9) as a sort of prop in aid of his campaign to restore calm to the troubled population of Wittenberg, who felt more comfortable if nothing was changed. This kind of dissimulation was one of Luther's favorite stratagems in making his revolt palatable to those who opposed change. Let surface appearances remain unaltered while revolutionizing the reality hidden beneath. There is a further explanation of Luther's failure to discard the cowl even though "celibacy and monasticism are condemned by

God." The monastery building he retained as his residence having
been provided by the Elector of Saxony for the Augustinians, it
would be 'wrong' for him to live there without the habit. Toward the
end of 1523 in a letter to the Elector he reveals his concern about
this problem. He and the Augustinian prior are the only remaining
members of the former community and the prior wants to leave. He
writes:

> I have now detained this prior longer than a year for my service.
> I neither may nor want to detain him longer because his conscience
> forces him to change his manner of living . . . . When the prior
> departs, my stay here should come to an end.[20]

Luther then proceeds to ask the Elector for the gift of a small adjacent monastic property where he might live; otherwise it would be
grabbed by the town council, as was the practice in other German
towns.

Another aspect of this problem is apparent in Luther's removing
his habit when he went out for an evening on the town, as was noted
in the report of Dantiscus. Such conduct Luther apparently felt un-
becoming in a clergyman, and he therefore changed his identity by
putting on a layman's attire for his evenings out. Luther was greatly
concerned to avoid any kind of scandal both in his own person and
among his followers. But scandalous conduct among his followers
was inevitable for in these years there were in the German monasteries and among the secular clergy innumerable persons without a vocation for religious or clerical life who eagerly accepted Luther's invitation to plunge into evangelical liberty. Luther refers to these
characters in the letter to Lang quoted above and Erasmus has this to
say of them:

> Some German cities are filled with these vagabonds, monks who
> have left their convents and married priests, many of them starv-
> ing and ill clothed. There is nothing but dancing, eating, drinking,
> and getting into heat. They neither teach nor study; there is no
> sobriety of life or integrity. Wherever they are, one finds an end
> of good learning as well as piety.[21]

Luther reports such a scandal in his own house. In a letter to Link
(December 19, 1522) he describes the liberation of one of his fellow
Augustinians:

> John P. ran off because he was guilty of shameful behavior
> that disgraced us all. The police found him drunk and in layman's
> clothes in a brothel.[22]

iii. The vendetta against the mass

By the end of 1522 Luther had become acclimated to his situation as 'outlaw.' He could move freely about the Elector's dominions without molestation, for the Edict of Worms had never been anything but a dead letter there. He was allowed to print a violent attack on the German bishops and a scurrilous rejoinder to Henry VIII of England, who had dared publish a criticism of the "Babylonian Captivity." In the spring of 1522 Luther had instructed his younger colleague Gabriel Zwilling on the proper technique for spreading the gospel:

> Work only with the word . . . The Father wishes you to draw men to him only through Christ, not force or lead them by our laws and ordinances. First a contempt for wickedness must be implanted in hearts; then wickedness will spontaneously fall away, without effort. Love of goodness must be first introduced; then goodness will come spontaneously.[23]

This quasi-Rousseauistic message expressed Martin's euphoric mood of the first weeks after his return from the Wartburg. He obviously was in a different mood when he produced the tracts against the bishops and the king referred to above.

One of the situations in which his benign approach failed signally was at the Castle church of Wittenberg, where the canons of the chapter continued to say mass as they had done before, and to administer the Eucharist in one form. Luther's ideas on this last topic had undergone development since 1520, and the traditional practice which had then been tolerable he now declared an abomination. Since the hearts of the canons were evidently too steeped in wickedness to yield to the persuasion of the Word, a new way must be found. Luther's god being strictly anthropomorphic, there was no problem about his manifesting a different will in 1523 than he had evidenced in April 1522. Luther announced the new approach (and shift in the divine will) in a letter to Spalatin of January 14, 1523, which demonstrates his matchless artistry as a propagandist:

> I think [the Eucharist] should from now on be *freely* given and received in both kinds. Thus far we have been indulgent enough to the weak, and everywhere the matter has now been predicted and known of until they are almost used to bearing greater things. It is time to make place for the gospel, and those who take offense at a usage so well known and foretold are not weak but rather *obstinate*. Therefore let us use our *liberty* in this affair.[24]

The choice of such works as 'freely', 'liberty' and 'obstinate' to mask the intention of changing an ancient usage by force, in short, the destruction of someone else's freedom, represents a technique at which Luther excelled. The reason for the devious approach is that Luther is here writing to one of the agents of Frederick, the sovereign of Electoral Saxony, who does not approve of Luther's innovations. Furthermore, Frederick cherished the services at the Castle church and the treasury of sacred relics which he himself had accumulated. The campaign which Luther now undertook, to abolish the celebration of mass at the castle church, required two years of an unrelenting propaganda effort to bring to fruition.

In a previous chapter we examined a statement of Luther's that during an anxiety state toward the beginning of 1520 he had conceived the plan of attacking the mass in order to strike a mighty blow at the papacy. A most interesting corrobation of this intent is to be found in the reply to Henry VIII published during the summer of 1522:

> If I succeed in doing away with the mass, then I shall believe I have completely conquered the Pope. On the mass, as on a rock, the whole of the papacy is based, with its monasteries, bishoprics, colleges, altars, services and doctrines . . . . If the sacrilegious and cursed custom of the mass is overthrown, then the whole must fall. Through me Christ has begun to reveal the abomination standing in the holy place.[25]

It should be noted that in this extremely explicit statement Luther says nothing about an intent to rectify abuses that had developed during the later middle ages around the celebration of mass, such correction being sometimes alleged as the primary objective in his writings and sermons dealing with the mass. His conscious purpose is rather to destroy the mass in order to destroy the papacy. That there is also an unconscious purpose will be shown later in this section. He does at times refer to the abuses but only because they provide him with useful ammunition in his propaganda effort.

In a review of this two-year campaign to end the celebration of mass at the castle church, the editors of the Weimar edition list in the neighborhood of 50 documents.[26] These include letters by Luther and his associates, instructions from the Elector, sermons and a tract with an odd title which I translate "That the Canon of the Mass is an Abomination." From this store of material it will be possible to select a few items which indicate the nature of the campaign Luther waged.

The first step was a threatening letter directed to the Provost and canons of the chapter:

> For more than a year we have tolerated practices in your church and worship that conflict with our gospel . . . . This tolerance

having become an occasion of stubbornness and derision toward the gospel . . . I must finally perform my duty. Wherefore I first remind your worships privately, in Christ, of evangelical standards, and demand that you undertake as a group effort to abolish all the intolerable abominations concerning the gospel that have been tolerated up to now . . . . Let your worships do voluntarily what you know very well must be done, lest I find it necessary to attack you publicly.[27]

Some of the canons, being acquainted with Luther's merciless tongue and pen, appealed to the Elector, and he instructed them to carry on as before. Not all of the members of the chapter were involved in this appeal; indeed, one of them, Amsdorf, was a crony of Luther's and the Provost of the chapter was no other than Jonas, an extremely devoted admirer. Just a week after the letter quoted above, we find Luther attending a christening at Schweinitz, several miles out of Wittenberg, in company with Jonas and his bride of a month. The wine has been flowing freely and Luther is in such a relaxed mood that he dashes off a letter to Spalatin in the nearby castle of Lochau, the seat of the Electoral court:

Being so close by that I could see Lochau, I had to write you, my Spalatin, that you would know we are or were here. We've been drinking good and pure wine from the main cellar, and should become beautiful evangelicals if the gospel feasts us this way . . . . Hail, and make our excuses with the Prince because we enjoyed so much of the Gorenberg wine. Jonas, together with his wife, greets you, cofather and comother with me. We are three virgins here, at least we call Jonas a virgin because he hasn't yet begotten a child.[28]

Luther renewed his assault in a second letter to the canons in July and the following day, a Sunday, he attacked them publicly in his sermon in the parish church. The scribe notes that he spoke very sharply against the canons. Again they complained to Frederick, who made a rather evasive reply. Luther proceeded to attack them in another sermon on August 2:

Their excuse for this godless behavior is that the Elector commanded it. But in these matters, what do we care about what the Elector commands? The Elector is a secular ruler whose concern is with the sword, not the office of preaching. They know that they must obey God rather than men in these things . . . .

I am the preacher here, and because this is all one congregation it is not to be tolerated that they despise my teaching and refuse to accept it. If they were so weak that they couldn't understand it, we would have patience with them, but since they are so obstinate and won't listen to it, we must punish them.[29]

On this occasion Frederick dispatched a message for Luther to a committee of three at Wittenberg, who were to induce Luther to refrain from this insubordinate behavior. They replied that Luther refused to stop the preaching, though in fact he did do so and sent the canons a third written warning. The next development in the campaign was a protracted discussion on possible changes in the manner of celebrating mass. After several months of uneasy peace Luther erupted again upon receiving a report that a communicant at the castle church had chosen to receive the Eucharist in one kind. On November 17, 1524 he wrote the canons a fourth warning:

> I have again learned that in your church the sacrament is given in one form, contrary to agreement . . . . Seeing that our great patience, which has up till now borne with your devilish habits and the idolatry in your church, is unavailing; . . . furthermore, as you have decided to divide our congregation and unity, if you can, and bring in factions and sects . . . I am forced, as a preacher of this congregation . . . in order to clear my conscience and put out the fire which is now glowing in the tinder, to take counsel and remedies against this . . . .
>
> It is therefore my friendly request and earnest desire that you make an end of this factional and sectarian game of masses and vigils . . . . But if you won't do that, you may well suppose that I will not rest, but with God's help see that you do it whether you will or not . . . . And I demand a plain, direct, straightforward answer, yes or no, before next Sunday, that I may be prepared accordingly.[30]

This brought forth another appeal to Frederick in which was included a complaint about Jonas. The Elector thereupon instructed Luther to desist from inciting violence against the canons. On Sunday November 24 Luther preached a new kind of sermon in which he systematically heaped ridicule on the mass, a sermon which formed the basis of the tract on the canon of the mass referred to above. He also wrote a furious letter to Spalatin, so insulting in tone toward both the Elector and Spalatin as to indicate — along with the sermon — that the manic symptoms had become more severe.

By this time the number of canons in the chapter who wished to continue the celebration of mass had dwindled to three. During December they finally yielded to the combined pressure of Luther's abusive language, the animosity of some of their colleagues and their fear of physical violence on the part of Wittenberg hoodlums stimulated to action by Luther's verbal assaults. By the end of 1524 the celebration of mass was officially prohibited in the Castle church and a set of ordinances was published stipulating what liturgical services were permitted there on the Sundays and feast days of the ecclesiastical year. Thus the wheel had come full circle from Luther's repudiation of force and human ordinances in April 1522 to his application of them for his own purposes in December 1524.

During the next several years various liturgical innovations were adopted in Wittenberg to replace the celebration of mass, indeed, such changes had been started — by Carlstadt — while Luther was still at his Wartburg hideout. It is not our purpose in this study to describe the new services. Luther's own role in this endeavor was primarily to do away with the essential character of the mass while concealing from the laity that a revolution was taking place. In the 1522 tract on administering the Eucharist in both kinds he had stated the guiding principle for the clergy in surreptitiously instituting the changes: "The priest will easily be able to arrange that the common people learn nothing of it and take no scandal."[31] In later years he speaks with complacency of the success of this large scale deception of the faithful of Saxony:

> Thank God, in indifferent matters our churches are so arranged that a layman, whether Italian or Spaniard, unable to understand our preaching, seeing our mass, choir, organs, bells, chantries, etc., would surely say that it was a regular papist church, and that there was no difference, or very little, between it and his own.[32]

In view of his eulogy of this elaborate sham, Luther's apparent hypocrisy would be compounded by his own comments on the 'immorality' of celebrating mass. Consider, for example, this remark in a sermon of 1523: "I have celebrated many masses. Would that I had rather committed murder or run off with another man's wife."[33]

Luther's hypocrisy should be called apparent because it would be as irrelevant to describe him as a hypocrite as to call him, say, a devout Christian. From 1520 onward he is a psychotic desperately striving to avoid complete regression to an infantile level. He continues to use the language and symbols of religion because they constitute his principal inheritance from his pre-psychotic past, and he could hardly be expected to develop a substitute. His writings and oral utterances are suitably described as a manipulation of this symbolic material with the (unconscious) object of preserving some hold on the adult world. His utterances on the mass appear more bizarre than those on a number of other topics because the mass was so deeply integrated into his intrapsychic conflict.

It has been indicated previously that Luther's early experience as a celebrant of the mass became involved with his pathological fear and hatred of God, usually repressed to a subconscious level but

surfacing into consciousness during his anxiety states (*Anfechtungen*).
It may be advisable to point out to the uninitiated that to the believer, especially the youthful believer, proximity to the altar and the
tabernacle can be an awesome experience. To the young Luther it
must have been (at times) absolutely shattering. He has left us too
many reminiscences about these terrors to make any other inference
possible. To this basic source of fear there was added another – the
sinful consequences to a celebrant of specific errors of omission or
commission in performing the prescribed liturgical actions. One may
likewise be sure, from his numerous reminiscences in later years, that
the young Luther took these ordinances and penalties very seriously.
His abnormal reaction to them must be in large degree responsible
for his subsequent denial of the authority of the Church to 'bind and
loose.'

The tract "That the Canon of the Mass Is an Abomination," published in 1525 some weeks after the sermon of the previous November, may be viewed as the ultimate expression of this aspect of his
psychopathology.[34] Structurally the tract has the form of a running
commentary on a text. His procedure is to print a German translation, paragraph by paragraph, of the Latin text of the canon and
then ridicule either the language of the text or the actions of the
celebrant prescribed for the paragraph in question. Much of the tract
sounds like the production of a malicious fourteen-year-old using
adult language to express his immature wisecracks.

By way of illustration consider the comment on a text occurring
between the consecration and the priest's communion. The celebrant, placing a portion of the consecrated host in the chalice, says:

> May this mingling and consecration of the Body and Blood of
> our Lord Jesus Christ be unto us who receive it effective unto life
> everlasting. Amen.

> Luther's comment:

> This is a blasphemous expression. I would certainly like to
> know how the body and blood can be mingled when there is but
> one Christ. It is the bread and wine that he mixes. But it is far
> more scandalous to speak of the consecration of the body and
> blood, just as if there were something in Christ to consecrate. And
> to say in addition that this mingling shall be effective to him who
> receives it for life everlasting, that is, to be accomplished by a
> work. What happens to the word of life? It is all done by us and
> based on the sacrifice.

At this point there is a rather remarkable omission. After the
prayer just quoted, the celebrant intones thrice: "Lamb of God
[*Agnus Dei*] who takes away the sins of the world, have mercy on
us." Luther has been asserting since 1520 the 'Pope' teaches that the

penitent obtains forgiveness of sin by his own 'works,' and he continues to assert this fabrication till his death. It would seem that rather than expose his mendacious habits by printing the *Agnus Dei,* he chose to suppress it altogether.

During his commentary on passages in the canon, Luther refers to the celebrant variously as a 'wretch,' a 'parson' and a 'fool' [*Narr*], the latter being the epithet of choice. At the end of the tract he proposes the celebration of mass be treated as a crime:

> If some insolent rascal off the streets openly blasphemes, curses and dishonors God, and the government puts up with this and doesn't punish him severely, as it is bound to do, then in the sight of God the government official shares in this evil deed . . . . In the case of celebrating mass the civil authority should protect society and administer punishment, because slandering and reviling are as obvious in the mass, are done as openly, as when some knave from off the street blasphemes.

In summary, Luther's attack on the mass after his return to Wittenberg represents his most continuous and energetic effort in these years to establish the new schismatic church of Electoral Saxony. It also demonstrates his skill in handling the principal weapons he employed in this task: deceit to beguile the uninstructed and force to compel the obstinate.

iv. Designs on Ducal Saxony

During the early post-Wartburg years, Luther's effort to abolish monastic life ranks in importance close behind the campaign to eliminate the mass. In the next chapter we look at his attempt to subvert a portion of Paul's first epistle to the Corinthians to this end. About the same time (1523) he devoted his attention particularly to reducing the population of the convents for women. For many years it had been the practice among families of the lesser German nobility to treat the convents as a haven for disposing of unmarriageable daughters. The girls were ordinarily placed in a convent early in life and encouraged to make their profession some years later when they had reached a suitable age. It could hardly be expected that many such persons had a vocation for the religious life. But without a dowry they could not leave the convent and find a husband to support them, opportunities for employment other than as servants were rare, and their own families had by their action indicated unwillingness to care for them. Faced with these alternatives, it would appear that such women ordinarily remained in their convents unless a domineering superior made life there unbearable for them.

In the spring of 1523 the message went out from a Cistercian convent at Nimbschen near Grimma in Ducal Saxony that a considerable number of dissatisfied nuns wanted to leave. Accordingly, a Torgau merchant, Leonard Koppe, who made regular deliveries at the Nimbschen convent, arranged to conceal the nuns in his wagon during a trip there and bring them to Wittenberg. (Two years later, we find Luther ordering from Koppe a keg of the best Torgau beer for his own wedding celebration.) The plan appears to have gone off without a hitch. On April 4, the Saturday preceding Easter Sunday, twelve nuns crowded into Koppe's wagon while it was parked in the convent grounds and were surreptitiously driven away. Three of them were taken in by their families without delay. The remaining nine were delivered by Koppe on the following Tuesday to the Black Monastery at Wittenberg, now depopulated save for Luther and the prior.

Luther took this occasion to issue what was becoming for him a preferred means of broadcast, a circular letter nominally addressed to Koppe setting forth his views on Koppe's exploit.[35] The letter was to some an extent an apology, though truculent in tone rather than apologetic, because the abduction of a nun was a capital offense in Saxony and Luther wanted to avoid the implication that he had broken any law. After a page or so of boastful self-justification, he entered on the subject of real interest, namely, why nuns should be given help to leave their convents. The first reason — sufficient by itself — is that only by 'escaping' can they hear the word of God, i.e., the gospel according to Luther. His discussion of this point throws an interesting light on Martin's proselytizing zeal. It disturbed him that even one group of his fellow citizens was in effect cut off from exposure to his doctrine. As matters turned out, this was just a temporary situation, for during the 1520s as one German city after another joined the schism, supervision of the local convents fell into the hands of the town councils. We hear in particular from the records of Nuremberg of how those nuns who braved the popular agitation against the practice of their vocation were obliged to listen to harangues and gibes from preachers trained in Wittenberg and forced on them by the city government.

The lion's share of attention in the circular letter is given to an attack on celibacy, a continuation of the one Luther had earlier delivered in his "Judgment of Monastic Vows." Here also he introduces the subject as a question of the three monastic vows, but his preoccupation is made manifest by his giving exclusive attention to celibacy. In the earlier tract his arguments dealt essentially with monks. Now that he is concerned with women, he develops a new angle. By entering a convent a woman escapes child bearing. But it is her duty — cf. Genesis 3:16 — not only to bring forth children but to bring them forth in pain. Hence the nun's vow of chastity, by permitting her to avoid the pangs of childbirth, is a deliberate violation of the divine command and therefore lacks validity. The extraordinary ingenuity which Luther displays in this short piece (and at much greater length in the "Judgment") in contriving arguments to prove the vow of chastity does not bind is ample evidence of the inner turmoil generated by his desire to break his vow.

By midsummer of 1523 Luther became aware of certain problems arising from his anti-monastic propaganda efforts. The monks who so readily abandoned their profession upon exposure to his siren call were not very admirable human types. Furthermore they made a nuisance of themselves by descending upon the Pied Piper of Wittenberg, availing themselves of his hospitality and wasting his time. In a letter to Spalatin (July 11, 1523), which betrays not the slightest awareness of his own responsibility for these annoying visitors, he gives vent to his indignation:

> I am most irritated by the great number of renegade monks who assemble here. What especially disgusts me is that while they are the sort of men who are good for nothing they want to take wives at once. Every day I try to think of what can be done to stop this.[36]

We now turn to a major aspect of Luther's proselytizing effort: the dispatch of letters from his haven in Wittenberg to heads of state urging them to adopt his gospel and impose it on their subjects. We shall examine three of these ventures, beginning with his attempt to convert the ruler of Ducal (or Albertine) Saxony, Duke George (a cousin of the Elector Frederick), whom we encountered previously at the Leipzig debate in the summer of 1519. Duke George was quite a different sort of person from his rather retiring and non-intellectual cousin. As a younger son in a princely family he had been educated for the Church, but upon the untimely death of his older brother he became heir to the Duchy of Saxony and the Margravate of Meissen. His territory, of smaller extent than Electoral Saxony which it adjoined, included the cities of Leipzig and Dresden. He manifested intelligent concern about theological questions and supported efforts to rectify abuses in ecclesiastical affairs. His relations with Erasmus provide an indication of his interests: in the collected edition of Erasmus' correspondence there are a score of letters from Erasmus to George and half that number from him to Erasmus. In contrast there are only three or four letters from Erasmus to Frederick and his brother John (who succeeded him in May 1525) and but one (from Frederick) to Erasmus. It was George who became alarmed at the disorders in Wittenberg of 1521-22 that brought Luther home early from the Wartburg. As a temporary measure, he prevailed upon the committee of German princes in charge of imperial affairs during the absence of the Emperor to enact an ordinance prohibiting changes in religious worship until such questions could be debated at a session of the Reichstag. It was this action which provoked the retaliation from Luther described below.

About a fortnight after his return from the Wartburg, Martin, still very high, wrote a rambling diffuse letter to Hartmuth von Cronberg, a member of the group of German knights who under the leadership of Francis von Sickingen staged an abortive military revolt later that year. The letter to von Cronberg, much too long to quote here, provides a most interesting revelation of Luther in the exalted phase of his disorder. [An English translation is in Smith II, #536, and Luther's Works, 43.] Its quasi-religious fervor makes him sound like one of the enthusiasts he was presently to disparage as 'fanatics,' and it contains a paragraph loaded with insults about George. The letter, with the Duke's name inserted, was printed four times during 1522. When it came to the attention of George he wrote a courteously phrased inquiry to Luther asking him "what position do you take in it?" Luther's reply, quoted here in part, offers one of the numerous exhibits of the manic hostility that characterized this period of his life.[37]

> Instead of greeting me, stop raging and roaring against God and his Christ. Ungracious Prince and Lord! I have received your Disgrace's letter along with the tract or letter I wrote Hartmuth von Cronberg and have had read to me carefully the place about which your Disgrace complains as most injurious to your soul, honor and reputation . . . . Since your Disgrace would know what position I take in it, here briefly is my answer: it is all one to me regarding your Disgrace whether I am standing, lying, sitting or running . . . . If your Disgrace were in earnest and did not lie so uncivilly that I came too near your Disgrace's soul, honor and reputation, you would certainly not slander and persecute Christian truth so shamefully . . . . I offer to serve your Disgrace in any way I can save for base requests. If that offer is despised I can do no more. I will not be scared to death by any bladder . . . . ("Bladder" was one of the insults in the letter to von Cronberg.)
>
> Martin Luther, by the grace of God
> Evangelist at Wittenberg

Duke George, long aware that Luther was trying to replace the traditional faith of Christendom with his own concoction, had so far as possible kept the Lutherian propaganda out of his territory. In particular he had forbidden the sale in his dominions of Luther's German N. T., itself a work of propaganda because of the anti-papal cartoons and comments it contained. The preservation of the old religion in Ducal Saxony during the lifetime of George shows clearly that the propagation of the Lutheran schism in Germany was possible only with the support or connivance of the local governments. Mortified by the failure of his 'movement' in this neighboring province, Luther at length decided on a new approach. Near the end of 1525 in a letter somewhat reminiscent of one to Henry VIII a few months earlier, (see below) he again throws himself at the feet of a prince he has egregiously insulted in the past, and excusing his "fierce and bitter" attacks on the Duke, begs him to let down the bars to the 'gospel.'

Seeing that your Grace does not desist from ungraciousness but still continues in it, I have decided once more to make a humble and friendly request of your Grace in this letter – perhaps for the last time . . . . So I come now and sincerely fall at your Grace's feet and ask your Grace in all humility to abandon the ungracious policy of persecuting my doctrine. Not that much harm could befall me by your Grace's persecution: I have nothing more to lose than this bag of maggots that daily hastens to the grave . . . . Although your Grace will not believe my doctrine is God's word, . . . I know it is and am certain of it, and at the peril of my soul will care for your Grace's soul, pray, weep and admonish that I may achieve something. May your Grace have no regard for my poor person, for God "once spoke through an ass." . . . Neither your Grace nor any man can dampen or prevent my doctrine . . . for it is not mine.

I wish to vindicate myself before God and your Grace's conscience because I have done my part and am ready and willing to do or to leave undone whatever your Grace wishes, apart from my doctrine. That I cannot abandon in conscience . . . . If only your Grace will give in on that one point, all will be simple – that Christ's word, brought to light by me, be free. Then without doubt all the angels in heaven will rejoice over your Grace. Your Grace should know that thus far I have prayed earnestly for your Grace and still pray, and the more gladly come with this letter that I may not be forced by circumstances to pray against your Grace. For although we are a poor little group, if we were to pray against your Grace . . . nothing good would happen to your Grace, for we know that what Christ has promised us he will stick to . . . . And perhaps your Grace will see that it is not the same thing to strive against Luther as against Muentzer. But I had rather this did not happen to your Grace.[38]

As noted elsewhere, Luther could maintain a certain control of the hostility if there was a prospect of advantage in doing so. But it was lurking just below the surface and shows itself in the threat to "pray against" Duke George if he continues to ban the Lutherian

propaganda, i.e., not let the "gospel be free." The practice of "praying against" his adversaries is an instructive example of Luther's
singular conception of the Christian faith. We shall examine this
feature of his pathology in a later chapter.

To this mixture of appeal and threat George replied promptly and
in a spirit of Christian fellowship. His letter is of interest as representing the attitude of an informed layman who had followed the development of Luther's ideas from quite early on, and because it
presents some first-hand information on the Leipzig disputation.

> Your letter came to us on Christ's birthday, whose peace and
> grace we wish you as you did us, and also a knowledge of your-
> self . . . . You attacked us bitterly against the divine law and the
> gospel . . . as a tyrant and denier of the gospel, vilifying our
> person, our body and mind with a great deal of wanton, sophisti-
> cal language you did not find in the Bible, to which you would
> liken your abusiveness.

> You boast about your many praiseworthy writings. We will not
> deny that at first we admired your writings very much. Also we
> were pleased to hear the disputation at Leipzig, for we hoped from
> it a reform of abuses among Christians. We were there when Dr.
> Eck charged you with being a supporter of the Bohemian sect,
> which you then most vehemently denied. We proceeded as one
> who agreed with your position, and called you to us true-heartedly
> for a private discussion . . . . We advised you in a brotherly spirit
> to write against the Bohemian sect, which you did not favor, to
> clear yourself of suspicion.

> You remind us of death, of which we are certain. What would
> happen if we accepted your gospel and died? Would not God say:
> 'Why are you with one whose gospel bore so much bad fruit?
> Haven't I said: You shall know the tree by its fruit?' If we replied:
> 'Luther said it was the gospel that lay under a bench,' God would
> say: 'You heard the Christian Church speak otherwise. Since you
> say every day you believe in the Christian Church, why did you
> believe Luther and not the Church?' No, Luther, keep your gospel
> which you pulled out from under the bench; we will stay with the
> gospel of Christ which the Christian Church received and holds.[39]

We have Luther's immediate reaction to the Duke's response in a
letter to a friend dated January 2, 1526:

> I wrote a humble and most sincere letter to Duke George, and
> he answered me in his typical style with a particularly foolish
> letter and breathing that ferociousness of a peasant he inherited
> with Bohemian blood.[40]

This comment provides an interesting example of the projection of

Luther's own unrestrained peasant manners onto a courteous member of the German ruling class. A few weeks later in a letter to another friend Luther recurs to the Duke's reply:

> I wrote to Duke George with good hope but I was mistaken. I have lost my humility and will not answer him anything. Nor am I at all moved by his lies and curses.[41]

These excerpts from Luther's correspondence make clear how completely insensitive he was to the rights of anyone who chose to disagree with him, and how irresponsible were his comments on the expression of views opposed to his own.

v. Foreign ventures: Savoy and England

In the summer of 1523 Luther came to believe that Charles, Duke of Savoy, had an interest in his doctrine. In consequence he composed an epistle to this "most distinguished and illustrious prince and lord" designed to extend his influence to the south.[42] This letter is of interest as showing the way Luther dealt with the problem of how to set forth 'my theology' intelligibly to a stranger. Instead of giving a straightforward summary of his teaching (as Melanchthon had done in 1521 − see Ch. 7) based on man's inescapably sinful condition in a deterministic world, he contrived a devious approach. No extraordinary perspicacity is need to appreciate the awkwardness of asking a potential convert to choose a new religious outlook which emphasizes the view that he lacks the power of choice. Presumably to enhance the appeal of his proselytizing effort, an approximation to the Pauline teaching of the inner renewal of the human person who commits himself in faith to Jesus makes a rare appearance in Luther's writings. It is the evidence that Luther evinces some grasp of this Pauline doctrine, and on this occasion deceitfully claims that he himself subscribes to it, that helps make the letter significant.

The opening paragraph, devoted principally to fulsome praise of Duke Charles, ends with an attack on the papacy. Then, after presenting as his first heading the ordinary Christian teaching that man's salvation depends on the sacrifice of Christ, Luther, as indicated above, blatantly falsifies his own doctrine of total depravity, substituting for it the Pauline doctrine that a living faith totally changes a man.

Luther then digresses into a violent attack on the Church, declaring that all monasteries, cathedral chapters and other such abominations must be destroyed. His second heading is a restatement of the first in different language. Included is the remarkable phrase that "like the good trees which are known by their good fruit, we are now sinless." This of course also constitutes a repudiation of his usual teaching. Heading number three asserts that the traditions or decrees of the Fathers and the decisions of councils are unnecessary and not binding on the faithful. This point naturally leads to another assault on the papacy and prepares the way for a bit of self-justification. Next he declares there must be freedom in the choice of religious ceremonies and that the Eucharist must be administered in both kinds. Following a routine attack on the mass comes the peroration. Apart from the large number of references in it to Satan and Antichrist, its most noteworthy feature is the revelation of what Luther hoped to achieve by his epistle to Duke Charles. May the conflagration enkindled in Savoy (by this letter) spread through all of France. Thereby the kingdom which is now impiously called 'most Christian' may, once released from the power of Antichrist, become most Christian in reality.

As it turned out, Luther's epistle to Duke Charles of Savoy bore no fruit. The Duke did not even reply to the Apostle of the Germans. But apparently he at least looked over the epistle, for one of his courtiers in a letter to Erasmus dated the following January mentions the incident. Although Charles "failed to answer Luther, this was not because he held him in low esteem but rather because he was little interested in what Luther had to say."[43] Whether Luther would have been more effective if he had imitated St. Paul to the extent of journeying to this missionary region and preaching to the gentiles there must remain a matter of speculation. Unlike Paul, Martin was preoccupied with the matter of his personal safety and showed no inclination to venture outside the region where he felt secure from harm. Not being gifted with prophetic powers, he could not foresee that one day his ideas would indeed be spread across France but under the auspices of a prophet he would have branded as heretical.

Luther's attack on the mass and sacramental teaching in the 1520 tract, the "Babylonian Captivity," was calculated to be highly offensive to any knowledgeable and sensitive member of the Church. For example, the chaplain of the Emperor Charles V declared upon reading it that he felt as if he had been whipped with rods from head to foot. Among those who responded to the "Captivity" in print was no less a personage than Henry Tudor, King of England. A copy of the tract reached him early in 1521 and during the summer he published his "Assertion of the Seven Sacraments" (in Latin). Henry had received rather more education than many princes of those times and had some academic acquaintance with theology. His tract assumed an imperious tone toward the German monk, who was not only a mere commoner but an excommunicated heretic as well. For this deed Henry was honored by Leo X with the title "Defender of the Faith," a distinction to which British royalty has clung tenaciously ever since.

With such provocation Luther decided to give Henry the full treatment designed for the proud and stubborn rejectors of 'my theology.' His *Contra Henricum Regem Angliae* ("Against Henry, King of England") dated July 1522 is accordingly one of the most abusive products to come from his pen during the period of the manic symptoms. Especially galling to the monarch would be the gibe that the "Assertion" was so full of lies and scoffing it had probably been composed by a member of the court rather than the King himself. Apart from the billingsgate, Luther's tract is a tedious harangue of such a low intellectual level that it does not appear to have been reprinted in modern times save in the Complete Works.

Perhaps because Henry's "Assertion" was presently translated and published in German, Luther also composed a German answer to it. Appreciably shorter than the Latin version, it twice repeats the charge that the "Assertion" was probably from another hand than the King's. In both versions he alters Henry's new title, "Defender of the Faith," to "Defender of the Church," saying he is glad not to be a member of a church — 'the Whore of Babylon' — defended by Henry. His motive for this may be surmised as an unwillingness to see Henry praised with his own favorite word. Also during the period following the excommunication Luther held the term 'church' in very low esteem.

There is a curious difference between the versions in regard to the abusive language. In the Latin form Luther repeatedly injects the name of Thomas (Aquinas) as a term of contempt, sprinkling his pages with it as noun, adjective, adverb and even verb, well over a hundred times. In the German version he uses the name hardly at all. As is apparent from a letter to Spalatin dated September 1, Luther chose to regard Henry as a 'Thomist':

> I knew that what I wrote against the King of England, that foolish and poisonous Thomist, was highly offensive, but it pleased me and indeed had to be done for a number of reasons.[44]

Luther in his pathological hostility toward Thomas chose to associate him with the teaching of the Church on the seven sacraments. Despite Luther's extensive ignorance of the history of matters ecclesiastical, he was at least in a position to know from his earlier training that Peter Lombard, a century before Aquinas, systematized the doctrine of the sacraments. But since Luther retained a certain affection for Peter, the 'onus' of the sacramental teaching opposed by Luther had to be transferred, and Thomas became the target. The marked difference between the Latin and German versions is of interest as showing Luther's ability to control his abusive language. Apparently he skipped these epithets in the vernacular on the assumption that his dear Germans were too uninstructed to ap-

preciate them. The German version ends with a choice bit of the
Lutherian brand of (unconscious) humor; he must break off this
scurrilous attack on a fellow human being in order to hasten back to
his translation of holy writ.

Outraged at Luther's response, Henry struck back in various ways,
including the dispatch of a letter of complaint to Frederick and his
brother. A few years later Luther imprudently gave him an opportunity for far more effective reprisal by sending Henry a proselytizing letter which provides an interesting comparison with the 1523
epistle to Duke Charles of Savoy. Luther had received what turned
out to be misinformation from the King of Denmark that Henry was
beginning to take an interest in Wittenberg theology. Enthralled
at the prospect of such an influential convert, Luther sent him the
letter quoted in part below (September 1, 1525). This enterprise
bears witness to the characteristically defective judgment of the
psychotic. Particularly notable is Luther's attempt to deceive a man
already quite familiar with the "Babylonian Captivity" as to the
nature of his teaching. The italicized words express the more
egregious falsehoods in the letter; there seems no reason to regard
them as examples of the denial mechanism. Rather they illustrate
Luther's habit of asserting whatever he thought would help promote
the spread of his movement.[45]

> I should properly be afraid to write your Royal Majesty because
> I realize I have greatly provoked and offended your Majesty by my
> little book which I foolishly and hastily published against your
> Majesty *not on my own initiative but at the urging of those who
> do not wish well to your Majesty* . . . .
> *I have learned from reliable sources* that the book which went
> out against me under your Majesty's name *was not written by the
> King of England* but rather by crafty sophists who misused your
> Majesty's name and failed to see the danger they incurred by this
> abuse of the royal name. Especially *culpable is that monster,* the
> manifest enemy of God and man, the *Cardinal of York,* the
> scourge of your kingdom. [This was Thomas Wolsey, Henry's
> most valued servant and Lord Chancellor; Luther probably meant
> Edward Lee, a member of the diplomatic corps, who had been in
> controversy with Erasmus. This careless assertion of erroneous
> opinion as fact is one of Luther's most conspicuous traits; here it
> led him into an astonishingly bad tactical error.] I dare not raise
> my eyes to your Majesty so great is my shame that I so readily let
> myself be moved by these evil characters; indeed I am an un-
> worthy man, a worm who should be looked down on by all with
> contempt, or ignored.
> I am moved to write, lowly as I am, because your Majesty has

begun to be well disposed to the Gospel and feel great displeasure toward such base men. This news was a true gospel to my heart, that is, joyful tidings. Therefore with this letter I cast myself at your Majesty's feet, as humbly as I can, and pray and plead that for the love and suffering of Christ and his honor your Majesty will deign to forgive and pardon me for my offences . . . .

Furthermore, if your most serene Majesty should think it not too unworthy for me to write a public recantation and restore the honor of your Majesty's name, will you graciously give me some indication and without delay I shall do this most willingly. Although I am a mere nothing in comparison with your Highness, it may be hoped that no small good may result for the gospel and the glory of God if it is granted me to write to the King of England on the evangelical cause.

In the meantime, as he has begun, may the Lord increase your Majesty, that you may obey and favor the gospel with all your soul. And may he refuse to allow your royal ears and soul to be concerned about the poisonous songs of those sirens who can do nought but call Luther a heretic. May your Majesty think within yourself: what evil can I teach *who teach nothing other* than faith in Jesus Christ, the Son of God, who suffered and rose again to bring us salvation, as the apostolic gospels and epistles give witness. [To find time to compose his epistle Luther had to stop work on the "Enslaved Will," in which he went well beyond faith in Christ.] For this is the head and foundation of my teaching, on which I build and teach love of neighbor, obedience to civil authority and mortification of the body of sin, as Christian doctrine prescribes. What is evil in these doctrinal topics? It is common practice that one first listens and then judges; why am I condemned when neither heard nor proved wrong? Moreover, I criticize the abuses and tyranny of the bishops, who teach other matters than these topics, nay *who teach the opposite of them* . . . . Why do they not reform themselves and teach rightly if they want to avoid hatred and censure?

Your most serene Majesty sees how many princes in Germany, how many cities and how many wise men are of my party and (by God's grace) desire to be saved . . . . May Christ include your Majesty among this number and set you free from these tyrants of souls . . . .

If it should be your Majesty's will, I await your merciful and gracious reply.

Your Majesty's most humble
Martin Luther

To this most distinguished forerunner of Uriah Heep Henry indeed replied, but in a style neither merciful nor gracious. He printed this extraordinary letter to pillory its author, and added a lengthy and blistering attack of his own. He began by assailing Luther for again doubting his authorship of the "Assertion" and took him to task for the slander against his favorite Cardinal Wolsey. Then he expressed his outrage at the assumption he had only lately become concerned with the gospel. This is the kind of gracious answer Martin received:

> When you say you are ashamed of your book, I don't know whether you speak the truth. But I well know that is reason enough for you to be greatly ashamed not only of this book but of almost all your books, which contain hardly anything but shameful errors and foolish heresies. These are neither grounded in reason nor supported by learning, but are put forward and confirmed by nothing more than the obstinate presumption you are such a great teacher your equal can be found neither in our time nor ever before.[46]

After a great many pages like this on the teaching, Henry turns briefly to the life. He upbraids Luther for living in sin with a nun, bids him put the poor woman back in a convent, and himself return to a monastery to do penance the rest of his life for his sins, particularly for leading so many souls into the pains of hell.

Henry published this work in 1526 and toward the end of the year sent a copy to Duke George. Early in 1527 there appeared a reprint in Dresden which featured on the title page the allegation that Luther was recanting. This was followed very shortly by a German translation whose title page bore the same phrase. Luther appears to have been crushed by this long overdue response to his letter of September 1525 and puzzled to know who was responsible for the title. He lost no time in getting a response in print, which he called: "Luther's Answer to the Libelous Title of the King of England." For the student of Luther's character this is one of the most fascinating documents to come from his pen, though it has received little attention. Its primary objective is to kill the suggestion he has recanted any of his doctrine. "Nein, nein, nein," he says in paragraph two, no matter how vexed kings, emperors, princes or devils may be at his denial.

In this crisis, one of the most serious he has yet had to face, Luther comes before his public to demonstrate he can still rise to the occasion. So anxious is he to dispel the nightmarish charge he has recanted that he almost forgets to favor Henry with more than perhaps a dozen insults. Of particular interest is the revelation of how much his heart is set on converting heads of state to his doctrine. The disclosure of his emotional state on hearing the news that

Henry was a likely convert is expressed in rather disconnected language, as though he were telling it under duress, but is composed with his customary rhetorical artistry.

> The most gracious King Christian of Denmark so filled me up with hope about the King of England that I was like a drunken man. He kept at it with speeches and letters, poured so many fine sayings into me — I need only write humbly; it would turn out well, etc. — until I became drunk over it and staggered around by myself. But who knows? There are twelve good hours in the day and if you can grasp one good hour, in God's name, and win over the King of England you are certainly bound to do it; and if you held back you would commit a sin. And so, a poor drunkard, I vomited up this humble and ill-fated letter. Now the swine devours and tears me; and I still think it was something holy. It's too bad I paid no heed to Christ's warning in Matthew 7 — "that I should not cast pearls before swine."[47]

In the interest of veracity it must be said that the King of Denmark played a more slender role in this operation than Luther here ascribes to him (cf. Luther to Spalatin, June 21, 1525 in WBr 3, 540). Much of the tract reads like an exercise in free association, and as befits a piece of self-revelation it is carried on largely in the first person singular. A propos of the topic of humility there is the stereotype of how he has now humbled himself three times — before Cajetan at Augsburg, before the Emperor and princes at Worms and to Duke George in a letter. With regard to his humbling himself about his life, in contrast to his doctrine, about which he is as proud as can be and never humble, there is a rather novel distinction. He will be humble before everyone about his life — even before a child — but only on condition the persons so honored are not enemies of the gospel. These latter people, however, "must regard me as a living saint."

His enemies having been mentioned, he now goes through his enemies list, distinguishing first those who are mere "nits." "The truth is that nits you are, lice you have not yet become." This type of discourse is carried on through the final third of the piece in a sort of elegiac mood. But near the end, abandoning his "idle talk" [*Geschwaetz*], Luther recalls why he is writing the "Answer." "I have not recanted my teaching nor will I." The "Answer" with its display of grandiosity and hostility, its utter egocentricity and its general lack of any clear direction serves to remind us that when he wrote it Luther was only six months away from the most severe depression of his life.

Chapter 5

In Conflict With The New Testament And The Rival Preachers

i. Luther as expositor of Scripture

The somewhat erratic course through the writings of the Old and New Testaments that marked Luther's career as professor of Scripture (1513-1545) can be best understood in the light of his psychic history. As noted earlier, he undertook this work not of his own choice but in obedience to his monastic superior. At the start he acknowledged he was not really qualified for the task and began his lecturing with the Psalms as the book he was most familiar with. During the first two years he developed a degree of self confidence that permitted him to tackle next one of the most difficult of the N. T. writings, Paul's epistle to the Romans. The reason for this radical shift in subject is probably related to his interest in Paul's remarks on justification in this epistle, which Luther was exploring as of possible assistance with his psychic problem. His propensity for identifying with Paul helps account for his next choice of topic, the most personal of the Pauline epistles, to the Galatians. By the time he had finished that he was started on the development of the *sola fide* defense, and next began lecturing on the epistle to the Hebrews as providing material congenial to this endeavor.

From mid-1518 on, Luther's career as professor of Scripture lacks direction. To the worsening of his psychic disorder was added the major distraction of the heresy prosecution. Instead of embarking on something new, he retreated to the book of Psalms, and likewise reworked the lectures on Galatians which now had additional relevance for him as he saw his conflict with Rome mirrored in Paul's conflict with Peter related in that epistle. Following the Worms-Wartburg episode, being now technically an outlaw, he was at first not permitted to resume his academic lecturing. As a substitute, in his living quarters he gave a series of informal talks on the epistles of Peter, whose observations on faith appealed to him in his new situation. When it became apparent that the edict of the Diet of Worms, prescribing for him the penalty of a condemned heretic, was a dead letter in much of Germany, he resumed the formal lectures. On this occasion it would appear that his choice of subject was influenced by the progress of the O. T. translation currently under way in Wittenberg. The fifth book of the Pentateuch, Deuteronomy, was completed in December of 1522 and two months later Luther began a course of lectures on it. He continued along this line during the remainder of the 1520s, lecturing on the minor and major prophets. (Exception must be made for the period of severe depression beginning in mid 1527, when, as described in the following chapter, he shifted to the first epistle of John.) His final excursion into the N. T. occurred in 1531 when, apparently in reaction to the emotions generated in him by the Diet of Augsburg, he once more held forth on the epistle to the Galatians.

After this he again had recourse to the Psalms to provide material for his academic lectures. During the next few years this activity appears to have been frequently interrupted by illness. Finally in 1535 he began his last series of lectures, on the book of Genesis, stretching it out for an entire decade. In earlier years he had preached a good many sermons on Genesis, and his consequent familiarity with it made it more suitable for this period of reduced intellectual power.

Because he concentrated on O. T. writings during the later decades of his academic career, Luther has been referred to as a professor of Old Testament Scripture. For an independent judgment on the quality of this work it is illuminating to turn to the man commonly referred to as the father of modern Biblical criticism, the 17th century French scholar Richard Simon. In his own lifetime Simon, who enjoyed unusual expertise in the languages of Scripture and raised fundamental questions about the texts and the composition of the O. T. writings, was a controversial figure. His writings, which he published in Rotterdam, aroused such a storm of protest in France he was ejected from his religious order and, exiled from Paris, died without honor in the town of northern France where he was born. Of Luther's O. T. commentaries he says they are

> rather lessons in theology and disputes than real commentaries. . . . . He thought that by giving moral instruction and crying out loudly against those who disagreed with him he threw a great deal of light on the word of God. But it is apparent from his writings that he was never more than a blunderer and a hothead who possessed only a certain lively wit and a spark of imagination . . . . Having studied theology, he produced a collection of theological problems, not a commentary on the text of Scripture.[1]

Among the handicaps Luther suffered as an interpreter of Scripture — and one of which he was himself aware — was a lack of the linguistic background demanded for serious work in this field. His attempts to acquire proficiency in Hebrew and Greek were unsuccessful, partly because he had little natural aptitude for language study, and partly because his time was taken up with other problems. On Luther's knowledge of Hebrew Simon comments: "Luther sometimes charged himself with following the interpretations of the rabbis too closely. But he should be exonerated of this fault, of which he was by no means guilty, because he was incapable of reading their books."[2]

Of comparable importance to his linguistic incapacity were the consequences of his psychic disorder and his practice of forcing scriptural passages into his system of defenses. We have previously noted his basic exegetical principle that understanding of Scripture must proceed from the 'inspiration of the Holy Spirit' rather than from study and research. From these considerations it is not hard to appreciate why a real Scripture expert like Simon should dismiss Luther's commentaries with such disdain. Because Luther's defensive use of Scripture involves primarily the N. T. writings, in this study we shall not be concerned further with Luther's lectures on the O. T. except for some of his dealing with the Psalms.

One of the remarkable aspects of Luther's long career as expositor of Scripture was his ambiguous attitude toward the N. T. writings. Though after his regression he made the grandiose boast of being the first man in history to have really understood the Christian revelation, he nevertheless carefully avoided presenting this understanding to the Wittenberg students in the form of a lecture series on any of the gospels, the Acts of the Apostles, the Apocalypse or the major Pauline epistles (save Galatians). As we have seen, he also refrained from publishing his early lectures on Romans and the epistle to the Hebrews. What inhibited Luther from lecturing on the books of the N. T. after 1520 was his realization that their teachings are in fundamental contradiction with the *sola fide* defense. We have previously commented on Luther's indirect avowal of this fact in the prefaces to the German N. T. in which he belittled more than three-fourths of the material in this new translation as not worth the attention of a mature Christian. For his exposition of the N. T. writings during the 1520s and later, therefore, one must examine his sermons, delivered for the benefit of the presumably immature Christians of the Wittenberg congregation, and certain of his polemical tracts.

Elsewhere in this study we noted some of Luther's defensive remarks about the symbolic gift of 'Keys' to Peter and the associated texts dealing with the authority of the Church to 'bind' and 'loose,' an authority he was forced to deny in an attempt to avoid the terror of certain damnation he must face for disobeying it. His continuing preoccupation with these texts is shown by his return to them in the 1530 tract called "On the Keys." Here he finally confronts the question of the scriptural meaning of 'bind' and 'loose.' His discussion of this subject is conducted in a manner that indicates the depth of his regression in this area and gives the impression of an individual ignorant of the most elementary standards of scriptural exposition:

> What schools teach such Latin or German as this: that 'to bind' means to command or to establish laws? What mother teaches her child to speak like that? Where do our key-explainers find the interpretation that 'to bind' means command? What else can they say but that it comes from their wanton verses or drunken dreams? This is to say nothing more than that they falsify God's word and truth with their lies and mislead Christians and serve the devil.[3]

To interpret this extraordinary outburst, it will hardly do to suggest that by 1530 Luther has forgotten the language of the N. T. is Greek. The scandalously abusive epithets may be taken to indicate that he was extremely disturbed when he wrote this tract and that his pathological defense mechanisms were in full control. Since he is writing in German, that is, for comparatively uninstructed readers who know of the Bible only as a book written in German (and perhaps Latin), there is no occasion for mentioning Greek. It hardly needs saying that the tract "On the Keys" throws little light on the word of God.

After his return from Coburg in late 1530, Luther was asked to replace Bugenhagen in the pulpit of the parish church of Wittenberg while the latter was absent. To this circumstance is owing the delivery of a sermon series on Chs. 5 to 7 of the gospel of Matthew that ran on through the next year because the pastor remained away much longer than anticipated. It is of interest to note that in these sermons Luther again resorted to the denial mechanism to downgrade the Synoptic gospels. A new falsification had to be concocted since Chs. 5 to 7 of Matthew, commonly but inappropriately called the 'Sermon on the Mount,' contain the longest continuous collection of 'Christ's words' in this gospel — and no 'deeds.' Confrontation with this material made the earlier falsification inoperative. The new one consists in the declaration that John's gospel is supreme because of its emphasis on the 'profound doctrine of Christ' while the Synoptics put more stress on good works so they 'won't be forgotten.'[4] This deprecatory remark about the teachings of Jesus collected in these three chapters of Matthew is mild in comparison with the abundance of defensive material, i.e., slanderous falsification, Martin directs against monastic life in these sermons. It would seem that reviewing the lofty moral teaching of the 'Sermon on the

Mount' aroused in him painful recollections of his abandoning the attempt to practice these precepts himself as a monk and thereby actuated his favorite defense mechanism.

It is of interest to observe how Luther fields the adjuration to love your enemies and the accompanying sanction that if you do not forgive others, your heavenly Father will not forgive you. This is doubly obnoxious to him, for the number of 'enemies' he cannot love or forgive has been increasing steadily for the past decade, and any suggestion that the forgiveness of sin is not absolutely free for the taking but tied to a condition represents a frontal attack on the gospel according to Luther. He explains away the condition on the forgiveness of sins by an artful contrivance: when I forgive others, that is an 'outward sign' that I myself have 'inward forgiveness' of my own sins, not a condition for my being forgiven. Contrariwise, if I don't forgive others, that is an 'outward sign' that I lack forgiveness myself. His further resort to the denial mechanism when faced with the command to love your enemies while more heavyhanded than that applied to forgiveness is much better designed for crowd appeal. It reduces to: my enemies are the enemies of God. If therefore I do not curse them with all my might, I too will be classed as God's enemy.

Among other passages in Matthew that Luther found painful to contemplate was the story of the rich young man (Matt. 19:13-21) who asked Jesus what he must do to win eternal life. The latter part of the reply: "If you seek perfection, go, sell your possessions and give to the poor . . ." as traditionally interpreted, had inspired the foundation and flourishing of the religious orders. After Luther renounced his vows in 1521, such scriptural passages provoked in him a strong defensive reaction. This sometimes took the form of rewriting the gospel in a Lutherian sense, as in the following excerpt from a sermon delivered early in 1531. After repeating a characteristic slander against monks, he proceeds:

> 'If you would become a son of God, possess eternal life and be freed from sin, this is the way: accept my will and my Father's. That means to believe in me, and that I am the bread of life.' A Christian must seek righteousness only in Christ if he is to accept the will of the Lord Christ and the Father. Thereafter let him proceed to be a judge, magistrate, father or mother, master or mistress, servant or maid, and do what is pleasing to God.[5]

The purport of the last sentence is to express Luther's conviction that no form of human behavior has any religious value.

Luther's practice of boldly replacing the text of Scripture with his own words in passages he found disturbing appears well established by the beginning of what is here designated as the paranoid phase of his disorder. Perhaps the most notable example of this defensive maneuver is his treatment of Matthews's parable of the Last Judgment. It is evident from numerous allusions that as a boy Martin had been badly frightened by the sight of a painting of the Last Judgment, which was a popular theme among artists in the latter half of the fifteenth century. In these paintings Christ as Judge is often depicted enthroned on a rainbow. It is not improbable that his parents or another adult had utilized such a painting to put the fear of the Lord into Martin when he was being contrary. In later years we find him condemning the painters' use of this theme; his early experience may help account for his rather indifferent attitude to the art of painting in contrast to his love of music. We may also infer that this youthful encounter with the Last Judgment was one of the sources of his pathological fear of damnation, and this in turn was a prominent factor in the motivation of the *sola fide* program. From these considerations it appears inevitable that when Luther had regressed to an appropriate level he would replace the text of the scriptural parable with something acceptable to himself. His personal version appears in a sermon preached shortly before the one quoted above. Early in the sermon he refers to a painting:

> This disgraceful and blasphemous picture or painting depicts Judgment Day with the Son kneeling before the Father and showing him his wounds, while St. John and Mary pray to Christ to spare us in the Judgment, and the mother shows the Son her breasts . . . . Such paintings should be done away with because they have been used to frighten tender consciences and make people imagine they must fear the dear Savior and flee from him, as if he would drive us away from him and punish us for our sins.[6]

After going on at length about the erroneous view of Christ as a judge he speaks of the parable (Matt. 25:31-46), saying that only for the wicked will Christ act as judge. Luther then throws out the well known passage beginning "I was hungry and you gave me to eat," etc., replacing it with his own invention.

> Christ will say to the pious and God-fearing: 'You came to me and believed in me . . . . I will not cast you out.' But to the others he will say on Judgment Day that he will be their judge because they did not come to him. Then there will be two groups, and he will divide the godless from the Christians and separate the goats from the sheep and say to the godless:
> 'You did not want me and did not believe in me. But you persecuted me, killed my Christians, blasphemed my word and cast out me and mine. Therefore go from here into hell's fire . . . .' The rainbow on which he sits does not frighten me but helps me to be saved.[7]

The remark about the rainbow indicates that Luther is here recalling

a different (and more customary) representation of the Last Judgment scene than the one he had in mind at the beginning of the sermon passage quoted here. The picture of Christ enthroned on a rainbow appears to be one of the terrifying images of him that from time
to time invaded Luther's consciousness. It might also be noted that
in the speech invented for Jesus in this sermon to replace the scriptural text we are witnessing another Lutherian projection. The treatment said to be accorded 'me' and 'my Christians' refers to the fate
of Luther and some of his disciples. 'I' was 'persecuted' and 'cast
out,' i.e., excommunicated as a heretic (but not put to death like
Christ); 'my Christians' were killed, i.e., burned at the stake for cleav-
ing to the Lutherian heresies.

ii.   Anomalies in Luther's relations to Jesus and to Paul

One of the most obvious indications that Luther lacked a real attachment to the person of Jesus is that he avoids the simple name
Jesus in his references to the Lord, preferring the designation Christ,
or 'that Man.' The contrast between Luther's practice and the multitude of references to Jesus in the "Imitation of Christ," for example,
is most striking. The source of this trait in Luther is to be looked for
in the mixture of fear and hatred of the Christ figure in the role
of Judge that he experienced especially during the anxiety attacks. In
the sermon of 1531 quoted above to illustrate Luther's rewriting of
the Last Judgment parable there are a number of allusions indicating
his pathological attitude toward Jesus as well as his struggle to overcome it. Note the projection in this passage:

> The heart is by nature so timid it always labors under the im-
> pression that Christ is a hangman or judge and will administer the
> law harshly against us. We always want to make him a Moses or
> lawgiver. This depravity I can overcome and free myself from as
> little as I can free you . . . . And even if I became as it were a
> martyr, depriving myself of all things, still my heart would not be
> at peace.[8]

This self revelation is followed by praise of the *sola fide* as the only
way to master the despair induced by this fear.

During his later years Luther freely projects his own psychic
states on Jesus. For example, consider his remarks (1531) about a
passage in John 12 in which Jesus is reported as saying his hour is
come and calls upon the Father to glorify his name, whereupon a
voice from heaven is heard: "I have glorified it." Luther projects into
this account his own extremely personal distinction between 'law'
and 'gospel,' which he declared too difficult even for Jesus to grasp:

> Even the man Christ was so lacking in understanding when in

the vineyard that an angel came to console him; though a doctor from heaven he was encouraged by the angel.[9]

In a sermon on John 4 delivered in 1540 Luther projects on Jesus his own extreme fear of physical danger to his person. The opening verses of this chapter relate that Jesus, upon being told the Pharisees had learned of his greater success in winning converts than John the Baptist, left Judea and returned to Galilee. Luther here attributes Jesus' action to fear of the Pharisees. To make his point Luther consistently mistranslates the verb *leave* (Gk. *apheken;* Lat. *reliquit*) as *flee:*

> Jesus *fled* from Judea . . . . Well, instead of *fleeing,* shouldn't he have stood fast? Now we must learn to understand this correctly. For whoever really knows this man has the Holy Spirit in him and can judge and censure all matters . . . . Here it was said he *fled* from the Pharisees. *Where is the man in him?* He wants to be Lord and yet *fears the Pharisees* and *flees* into Galilee.[10]

All told, Luther repeats these slurs on his Savior 8 or 10 times during this sermon and in its successor the following week, thereby indicating his shame at his own cowardice which is so painful to him as to precipitate the projection mechanism. (In his last sermon preached shortly before his death (see Ch. 10) Luther describes his solution of the problem of relating to Jesus.)

Turning now to Luther's attitude toward Paul, we note first another use of the same defense mechanism. In a Table Talk item of 1531 Luther projects his own pathological attitude to God on Paul: "I believe even Paul felt hostile to God because he couldn't believe as he would have liked."[11] In view of Luther's strong tendency to identify with Paul it is appropriate to compare some of their personal traits. In contrast with Paul's wish that all Christians could be unmarried like himself for the sake of devoting their lives more exclusively to the service of God, Luther urged all Christians to marry as young as possible and all religious who had taken the vow of 'unclean celibacy' to break it at once. Paul was a man of great personal courage who traveled through many strange lands to preach the gospel, was often imprisoned, beaten and otherwise maltreated, and ultimately gave his life for his faith. Luther, however, took extreme care of his personal safety, remained in territory where he was safe from harm, and during the last two decades of his life would not even leave Wittenberg without a bodyguard. His attempts to convert other peoples than his own were carried on exclusively by correspondence. No other Scriptural writer so explicitly emphasized the unity of all Christian believers as did Paul. The phrase "One Lord, one faith, one baptism" has become almost a byword to signify this aspect of the Pauline message. Luther, on the other hand, has few rivals in ecclesiastical history for the title of chief Apostle of Discord.

While the teaching of Paul is God-centered and Luther's doctrine is more like an anthropology, there is enough overlap to permit some meaningful comparisons. A central emphasis in Paul is that the Christian, however unsavory his past life may have been before his conversion, thereafter leads a new life in Christ, free from the domination of sin and in a state of charity with God and his fellow men. But Lutheran man experiences no such renewal. He remains sinful to the grave, being permanently the slave of sin; the only relief he experiences comes from his 'faith' that God will overlook his sinful state provided he can make himself believe that God is favorably disposed toward him. In the expression of this highly un-Paulinian point of view Luther composed some of his more striking paradoxes. Everyone has heard of his slogan "always a sinner and always justified." Less well known is his definition of the Christian religion as "a perpetual exercise in making believe you do not have sin even though you have sinned."

> It is sacrilegious for you to look upon sin as in your heart, because the devil put the sin there, not God. Rather look at Christ and when you see your sins clinging to him you are secure from sin, death and hell . . . . It does indeed take great effort to be able to grasp this in faith and to believe it, saying: "I have sinned and I have not sinned," and thereby overcome that most powerful master, the conscience, which often drives men to despair, to the sword [i.e., suicide] and to the snares of men.[12]

The two epistles to the Corinthians were not on Luther's recommended list of N. T. writings. It may be surmised that 1 Corinthians was omitted both for the strongly anti-Lutheran position on celibacy in Ch. 7 and the equally un-Lutheran declaration of the superiority of charity to faith in Ch. 13. Luther's attitude toward Christian charity is a consequence partly of the *sola fide* but more basically of the psychic disorder, which prevented him from enjoying a real experience of love with any human being, let alone with God. It is true that during the 1520s the word 'love' — coupled with 'faith' — is often on his pen, but the reality is conspicuously missing in much of his conduct toward others. As the years went on, the word love gradually became more and more inconspicuous in his utterances. In the early 1540s he said out loud what had been his practice for a long time, that charity is a secondary virtue.[13] In summary there is probably no position in the Pauline writings that Luther repudiated more emphatically than that in 1 Corinthians 13: "The greatest of these is love."

Despite his urge to identify with Paul after his regression, Luther devoted rather a small proportion of his time to Paul's epistles. In

1523 he published a tract on Ch. 7 of 1 Cor.[14] This is actually a polemical work despite its superficial resemblance to a commentary. Its primary object is to mount still another attack on clerical and monastic celibacy by adroit manipulation of Paul's words. Inasmuch as in three places Paul discusses the superiority of dedicated celibacy to marriage it might be thought Luther had his work cut out for him in using this chapter to attack clerical celibacy. But in the area of his disturbance a psychotic lacks ordinary judgment and does not scruple to say anything that suits his purpose. One line Luther takes is that hardly anyone is capable of following Paul's recommendation. In a tract on marriage he had written the preceding year Luther asserts the number of those capable of celibacy to be not even one in a thousand. Confronted with the challenge of 1 Cor 7 he raised the figure to a hundred thousand. Paul's advice that men and women should marry if incapable of living chastely as celibates is twisted into the statement that "God commands marriage" for practically all men.

One of Luther's more eccentric comments deals with the so-called Pauline privilege, i.e., the case of a Christian and a pagan spouse who have a falling out over differences in religion and separate. For this situation Paul makes an exception to the general rule that a married person separated from his spouse commits adultery by marrying another, and permits the deserted Christian partner to remarry. Concerning this Luther asserts it is therefore legitimate for the Christian to remarry — in succession — a whole string of pagans, even ten, if each pagan spouse in turn runs off. But Luther repudiates Paul with respect to the case in which the (separated) spouses are both Christians; according to Luther the abandoned husband may lawfully take another wife if he can't live alone. Presumably to reduce the incidence of abandoned husbands Luther declares the state should force the wife to return; if she refuses, she must be put to death.

As it happened Luther had occasion to practice his modification of the Pauline privilege not long after announcing it. His client was one Michael Cramer, a pastor in Ducal Saxony who had migrated to Electoral Saxony to take advantage of the facilities for clerical marriage available there. Cramer seems to have been more remarkable for his appetite for women than his ability to get along with them. His first wife having left him, he presently took a second. But wife number two apparently found him as unbearable as wife number one and departed only 24 days after their union. Though forcibly returned to him, she ran off again at the first opportunity. This occurred in July of 1525. In August, Cramer and the town council of Dommitsch, where Luther had helped install him as preacher the year before, appealed to Wittenberg for relief on the grounds that Cramer was a man whose nature required a bedfellow. Luther ruled that since the errant wife was an 'unbeliever' the Pauline privilege could be invoked. By November Cramer had found a third woman willing to take a chance with him. Subsequently when questioned during the visitation of Saxony parishes he displayed Luther's letter of authorization as a guarantee that wife number three was legal.[15] History does not record whether in later years Cramer made further progress toward the theoretical limit of ten marriages.

In the tract on 1 Cor 7 as in other writings on marriage Luther regards women as second class citizens, in accord with the prevailing opinion of his times. In the preface to the tract he provided a distinctively Lutherian argument on why all women should marry (and not, for example, enter convents). "The word and the work of God demonstrate that women must serve either as wives or prostitutes." The latter alternative being ungodly, they must all become wives. This prefatory comment in effect states the theme of Luther's exposition of 1 Cor 7; it also reveals how little regard he shows in the area of his disturbance for the teaching of Paul.

iii.   Carlstadt and the cost of non-discipleship

The story of Luther's life in the decade of the 1520s is to a considerable extent an account of his response to the challenge provided by Carlstadt, Thomas Muentzer and the Swiss Zwingli. We deal with these individuals only insofar as they provoked Luther into action that furnished information useful for his portrait. Our concern with them is confined mainly to the 1520s because two of them died early and violent deaths, Muentzer in 1525 and Zwingli in 1531, while Carlstadt departed permanently from Luther's proximity by 1530. It is of interest to note that the four members of the clergy who may be described as the intellectual leaders of the revolt against traditional ecclesiastical authority during this decade included a psychotic, a rather special type of crackpot (Carlstadt), a man with a severe personality disorder (Muentzer) and an ambitious politician (Zwingli).

It is ascribable to Luther's regressed state, that is, a condition characterized by lack of normal judgment, that in 1523 he announced a principle most inimical to his own presumptuous claims. It appeared in the tract entitled "That a Christian Assembly or Congregation Has the Right and Power to Judge All Teaching and to Call, Appoint and Dismiss Teachers, Established and Proven by Scripture." According to this principle the local congregation has the power to judge what is 'pure' doctrine. To support this position, Luther advanced one of the more preposterous examples of his scriptural exegesis, namely, that this power is vested in these people by the verse in John 10: "My sheep know my voice." As might be surmised, this anarchical doctrine enjoyed but a brief period of residence in the gospel according to Luther. For while he was not sufficiently rational to foresee what it would lead to, he was at least able to discern that sheep turned loose in the scriptural pasture rapidly developed un-Lutheran notions. His motive for endowing the ignorant and untrained with such an estimable power of criticism was that at the time he was conducting a belligerent campaign against the German bishops and this seemed to him a useful stratagem.

Carlstadt, who was capable of exhibiting shifts in outlook almost as radical as Luther's, was at this period also making a strong pitch to the uneducated. Like so many of his contemporaries, it appears he had originally 'gone into religion' for what he could get from it. He began his academic career about 1505 at Wittenberg, which presently granted him a 'quickie' doctorate in theology after a few years as teacher of philosophy. In 1508 he became a canon in the chapter of the Castle Church and not long thereafter was promoted to Archdeacon, the second ranking position in the chapter. His next move, in what proved to be a vain attempt to take over the top job in the chapter, that of provost, was to spend some months at an Italian university from which he returned to Wittenberg with the doctorate in both canon and civil law. He then joined forces with Luther in the attack on scholastic theology and, as we have seen, took part with Luther in the academic disputation at Leipzig in 1519. While Luther was at the Wartburg, Carlstadt came out strongly against monastic vows (in advance of Luther) and the mass, and at the end of 1521 became one of the first of the clergy to take a wife. It was at this time that his anti-academic phase commenced. He hailed the virtues of life on the farm, in lay garb mingled with the peasants, and as brother Andrew helped them load their carts with hay or manure.

As Archdeacon he enjoyed the revenues of the rural parish of Orlamuende. Being a compulsive verbalizer like Luther he found the silence imposed on him in Wittenberg intolerable. To obtain relief he abandoned his academic duties and repaired to Orlamuende, where he let the curate go and as pastor introduced the liturgical innovations he had earlier promoted in Wittenberg. His approach made a hit with the local peasantry and presently he succeeded in establishing a new propaganda center in opposition to Wittenberg within Electoral Saxony. Like Luther he disseminated his views in both pamphlets and sermons, thereby making numerous converts outside as well as within the Elector's domains.

In addition to committing this monstrous offense, Carlstadt abolished the mass openly instead of covertly in the Lutheran style. Also he not only denied, like Luther, that at the consecration the bread and wine are transformed into Christ's body and blood, but found unacceptable the Lutheran subterfuge that during the celebration for a brief but unspecified interval Christ is physically present in the bread and wine. To stifle this threat to the Wittenbergian monopoly on innovations in religion pressure was put on Carlstadt to return to the university where he could be kept under surveillance. This maneuvre failing, Luther decided to intervene personally and in August of 1524 journeyed to Orlamuende. At a meeting with the congregation, most of them peasants, he displayed both his will to domineer and his incapacity for any real rapport with what was by far the largest class of German citizenry, the peasants, whom he was to categorize the following year as enemies. Although his mission was unsuccessful, his recommendations to civil authority appear to have been instrumental in the banishing of Carlstadt from the Electorate in September.

Luther next proceeded to attack Carlstadt in a long ill-organized tract called "Against the Heavenly Prophets." A feature of the attack was the falsification that because Carlstadt destroyed images he had a murderous character — like Muentzer — and if tolerated would presently be killing off his adversaries. Actually Carlstadt had as little stomach for physical violence and the sight of blood as Luther himself. Among the diverting sallies in this onslaught on his one-time colleague are the reproach that Carlstadt should have suffered his exile in silence (instead of complaining about the illegality of the edict), and that since "he has no respect for me, he won't respect any of us." Perhaps the highlight of the tract is Luther's discussion of an eccentric bit of scriptural exegesis fathered by Carlstadt to support his denial of the Real Presence in the Eucharist. According to this expository gem, when Jesus at the last supper held out the bread and uttered the words of institution, "Take you and eat, this is my body," he also pointed to himself to show what "this is my body" means. If the reader is puzzled to hear that Luther devoted more than a dozen pages to refute this infantile interpretation, the explanation is that Luther had elsewhere himself stooped to the same level in explaining away the famous "Thou art Peter, and upon this rock I will build my Church." According to Luther "this rock" is not Peter at all, but instead, Jesus is here referring to himself. It is indubitable that one of these interpretations inspired the other, but which man deserves credit for priority I do not attempt to determine. That Luther was greatly disturbed at here being in the same bed with Carlstadt is evident from the many pages of childish argument proving the two interpretations have nothing in common.

For the better part of a year Carlstadt roamed about southern Germany and Switzerland, nowhere finding an abode or means of livelihood. As early as February 1525 he wrote Luther on the possibility of a return to Saxony. Finally in June after submitting a written apology for the disturbance he had caused, he was granted conditional entry. For about three months he resided in the Black

Monastery with Luther, where he wrote a second apology for his Eucharistic views. The two apologies were printed with prefaces by Luther. Far more repugnant to him than the apologies was the recantation Luther composed and forced him to sign:

> I recognize before God, without jest and from my heart, that all I wrote, spoke or taught from my own brain or discovered for myself is human, false, unpraiseworthy, deceitful, satanic and to be shunned and avoided.[16]

Carlstadt said the Turks would have treated him better, but he was under duress. He and his family were in danger of starvation and he had been, like Luther, terrified by being caught in the area ravaged by the Peasants War. In a letter to the Elector, Luther remarked on the advantage of having Carlstadt under his control: "It helps mightily against all who have accepted his errors and discourages them that he lives in dependence on our favor and grace."[17]

After this humiliation Carlstadt was permitted to try to earn his living on a farm several miles outside of Wittenberg, and forbidden to preach, teach or publish. There followed a year of dismal failure as a farmer after which he again appealed to Luther:

> I have to leave the farm at Berkwitz. I keep on losing my horses; recently a great strong carthorse together with another stallion that I would not have taken 15 florins for both died in one week. So I hastened to sell the farm cheap lest I become a beggar and the fields through my fault lie fallow. I hope no one will blame me for still another change or accuse me because of it, for I have now lost seven horses and endured unbelievably great losses besides . . . .
>
> Because I have kept so quiet and . . . people no longer speak of Carlstadt's teaching, also because I am no longer desirous of taking part in the affairs of the very learned . . . I ask your reverence to write the most honorable prince and lord, Duke John of Saxony . . . for permission to go to Kemberg to support myself in association with other townspeople and earn food and clothing for my poor children.[18]

Luther acceded to this petition and the Elector allowed Carlstadt to reside in the village of Kemberg a few miles south of Wittenberg, where he lived barely at a subsistence level as a shopkeeper. But Luther's persecution of the hapless ex-professor continued. The following year he was again required to state his views on the Eucharist and also to write against Zwingli. In the summer of 1528 Carlstadt complained to the Elector about Luther's treatment of him, and of his inability to agree with Luther's opinions. Following this, Luther recommended that Carlstadt be thrown in prison. Imprisonment for heresy, defined as public refusal to accept Luther's current theological opinions, became settled Wittenberg policy in the 1530s.

But Carlstadt had no inclination to become a victim. Early in 1529 he fled from Saxony and after more wandering about found a berth in Zwingli's church as preacher and later (1534) returned to academic life as a professor of theology at the university in Basel. Whatever his mental limitations, he made at least one penetrating remark about Luther's character, singling out what would be called today Luther's defensive stance:

> It is your specialty always to speak in such a way as to safeguard your own reputation and cast the odium on others.[19]

By way of contrast with the treatment meted out to Carlstadt, we may remark on the later career of Gabriel Zwilling, the Augustinian rowdy who had briefly shared the limelight with Carlstadt at Wittenberg. Having accepted the Lutherian gospel, he was forgiven his misconduct and awarded a preaching job in Saxony for life.

iv. Muentzer and the Peasants Revolt

Thomas Muentzer, five years Luther's junior, was born in Stolberg, only twenty miles from the village where Luther spent his boyhood. Muentzer enrolled at the University of Leipzig in 1506 and at Frankfort on the Oder in 1512. Possibly at the wish of his mother he was ordained to the priesthood. He was bookish rather than academic, his formative years being spent largely in private study. Nowhere did he put down roots; his longest residence at one place after his college days seems to have been two years. The restlessness indicated by this continual moving about reflects an inner strife which in later years he described as a sort of despair necessarily preceding the acquisition of 'faith.' In this account one notes the Lutherian practice of characterizing a personal psychic problem as the norm for man's spiritual development. Muentzer found Luther's writings of such interest that he visited Luther at Wittenberg in 1518 or 1519 and attended the Leipzig debate between Luther and Eck. It was doubtless hearing their discussion of papal and conciliar authority that prompted him to engage in a course of reading on early ecclesiastical history as well as on the more recent councils of Constance and Basle.[20]

In May of 1520 he served as preacher in a Zwickau church during the absence of the incumbent and later in that year transferred to another church in the city with a congregation composed largely of weavers. It was his experience in Zwickau which helped establish Muentzer in his metier as the prophet of the working class man. By this time he had developed his own distinctive religious theme — that the only people who count are the Elect. It was a theme which had a strong appeal to those who were hopelessly at the bottom of the social and economic ladder. Apart from this, following Luther and others, he banged away also at the anti-clerical theme so popular in those years, especially among the working men. The bookish recluse became so embroiled in factional disputes in the city that in April of 1521, after not quite a year at Zwickau, he was dismissed from his parish.

Muentzer spent the latter half of 1521 in the city of Prague. Toward the end of his sojourn there he issued a proclamation about himself which reads in part:

> I, Thomas Muentzer, confess before the entire church and the whole world that I, with Christ and all the elect who have known me from my youth, am able to testify that I have labored more strenuously than all other men I have known to acquire or obtain a more elevated understanding of the holy and unconquerable Christian faith. During my whole life (and God knows I am not lying) no monk or priest has taught me the proper exercise of faith and the usefulness of trials (*Anfechtungen*), which illuminate faith by the spirit of the fear of God . . . . These things are unknown to those who would be Christians and especially to the damnable priests.[21]

This grandiose boasting, together with the use of *Anfechtungen,* so reminiscent of Luther, suggests that Muentzer has learned more from Wittenberg than he cares to admit — and, as we shall see presently, more than Luther is willing to acknowledge. At this point it is desirable to draw up a comparison between the two prophets. Each has a radically egocentric nature, with no real insight into other human beings, and each man attempts to restate the Christian faith in the light of his own psychic problems. Each man has an uncontrollable drive to instill his views into as large a part of the human race as possible. Each man considers that he is the first in the history of Christendom since the days of the Apostles to discover the essential Christian message. Muentzer is only somewhat more blatant than his older counterpart about this claim, asserting that the gates of hell prevailed against the Church soon after the death of the last Apostle. Each uses Scripture as a taking-off point and there is only a difference of emphasis between the two on the role of the 'Spirit' as the real source of his unparalleled understanding of the Christian faith. It is partly an accident of history that Luther's preaching had its strongest appeal to the middle class Germans, especially those with mild neurotic anxiety about their salvation, while Muentzer went after the uneducated proletariat — not many others would listen to him. Muentzer actually did make a pitch to the ruling classes but he had nothing new to offer them. They got what they wanted from Luther — abundant exhortation to the populace on civil obedience and a free hand to take over with a 'good conscience' the immense real estate holdings of the monastic orders and other religious foundations (see below). Indeed Muentzer diminished the value of this property by inciting his followers to plunder the buildings and then burn them to the ground. Civil disobedience became his principal rallying point in haranguing the proletariat.

A fundamental difference in character between the two is that while Luther feared and shunned physical violence (as a potential threat to himself) Muentzer enjoyed and promoted it. [Muentzer's anti-social attitude, general irresponsibility and grandiosity are some of the symptoms of what in our time is diagnosed as a 'character' or 'personality' disorder. For an illuminating discussion of this form of psychopathology, see Norman Cameron, *Personality Development and Psychopathology* (Boston, 1963) Ch. 19.] What might be termed the fanaticism of violence is given inimitable expression in this remark from a sermon of 1524: "The godless have no right to live except as the Elect wish to grant it to them." Another pulpit utterance: "All public officials should be strangled like dogs," was not heard until Muentzer had lost hope of converting the rulers to his gospel.[22] As against this Luther would have sent the 'godless' into exile, and if they starved as a result that was God's justice catching up with them.

Like Luther, Muentzer was quite unconcerned about monetary matters. In the spring of 1521 during his early thirties he inherited his mother's estate; two years later he was penniless. From this condition he was rescued by being appointed (April 1523) to the small parish of Allstedt in Electoral Saxony. His tenure of this living throws light on the relaxed attitude of the Elector toward his administrative responsibilities in ecclesiastical affairs, the same attitude that provided Luther a haven after the Edict of Worms and tolerated his unrestrained propaganda activities against the Church apart from an occasional wrist slapping. The Elector as patron of the Allstedt parish was required to ratify the selection by the town council of a new incumbent. Not only did he omit to do this but virtually ignored a complaint by the Count of Mansfeld in September 1523 against Muentzer's numerous (and illegal) innovations. It was not until the following summer that any official action was taken against the Allstedt pastor. By then he had given abundant demonstration of his talents as a religio-political agitator, having formed the quasi-military 'League of the Elect' and instituted the campaign of church burning that came into full bloom during his involvement in the Peasants Revolt in 1525. Duke John, the Elector's brother, held a hearing on the Allstedt problem in August 1524. He outlawed the printing press in Allstedt by means of which Muentzer disseminated his propaganda throughout Germany, and ordered Muentzer to remain quietly in

Allstedt. But Muentzer had the same compulsive need for access to a press as Luther. Abandoning Allstedt (and the ex-nun he married in April 1523) he proceeded to Nuremberg to print an answer to Luther's recent pamphlet attack on his person and doctrine and then sojourned in Switzerland until the following spring.

Luther's encounter with Muentzer might be described as the meeting of two impenetrable minds. Though both men pursued the goal of eradication of the ancient Church, neither had appreciable sympathy for the other's approach and the Lutherian pamphlet just referred to established them as irreconcilable enemies. It was published in late July 1524 in the form of a communication to Luther's sovereign, being called "A Letter to the Princes of Saxony on the Rebellious Spirit." Only about ten pages in length (in the Weimar text) it is yet Luther's most considerable piece of writing on his Thuringian rival. In keeping with the devious style of some of his polemical work, the name of Muentzer nowhere appears in the tract. The word 'spirit' is employed with deliberate ambiguity, now referring to Muentzer's claim to be graced with an indwelling of the Holy Spirit and at other times to Muentzer himself, who is typically identified with the evil spirit Satan.

To appreciate the rhetorical mastery of the "Letter to the Princes" one must be aware of the extremely difficult problems that confronted Luther on this occasion. First off, there are now two men, both with considerable oratorical talents, claiming to have the singular distinction of being summoned by the Holy Spirit to restore the Christian gospel after fifteen centuries of darkness and unbelief. Both have been successful in winning a following even though their presentations of the gospel are in sharp conflict. In the second place the rival prophet has been boldly traveling about, preaching now in the diocese of Brandenburg, then in turbulent Zwickau, after that in even more turbulent Prague, and at the moment is enjoying spectacular success in Luther's native land. Luther could not possibly have dared do this. And yet which of the two is more like Paul — outwardly, that is — the apostle Luther tries to identify with? A third problem is that he must now repudiate a principle he had advanced with great fervor during the past year in the tract called "On Secular Authority." Here he had established as one of the eternal verities that

> It is never possible to overcome heresy by force . . . . My good sir, if you want to get rid of heresy, the first thing you must do is find a means of tearing it out of men's hearts and altogether changing their wills [provided for the occasion]. You won't end it with force but only make it stronger . . . . But God's word illuminates hearts and in that way hearts will spontaneously be freed from all heresy and error.[23]

This particular verity, it is true, stems from the post-Wartburg era of manic exaltation, i.e., the spring of 1522, and by the spring of 1524 Luther, now in his more usual unexalted state, was complaining that the word of God was spreading rather slowly for his taste. By the summer of 1524, that is at this very moment, it may be recalled that he was in the thick of the battle to drive the mass-priests out of the temple in Wittenberg, an affair in which force was really to come into its own and permanently bury the word as a primary instrument of Wittenberg policy. At this moment, however, Luther could still speak with enthusiasm of the power of the word and boast of all the convents he had emptied solely by this power. But as for using force rather than the word against Muentzer, that was perfectly legitimate, indeed was commanded by God, because that limb of Satan was himself using force. Only the noticeably excessive number of words that Luther devotes in the tract to this pat solution of the word-force problem reveals his actual uneasiness about his latest betrayal of a sacred principle.

The more formidable of his problems, however, is to establish himself as the true prophet and Muentzer the false one. For obvious reasons he is barred from employing his favorite tactic of rebutting claims by fellow enthusiasts to possess the Spirit, — "let them prove this by working miracles." His approach is rather to discredit Muentzer by other arguments while modestly setting forth the evidence of his own superiority. In the opening paragraph he uses the aforesaid argument of identifying Muentzer with the devil. "Satin . . . has settled in your Grace's electorate at Allstedt and has made himself a nest."[24] The geographical reference is indispensable for identifying the object of his attack without naming him, a device which doubtless puzzled the Elector and his brother. Luther then proceeds to congratulate himself that "they" — here Muentzer for Luther's convenience takes on the plural number — brag of receiving their diabolic teaching direct from heaven rather than from Wittenberg. They hear 'heavenly voices' or 'God's voice,' a phrase which Luther introduces early and repeats on at least every other page throughout the tract as a means of ridicule. Luther is at pains to establish Muentzer's independent source of inspiration, for a few years earlier not only had Muentzer been preaching Lutherian material but had actually paid one or two visits to Luther at Wittenberg, which are described in this enigmatic remark: "Once or twice he was with me in my cloister at Wittenberg to have his nose punched."

The technique Luther employs to discredit Muentzer and validate his own claim is simple — whatever Muentzer is or does is bad, and Luther is the opposite. It is a sign of pride to brag of the 'heavenly voices'; therefore Luther never hears them. There are few places in Luther's works where we hear so much about his humility as in this little tract. He is a veritable model for Uriah Heep. In one such sally he tosses off the following exquisite morsel: "My poor, retiring spirit has had to stand free like a flower of the field . . . prepared and ready to answer every man, as St. Peter teaches."

This botanical simile follows hard upon one of the most striking uses of the denial mechanism in the tract, always an indication that Luther is in some sort of trouble. (As a sign of what is in the wind, St. Paul makes an appearance at the beginning of the passage.) Here Luther is making out that Muentzer is the coward and himself the man of dauntless courage. To support this interesting reversal of fact, Luther rehearses his favorite trio of exploits, each ornamented with a characteristic falsification:

> At Leipzig I stood and debated before one of the most dangerous assemblies. I was in Augsburg without a safe-conduct to appear before my greatest enemy. I was at Worms to answer to the Emperor and the entire Diet, though I knew very well they had broken my safe-conduct and were planning strange and savage tricks and treachery against me.[25]

These inventions were picked up by Muentzer in his rebuttal and have subsequently aroused comment by writers on Luther. Basically they are no different from the countless thousands of uses of the denial mechanism to be found in his writings and were presumably motivated by his shame at his own most unPauline timidity.

Luther's invitation to the German ruling classes to plunder the monastic property and other ecclesiastical real estate is presented with consummate artistry in this "Letter to the Princes." (In later years he was to complain bitterly and repeatedly that these same characters refused to give financial support to his new church establishment.) He introduces the topic by way of contrasting his own policy of non-violence with the pillaging activities of Muentzer and his followers:

> Preaching and suffering is our office, not to strike with the fist and defend ourselves. Thus Christ and his apostles did not destroy churches nor break images, but they won hearts with God's word, whereupon churches and images fell down of themselves. We should do likewise: first draw hearts way from the cloisters and foundations. When they have departed, the churches and cloisters will be deserted. Thereupon, let the lords do what they wish with them. What do wood and stone mean to us when we have entry to hearts?[26]

It hardly needs pointing out that this part of Luther's message made a strong appeal to the hearts of the ruling classes and proved most effective in the promotion of his movement in Germany and Scandinavia. As might be expected, Luther subsequently reversed his position after he had observed the extent of the plundering operation in Saxony. Writing to Spalatin on the first day of 1527, he declares he is greatly perturbed about this grand larceny, and goes on to describe how on a recent occasion he even intruded into the bedchamber of Elector John to deliver a personal complaint.

It was especially irksome that Muentzer could in any way benefit from Luther's revolt:

> How well do they use and enjoy our victory, take wives and put an end to papal laws, though they have not fought for this or endangered their lives. But to obtain it I had to risk my body and life.

Having gone thus far, he casts off the mantle of Uriah Heep, though ready at any moment to put it back on:

> I have to boast, as St. Paul also boasted, although it is foolishness and I had rather not if it weren't for the lying spirits . . . I know and by God's grace am certain that I am more learned in Scripture than all the sophists and papists, but God has graciously preserved me thus far from pride, and will continue to preserve me.[27]

Muentzer's pamphlet in response to Luther's may have contributed further to this preservation, for on the title page Luther was saluted as the "unspiritual, soft-living flesh of Wittenberg" and elsewhere by a rich variety of epithets, one of the more colorful being Dr. Pussyfoot. Muentzer was especially resentful that as one of the Elect he should have been dishonored by Luther with the name of Satan. If Muentzer had restricted the expression of his resentment and hostility to namecalling, an art in which he was far more adept than that of guerilla warfare, he might have enjoyed a longer life. But he chose instead (or was driven by an uncontrollable urge) to put into effect his teaching about the God-given right of the Elect to rule the world. He found his opportunity in the spring of 1525 when from a base in the unruly city of Muehlhausen he led a large group of disgruntled peasants and miners on marauding expeditions through Thuringia. In mid-May, near Frankenhausen, an enthusiastic army of peasants with very little fire power was surrounded by the mercenary soldiers engaged by some of the German princes and thousands of the rebels were put to the sword. Muentzer and other leaders were captured and promptly beheaded.

About a month before this date Luther had traveled to Eisleben with some of his Wittenberg associates for the dedication of a school. During the last ten days of April he delivered sermons in various Thuringian towns in an effort to calm the disturbance. He witnessed some of the destruction wrought by the marauding bands of peasants and at length became so frightened that he gave up and headed back for Wittenberg. En route at Seeburg, a hamlet near Eisleben, where he apparently stopped for the night of May 4-5, he wrote a most interesting letter to his relative John Ruehel in Eisleben. He had just learned of the death (or imminent death) of his protector, Frederick the Wise, which occurred May 5 after a lingering illness. This was not a blow to Martin because Frederick's successor, Duke John, unlike his older brother, was an enthusiastic supporter of the 'gospel.' Much of the letter is devoted to the current civil strife, but in the final third Luther introduces some personal touches:

> The devil wants to kill me, for he is angry that thus far he has failed to accomplish anything by either deceit or force. He thinks if I were out of his way he could pursue his own aims and turn the whole world topsy-turvy. I almost can believe I am the reason the devil can go on like this in the world so God can punish it. Well, if I get home . . . . I will await my new masters, the murderers and robbers, who tell me they wish harm to no one . . . . But before I will approve and justify what they do, I will lose my head a hundred times . . . . If I can do so before I die, I will take my Katie to wife when I hear they have gone away. I hope they won't take away my spirits and peace of mind.[28]

This letter indicates Luther is greatly perturbed — not surprisingly — after receiving what was perhaps the greatest shock of his lifetime. Apart from the spectacle of widespread violence with no end in sight (the date is ten days before the sanguinary rout of the peasants referred to above) Luther is aroused because there is talk of his writing and preaching being responsible for the tumult and destruction. We quote below some passages from his writings that show how disturbed he was at this period. Yet it is in the midst of this tragic hour for Germany that he is planning to get married. He reached home the evening of May 6 and proceeded to publish a brief but violent pamphlet called "Against the Robbing and Murdering Hordes of Peasants." Its theme is that since the peasants are revolting against God as well as their fellow men, it is the duty of the civil rulers to destroy them without mercy, for they are like mad dogs. "These are such wonderful times a prince can merit heaven with bloodshed better than others with prayer." After the defeat and slaughter of peasants at Frankenhausen the killing continued for some weeks; it has been estimated that a hundred thousand were slain. Luther was now widely charged with responsibility for the mass killings and this provoked him into writing another pamphlet "On the Harsh Book against the Peasants," probably soon after his wedding feast on June 27 (which followed the hasty wedding ceremony by a fortnight). This pamphlet, like much of Luther's writing, is an attempt to justify his conduct of the present moment. In attacking the excuse offered by many of unhappy peasants that they were forced to join the rebels, he demonstrates his state of confusion: "Who ever heard a man can be forced to do good or evil? Who can force a man's will? That [statement] won't stand up."[29] After this unconscionable repudiation of his basic position on the enslaved will, he proceeds on the next page to reverse himself:

> Where is there a sin the devil, the flesh and the world don't drive and as it were force us into? . . . . Who is master of his heart? Who can withstand the devil and the flesh? We are unable to resist even the smallest sin . . . . We are prisoners of the devil, as our prince and god, and must do what he wishes . . . . But should that go unpunished and be called right? Not at all.

It is not to be wondered at that Luther's audience could not grasp his teaching. In the earlier pamphlet he had urged the princes to merit heaven by slaughtering the peasants. This shameless repudiation of the *sola fide* having been pointed out to him, he replied to his critics in an equally shameless rejoinder:

> How men spy on me! . . . . I hope they will let me use the words and expressions of everyday speech and of the Scriptures . . . . But it is still true that works count for nothing in God's sight; faith alone matters.[30]

Seldom has Luther so heedlessly juxtaposed his assertions and self-contradictions. In the earlier pamphlet he had addressed himself to all the princes, whether 'Christians' or not. Those who do not 'tolerate the Gospel' are right and praiseworthy to smite the peasants at once without waiting for prior legal proceedings. The 'Christians, who tolerate the Gospel' should first consult God, pray for help, and offer peace to the peasants. When the offer is rejected, let these princes join their non-Christian peers in wielding the sword. In his "On the Harsh Book" Luther resorts to the denial mechanism here likewise. Readers of his earlier book can see "I was instructing only pious Christian rulers."[31]

A consideration of these matters makes clear the serious impact of the Peasants Revolt on Luther's psychic state and subsequent life. The guilt feeling which is reflected in the incoherent attempt at self-justification clung to him for many years. In 1533, for example, as we shall see later on, it inspired a remarkable instance of projection in a further attempt at ridding himself of his guilt. Despite his bold words, he feared the peasants had become his mortal enemies and thenceforth would not risk going far outside the walls of Wittenberg without a bodyguard. This experience seems to have contributed significantly to the formation of his persecutory delusions. To those above a certain level of education who took the trouble to read his writings, he appeared to be an unconscionable liar who would say anything to promote his cause. This loss of face among contemporary intellectuals was promoted by the publication later in the year of his "Enslaved Will" in answer to a critique by Erasmus.

v. Encounters with Zwingli and the Anabaptists

There are obvious parallels between the German Luther and the Swiss Zwingli, each of whom led a revolt against the Church in his own country, developing an effective propaganda campaign in pulpit and in print and acting through governmental organization to solidify his conquests. Their doctrinal and disciplinary innovations have much in common, allowing for the fact that each read his own personal meanings into such key terms as faith and grace. Finally, each hoped to extend the influence of his teaching beyond his native land; for a time Zwingli thought Italy, Spain, France and Germany would fall into line behind him.

But in character the two men were radically different. Zwingli had been educated for the priesthood by an uncle who was himself a clergyman, and in taking holy orders and accepting a benefice as a means of gaining a livelihood rather than from religious motives, he exemplified one of the gravest and most widespread abuses in the late medieval Church. The fact that during his first parish assignment he carried on an affair with the local barber's daughter, acknowledging that the child she bore might be his or another man's, is only one of the rather obvious indications he lacked an authentic religious life. In late 1518 he transferred from a small town parish to an assignment at the cathedral in Zurich, the leading Swiss city, where he found an opportunity to satisfy his ambition to rise to a position of power and influence. On this occasion he answered a question about his promiscuous behavior (which he had tried to keep secret) with the statement that at least he had always been careful not to deflower a virgin, commit adultery with a married woman or ravish a nun.

Zwingli was the only one of the revolutionary leaders dealt with in this chapter who could qualify as a normal human being. In fact he could appropriately be called *un homme moyen sensuel.* His role as a churchman and his occupation with theology were historical accidents. In our time such a man would most likely start his career in the business world and, since his talents were mainly in the area of politics, he would eventually rise to the office of senator or governor. At the time he moved up the organization ladder to Zurich, the perennial question of church reform was receiving fresh emphasis, partly from the writings of Erasmus, who had long been admired by Zwingli, and more recently by the activities of Luther. As this was a

most promising field of operation for an ambitious young churchman — Zwingli now 35 was the same age as Luther — he decided to
go in for reform. At that moment there appeared to be no divergence
between the direction of reform advocated by Erasmus and that by
Luther.

In his first few years at Zurich Zwingli devoted his efforts to con-
solidating his position with the city council because that is where
political leverage could be best exerted on the local churches. In
1520 he renounced the papal pension he had received for a number
of years. In further witness of his patriotism he worked to end the
practice of Swiss soldiers hiring their services abroad as mercenaries.
It is not known how early Zwingli elected to follow the Lutherian
pattern of schism rather than the Erasmian objective of reform within the Church. Zwingli published nothing that would show his hand
until 1522, when during a local controversy concerning laws on fasting he declared these laws not in harmony with Scripture. Also this
year he privately married a well-to-do widow, keeping the fact secret
for the next two years.

Following a calculated plan, in 1523 he arranged public disputations under the auspices of the city council in which much of the
Wittenberg program was defended and officially adopted by the
council. During the next two years innovations similar to those of
Saxony were carried out in Zurich — abolition of the mass, the sacraments of penance and extreme unction, abrogation of various ecclesiastical laws such as on clerical celibacy, expropriation of Church
property and the destruction of paintings, images and sacred vessels.
Luther's *sola scriptura* was promulgated as the basic theoretical
principle of the new state church of Zurich with Zwingli as the sole
authoritative interpreter. A program of harsh repression was carried
out against citizens who chose to read Scripture their own way, their
punishment being imprisonment, exile or death. Within a few years
this system spread to other Swiss cities but as in neighboring Germany a number of territories (cantons) remained attached to the
ancient church.

Our primary interest in Zwingli in this study concerns his treatment of the Eucharist, because it was on this subject that he provoked Luther into action. Toward the end of 1524, some months
before the celebration of mass in Zurich churches was finally stopped,
Zwingli leaked the following statement to the press by inserting it
in a letter that was published shortly afterward. "I do not believe
that anyone ever believed he ate Christ bodily and substantially in
the sacrament."[32] This was Zwingli's calculated announcement of
his own disbelief in the Real Presence, which thereby became official
Zurich doctrine. The implication of this statement is that Zwingli
never did have a belief in the Real Presence even though he had

accepted ordination as a priest and been celebrating mass since the age of 21.

At the time Zwingli issued the statement Luther was composing his long attack on Carlstadt ("Against the Heavenly Prophets") for promulgating essentially the same position as Zwingli. It is of interest that Luther's hearty approval of the changes in religious practice Zwingli introduced into Switzerland was more than outweighed by his disapproval of Zwingli's doctrine on the Eucharist. Instead of joining in their campaign against the papacy, the two men became enemies. After a preliminary skirmish in 1526, Luther wheeled up the heavy artillery at the beginning of the next year. In one of his longest tracts since leaving the Wartburg entitled "That the Words of Christ 'This is My Body' Still Stand Firm Against the Enthusiasts," he belabored Zwingli and Oecolampadius, his chief supporter. One notes Luther's usual technique in the choice of title, omitting the names of his targets and incorrectly terming them *Schwaermer,* a term which may be rendered either as 'fanatics' or 'enthusiasts.' This tract elicited a rebuttal from Zurich to which Luther replied the following year (1528) with the much longer "Confession Concerning Christ's Supper."

In the earlier of these two tracts Luther gives three reasons for writing: to present the truth about the Eucharist, to win back some of Zwingli's converts or strengthen the weak, and by giving testimony of the true, i.e., Lutherian teaching to clear himself from complicity with Zwingli in the destruction of souls. We hear at this point the familiar "I am innocent." Likewise in the second document, the "Confession," he gives much the same explanation. From this it would appear his anxiety had been aroused by the thought that his own attack on the teaching and practice of the Church had fathered the rapidly spreading disbelief in the Real Presence.

Much of the substance of these tracts may be regarded as a *reductio ad absurdum* of the *sola scriptura* position. Luther and his opponents exhibit the same radical misunderstanding of the role of the N. T. writings in the early Church. One of the more revealing instances of this misconception is found in Luther's statement that without the texts on institution in Luke (22:19) and liturgical practice in Paul (1 Cor 11) "we would not have had this sacrament." Other self-disclosures of interest here are Luther's disclaimer of having an expert knowledge of Greek and that the purpose of exegesis is to provide "a good sure foundation for my conscience."

It was pointed out earlier that the source of Luther's rejection of the ancient teaching that in the Eucharist the bread is transformed into the body of Christ is to be found in his psychic disorder. His pathological fear of the Eucharist was bound up with his belief in the Real Presence; with his susceptibility to sudden attacks of anxiety, the Eucharist could be like a Damoclean sword threatening him with annihilation. Yet despite his fear, he regarded reception of the Eucharist as a useful consolation because it signified to him that his sins were forgiven. A paragraph in the "Confession" provides unmistakable confirmation of this anlysis. In discussing the parallel question of the relation between the wine and the blood of Christ, Luther asserts he doesn't care what interpretation is made so long as the Real Presence is preserved. "Rather than have mere wine with the fanatics, I will have *blood alone* with the Pope."[33]

While this is grossly inconsistent as a theological statement with his position on the body of Christ, it is psychologically understandable. For the contents of the chalice are consumed by the celebrant at mass; the precious blood is not preserved in the tabernacle like the sacred host to serve as a continual threat to him. That Luther believed the wine is really transformed into Christ's blood is attested by an incident in the Wittenberg church in 1541. A woman communicant accidentally upset the chalice, its contents spilling on her lined jacket, her coat and the communion chair (*Stuhl*). Luther rushed over, with Bugenhagen, and they reverently licked up the spilled contents as well as possible. "Luther was so upset his eyes filled with tears." After the service he cut away the lining of the jacket which could not be licked clean and burned it; also he had the chair back planed and the shavings burned (WBr 10, 337). These precautions would be superfluous if after the service the spilled matter reverted to mere wine, as he at times affirmed that it did (cf. WBr 10, 348). When one compares the scores of pages of impassioned argument defending his purely arbitrary interpretation of the words 'This is my body' with his casual dismissal of the same argument applied to 'This is my blood,' there can be no question of what constitutes the driving force of Luther's pronouncements on matters of religion.

The year following this final repudiation of Zwingli, Luther was persuaded to attend a parley in far off Marburg sponsored by Philip of Hesse for the purpose of promoting a military alliance between the Germans and the Swiss cantons that had joined Zwingli. Among the political heads of the new territorial churches that were being established in Germany in the 1520s Philip was the most active and ambitious. Aware that the bitterness between Luther and Zwingli arising from their doctrinal differences might frustrate his plan, Philip sought to dispel this through a conference that would produce a harmonious doctrinal statement. Philip's effort was wasted. Although differences were patched over on other topics, on the subject of the Eucharist the two men were irreconcilable. At the close of the Marburg meeting Luther refused even to shake hands with Zwingli. From this episode it is apparent that the reputation Luther had acquired from his stance in the Peasants Revolt as a 'toady of princes' was quite inaccurate. He could be extremely obsequious in his approach to any of the princes when he saw a chance of conversion to his gospel. But he "lost his humility" if the prince rejected his doctrines. Luther, however, did remain on good terms with Philip even though the refusal to come to terms with Zwingli doomed the proposed military alliance.

Two years later (1531) Zwingli was permanently removed as an antagonist by his death on the battlefield in a Swiss civil war. Luther did not fail to cite the appropriate Scripture text about what happens to those who take the sword. He interpreted his own survival and the spread of the territorial churches in Germany in contrast with the abrupt elimination of Muentzer and Zwingli as proof of divine favor for his cause. He could hardly be expected to make the opposite interpretation that in this life it is likely to be the wicked who prosper while the just man suffers. Nor could he admit that his gospel prospered primarily because it was acceptable to his sovereign, the Elector of Saxony, without whose protection Luther would have been forced into exile like Carlstadt and could hardly have enjoyed a secure bastion from which to launch his propaganda.

Since after the death of Zwingli Luther gradually lapsed into comparative silence on the Eucharistic controversy which had made them irreconcilable enemies, it is appropriate to ask why he remained so adamant. As early as 1520 he had announced in "On Christian Liberty" (or "The Freedom of the Christian") that the word of God alone is necessary for salvation. As if to underline his view that the Eucharist is not necessary, he repeatedly denied there is any eucharistic reference in the Johannine account (6:52-61) of Jesus telling his followers they must eat his flesh and drink his blood to possess eternal life (a maneuvre indispensable for saving the *sola fide*). Yet rather than compromise his own innovative position on this non-essential rite, he appeared bent on blocking any attempt to unify the Germans and Swiss who had separated from Rome at his bidding by grossly insulting the leading spirits among them who differed with him on it. The explanation of this paradoxical behavior is to be sought in the precariousness of his defensive array that made any dissent from his views on defensive matters intolerable. If the dissenters were associates, no matter what their importance to him earlier they must depart; *aus mit ihm* was the inescapable rule. This was the story for Adrian, the professor of Hebrew, in 1520, for Carlstadt in the mid 1520s, for Agricola in the 1530s; later we shall cite Melanchthon's private complaint on Luther's despotic nature. Dissenters at a distance were covered with abuse from the pulpit and in print. By these measures Luther was able to ward off their threat to his defenses. While the Eucharist was not essential for salvation — which required faith alone — it was, as noted above, integral to his defenses. A limited Real Presence in the bread or an unlimited one in the wine could give him the next best thing to salvation, namely, a 'comfortable certainty' of it.

The dissident religious groups that flourished in Luther's day are considered here only insofar as his interaction with them throws light on his character. For our purposes the account begins with the Zwickau prophets whose visit to Wittenberg at the end of 1521 helped speed his homecoming from the Wartburg. He dubbed these men 'fanatics' and this became a favorite appellation applied indiscriminately to almost any of the heterodox who disagreed with him. *Widertaufer* or 'Anabaptist' was a widely used term for groups whose members rejected infant baptism but actually held a number of other distinctive beliefs.

Luther, essentially an academic type who enjoyed exchanging verbal brickbats with academic opponents, was rather at a loss to cope with the Anabaptists. Not only were the rank and file from the lower orders of society and thus hardly remarkable for literacy, but on the whole the preachers who converted them were less inclined to publish than to talk. During the 1520s Luther issued only one tract specifically against them, "On Rebaptism" (early 1528). Four years later he attacked the Anabaptist preachers in an open letter or tract called "Sneaks and Undercover Preachers." Also of interest is a sermon of this period on a text about 'false prophets' (Matt. 7:15).

The groups designated as Anabaptists are too heterogeneous in motivation and doctrine to permit much useful generalization. For example, some of them, under Muentzer's influence, exhibited his seditious leanings. Others, in contrast, advocated a policy of pacifism or non-resistance. The gospel according to Luther, so far from satisfying the religious needs of a large fraction of his contemporaries, instead diverted attempts to meet these needs into new channels. The practice of rebaptizing adults on the ground that only adults can have the kind of faith required for baptism, which gave the Anabaptist movement its name, is an obvious consequence of the *sola fide.* It was this practice Luther examined in the early 1528 tract cited above. Since the sacrament of baptism lay outside the area of his disturbance, his reaction was basically that of the pre-1520 Luther. He defended the position that the validity and justification of infant baptism derive from the fact that the mode of administering the sacrament was handed on by the Apostles to later generations. This tradition guarantees the integrity of the practice of baptizing infants.

In line with this thoroughly orthodox position the *sola fide* is ignored. The tract "On Rebaptism" is of interest as demonstrating a fundamental trait of Luther's: that when he is involved with a theological topic unrelated to the sources of anxiety the *sola fide,* devised to cope with anxiety, remains as it were disengaged. Furthermore, the *sola scriptura* position is in this tract not merely ignored but grossly contradicted. So far from being concerned about the lack of a 'clear text' justifying infant baptism, Luther here assumed what might be called an anti-*sola scriptura* posture. A doctrine or practice supported by tradition must be accepted by the faithful unless there is a clear text *against* it. So engrossed in this line of argument does Luther become that he almost finds himself back in the papacy. For years he has not had so many kind words for it. He can even call the papacy a "work of God" but not a "work of Grace" and that for just one reason: "Scripture [no text cited] is against it." (It must be recognized that at the moment of composing the tract there is no overt threat to Luther from the papacy and he is just recovering from the long depression of 1527, characterized by a marked diminution of hostility.) At this juncture with both of his sacraments under attack from the other innovators, Luther will not reject support from Rome though he will presently be twigged by some of them on this account.

The Anabaptists' position on baptism was in fact only subsidiary to their more central object of trying to live according to their conception of the way of life of the early Christians. Not being historical scholars, the Anabaptists could not be expected to possess a very accurate notion of conditions in that remote age. But they could hardly be faulted for holding that the Christian way of life demanded renunciation of self and some share in the sufferings of Jesus Christ. It was this outlook that brought them into conflict with the Lutherian gospel. For their part, they judged the Lutherian community according to the scriptural rule of "by their fruits you shall know them." Their scrutiny revealed a community whose moral behavior suggested no familiarity with the teachings of the N. T.

Luther did not deny the accuracy of this criticism but rather the right of these interlopers to make it. In his pulpit series on the 'Sermon on the Mount' (referred to earlier) he finally teed off on the Anabaptists, utilizing the text "Beware of false prophets." In his enemies list of February 1527 he had not even mentioned them by name. A year later in the tract "On Rebaptism" he had expressed relief that the Elector's territory was free of Anabaptists and confined his rather mild comments on them to the relation of faith to baptism. But now (early 1532) they have infiltrated and are trying to abolish true doctrine. There has also been an inner change in Luther since 1527: the paranoid symptoms are now more strikingly in evidence. Here is an illustration of paranoid suspicion from his sermon:

> I must not put up with or yield anything but be on guard and watchful even with my own brother . . . trusting no man who is

with me now, for today he can be with me and perhaps tomorrow preach against me.[34]

As reported elsewhere in this study, by the second half of the decade of the 1520s the better informed observers who had at first welcomed Luther as one who could help bring about a renewal of religious life were disenchanted with him. They came to regard him as a prophet of discord rather than renewal, with an essentially negative message. His complaints about the Anabaptists in this sermon on 'false prophets' indicate that a comparable attack on his doctrine had been made by these people from the opposite end of the social scale. Among them were men and women making a serious attempt to live according to the precepts of the Gospels. Their harsh experience of life made them reject the complacency of the *sola fide* with its promise that by asserting their faith they would automatically and effortlessly acquire the holiness of the Lord.

Faced with this challenge from within and the loss of earlier converts to the *sola fide* program, what does Luther do? He identifies the Anabaptists with the monks he has been attacking for the past decade even though they do not shut themselves up in convents but stick to their jobs as 'harvesters' or 'at charcoal kilns.' For some years he has been saying that such activity is truly a 'good work' in God's sight. But the Anabaptist workingmen are condemned as 'work-righteous.' In his regressed state, Luther can no longer invent new epithets to describe this new breed, but falls back on the well-worn vocabulary of 1520. As for the call of Jesus to "him who would come after me, let him sell all he has, etc.", Luther in effect denies there are any such words in the New Testament.

One of the novelties of the Anabaptist creed was that its adherents were advised to shun contact with civil government. In an age when churches were intimately linked with civil authorities and often dominated by them, this alone was enough to arouse suspicion. It helps account for the Anabaptist preachers being hunted down and either imprisoned or executed if they refused to recant. To carry out their mission they were forced to operate in a clandestine fashion. It was for such tactics that Luther excoriated them in the 1532 tract "Sneaks and Undercover [literally, "in a Corner"] Preachers", whose principal theme is the legalistic argument that these preachers lack an official 'call.' For this reason, even though they were to teach nothing but 'pure doctrine,' they must be avoided by the faithful and reported to the authorities. In this tract Luther underlines the inferior status of the layman as compared with the official preacher and is silent about the 'priesthood of the believer.' The layman must keep quiet even if false doctrine is preached to him (by the Lutherian preacher). This champion of evangelical liberty advocated punishing

Anabaptists by exile or imprisonment, but was opposed to the death penalty. However, at length he succumbed to the pressure of his associates and signed a document emanating from the official theological bureau of Wittenberg prescribing death for conviction of the crime of Anabaptist heresy.

Chapter 6

Luther's Problems
With Sex And Depression

i. Second thoughts on celibacy

The sexual life of Martin Luther is not a subject his biographers have pursued with enthusiasm. Indeed it is one of several topics of Luther lore passed over with scarcely a mention. A few have been so bold as to maintain — without evidence — that he remained perfectly continent until the night of June 13, 1525, when at the age of 41 he first went to bed with Catherine von Bora. Such a view happens to be consistent with the conclusions of this study, as will appear presently, despite the fact that Martin had been asserting for the past several years with all the eloquence at his command that continence was impossible for man. But let us hear some of the magnificent rhetoric with which he seeks to establish his copulative imperative, the following passage being from a letter of March 27, 1525. It is written to Wolfgang Reissenbusch, a wavering clergyman, with the aim of convincing him of the obligation of all men to copulate and shows that Wilhelm Reich, the famous sexologist of the twentieth century, might well have taken lessons from Martin on his favorite subject. Reich being a man of the twentieth century did not require the divine sanction that is so heavily stressed by his sixteenth century forerunner, but the overall message is much the same: "Nothing is better than to comply with our sense as early and as fully as possible."

This is the word of God through whose power seed is produced in man's body and the burning natural longing for a woman is created and preserved. It may not be prevented by either vows or laws, for it is God's word and work. Whoever would be alone can put away the name of 'man' and prove he is an angel or spirit. For God does not bestow this state on man in any fashion . . .

Therefore it is to be taken as true that one who wants to be alone is striving for an impossibility because he harms himself and

174

opposes God's word and the nature that by his word is created, preserved and empowered to act. Those who struggle in this way will end in fornication and all impurity of the flesh in which at last they will drown and be forced into despair.[1]

Martin, it will be recalled, entered the Augustinian monastery at Erfurt at the age of 21 and took the vow of chastity after a year's novitiate. There is no evidence he experienced intense sexual craving at that more ardent age. Several years afterward he persuaded one of his favorite teachers at the University of Erfurt to follow him into the same chapter house. As late as 1518 he is asserting the best way to lead a Christian life is in the monastery. It is in 1519 that we first begin to hear, faintly, of sexual difficulties, but by 1521 the voice has grown loud and the theme developed in the letter of March 1525 is established. Yet Martin does not take a woman until June of 1525. The student of Luther may well ask what is responsible for the change in 1519? And once having decided every man must have a woman, why does he wait four years to consummate his desire and then celebrate the joyful occasion at a time when Germany is disrupted by a bloody civil war in which he was more than a little involved? We shall see that the second query has a simpler answer than the first.

To appreciate how radical was the change in Luther in the period 1519-21, consider what he was saying in 1515 at age 31:

Since the glory of the body is in chastity and continence, or at least in a proper use . . . our body is intended either for honorable marriage or for a more honorable chastity.[2]

Here be it noted he states traditional ecclesiastical doctrine, which from 1520 onward he was to misrepresent grossly on countless occasions. Another passage from the same work (Lectures on Romans) makes a recommendation at the opposite pole from that given to Reissenbusch:

No victory over fleshly desire is preferable to flight and turning from it in devout prayer. For the flesh soon grows lukewarm and cools off when opposed by fervency of spirit.[3]

In 1519 there was printed a report of a sermon given by Luther on the married state. In it he is represented as saying:

It is well known that youthful flesh has no peace. I don't have it in me to contain myself. There is a book written about how one can do this, about how it is so impure and unclean to [desire] a woman. Ovid's *Remedio Amoris* has the same purpose but reading it excites one even more. For when the temptation comes and the flesh is kindled, you are already blinded, even if the woman is not pretty.[4]

Luther was so perturbed at this unauthorized version he prepared a new one without the self revelation. Whether he was misrepresented or not is of less interest than his shame in 1519 at what a year or two later he was publicizing himself.

According to commonly accepted interpretation of such texts as Matt. 19:12 — "Let him take it [renunciation of sex for the sake of the kingdom of God] who can" — dedicated celibacy is possible only with the help of divine grace. Luther professed this belief until about 1520, after which he said that such renunciation is possible for only a very tiny number, in other words is impossible for virtually all mankind. In view of his disorder some kind of sexual abnormality is not unexpected. For him the problem appears to have been heterosexual craving which was not directed at a specific woman; it became manifest by the time of his stay at the Wartburg in 1521, as indicated in the following anecdote from the Table Talk.[5]

One night the wife of the Electoral official in charge of the staff that Frederick maintained at the castle expressed a desire to sleep in Luther's bed. So he withdrew from his quarters, while the woman came in and spent the night alone there. We would recognize this story as fictitious even if we did not know that the official in question had no wife at the time. Luther, of course, recounted the story in later years as an actual experience. It may originally have been a dream but might also have been a daytime fantasy. From 1521 on fantasies, especially of a defensive type, appear in Luther's writings and they are common by 1530.

We next examine Luther's disclosure of his problem in the Wartburg correspondence. In a letter to Melanchthon in early July of 1521 he describes what appears to be the kind of mild depression to which he was subject prior to 1527:

> For the past eight days I have written nothing and neither prayed nor studied, partly from temptations of the flesh, partly because I am beset by other troubles.[6]

Earlier in the letter he had said:

> I sit here idle, without feeling and callous, Oh woe is me! I pray seldom and do not sigh for the church of God. I burn in the great fires of my uncontrollable flesh. In short, I who should be fervent in the spirit am fervent in the flesh, in lust, sluggishness, idleness and drowsiness, and because you don't pray for me, I wonder whether God has turned away from me.

During the summer of 1521, as can be seen especially in the letters to Melanchthon, Martin was preparing himself psychologically for the all-out attack on clerical celibacy which he completed in November under the title "Judgment of Monastic Vows." What offends him mainly about the monastic life he had been leading for the past 15 years is the vow of celibacy, which he refers to in a letter dated November 1 to Nicholas Gerbel, a lawyer friend in Strasbourg, as "this impure celibacy, which must be condemned for causing either a constant sexual craving or filthy pollutions [emissions] . . . . I think marriage must be a paradise."[7]

A letter to Spalatin dated November 11 announces the tract on vows as forthcoming. (This letter opens with an outburst of psychotic hostility against Spalatin and the Elector because they suppressed a violent attack on the Archbishop of Mainz Luther had sent them for publication.) Toward the end of this letter Luther writes:

> I am determined to attack monastic vows and liberate youths from this hellish celibacy with its most filthy and damnable sexual craving and pollutions. I write partly because I have suffered these things; partly because I am angry. I hope you agree with me. There is not just one devil with me, or rather against me; I am alone, but sometimes I am not alone.[8]

In the letter to Gerbel previously quoted Luther had written:

> I believe that a thousand devils are after me in this idle wilderness. It is so much easier to fight against devils in the flesh, that is, against men, than against spiritual wickedness in celestial regions, and I often fall.

From these revelations of his psychic state at the Wartburg, one can better appreciate why his associates, as mentioned in an earlier chapter, persuaded him to begin translating the New Testament.

The "Judgment of Monastic Vows" belongs among the last few Latin writings of Luther's career even though he lived on for a quarter-century after composing it. Indeed the only other considerable work in Latin he produced after this was the "Enslaved Will" of 1525. He had begun the process of cutting himself off from the Christian past by attacking sacramental teaching and practice a year earlier with the "Babylonian Captivity." The "Judgment" may be said to complete this process. For in this tract he is not opposing late medieval abuses in monastic life but rather attacking the monastic ideal itself, which is a development not of the medieval but of the early Christian centuries.

What may be called the theoretical foundation of the monastic ideal (discussed above in Ch. 1) goes back at least to Origen in the first half of the third century, among the first Christians to practice it being the anchorites who left the cities of Egypt for the desert. Monastic life began to flourish after the peace of Constantine made it possible for settled communities of men and women to live undisturbed by the intermittent persecutions formerly carried on by Roman emperors. Hence during the fourth century, beginning within

a generation or so after Constantine, monastic communities are promoted or encouraged by most of the leading churchmen: Athanasius,
Basil, Ambrose, Jerome, Augustine, to mention only the most illustrious names. It is a matter of no small interest in the history of the
Christian religion that a Germany saturated with Lutherian propaganda was as inhospitable to the monastic ideal as was the pagan
Roman empire.

Augustine, for example, discovered monastic life by observing
communities Ambrose had established in and near Milan, and from
the time of his conversion at the age of 32 embraced this mode of
life as the most suitable for a Christian. When he returned to his native Africa, he formed a monastic type of community with other laymen, and was reluctant to accept the bishopric of the city of Hippo
because this step required him to give up monastic life. But even as
bishop he followed the monastic pattern as far as the duties of the
state permitted, relinquishing all his property and requiring the
priests of his diocese to do the same and live together in a monastic-
like regime. Writers who allege some sort of spiritual kinship between
Luther and Augustine do not seem to consider how Augustine would
have looked upon this ex-Augustinian. As the author merely of this
one tract against the monastic life, apart from many other comparable writings, Luther would have been regarded by Augustine with
profound disgust.

Luther's intention in writing this work, by which he hoped to
destroy the monastic institution, was to persuade himself that
monastic vows are not binding and that he is free to take a wife without arousing anxiety over his salvation. In this endeavor can be seen
one of the many reversals of his theological views dictated by
changes in his psychic condition. He had written as recently as three
years earlier (in his tract on the Decalogue) the following condemnation of what he was now urging men and women to do:

> For the religious, the breaking of vows is the most serious
> sacrilege, for after voluntarily consecrating themselves to the Lord
> they withdraw from him.[9]

And in the "Commentary on the First Twenty-two Psalms" Luther
mounts an attack — based on Scripture — against the well established
practice of releasing monks and priests from their vows of religion
by action of an ecclesiastical court:

> The prophet demands that vows made to men be kept as neces-
> sary for salvation. The obligation not to dissolve vows or promises
> offered to God is even more binding .... Yet despite many exam-
> ples [provided by Joshua, Ezekiel, etc.] this heretical opinion
> [about dissolving religious vows] prevails.[10]

In this attack of 1520 Luther abuses the Pope for dissolving religious vows; in the attack of 1521 he abuses the Pope for not dissolving them. We call attention to this situation not so much because it exhibits one of Luther's most conspicuous traits as because it helps establish 1520 as the year of his major psychic change.

The arguments of the "Judgment" are arranged in five sections of about equal length showing why vows are opposed to (1) the word of God, (2) faith, (3) evangelical liberty, (4) divine precepts and (5) reason. Then follows a conclusion about twice the length of one of these sections in which Luther shows that since a religious is sometimes released from the vows of poverty and obedience he should enjoy the same freedom with respect to the vow of chastity. One may be surprised to see 'reason' included as opposed to vows since Luther's favorite epithet for human reason is 'Devil's whore.' But when he once gets started on a polemical attack, he is bound by no scruples and any notion of consistency is simply irrelevant. To observe one of the most accomplished masters of sophistry, double talk and slanderous invective in Western literature operating in the area of his highest skill, one should read the "Judgment" (there are translations into English, German and French). But to savor this exhibition to the fullest extent one must be fairly knowledgeable not only about monastic rules and practices but also about Luther's own positions expressed in earlier writings. The unwary reader should be warned not to take seriously anything Luther says about monastic orders, for the tract abounds in examples of the denial mechanism; if the author were not known to exhibit psychotic symptoms, he would have to be put down as a colossal liar. The typical ex-monk of Luther's day, having had only a shallow commitment if any to the monastic ideal, simply walked out of his monastery and disported himself in the frivolous manner described by Erasmus (see Ch. 4). For Luther, on the other hand, the display of pathological hostility in the "Judgment" may be taken as a measure of the depth of his former dedication to the monastic profession.

An indication of how Luther's disturbance affected his judgment can be seen in his arbitrary interpretation of a Pauline text:

> Some will heed deceitful spirits and things taught by demons through plausible liars . . . who forbid marriage and require abstinence from certain foods. (1 Tim 4)

Luther seized upon the phrase "forbid marriage" as a scriptural condemnation of clerical celibacy, saying the "Pope teaches doctrines of demons."[11] His discussion of this passage in the "Judgment" shows his awareness that responsible exegetes view it as referring to Manichean or dualistic teachings on matter as inherently evil. But henceforth he repeats this defensive interpretation on innumerable occasions.

Luther's return to life in society in March 1522 after his seclusion
in the Wartburg did not provide relief from his sexual craving. A
pamphlet he wrote the following July — "Against the So-called
Spiritual Estate of the Pope and Bishops" — is illustrated with phallic
imagery he avoids in his other published writings and contains one
of his most explicit references to his emissions. Luther was motivated
to write this tract because of the punitive action taken by some of
the German bishops against clergy under their jurisdiction who had
violated the imperial law forbidding clerical marriage. His inner conflict over the problem of law and order helps account for the hostility
displayed here. For Luther at this period was in a most frustrating
position. With respect to two of the three jurisdictions to which he
owed allegiance: the empire, Electoral Saxony and the Church, he
was officially an outlaw. For a man with such ingrained loyalty to
public authority — except where it conflicted with his personal
interests — this was an intolerable situation. To accommodate himself to it he must devote the first several pages of the pamphlet to
proving by abundant reference to Scripture that he is commanded by
God to deliver this violent attack against the bishops (the Pope is
named in the title mainly for rhetorical purposes). Elsewhere in his
writings and sermons Luther is very strong on the duty of the citizen
to obey his government because Scripture commands him to do so.
That he is now acting in flat violation of one of his most cherished
positions helps explain his agitated tone as well as the otherwise
irrelevant claim at the beginning that the voice of Luther is the voice
of God.

Another source of his frustration during this period of the early
1520s was the ambiguous position he occupied with regard to his
taking a wife. He has uncompromisingly asserted that all men who remain single must be either fornicators or "commit the secret sin
which St. Paul calls uncleanness and effeminacy" — both inexpressibly
offensive to God.[12] Yet Luther remains single, and for an inglorious
reason. His territorial prince and protector, the Elector Frederick, is
very much opposed to violation of the imperial law against clerical
marriage and Luther is afraid to arouse his ire by such an overt act
of disobedience. As we shall see presently, Spalatin, Luther's pipe-
line to the territorial government, himself remains single until six
months after Frederick is dead and buried, while the more impetuous
Luther waits barely a month. In the meantime he is in the position of
the military leader who calls out: "Go forward bravely, men, and
attack the enemy, while I remain back here where I am safe from
danger." Or as Luther puts it in the tract, after proving the prohi-
bition against the marriage of priests is a command of Satan, the
priests 'should have a good conscience' about their marriage. "A man
who doesn't want a wife should take one anyhow so that he can

injure and defy the devil and his teaching."[13]

Shifting his attention from priests to nuns, Luther claims to be most knowledgeable about the fair sex. He admits: "In my time I heard no nun's confession. But I can nevertheless understand from the Scriptures [no citation provided] how it is with them, and you know I am not lying. A maiden, unless she enjoys great and extraordinary graces, can no more get along without a man than she can get along without eating, drinking, sleeping and other natural needs. . . . The nuns in the cloisters don't want to live chastely and not have men."[14] This passage, apart from being an interesting example of projection, reveals how little Luther needs to depend on direct sources of information for what he claims to know; whatever he wants to impress upon his audience is true because 'the Bible tells me so.'

The most specifically phallic imagery in the tract is employed in the attack on the bishops' reputations. Luther works his way into this material by identifying the Moabite idol Baal-Peor (from Numbers 25) with the Greek god Priapus. He then makes a bogus apology for introducing such an unseemly character, which he is compelled to do from the highest of motives:

> I would much rather remain silent about him on account of my chaste readers. But I am forced by St. Peter's words to honor our clerical big-shots [the bishops] by displaying their virtues. . . . Priapus was a statue of a naked youth with uncovered genitals executed in the crudest, most shameful and indecent fashion like a god of unchastity. [Luther may here be recalling Michelangelo's *David*, which was on location outside the Palazzo Vecchio when he stopped off in Florence in 1510 on the Rome journey. The references in the 1522 tract suggest that this masterpiece of Renaissance art was shocking to the young monk from provincial Saxony.] . . . The most honorable lady in the city had to place a garland on the abomination and indecency of this statue . . . and then all the brides had to place themselves on this shameful indecency.
>
> Baal signifies a man who attaches himself to a woman and includes the meaning of 'lying with' and 'male activity.' . . . Baal-peor is a man who keeps his mouth open, what we call in German a 'gaping idler' (*Maulaffe*). Such a one has nothing masculine about him except that he can lie with a woman . . . . What else can a statue of a naked, shameless youth stand for than a gaping idler and an indecent lady's man? . . . . And though our clerical big-shots do all this in a spiritual way, as we are about to hear, they are of such high station they also do it bodily . . . . What else can they do but ride handsome horses and gorgeous girls?[15]

So Luther goes on for page after page of abuse of the higher
clergy, reveling in this pious duty of bespattering his targets with
erotic imagery. Toward the end of the tract he provides a biological
explanation of the emissions about which he is so conscious during
this period of his life:

> Nature carries on with her work; the flesh produces seed as God
> ordained and the blood vessels likewise perform as they are in-
> tended to do . . . . If I may speak coarsely, if it does not flow into
> the flesh, it will flow into the shirt.[16]

To round off this scientific exposition, Luther later provided the following note, recorded in the Table Talk (# 3921):

> If anyone feels himself a man, let him take a woman and not
> tempt God. This is why a maiden has her little paunch, to provide
> him a remedy by which pollutions and adulteries may be avoided.

Just how the adulteries could be committed in the absence of the
little paunch, Luther doesn't make clear, but he was never known to
be a rigorous thinker.

ii. Luther's wedding and some post-nuptial reflections

The disturbed political situation at the time of Luther's wedding
was referred to in the preceding chapter; here we review some of the
subsequent developments. The wedding ceremony was held in
Luther's domicile, the former Augustinian monastery, since the bride
had no home other than the residence where she had been employed
as a domestic. Witnesses included the two faithful retainers, Jonas
and Bugenhagen, likewise the well known painter Lucas Cranach.
Melanchthon was not invited since he thought it inappropriate for
Luther to take a wife. The affair was arranged in such haste that the
wedding feast was scheduled for two weeks later.

Soon after the ceremony, which occurred on Tuesday evening,
June 13, Luther began sending letters of invitation to the wedding
banquet. In some of the letters he offers an explanation of why he
married. One of the first letters, written on the Friday of that week
to his friend Spalatin, sounds less than cheerful:

> I have closed the mouths of those who defame me with Cath-
> erine Bora . . . . This marriage has made me so cheap and con-
> temptible that the angels laugh and all the demons cry out.[17]

For his friend Link, at one time prior of the Wittenberg monastery,
he has quite a different account: "The Lord has suddenly and marvelously joined me in marriage with Catherine Bora, the nun."[18]
To another intimate, the bachelor Amsdorf, there is a third
explanation:

The story is true that I suddenly took Catherine to wife, before the tongues that are always noisy about me could be heard. I hope to live a while yet and would not refuse my father's recent request for descendants. Also I would confirm by deed what I have taught, for I find so many faint-hearted in the great light of the gospel. Thus God has willed and caused me to act. For *I neither love nor burn for my wife, but esteem her.*[19]

The italicized sentence, written a week after the wedding night, appears to represent Luther's attitude toward Catherine without substantial change from then on apart from the fact that he discovered her to be useful to him in his struggle against anxiety. For this service he probably added a feeling of gratitude. Whether he appreciated her considerable accomplishments as a housekeeper is less certain. In a list of meritorious services a Christian may perform for others compiled in 1531 he includes "putting up with a cranky wife and an unmanageable family" and at times he felt her to be insubordinate. But their relations eventually turned out to be most amicable which, as anyone aware of what living with a psychotic can be like, gives immeasurable credit to Catherine. Indeed the marriage with Catherine may be described as perhaps the most fortunate decision of Luther's entire life, though since it appears to have been a purely impulsive action, it could not be accurately termed the most judicious.

The conflicting explanations Luther gave for his marriage to Catherine seem to have perplexed his biographers, who debate over what the actual motive might have been. From the material quoted in this chapter it is apparent that he took a wife to satisfy his craving for a sexual outlet more satisfying than emissions into his shirt. It has also been noted here that he did this as soon as possible after the obstacle represented by the Elector Frederick had been removed. And he took Catherine rather than another woman because there was no other woman available on such short notice. If Frederick had been obliging enough to die six months earlier, the chances are he would have asked Ave von Schonfeld (see below) instead of Catherine.

Melanchthon's opinion about Luther's motive confirms this interpretation. In a letter to a friend two days after the wedding he writes: "I think that he was compelled by nature to marry." The prevailing tone of Luther's remarks to his intimates in the period immediately following the wedding night is one of expectations disappointed. This conclusion is also supported by Melanchthon's words in the same letter:

When I see Luther to be in a state of sadness and disturbed about the change in his life, I try to console him as kindly and affectionately as I can. Nor do I venture to condemn this deed as an error or mistake.

Yet Melanchthon acknowledges that his correspondent might

> marvel that in this unhappy time when good and honest men are
> everywhere in great trouble he not only is unconcerned over their
> distress but appears not to worry at all about the evils which are
> taking place before our eyes, although in the meantime his reputa-
> tion is being diminished when there is the greatest need in Ger-
> many for his lofty spirit and worthiness.[20]

From Luther's rather unhappy reaction to his first days of wedded
life it may be inferred that his long awaited heterosexual experience
was something of a letdown as compared with the sexual fantasies on
which he had been feeding since his regression in 1520. Another
legitimate inference is that the disenchantment with sexual experience he now exhibited (compare the earlier "I think marriage is
paradise") demonstrates that this was indeed his first 'carnal
knowledge of woman.'

Luther's habit of uncouth jesting, which Melanchthon found so
hard to endure and hoped the marriage would put an end to, shows
up in another letter to Link the following month. At the conclusion
of the letter, which was written in Latin, Martin adds a punning
sentence in German, followed by some more Latin:

> Ich bin an Kethen gebunden und gefangen, und liege auf den
> Bore, scilicet mortuus munda. Salutat autem te tuamque mea
> Catena.[21]

> [I am bound and captured by Katie (chain) and lie on the Bora
> (bier) as though dead to the world. My Katie (chain) also greets
> you and your Katie (chain).]

In addition to Catherine von Bora, two other of the nine nuns
from Nimbschen that Luther had sheltered in the monastery during
the spring of 1523 remained in Wittenberg until 1525. He appears to
have taken a strong liking to one of these named Ave von Schonfeld. But she found a husband early in 1525, as he indicates in a
reminiscence in the Table Talk in 1538. It is presumably a continued
longing for Ave that accounts for the following remarkable projection of Luther's consciousness of being an adulterer; the projection
appears in a sermon delivered some months after his wedding (5
November 1525) dealing with the commandment "Thou shalt not
commit adultery":[22]

> It is a great and fine honor for the world that God has made of
> it a stable full of adulterous men and women. God well deserves
> to have us as enemies for dishonoring us in this way, defaming
> and covering us with shame. And He excepts no one, not even our
> monks, though they have taken a vow of chastity. You see that
> God hasn't enough confidence in us to believe that there is even

one married man who is satisfied with his wife or she with him . . . .
A pious man might say, "Why do you take me for such a person?"

But God spares no one; in this commandment He accuses all of
us men and women of adultery. All, He says, without exception . . .
are whoremasters, if not openly before the world, then at least in
our heart, and whenever we have the opportunity, the time, the
place and the occasion, we all commit adultery. This tendency is
innate in all of us without exception. This earth is a vast hospital,
where men and women, young and old, all are tainted with this
malady. And this evil is not like a red coat that we can put on or
take off; we have all contracted it in our mother's womb and since
then we bear it with us. It has penetrated through skin and flesh
into the marrow of our bones, it has poured through all our veins.

This is perhaps one of his most ingenious attempts to rid himself
of guilt feelings, on the one hand by claiming kinship with the whole
human race, including the monks, and on the other representing the
guilt as an unavoidable inheritance — man's total depravity. This projection, which his congregation must have felt as a self-accusation
that set tongues buzzing, is reported again several years later in the
lecture room when he is discussing the Pauline epistle to the Galatians:

If anyone examines himself conscientiously (and I am speaking
here of a pious spouse of either sex), he will discover without any
doubt that the appearance or manner of another woman pleases
him more than his own. He becomes tired of his wife and loves
one who is forbidden him.[23]

There appears to be no evidence on whether at this time (1531) he is
still wishing for Ave or has found a new flame. Since the Table Talk
reference to Ave comes a number of years later on, it is not unlikely
that she is the 'forbidden' one alluded to here.

As might be expected, after Luther's marriage the frequent complaints about his emissions characteristic of the first half of the
1520s disappear. Also some distorted views about marriage,
attributable to his exaggerated notions of his own sexual potency, no
longer crop up. For example, this view of the chief duty of woman,
in a 1522 sermon on the married state:

If women wear themselves out and finally die from child bearing, that does no harm; let them breed themselves to death, that is
what they are for.[24]

After he has become the father of a family one no longer hears this
astonishingly heartless comment on what women are for.

By his advocacy of bigamy in the earlier 1520s Luther was making provision for future contingencies so that when he finally had the
opportunity to take a wife he could have two if one failed to satisfy

him. He describes the psychic preparation for getting wife number two in a letter dated January 27, 1524 to Gregory Brueck, Chancellor of Electoral Saxony; the husband who wants a second wife should

> assure himself in his own conscience firmly and with certitude by the word of God that this is permitted. Let him seek out those [like me] who aided by the word of God can assure him of it.[25]

Luther was aware that according to the word of God in the N. T. what he here describes to the Chancellor is simple adultery. He was evading the teaching of the N. T. by an appeal to the O. T., which on other occasions he repudiated as abolished by the N. T. Perhaps the most interesting feature of the above quotation is the light it sheds on what 'conscience' means for Luther: an elastic organ that may be stretched to accommodate to whatever one's nature demands. In a reference to Deuteronomy 25 in August of 1525 on the practice of a childless widow marrying her husband's brother to produce offspring in his name he states: "Thus it fell out that a man had several wives, and this was an excellent rule."[26]   This citation of the O. T. in opposition to the authority of the N. T. is best understood in terms of his own sexual craving at this period of his life. He was preparing the ground for obtaining all the sex he might need at a future date.

Toward the end of the following year after discovering the modest limits of his own sexual potency and no longer interested in more than one wife for himself, he not unexpectedly reversed his position in accord with his basic policy of following Scripture faithfully — when it did not interfere with his own purposes. In a letter to Philip of Hesse (November 28, 1526) he writes:

> No one, especially Christians, should have more than one spouse, not only because it is an occasion for scandal and no Christian should give scandal but must avoid it with all his might. But also because no word of God shows it is pleasing to God where Christians are concerned . . . . It will not do for a Christian to consider what the patriarchs did; he must also have a divine word to give him certitude, as they themselves had . . . . For this reason I cannot advise bigamy but must instead advise against it, especially for Christians.[27]

This radical change in the meaning of the word of God for Luther in the interval between January 1524 and November 1526 obviously has a psychological rather than theological basis. It should be noted that Luther's correspondent at the later date is the principal in the famous bigamy case in which Luther became involved at the end of the 1530s.

The expansion of Luther's life style beginning on 13 June 1525 not only provided an additional source of material for the uncouth jests that Melanchthon deplored but also gave him the opportunity to display his native ingenuity in new ways. As noted earlier, Spalatin did not, like Martin, rush precipitately into wedlock upon Frederick's death, but waited a more discreet six months. Naturally he expected his best friend to be present at his wedding festival as he had been present at Luther's. The friendship between the two men, who were of a like age, dated back many years before this time, and it was to endure until Spalatin's death not long before Luther's. Like so many of Luther's intimates, Spalatin suffered from neurotic anxiety, and nearly a score of years after this date we find Luther attempting therapy (by correspondence) with Spalatin, who had developed symptoms of depression [letter of 21 August 1544 in WBr 10, 638].

The letter Spalatin received from Wittenberg in mid-November announcing that Luther was not coming to the wedding must have been a grievous disappointment to him. It will be recalled that by the second half of 1525 Luther's persecutory delusions had developed to the point that he no longer dared leave Wittenberg without a bodyguard. [The earliest extant evidence of Luther's fears seems to be a letter of June 15 to some friends in Mansfeld: "Now lords, pastors, and peasants are all against me and threaten me with death" (WBr 3, 530).] On this occasion, so soon after the Peasants Revolt, he was afraid to venture as far as Altenburg (about two days journey) even with one. Characteristically, in declining Spalatin's invitation, he tried to put the onus for his refusal on someone else, saying: "The tears of my Katie keep me from coming to you; she thinks you actually want me to be put in danger."[28]

In a second letter written a few weeks later and after the wedding, Martin tries to make amends for his churlish refusal to be a guest. After repeating that the roads are not safe and the traveler must fear dens of robbers and traitors, he asks Spalatin to convey greetings to the bride (like Martin's also named Catherine).[29]

> When you have your Catherine in bed most sweetly embracing and kissing her, reflect within yourself: 'My Christ, to whom be praise and glory, has given me this being, the best little creature of my God.' And then when I have guessed the day you will receive this letter, on that very night I will also love my wife with the same act in memory of you. Thereby I will give you like for like. My rib greets you and your rib. Grace be with you. Amen.
>
> Yours,
> Martin Luther

It may be doubted that Spalatin regarded this promise of synchronized copulation, marked though it is by the style of Martin's peculiar genius, as an acceptable recompense for the empty chair at the nuptial banquet.

It was inevitable that Luther would endeavor to put his sex life into service in some fashion in the battle against anxiety. How soon he began this practice is not known. The earliest record of it appears to be a Table Talk entry dated early 1533, by which time it seems to be well established. This is upwards of a year and a half after the 'devices' letter to Jerome Weller, quoted above in Ch. 3.

> These evil thoughts trouble me more than all my endless labors. How often have I grasped my wife [in bed] and rubbed against her naked body that by arousing sexual desire in this way I might drive away those thoughts that come from Satan. But it has not been very effective; he refuses to give up. For Satan is the author of death; he has so defiled our nature that we do not accept consolation. Hence let everyone strive to expel these diabolical thoughts by arousing in himself other thoughts such as of beautiful girls, or by hearty eating and drinking, or by stirring up in himself some other powerful feeling. I recommend these things, although the best of all remedies is to believe in Jesus Christ.
>
> Often I have been angry with myself that during these struggles with temptation I could not conquer them by thoughts of Christ. Despite all I have read and written and preached about these things, I still can't manage them myself. Therefore as Scripture says, "let us rejoice in the Lord." (T.R. #3298b)

The modern reader might pause to reflect on this spectacle of the man who proclaimed himself the greatest Christian teacher since apostolic times practicing the device described here on his bedfellow in a futile effort to arouse sexual desire capable of swamping his urge to blaspheme the anthropomorphic god he can hate but cannot love. This spectacle tells us immeasurably more about the ultimate sources of 'my theology' than whatever Scripture texts Luther could assemble to prop it up.

The scribe who preserved for posterity these words of advice uttered over the dinner table to Luther's boon companions also records that during this conversation Catherine fled into a nearby bedchamber and fell into a swoon. An unfeeling modern editor wonders what made her do this, for she was not known to be pregnant at the time. Apparently Catherine is not to be credited with possessing the normal sensibility of a wife on hearing the intimacies of the nuptial couch described to an audience. Luther himself appears similarly insensitive, for when Catherine rejoined the company he inquired of her what thoughts had come into her head during the fainting spell.

To illustrate the view that Luther's doctrine is a product of deeply felt personal experience, it would be difficult to find a more effective example than his utterances on sex. Earlier in this chapter we have noted how changes in his experience with sex have been faithfully mirrored by shifts in doctrine. This phenomenom becomes even more pronounced in his later years. After all the outcry in the first half of the 1520s about his being criminally prevented from satisfying his imperious need to copulate, a need so imperious that to satisfy it he demands the total destruction of the monastic way of life, he ends by wishing for greater sexual potency. In what may be described as his existential commentary on the gospel passage about becoming a eunuch for the sake of the kingdom of heaven (Matt. 19:12) Luther makes the following remark about the sacrifice of his own testicles: "Rather than having one pair cut off, I would sooner have two pairs fastened on." (T.R. # 2865a)

By his mid fifties, Luther seems to have been finished sexually. His last child was born in 1534, Luther being then 52 and Catherine 35. (Some years later she suffered a painful and disabling miscarriage.) The indication of the doctrinal change in Luther comes in a letter dated August 31, 1538 in which he advises a colleague strongly against a second marriage:

> If I were a young man but nevertheless well acquainted with the troubles of this world, I would choose death rather than marry again, even if a queen should offer herself to me after my Cathy.[30]

As Luther continued to age, so also continued the retreat from his demands for unlimited sex. The celibate life of the monks and the clergy which in the 1520s was a blasphemous offense against God miraculously returns to favor as preferable even to matrimony. Those who doubt the possibility of this antisexual revolution in the author of the 1525 letter to Reissenbusch have only to read a Table Talk item from the winter of 1542-43 when Luther was 59 years of age:

> A man can find a woman in short order, but to enjoy love continually thereafter is most difficult and he who does have it may well give thanks to our Lord God. Therefore if anyone is minded to take a wife, let him first reflect seriously about this step and pray to our Lord God: "Dear Lord God, if it is your divine will that I should live without a wife, please help me. Otherwise, please provide me with a good pious maiden to live with so that I may love her and she love me." As for copulation, that profits nothing. There must be harmony in taste and manners. *Copulation is no help at all.* (T.R. # 5524)

iii. Eyewitness report of an anxiety attack

Viewed from the outside, Luther's situation in 1527 would appear to be reasonably stable and secure. He is living on excellent terms with his territorial sovereign, Elector John, who heartily supports the new Wittenberg doctrine and is capable of protecting Luther from threats by either Emperor or Pope, although at this time there are no threats from either of them. At home Luther has settled down to family life in a dwelling which will become the joint property of himself and his wife by gift of the Elector. He is once more living an orderly existence under the rule of a determined housekeeper with whom he has learned to get along as he did formerly under the monastic regime. He is the father of a son named Hans after the grandfather, and a second child is expected at the end of the year.

Professionally, likewise, all seems well; he is lecturing on his cherished Scriptures to admiring and attentive students and enjoying harmonious relations with the Wittenberg faculty. As for theological opponents, Erasmus has been disposed of, Carlstadt is under his thumb, and Zwingli is providng him with an opportunity for the verbal combat he so keenly relishes. Nevertheless, in the middle of this year 1527 Luther went into a severe depression of which the symptoms were still evident six months later. On the last day of the year he writes to a friend James Propst of Bremen that, while enjoying bodily health, inwardly he suffers attacks from the 'devil and his angels.' The next day, January 1, 1528, he writes to another friend, Gerhard Wiskamp of Herford, what is to the Luther biographer one of the most useful items in all his correspondence:

> In truth this trial [*tentatio*] is extremely burdensome. And although such trials have been occurring since my youth [*adolescentia*], I did not anticipate they would grow so much worse now. Nevertheless, Christ has triumphed thus far, but he keeps me hanging by a very slender thread. I commend myself to your prayers and your brothers'. I have saved others; I cannot save myself. Blessed be my Christ, even in the midst of despair, death and blasphemy.

In passing, we should note the appearance of the grandiose delusion in the next to the last sentence, which (in the Latin original of the letter) is an exact quotation of the Vulgate Gospel according to Matthew (27:42) — "He has saved others, himself he cannot save." This is the gibe uttered by the chief priests and scribes to Jesus as he hung on the cross, with only the grammatical shift from the third person to Luther's favorite first.

What this letter tells us, in short, is that ever since he was a teenager (*ab adolescentia*) he has suffered attacks of anxiety accompanied by (presumably mild) depression. This fact would have to be inferred anyhow from all the other biographical data, but it is nonetheless most helpful to have this unmistakable confirmation from Martin himself.

We now return to the day of July 6, 1527, for an eyewitness

account of the dramatic onset of the depression. This report has been published only once previously in English translation and despite its great importance to the student of Luther has been passed over in silence by the Luther biographers. In his pioneering study of Luther's psychosis, Dr. P. J. Reiter made this report, along with the score or so of Luther's letters during the second half of 1527 referring to his symptoms, the key to his analysis of the illness. In view of the very great advances in the understanding of psychic disorders made since the 1930s when Reiter's study was conducted, it is now possible to take a different approach. Here we utilize material from the enormous quantity of data on Luther's disorder, not all of which is discussed in the Reiter study, to interpret the report. Our present understanding of the disorder would not have to be modified if the report were not available, but like the letter to Wiskamp it is a most useful document.

The background of the report is as follows. On the morning of Saturday July 6 Luther suffered a severe anxiety attack, the immediate cause of which will be described after the report is quoted. In his distress he made his confession to John Bugenhagen, one of the faithful retainers always found in the company of men with a charismatic personality such as Luther's. At midday he dined with some local dignitaries at the residence of the Wittenberg magistrate, and after dinner visited Justus Jonas, another member of the inner circle and author of the report. An invitation to supper at Luther's home brought Jonas on the scene about 5 P.M. in time to witness the spectacle he describes in the report. A physician was summoned to assist Luther, and Bugenhagen also joined the group about 5:30.

Jonas was so deeply impressed by what he saw and heard there that he promptly wrote a report and sent it to Bugenhagen the next day with this covering letter:

> I did not wish those words, so full of most ardent feeling, which Dr. Martin used yesterday at the beginning of his distress, to be lost to us. I believe all of them have been retained in my memory as if written and fixed there, and have noted them faithfully on this paper . . . . I do not think such a misfortune should be made light of. Farewell in Christ and *do not communicate this to anyone else but keep it hidden.* It is enough that we should know it; otherwise *it would become too widely publicized.*[32]

Jonas' admonition to keep the report bottled up has been treated with the greatest respect by most Luther biographers.

Bugenhagen prepared a supplementary report, stating that he had received an urgent summons to Luther's home on the Saturday morning. After making his confession in a private room upstairs Luther requested Bugenhagen to administer to him the Eucharist

on the following day. Bugenhagen, noting that Luther seemed somewhat disturbed, remained with him until time for the dinner at which
he was also a guest. Some interesting self evaluation by Luther during
this morning visit will be quoted later in this chapter. At this point
we present a translation of the Jonas report, dated 7 July 1527:[33]

This is what befell our dearest father, Dr. Martin. As he confessed to us himself, he had undergone a severe spiritual trial
[anxiety attack] in the morning, and after somehow regaining his
composure was called by certain of the gentry (Martin Waldefels,
Hans Loeser, Erasmus Spiegel) to the lodgings of Schultheisen. He
came into my garden after dinner to rid himself of his sadness and
distress of mind. He sat there talking with me for two hours;
upon leaving he asked me and my wife to supper. So I went up to
the monastery about five o'clock. His wife said he was resting on
account of his state of health, and asked me not to be troubled
over the delay since he was unwell. While I waited, the doctor left
his couch to join us at supper. He complained of a loud and annoying ringing of his left ear, said by physicians to herald a fainting spell. Suffering from this ringing noise, the doctor presently
said he was unable to sit because of the ringing, went back up to
his room and reclined on his couch.

I followed him by myself, his wife stopping on the bottom stair
to request something of the maids. Before she reached his door,
though she was hurrying, the doctor fell into a faint, and suddenly
cried: "Oh Doctor Jonas, I am in bad shape; give me water or
whatever you have or I will die." Frightened and trembling, I
hastily poured cold water first on his face and then over his bare
back. At this time he began to pray: "Oh Lord, if you so will, if
this is the hour you have foreordained for me, your will be done."
Raising his eyes to heaven, he prayed the Our Father and the
entire psalm, 'Lord, do not denounce me in your wrath . . .' with
great animation.

Meanwhile his wife arrived and, seeing him in a state of col-
lapse, also became terrified and called out to the servants in a loud
voice. Presently the doctor asked to have his trousers removed,
and this was done immediately. Then stretched out quietly on his
back on the couch and feeling all his strength suddenly drained
away, he again had recourse to prayer: "Lord, my dearest God,
you know how gladly I would shed my blood for your word, but
perhaps I am unworthy. Your will be done if it is your will that I
die; let your name be glorified whether in life or in death. Had it
been possible, I would have preferred to live for the sake of the
godly, Lord, for the sake of your elect; but if the hour has come,
you are Lord of life and death. My dearest God, you have led me

into this affair; you know it is your truth and word. Do not glorify our enemies lest the heathen say: Where is their God? but glorify your holy name against the enemies of your most holy word. Lord Jesus, you gave me knowledge of your name; you know I believe you are true God and our true mediator and savior who shed your blood for us; be present now with your Spirit at this hour." And he repeated: "You know there are many whom you have allowed to shed their blood for your gospel, but I am not worthy; may your will be done. You know that Satan has plotted against me in various ways to destroy me spiritually and bodily by means of kings and princes, but thus far you have marvelously preserved me; continue to preserve me if it is your will."

Then he asked whether the physician had come, Dr. Augustine, who did come in soon thereafter and applied hot bags and other such remedies, cheering and consoling him lest he grow disconsolate. In the meantime there arrived the Wittenberg pastor Bugenhagen, to whom he had confessed that morning. Then he began to say to us, as he had said earlier to me, and to our wives standing there: "Please pray for me." We, on the other hand, asked him to pray to the Lord that we not be deprived of a faithful minister of his holy gospel. Then he went on: "My dear pastor, I made my confession to you today, and you gave me absolution; that is precious to me." Then as his faintness increased somewhat, he repeated these excellent words of faith: "My dearest God, you are truly a God of the sinner and the miserable; please help me." After this he said twice or thrice to his wife: "My dearest Katie, I ask you, if it is God's will, that you abide in God's will; you are my true wife, you will certainly not lose sight of that and will be guided by the rod of God." Then to Bugenhagen and me: "I thought I would still write on baptism, but your will be done."

During these remarks he did not cease to pray and began again: "Oh Lord Jesus, who said 'Ask and you shall receive, seek and you shall find, knock and it will be opened to you,' I beg you, Oh Christ, open now to the one who knocks! Oh you dearest God and Father, you have given to me many thousand more precious and noble gifts than you have given to others. If it were your will, I would gladly have let myself be used for the honor of your name and the benefit of your people. But your will be done that you may be glorified whether by death or by life." After that he added, "Oh how the fanatics will carry on after my death."

Then, sobbing, he shed an abundance of tears, and afterward went on: "My dear God and Father, if sometimes I have been loose in my speech, you know that I did so to relieve the sadness of my weak flesh, and not with a bad conscience." Then turning to us he said: "Be witnesses that what I wrote against the Pope on penance and justification I have not revoked but regard as God's gospel and God's truth. If to some I appear to have been a little too free and severe, I am not sorry. I have wished no one ill; God knows that." And again: "Lord if you wish me to die in bed, your will be done. I would have preferred to shed my blood, but then John the Evangelist, who also wrote a good strong book against the Pope, died in this way according to your will."

While the hot bags were being applied he began to ask about his son: "Where is my dearest little Hans?" The boy was carried in, smiling at his father, who then said, "Oh you good little child, now I commit my dearest Katie and you to my dearest and good God. You have nothing, but the God who is father of orphans and judge of widows will preserve and maintain you." Having finished this, he said something to his wife about silver cups, adding: "Apart from these, you know we have nothing." To all this his wife, frightened and dismayed, but trying to look hopeful and hiding the anguish of her heart, replied: "My dearest Doctor, if it is God's will, I would rather that you be with our Lord God than with me. It is not only myself and my child but many pious Christian people who still need you; but do not be troubled on my account, I commend you to his divine will. God will preserve you." When the hot bags were applied he said his strength was returning and he hoped he would sweat. They were asked to leave so he might rest. May our Lord Jesus Christ keep this man safe for us a long time. Amen.

Today [7 July] the doctor said to me: "I must take note of this day; yesterday I was at school." He said that yesterday's spiritual trial was twice as great as this bodily illness that followed it in the evening.

As pointed out by the American psychiatrist S. Arieti, a depression typically follows a distressing experience such as the death of a near relative or some comparable source of grief. The depression may occur quite suddenly and dramatically or its onset may be very gradual and almost imperceptible. As a rule milder attacks have occurred previously which either were not detected or were viewed as ordinary changes of mood.[34] The experience which appears to trigger the depression is often referred to as the 'precipitating factor.' Recognition of the factor which helped to bring on Luther's most severe depression has been blocked by the erroneous impression that he was a man of outstanding personal courage.

An analysis of the Jonas report reveals that the source of Luther's grief was the intense mortification arising from his awareness of his unseemly cowardice. Of particular interest is his outcry, "Dearest God, you know how gladly I would have shed my blood for your word, but perhaps I am unworthy." The claim of willingness to shed his blood despite the extreme fear of death he manifests at this (and other) times is especially interesting, for Luther is here addressing his Creator, with whom no deception is possible. That Luther employs the denial mechanism even when addressing God (shedding his blood for any cause whatever being an act he would avoid at all costs) attests to the severity of his disorder. The excuse he offers of not being 'worthy' — also heard on other occasions — is too feeble to dispel the shame he feels for his terror at the thought of danger to his person.

What danger did he especially fear at this time? It will be recalled that under the new Elector John, the decision had been made to send representatives of his government throughout the parishes of Electoral Saxony to compile data on conditions that needed improvement. For this visitation, who was better suited than Luther himself, who in addition to his other qualifications had three years of professional experience as district vicar in examining religious foundations? Yet Luther remained in Wittenberg and the lay teacher of Greek, Melanchthon (now converted into a lecturer on the New Testament), went in his stead because, as pointed out earlier, Luther had been afraid to venture outside Wittenberg without a bodyguard for the past two years. There appears to be no record of the discussions that preceded the decision to send Melanchthon instead of Luther but we know very well why Luther did not go. Melanchthon departed from Wittenberg on Friday, July 5, the day before Luther's breakdown.

Now with the tremendous guilt feelings aroused by what he feels to be a cowardly dereliction of duty, he expects to die anyway. A number of other conflicts are stirred up in him; especially worthy of note is his fear that he may recant the *sola fide* defense, perhaps because of its obvious ineffectiveness in this crisis. Both Jonas and Bugenhagen record his request that they witness his fidelity to it. Also of interest is his claim of kinship with John the Evangelist, who according to tradition was the only one of the twelve apostles to escape martyrdom. To establish the identification, Luther interprets the Book of Revelation as an attack on the papacy, temporarily upgrading it (for purposes of this defensive maneuver) from the nonapostolic level to which he had consigned it in 1522.

At this point we shall examine some of Luther's remarks to Bugenhagen during their talk after the Saturday morning confession. The report of Bugenhagen has not previously been translated into English.

Because of the way I talk, my life is thought to be a bed of roses. But God knows what my life is like. I have often tried to serve the world with more dignity, with a stern countenance and the appearance of sanctity. But God did not grant me that gift. I have done the world no harm that it can justly condemn me for,

and yet in the judgment of the world, so far as I can see, it has
been injured. Perhaps in this way God wants to make foolish the
blind and ungrateful world that it may perish in its contempt.
Likewise, that the world may not see what outstanding gifts he
has given to me alone and not given to many thousands of other
men, that I may serve those whom he knows, and that while the
world may not honor the word of salvation which God offers it
through me, it may find in me what offends it and be slain. God
will recognize these judgments of his, for I will pray that my sins
may not be to others a source of scandal.[35]

An important feature of the symptoms of depression is that the
hostility the neurotic or manic individual directs against others is
turned against himself when he goes into depression. We can see
something of this in the passage just quoted from Bugenhagen's
report. Along with the grandiose and persecutory delusions which by
now are commonplace in Luther's symptomatology, we hear the admission, most unusual for him, that by his behavior he may be
setting a bad example for others. In fact the absence of the customary
attacks on the Pope and papists, religious orders and the various
sectarian groups that Luther found so troublesome is itself an indication of the onset of depression. For the next six months this hostile
attitude toward his favorite targets largely disappears from Luther's
utterances.

iv. The would-be suicide

Information about the course of Luther's depression from its
onset to the end of 1527 is provided mainly by his correspondence,
which after July averaged a dozen letters a month. (By chance there
is extant a letter to his friend Link, written on Friday July 5, the day
before the breakdown, in which Luther shows his ordinary cheerful
attitude and gives no sign of the impending emotional cataclysm.)
While he is reported to have engaged in preaching during this interval,
no sermon transcripts appear to be extant prior to Christmas. Under-
standably he wrote little for publication at this time. His lectures on
Scripture, which were transcribed by one of his hearers, began in the
latter part of August. They include a series on the first epistle of
John and on two of the shortest Pauline epistles (Titus and Phile-
mon). The lectures were delivered to a small audience since, as
pointed out below, the Wittenberg faculty and students had most of
them left town to escape an outbreak of plague.

In a large proportion of the letters Luther wrote during the latter
half of 1527 he alludes to the symptoms of his depression. His first
letter to Melanchthon in July has not survived; in another dated
August 2 he provides further information:

> Beyond those matters I wrote about recently, I was for more than a whole week really in death and hell, my whole body stricken so that my limbs still tremble. I almost completely lost Christ in waves and storms of despair and blasphemy against God. But moved by the prayers of the saints, God began to show mercy to me and raised up my soul from the depths of hell. Keep on praying for me as I do for you.[36]

His requests for others to pray for him, which appear in virtually all of his letters to friends, must on a conservative estimate have recurred many thousand times during the last quarter century of his life. It is of interest that during these same years he was damning monks and nuns as blasphemers and enemies of Christ for offering their prayers for fellow Christians, and likewise ridiculing the practice of his former co-religionists for beseeching departed saints to pray for them.

On August 12 he writes to Justus Menius in Erfurt:

> I am ill not only in body but very much so in mind, because Satan and his angels torment me with the permission of God our Savior. Therefore remember me particularly in your prayers that God may hear you and grind Satan under our feet. Amen.
>
> The infirmity of my head keeps me from my studies . . . . Zwingli and Oecolampadius have replied to me but I haven't yet read their writings nor will I be able to read them until I recover.[37]

On this same point he writes to Amsdorf the first of November: "I long to reply to the Sacramentarians but unless I become stronger in mind I can do nothing."[38]

Earlier, on October 8, he had written to another friend (Michael Stiefel in Tolleth): "For about three months I have been ill not so much in body as in mind so that I have written next to nothing, Satan has tormented me so much."[39] The other extant letter to Melanchthon of this period, dated October 27, reads in part as follows:

> Pray for me, a wretched and abject worm, much harassed by a spirit of sadness through the good will of the Father of mercies, who is glorified even in my wretchedness . . .
>
> I believe Zwingli, who acts against God's holy word so brashly and vilely, deserves a *holy hatred.* I have not yet read the *Hyperaspites* [of Erasmus] and why should I read, Christ's sick man, who scarcely keep alive, much less do or write anything?[40]

The defensive phrase 'holy hatred' we have encountered elsewhere.

Toward the middle of November, in a letter to Jonas now at Nordhausen, he is feeling especially low and the persecutory delusions appear:

I endure the wrath of God because I have sinned against him. Pope and emperor, princes, bishops and all the world hate and attack me; nor is this all, for my brothers have dragged me down so that my sins, death and Satan with his angels savage me endlessly. And what could preserve and comfort me if even Christ abandoned me, because of whom they hate me? But he will not leave the most wretched sinner at the end, for I believe myself to be the least of all men. Oh if only, and again if only Erasmus and the Sacramentarians might for a quarter-hour experience the misery of my heart. I am safe in saying they would truly be converted and saved.[41]

These lugubrious sentiments are followed by what seems to be the only such remark in all of Luther's output after 1520 — an expression of good will toward the Pope regarding the sack of Rome.

Luther's famous arguments with Satan, who can quote Scripture even more cleverly than the Wittenberg doctor himself, are the subject of a letter to Nicholas Hausmann, November 17:

I really believe that no ordinary devil but the prince of devils himself has risen up against me because he is armed against me with such great power and scriptural learning. My own knowledge of Scripture would not be enough if I did not have words from others. That is why I ask so much that you pray for me and that you may be able to recognize the depth of Satan, as they say, if this should happen to you.[42]

A month later Luther seems almost reconciled to being in depression, a not uncommon symptom for those afflicted with this disorder. He writes to Hausmann December 14:

I am not yet freed from my trial. Nor do I wish to be freed if it is for the glory of my God, the sweetest Savior, Amen. However, do not cease to pray for me and strive in this most bitter contest against the most powerful prince, Satan himself.[43]

We now consider the appearance in Luther of the suicidal tendencies frequently observed in individuals with symptoms of depression. Suicide was a topic in which Luther manifested considerable interest. He published no treatise on it but often discussed it in his correspondence and was always ready to provide counsel to potential suicides or their families. The prevalent attitude to suicide, that it was a heinous crime depriving the guilty — and successful — suicide of the right to Christian burial was not exactly shared by Luther. Instead he regarded the suicidal urge as the work of Satan and commiserated with the victim rather than damning him. He could try to console a widow by suggesting that when her husband jumped off the bridge he might have had a change of heart before hitting the water and received the divine pardon. But while Luther's preoccupation with suicide and sympathy for those inclined to it point to his kinship with other sufferers from depression, there were serious obstacles in the way of his ending his own troubles by this means. Foremost was his terror at the prospect of damnation to be expected from this violation of the command "Thou shalt not kill." Death would not be a way out for him if dying by his own hand could only assure him a place in hell. Another obstacle was his horror of physical violence. That he could hang himself or slit his throat was unthinkable.

There was, however, another way that had none of the drawbacks of the ordinary methods of self-destruction but did possess one serious defect — it might not work. By coincidence, a few weeks after Luther's depression began an epidemic of plague broke out in Wittenberg and those who could do so left town. Faculty and students found accommodations at a site well removed from Wittenberg and avoided the plague-stricken town until mid-winter when the contagion ended. Luther, however, remained at home. On August 10 the Elector wrote him, offering transportation for Martin and his family to the temporary university quarters. No reply is extant or known. For it appears that he had already begun to write his 'suicide note,' a tract entitled "Whether One May Flee Death."

This work has the format of a circular letter sent in reply to a Lutherian preacher, John Hess, in the town of Breslau. According to Luther, Hess had more than once requested advice on whether a Christian should flee to a safe retreat during an epidemic. It would appear that Luther thus chose Hess to be the nominal recipient of a circular letter in which he would justify his remaining in Wittenberg. It may be said that much of the tract does not bear on the question of whether one may flee death. In view of his depressive symptoms at this time, continuous and coherent development of a theme could not be expected. (A similar observation could be made about the lectures on 1 John discussed below.) Indeed it appears Luther spent around three months preparing this twenty-page tract for publication — in striking contrast with the prodigious output of 1520-1521 when the manic symptoms were evident. [The editors of the Weimar edition of this tract, who could hardly be expected to show understanding of the effect of psychotic symptoms, find the tone of the tract "singularly mild." (WA 23, 323 f)]

After some brief preliminaries, Luther begins his roundabout explanation of why he must remain in Wittenberg. By way of illustration, a man imprisoned for his faith in God's word must not try to escape by denying it, but rather suffer death. Similarly a preacher, like the good shepherd, must be prepared to lay down his life for his sheep. He may flee the threat of death only if there is a substitute to provide services for the congregation. Roughly the first third of the tract deals with examples of those who must not desert their charges even to escape death. Luther next explains how one may fortify his courage to stay in a plague-ridden community. The first method, the same as he recommends for anxiety attacks, is to scorn Satan, who is responsible for the sickness. The second way is to recall God's promises to help the poor and reward those who care for the sick. Such reflections will overcome his fear and the temptation to flee, which would be sinful. But equally sinful would be careless exposure of himself to the infection, in fact, that could make him a suicide. He must observe all reasonable precautions, and if despite that "God chooses to take me (*sic*) it is his responsibility not mine." The remainder of the tract (we are now somewhat past its midpoint) departs still farther from the question "Whether One May Flee Death."

Regarding additional evidence that the main thrust of this tract is to reveal Luther's plan to end his life without incurring the penalty of suicide, it may be pointed out that on other occasions Luther had indicated that death from the plague was one form of death he did not fear. He had seen many others depart this life from that cause and felt that they died peacefully and thereby would be rewarded for their obedience to the divine will. Luther had dealt with the question of flight from the plague in a letter eight years earlier. That the 'weak' should flee was to be expected, and tolerated. But the 'strong,' like Luther, will stay and passively await death without even asking for medical help. The suicidal intent is evident in his remark that those who are perfect *spontaneously seek death* and do not need a physician. (To Martin Seligman, October 14, 1519 in WBr 1, 532). Indeed Luther regarded his own fear of death to be a violation of God's will and therefore one of his serious sins. Another factor was that in such a death, as contrasted with the burning at the stake which would be his fate as a condemned heretic, there was no possibility of recantation. As noted above, the thought that he might at the last moment cravenly recant his doctrine to escape violent death was a very real source of anxiety for him.

A consideration that does not appear in Luther's tract concerns a man's responsibility for causing others to remain in the danger area. This was by no means an academic question. Justus Jonas, the author of the eyewitness report quoted above, remained in Wittenberg along with his wife and infant son to be near Luther. He remained, that is, until the son died of plague, whereupon he speedily departed with his wife to a safer locale. Likewise, Luther's faithful retainer and scribe George Roerer stayed on for the same reason, and thereby lost his pregnant wife to the dread disease. Luther, it will be recalled, at this time was the father of a year-old son, and his wife also was pregnant. As it happened they, like Martin, escaped the contagion. If the reader surmises the egocentric Luther says nothing in the tract about the matter of callously exposing his wife and child to the bubonic plague, the reader is right.

The lectures on 1 John, preserved in student's notes, are barely distinguishable from rather bland sermons. Luther presumably chose this epistle to lecture on because he found consolation in its message; also it is relatively simple. In his attack on the N. T. canon in 1522 he seems to have been on the fence about 1 John, excluding it from one of his preferred lists and including it in another. Doctrinally it has very little in common with his personal teaching, but he could find it consoling in his distress because of the 'promises' it contains and he found it possible to ignore the unacceptable (to him) conditions on which the promises are offered.

Many of the comments in the reported text of the lectures are from the point of view of ordinary exegesis irrelevant to the words of the epistle adjacent to them. They represent material which the language of the epistle has been instrumental in dredging up into his consciousness, unwelcome material which he has been unsuccessful in suppressing. For example, it is evident his excommunication and his rejection of the monastic vows are still a source of anxiety to him. Augustine, Benedict and Francis must be condemned for their guilt in promoting monastic life. Bernard, however, is saved from this fate by a rehearsal of the Bernard fantasy. Consider these obvious self-references: "If anyone were troubled because he had not celebrated mass"; or "The devil can disturb a person for having departed from the monastic life and can suppress the joy of his heart." Likewise his hostility to others, which he feels and interprets as hatred, is a particular problem for him in this epistle which treats hatred of one's fellow men as the most serious offense that can be committed by those who profess to be Christians, revealing them to be only pseudo-Christians.

Of particular interest is Luther's confrontation with the central teaching of 1 John as expressed, for example, near the beginning of Ch. 5: "We can be sure we love God's children when we love God and do what he has commanded. The love of God consists in this: that we keep his commandments — and his commandments are not burdensome." Luther regularly maintains that to love God is impossible in this life and that it is equally impossible to keep the commandments, and he continues to assert these positions in later years. But on October 28, 1527, having put himself on the spot by undertaking to lecture on 1 John, he must have recourse to the denial mechanism not only for the Scripture text but even for his own repeatedly expressed views. Note the tangle of falsifications in this passage. For John

> to keep God's commandments is *to believe*. Moreover, he means the *commandments of the gospel*, which are not burdensome. But

the Christians [in contrast with heretics] love God and keep all these commandments.[44]

Luther then says of the phrase: "The love of God consists in this" that it means the love with which God loves us. Luther's phrase 'the commandments of the gospel' is especially significant because one of his most firmly held positions is the distinction between the 'Law,' consisting of commandments, and the 'Gospel,' of promises. Anyone who wickedly tries to read commandments into the 'Gospel' makes Christ into a lawgiver, a Moses. In his present low state Luther can sacrifice a cherished position to achieve an accommodation with Scripture.

But he soon returns to safe ground by asserting that everything is contained in this word 'believe,' and he had stated in an earlier lecture that 'John always proceeds from faith to love for one's neighbor and from here he returns to faith.' Throughout the first epistle of John the word *love* (as noun and verb) appears nearly 50 times; the noun *faith* appears only once, in the last chapter, and the verb *believe* five or six times, not of course in the Lutherian sense. In fact it is probably John's strongly anti-Lutherian bias that provoked Martin in a lecture earlier in October to correct the famous 'Love covers a multitude of sins' (1 Pet. 4:8) to read 'Faith is the covering . . . . which covers countless sins.' Also one may attribute to the effect of this epistle, which condemns hatred of others so strongly, the very odd expression in his letter to Melanchthon of October 27, "I believe Zwingli is deserving of *holy hatred*."

It would appear, then, that Luther's lectures on this epistle were undertaken because of his unique situation in the late summer of 1527 — a state of depression requiring very special consolation and the presence of a small group of unquestioning listeners. It was this combination of circumstances that trapped him into commenting on a scriptural work with so many pitfalls for 'my theology.' The character of the lectures and the occasion on which they were presented throw considerable light on the question raised earlier about why, after his regression, Luther tended to steer clear of the N. T. in his academic work. These lectures show, however, that Luther's defensive system was equal to all the challenges and for a time had him almost believing that he too was capable of experiencing the love for God so ardently exemplified by the apostolic author.

This depression is unique in Luther's history for its duration. During the next two years, until the departure for Coburg in the spring of 1530, there are indications — gaps in his preaching schedule and remarks in his letters about his inner state similar to those quoted above — that he went into depression a few more times, but only for periods of weeks rather than months. The most likely explanation of the extraordinary length of the 1527 depression is that during this period Luther was cut off from the presence of Melanchthon, who was away from Wittenberg for more than six months, at first on the visitation program and later on account of the plague. A parallel situation earlier on was Luther's increasing emotional tension in the period 1516-18, which as suggested previously could be attributed to the extended absence from Wittenberg of Staupitz, Philip's predecessor in the role of maternal substitute. Luther's emergence from depression early in 1528 is probably attributable to renewed contact with Melanchthon.

Chapter 7

The Enslaved Will And
The Ten Commandments

i. Melanchthon as mouthpiece

In this chapter we look directly at Luther the theologian, who in 1525 summed up his view of theology as a doctrine that teaches "how to be liberated from sin, to acquire a good conscience and to make your heart joyous and peaceful in God's sight. This is the most important thing of all."[1] The outcome of such a merely practical approach to what is commonly viewed as a theoretical discipline was the practical contrivance known as the *sola fide*. To present it as a 'theology' required some sort of theoretical underpinning. But the author of the *sola fide*, having failed to inherit the type of mind that finds its chief satisfaction in a theoretical enquiry about the Divine Being, the human condition and their interrelations, gave little attention to these questions. His habit of referring to himself as a theologian stems at least partly from his living in an academic culture where theology was still top dog and from his own occupational involvement with it. It is to be doubted that he was in the least aware of how little he had in common with a genuine theologian.

The most readily available foundation which could as it were be slid under the *sola fide* to make it appear more than a mere how-to-do-it affair was some sort of theory about man's impotence in a deterministic world. Such a theory was congenial to Luther's experience in the anxiety attacks, but he seems not to have cared to address himself to preparing a systematic discussion of it. However, he was to be relieved of this task early on by his brilliant young disciple, Philip Melanchthon. Though engaged to teach Greek at Wittenberg, Philip was speedily impressed into the work of propagating Lutheran doctrine among the students. He was so successful in this endeavor that early in 1524 Luther wrote to the Elector requesting, indeed almost demanding, that Melanchthon be given permanent status as lecturer on Scripture and never again required to give 'childish' instruction in Greek.

The shift in Melanchthon's academic function was engineered by having him lecture on the Pauline epistle to the Romans, which was of course written in Greek and just happened to be a convenient locus for developing the principal themes of 'my theology.' Melanchthon continued the subterfuge by publishing in 1521 a treatise ostensibly summarizing the teaching of the Epistle. In it he perpetrated the remarkable falsification, worthy to stand beside one of Luther's and doubtless derived from him, that Paul had composed the epistle as a compendium of Christian doctrine. The tract was given the rather non-descript title "Theological Commonplaces." A more informative one might be: "All the Christian Need Know for His Salvation, as Manifested to the Rev. Dr. Martin Luther by the Spirit, Compiled and Edited by His Faithful and Adoring Disciple, Philip Melanchthon, M.A., and Personally Endorsed as Both Accurate and Entire by the said Dr. Martin Luther."

As mentioned earlier, Philip is in his own right as fascinating a character as Luther, much better endowed intellectually, personally attractive, and fully as zealous about his religion. At the time he composed the first edition of the "Commonplaces" he was still completely hooked on the charismatic personality of Martin and desired to be nothing more than a mouthpiece. Although their acquaintance dated back barely three years, he had thoroughly absorbed the Lutherian doctrine, which in his present state of naivete he identified with authentic Christian revelation, and had become a more able spokesman of it, if possible, than Luther himself. Apart from his superior native gifts two other factors contributed to Philip's speedy acquisition of the gospel according to Luther. One of these was the neurotic anxiety that made him an ideal receptor of the consolation available from the Lutherian scheme; the other, that he was relatively so uninstructed in theology upon his arrival in Wittenberg at the age of 21 that he could offer no critical opposition to Luther's seemingly erudite demolition of the Christian past. Hence such a charmingly naive statement in the "Commonplaces" as this: "Aside from the canonical Scriptures, there is no sound literature in the Church."[2] At the time he wrote these words, Philip could not have read as much as a hundred-thousandth part of this literature, rather a small sample for such a sweeping judgment. By name he airily dismissed Origen, Ambrose and Jerome; Augustine and Bernard do not fare much better. From the time of Jerome (later fourth century), he informs us, the more recent an author, the less Scriptural he is likely to be.

The first edition of the "Commonplaces" is a curious blend of humanism and anti-humanism, reflecting at once Melanchthon's own previous academic background and Luther's narrow and highly personal biblicism. Philip likes to draw his analogies from the ancient (pagan) historians, whom he *has* read, but as a true-blue Witten-bergian he must renounce the use of human reason and deny the freedom of the human will. Indeed this latter topic serves as the cornerstone of the entire work, the foundation of the Lutheran anthropology. For despite the title — "Theological Commonplaces" — in this book God is assigned a minor role, the divine attributes being dismissed at the opening as a topic unsuitable for theological discussion. Philip also has little to say about the Church. In 1521 he appears somewhat sensitive about the propriety of his undertaking this task but not on the grounds of his youth. Rather he tries to defend himself against the charge, by no means inaccurate, that he is only a 'professor of languages dabbling in theology.'

His picture of the depravity of Lutheran man is appropriately dismal:

> When is the soul of man not stewing in evil desires, of which the worst and foulest are not even perceived? . . . Who is there that does not sometimes experience them — arrogance, contempt, pharisaical vanity, despising of God, distrust in God, blasphemy? Few notice these chief passions [affections].[3]

This last word is a key term in the Lutheran anthropology; it expresses Luther's awareness of his uncontrollable emotional states and might be described as the existential basis for his denial of the freedom of the will. The ideological emphasis on feelings at the expense of reason is to be expected from one so completely dominated by his emotions as was Luther. One wonders whether the rather dainty-looking young professor of languages experienced the uncontrollable evil desires himself or merely took them on Luther's say-so, as he took the concept of the enslaved will.

The anthropomorphic god of Luther is briefly described in equally vivid language. He is an "angry God, threatening eternal death"; the aroused conscience "fears him as a cruel executioner, an avenger, and, what is most hideous, as being wicked."[4]

While Philip presents his material under more than 25 separate headings which, if read through as a list, are more likely to bewilder than inform, the treatise falls roughly into just two main divisions. The first is devoted primarily to the Lutheran anthropology and starts off with a lengthy account of man with an enslaved will, the helpless victim of his evil passions or sins. As for human reason, that must be renounced as the seat of ignorance of God, contempt of God, disbelief in God and other deadly pests. Elsewhere it is the 'impure heart' which plays the role here assigned the reason. For an expositor who has renounced the use of reason as 'flesh' such a contradiction is not surprising; without the reason to detect contradictions, about all that remains is to make assertions pleasing to the emotions. The follow-up to this picture of man is a description of 'Law,' primarily the Decalogue, whose function is by threats of eternal damnation to terrify the sinner into substituting for his reliance on his reason a trust in the promise of the Gospel. How he can be expected to take such action when hamstrung by his enslaved will is one of the ineluctable mysteries of the Lutheran anthropology.

The second main division is concerned with the Gospel and its benefits and includes such topics as the abbreviated list of sacraments in the "Babylonian Captivity." Two key terms in this division, grace and faith, taken over from traditional theology, are given the new Lutheran meanings. Each term, in fact is given two distinct and conflicting definitions. Grace is first the favor or good will of God. Although the God of traditional theology is unchanging, the Lutheran God is at times an angry, vindictive judge and at other times a benign monarch who looks with favor on the helpless wretches who constitute the human race. What Philip is at pains to emphasize is that grace can have no effect whatever on the human soul – as the foolish Sophists teach. When the soul comes to believe it has a gracious God willing to overlook its sinful state, the soul can feel happy but remains the same sin-drenched soul as before.

Faith is first defined as 'righteousness,' a term which Philip repeats ten times in various contexts – without defining – before equating it with faith. He then redefines faith as trust in the divine promise, which sounds rather different from righteousness, but in a universe of discourse from which reason is barred this can hardly be called surprising. At any rate, he has done the best he could with material never intended for coherent and systematic presentation, and for this accomplishment he received a magnificent reward from his mentor: the assertion that the "Commonplaces" of 1521 was the greatest theological work in Christendom, worthy to stand on the same shelf as the Gospels and Epistles.

The work is full of Lutheran touches and features many of Luther's falsifications of standard ecclesiastical teaching. The writings of the master himself are occasionally recommended for an authoritative explanation of the more important themes. In particular, to learn the meaning of 'faith' one must turn to the pages of that ultimate expression of the *sola fide,* "On Christian Liberty." One finds repeated sallies against the 'Sophists,' i.e., the scholastic theologians. Indeed there are no other enemies, for at this date Carlstadt, Muentzer, Zwingli and the 'fanatics' may already be maturing their felonious plans but are still below the horizon. There is much breast beating over reason and philosophy; the more recent scriptural commentaries are said to "reek of philosophy"; Plato – the begetter of 'reason' – is in as bad odor as Aristotle. Jesus is given a very slender role in this compendium of Christian theology, and clearly

Philip has inherited the policy of ignoring Jesus as a person. One of the neatest encapsulizations of the egocentric Lutheran 'Christology' is the phrase: "To know Christ means to know his benefits." On one topic Philip has to admit defeat — the impossibility of reconciling the conflict between the *sola fide* and the teaching on reward and merit in the Synoptic gospels. He has not yet had the benefit of Luther's remarkable use of the denial mechanism on the Synoptics, which is still a year in the future.

The errors committed by ecumenical councils, especially the Council of Nicea, are brought to the teacher's attention. Despite Philip's program of limiting his discourse to the most essential topics of theology, he finds room for such statements as that the bishops must not be obeyed and that the papal bull condemning Luther as a heretic must be ignored as contrary to divine justice. It was of course eminently desirable to indoctrinate the Wittenberg students with such fundamentals of theology. In general the language of the treatise is more restrained than the master's but at times rises to a Lutherian pitch, as for example, "Moral virtues stink, and the right-eousness of the saints is nothing but dirty, menstruous rags."[5] Finally, the basic Lutheran positions that believers are saved even though they continue to "have sin" and that they can be certain of this are given due emphasis.

As matters turned out Philip could not rest easy with the tremend-ous compliment for what he had accomplished in the "Theological Commonplaces." During the next several years as he continued to pore over the N. T. and began to read some of the authors he had dis-paraged unread in 1521, he became most unhappy with the concept of the enslaved will, ultimately dropping it completely and commit-ting the most grievous act of lese' majeste' by describing it as a "Manichean heresy." It is doubtful if Martin ever read the later revised editions of the "Commonplaces"; indeed he seems to have read less and less with advancing years and so could innocently continue its supertop rating after it had become a vehicle of counter - revolutionary propaganda. Philip's defection revealed one of the more engaging features of 'my theology' — that it could roll along as triumphantly as ever after its underpinning had been removed.

Posterity has not always treated the "Commonplaces" very kindly. Some of the theological specialists of the contemporary Luther cult appear to ignore it and even at times speak slightingly of its author, although they are careful to imitate his example of dumping the theory of the enslaved will. The modern reader who wants a con-nected and authoritative account of Luther's theological views in the early 1520s would be well advised to ignore the modern commenta-tors and read the 1521 edition of the "Theological Commonplaces." But he should avoid the later editions, which reek of Philipianism.

As a measure of the reactionary level to which Philip sank in later years, he opens the 1543 edition with a long section on the Divine attributes, and farther on even finds room for a short chapter on the Church.

ii.   Luther against Erasmus and Augustine

One of his writings Luther considered worthy of being read by posterity, the *De Servo Arbitrio* (On the Enslaved Will), appeared late in 1525 in reply to a critique called *De Libero Arbitrio* (On the Free Will) published the year before by Erasmus. The account of Erasmus given here is limited to background matters of interest to the controversy with Luther, for Erasmus is too complex a person to permit of summary treatment. In comparison Luther is but a simple lad from the country. Erasmus' literary and scholarly efforts had a two-fold aim: to renovate the educational system of Europe by promoting the study of classical letters, both Latin and Greek, and to renew theological studies (and hopefully religious life) by replacing the dessicated theology of the schools with intelligent reading of Scripture and the works of the great theologians of Christian antiquity, from Irenaeus in the second century to Augustine in the fifth. To prepare himself for this task he undertook the study of Greek in his mid-thirties, rather late in life for those times, and mastered it.

Erasmus left his native Holland as a young man and spent the rest of his life in various countries of Europe. By 1510, in his early forties, he had achieved European fame from his literary productions. He then concentrated on preparing a Greek edition of the N. T. accompanied by a new Latin translation and extensive notes. This appeared early in 1516, with a dedication to the reigning Pope, Leo X, and was soon followed by his edition of the letters of St. Jerome. While these publications together with his earlier works established him as the leading scholar and writer of Christendom from then till his death twenty years later, his edition of the N. T. provoked never-ending controversy with reactionary critics who were disturbed at seeing competition with the Vulgate, the standard Latin text of the N.T. in western Europe for the past thousand years. In one respect Erasmus was ill suited to his self-chosen task of reforming literary and theological study because he was very thin-skinned and abhorred partisanship and personal controversy. To make matters worse, he was master of an ironical style that infuriated his opponents. Thanks to his extraordinary talents he had many powerful and distinguished friends, but perhaps an equal number of Erasmus-haters.

Despite chronic ill health he was an indefatigable worker and during the last twenty years of his life (roughly from age 50 to 70) he edited the works of about a dozen ancient Christian writers, published a great deal of commentary on the writings of the N. T., repeatedly revised and expanded his numerous educational texts for schoolboys, and rebutted theological adversaries. In addition he carried on an enormous correspondence with important and unimportant personages throughout Europe. His rather frequent changes of address in his later years were to some extent occasioned by his search for a community where he could live in peace. When Luther first achieved prominence through the publication of the Indulgence Theses, Erasmus supported him as an ally in the endeavor to renew Christian piety. This support included a recommendation to Elector Frederick as late as October 1520 that Luther should be given protection from ecclesiastical authorities who wanted to suppress him. He had earlier advised Luther in private correspondence to exercise restraint in his attacks on theological opponents.

During the period 1518-20 Erasmus hoped to salvage Luther's positive contribution to the 'advancement of piety' while preserving peace. One of his later publications was an essay entitled "On Mending the Peace of the Church" (1533). Unfortunately this had as little practical effect as had his efforts to persuade Luther to be more restrained in his writings. Naturally Erasmus could have no understanding of Luther's drift toward psychotic regression and was appalled when he ultimately became aware of the display of manic hostility against the papacy that followed this change. Erasmus' efforts to defend Luther from the enemies of progress now seriously compromised his own status as a loyal member of the Church. He could retrieve his position only by some public criticism of Luther, but this step he hesitated to take because it would embroil him in still further controversy.

At length he chose to attack the deterministic denial of man's power of free choice which Luther had developed in some of his writings, for which he had been condemned in the bull *Exsurge Domine,* and which Melanchthon (acting as Luther's spokesman) had disseminated throughout Europe in the "Theological Commonplaces." Reacting to news of this impending event, Luther wrote Erasmus in mid-April of 1524 warning him to publish nothing against 'my theology.' The letter [Smith II, #620] presents an interesting display of manic grandiosity which included a spiteful belittling of the talents and courage of his most distinguished contemporary. In view of the obviously provocative and uncivil tone of this letter Erasmus might well have ignored it. But anticipating Luther's letter to him would become public anyhow, he chose to reply. His response [Smith II, #624] provides valuable insight into the dilemma in which he found himself as a result of Luther's revolt. Under continuing pressure from his adversaries and others to resolve the apparent ambiguity of his position, Erasmus published the "De Libero

Arbitrio" in September of that same year.

Aware of the difficulty of the philosophical and theological problems involved, Erasmus makes no claim that he can solve them and is unwilling to settle for a glib pseudo-solution, preferring to leave the thornier questions open. After reviewing the many scriptural texts that would appear meaningless in the face of a denial of man's personal responsibility for his conduct, he discusses other texts that appear to leave the issue of free will in doubt, and proposes interpretations to reconcile them with the passages cited first. Then he criticizes arguments against the free will presented by Luther in an earlier tract. Throughout the essay, his approach is even-tempered and urbane, without animosity toward Luther.

When Erasmus' essay appeared in the autumn of 1524, Luther was too occupied with extra-curricular activities to give it much attention. His personal conflict with Carlstadt had been a principal concern during the summer and he had decided to prepare a major literary attack ("Against the Heavenly Prophets") on his one-time colleague. Also during the summer he had entered the lists against Muentzer. Beyond this he was devoting major attention to the task of abolishing the celebration of mass in the Castle Church. In the spring of the following year he became involved in the Peasants Revolt and in the summer he got married. Thus the reply to Erasmus — the "Enslaved Will" — was not in print until late in 1525, about fifteen months after the publication of Erasmus' work, an extraordinarily long delay for Luther.

As an instance of Luther's incapacity to deal competently with the questions at issue, we cite one of his principal conclusions: the boast that everything in Scripture supports his deterministic posture. By way of comment on this assertion, consider this analysis from a modern Scripture manual; though written without reference to Luther, it provides a devastating exposure of his inability to understand scriptural material in the area of his disturbance.

The authors point out that while the Bible does not treat explicitly the question of the freedom of the will one can discern in its pages a definite and consistent point of view on the matter. In Scripture human beings are regarded as responsible agents who can choose and decide for themselves. Many key biblical terms are verbs which take for granted the freedom of the will, such as 'love,' 'repent,' 'forgive,' 'judge,' 'thank,' 'obey.' Anyone who rejects the freedom of the will must also reject these words as meaningless. In Scripture human freedom is contrasted with a state of bondage rather than a state of necessity; only naturally free beings can be forced into a state of bondage. Furthermore, the Bible relates freedom not to a condition of independence but rather to loving and being loved.[6]

In view of the insight presented here, the "Enslaved Will" may be regarded as a gigantic exercise of the projection mechanism. The denial mechanism is also much in evidence, cf., "Augustine, whom you do not refer to, agrees with me completely."[7] In fact, Erasmus would have been more effective if, instead of composing his own rather bumbling argument, he had published an edition of Augustine's essay "Grace and Free Will" with an appropriate introduction. Erasmus, of course, does more than refer to Augustine. He even quotes the same 'proof text' from Ecclesiasticus [15:14-18] with which Augustine had begun a lengthy demonstration of how God reveals in Scripture "that there is in man a free will" (Ch. 2). Such an approach by Erasmus might have inhibited subsequent mendacious claims by Luther of his agreement with Augustine and reduced the quantity of personal abuse he showered on Erasmus. Luther contradicts Augustine not only on the scriptural revelation of man's power of free choice but also on a fundamental argument from reason. In his philosophical masterpiece, the "City of God," Augustine had pointed out that God's foreknowledge does not take away the freedom of the will, and that man's power of free choice does not prevent God's foreknowledge.[8] He goes on to say that when a man sins he does so not as one compelled to act by fate or fortune but because he wills to sin, and the divine foreknowledge is a knowledge of this act of the will. Luther had studied the "City of God" in his earlier years but this passage he seems to have failed to comprehend. When he discusses the same point in his tract, he naturally makes no reference to Augustine.

It is not so certain whether Luther had read another work of Augustine, the dialogue entitled "On the Free Will" (*De Libero Arbitrio,* the title Erasmus chose for his own essay), but he must certainly have heard of it. Had he read it, he would have encountered an explanation of why he failed to grasp the truth of the argument alluded to above in the "City of God." For in the dialogue Augustine remarks that while one man is able to apprehend a certain truth rather easily, and another man can likewise grasp it but only with more difficulty, a third man can not get it at all. Augustine, it might be noted, had been a teacher with classroom experience.

To conclude this brief review of the radical divergence between the positions of Augustine and Luther on the free will, a divergence which Luther was not only at some pains to conceal but even to deny, there might be adduced a comparison of the two men which throws some light on Luther's attitude. Augustine occupies a most distinguished position in the line of the great philosophers of western culture. From an early age he exhibited this gift and after his conversion to the Christian faith he continued to view theological questions from the viewpoint of a philosopher as well as a fervent believer. Luther on the other hand not only lacked the ability to understand the philosopher's approach to reality but as a result of his unhappy experience contracted a violent hatred of philosophy. Thus, matters which were quite clear to Augustine could be opaque to Luther or even misconstrued.

Apparently Erasmus did not receive a copy of the "Enslaved Will" until late winter or early spring of 1526. In April he sent a bitterly reproachful letter to his Wittenberg foe complaining about the personal abuse. By his estimate, which may seem a trifle high, the slanders and calumnies directed against his person constitute more than a third of the tract. He writes: "In what way is the argument advanced by all the scurrilous invective, the mendacious accusations that I am an atheist, an Epicurean, a sceptic in matters of Christian belief, a blasphemer?"[9] It is not unlikely that these vicious falsehoods about Erasmus' character, the product of Luther's pathological hostility, have contributed to the unfavorable reputation Erasmus has enjoyed in some quarters even to the present day.

Another comment in the letter provides a view of Luther's character which was apparently shared by a large fraction of educated observers from the mid 1520s on, who could have little or no understanding of the fact that they were observing the behavior of an unrestrained psychotic. "With your arrogant, brash, seditious nature you have involved the whole world in destructive conflict, thrown good men and lovers of good letters against fanatic Pharisees, armed the restless and seekers after novelty to rebel; in brief, you so treat the evangelical cause that you confuse all things sacred and profane. It is as though you intend to prevent the tempest from finally coming to an end."

Luther did not reply to this letter or to the long tract, appearing in two parts, that Erasmus published in reply to the "Enslaved Will" during the next two or three years. Another serious exchange between the two started with a long abusive letter about Erasmus that Luther addressed to his friend Amsdorf in 1534. This was soon in print, and in due course Erasmus replied to it in a tract entitled "Against the Most Calumnious Epistle of Martin Luther." Earlier he wrote privately to a friend: "I have already seen Luther's letter, which is the product of a madman. He not only lies shamelessly and impudently but even promises worse things. What can people think who commit their souls and their future to a man so enslaved by his passions? Anyone who damages his own cause, on which he sets so great store, can have no judgment at all."[10] Luther's letter seems to have been motivated by the previously mentioned essay of Erasmus "On Mending the Peace of the Church." For his attempt to restore peace, he was vilified by the sage of Wittenberg as a heretic, atheist, blasphemer, etc. Two years later Luther was permitted to rejoice in the death of another of his adversaries.

Here we may add to the testimony of Erasmus that of another contemporary witness who avoided personal controversy with Luther, the celebrated scholar and jurist of Nuremberg, Willibald Pirckheimer. Like Erasmus, Pirckheimer was at first a supporter of Luther, so much so his name was included with Luther's on the bull of excommunication. Being a fellow German, he could read Luther's vernacular writings as well as the Latin ones and thus had a much clearer picture of his development than was available to Erasmus. Being a scholar, he acquired and read copies of Luther's publications as they appeared. At his death in 1530 his library contained more than 120 such items.

Pirckheimer like Erasmus observed with increasing dismay the remarkable changes in the man he at one time thought was capable of renewing religious life in Germany. The following passage from a well known letter of Pirckheimer's to a friend represents the reaction of a contemporary observer far better qualified than most to render an objective judgment of the Luther of the later 1520s.

> In earlier years almost all men applauded the name of Luther, but nowadays nearly all are overcome with disgust upon hearing this name. The good report of his notable virtues has not only waned, but practically died out.
>
> In addition to his insults and his audacity, impudence, arrogance and abusive language, he puts on such a bold front that he will stop at no lie. What he asserts today, without any shame he dares to deny tomorrow.[11]

Pirckheimer is here giving testimony to symptoms which in the twentieth century are identified as manic grandiosity along with the defense mechanisms of denial and projection. Elsewhere in his correspondence Pirckheimer expresses the view that Luther is 'insane.' While there is other contemporary witness to Luther's behavior in agreement with Pirckheimer's, his testimony is more valuable than perhaps any other contemporary witness because of his independent character, his personal acquaintance with Luther, his broad experience of men and affairs, his scholarly training and background, and his detailed knowledge of Luther's writings.

Turning now to the self-revelation that makes the "Enslaved Will" a document of perennial interest, we first listen to Martin describing what motivated his denial of human freedom:

> As for myself, I readily admit that I wouldn't want to be granted free will even if that were possible, or have it left up to me to strive after salvation. And this is so not only because, confronted with such great adversities and perils and attacks of the devil, I could not stand up against them and hold my own . . . . But even if there were no perils, no adversities, no devils, I would be

compelled to struggle in uncertainty, without letup, and beat the air with my fists. And if I lived and worked to eternity, my conscience would never attain to a *comfortable certainty about how much I must do to satisfy God.*[12]

This passage, as disarmingly ingenuous as anything in the *Confessions* of Jean-Jacques, reveals perhaps better than anything else he ever uttered the basic dynamism determining Martin's behavior. The italicized words indicate how remarkably distorted was his view of the Christian gospel, which neither promises 'comfortable certainty' nor requires that one 'satisfy God.' A comparison of the enslaved will fantasy with the *sola fide* makes clear that they are similar instances of a juvenile sort of wish fulfillment. The *sola fide* reduces to asserting: "I want forgiveness of my sins; therefore I am granted forgiveness of my sins as long as I believe I have it." The enslaved will thesis can be paraphrased as "I don't want to be held accountable for my behavior; therefore I am not accountable for it." This comparison suggests incidentally that the servile will doctrine does not really provide a foundation for the *sola fide.* They are independent productions of a disordered psyche that may be likened to the tentacles of an octopus reaching out for some kind of support in a threatening world. If one of the tentacles is lopped off, the others are unaffected. That is why the enslaved will doctrine could disappear publicly from Wittenberg theology by 1530 without creating a sensation.

As pointed out above, Melanchthon as Luther's spokesman excluded a treatment of the divine attributes from his 1521 compendium of the major topics of Christian theology. Perhaps one reason for this was that Luther had imparted to him such confused and contradictory views of the deity that he could not possibly reduce them to any coherent order. The "Enslaved Will" has some very interesting disclosures of these views and of the experience that generated them. Somewhat beyond the midpoint of the treatise he tells us that he has been bewildered and stunned at the thought that the merciful God revealed in Scripture can nevertheless choose to damn a certain portion of mankind to eternal punishment. Even more significant is his disclosure that the horror of this picture had driven him into such profound despair he wished he had never been born.

This aspect of Luther's psychopathology must be kept in mind for an understanding of the 'theoretical' solution he proposes for his dilemma. He advances the notion that there are in effect two gods. One of these, the one revealed in Scripture, is kind and merciful. This is the god of whom it is written that he wills not the death but rather the salvation and life of the sinner. The other god is completely hidden in his majesty, and although we can know nothing at all about the hidden god, we nevertheless know that he wants to have nothing to do with men except that for some inscrutable reason he wills that certain of them be consigned to hell for all eternity. Since the contemplation of the hidden god is most painful to Martin, comparatively little about this part of 'my theology' appears in the writings and sermons.

While it is simpler to present these views of Luther's in terms of two gods, in general his language suggests something if possible even more irrational. There are not really two gods but only one, with two different aspects: the merciful and the inscrutable — but merciless — aspect. It is the merciful aspect of this schizoid deity that Luther encounters when free of anxiety, and the inscrutable, terrifying one he struggles against during the anxiety states. In the "Enslaved Will" Luther decks out these concepts with his characteristic rhetorical skill, speaking of "God preached" and "God hidden" or of the "Word" (not in the Johannine sense) and "God himself." He divulges this production of his pathological psyche with his habitual self assurance, as though he had merely to assert such preposterous notions to assure their acceptance. The problem of the schizoid god incidentally throws light on what might be called the contingent nature of the *sola fide:* "If there were any way I could understand how this god is merciful and just although he manifests such great wrath and inequity, there would be no need for faith."[13] This passage also exhibits the fundamental difference between Lutherian and scriptural faith.

It is not always clear which aspect of his anthropomorphic god Luther is referring to. In the flashiest rhetorical passage in the essay, he compares man's will to a beast sought after by two riders, Satan and the god. If Luther's god, whether it be "God preached" or "God hidden" we are not told, climbs into the saddle, the will goes where the god drives it; if Satan manages to climb aboard, he is in control. The human automaton (i.e., beast) can neither choose the rider nor exercise any discretion as to the direction of travel. "The riders fight between themselves to determine which one gets on."[14] It would seem that in the excitement of working out this elaborate figure of speech Luther forgets that his god is supposed to be omnipotent. But if omnipotent, there could be no contest — and no rhetoric. And it is the rhetoric that counts, for Luther's aim here is to humiliate Erasmus, the 'enemy,' not to speak sensibly.

In his 1524 essay Erasmus had pointed out that Luther's only predecessors in the denial of human freedom were the fourteenth century English eccentric Wyclif and the third century Persian Mani, a pagan whose writings subsequently inspired a heresy in the Church against which Augustine was active. At times Luther appears to recognize the justice of this charge for he declares the authority of the Fathers must be held null and void and laments their "blindness."

None of them could appreciate "Paul's clearest and plainest words" against the freedom of the will. Elsewhere, as we have seen, Luther with the characteristic duplicity of the psychotic claims he is supported by Augustine. This off-again-on-again attitude provides helpful insight into Luther's character. From 1520 to the end of his life his guiding principle was to establish a "comfortable certainty of salvation." This purpose replaced in Luther the concept of truth that guides one who enjoys normal psychic health. For Luther the concept of objective truth is irrelevant. If on a given day he can feel more secure by claiming Augustine in support of his own personal views, he does so. On another day when his grandiose delusions help generate this feeling, he can depreciate Augustine as of inferior rank to himself — one chosen by God to reveal the true Christian gospel that was hidden even from Augustine.

Perhaps there is nothing relating to his doctrine of the slavery of the will about which Luther exhibits greater confusion than his attempts to justify it. His argumentative mainstay is the doctrinaire assertion, mentioned earlier, that everything happens of necessity because of God's omnipotence and foreknowledge. However, in contradiction to this he says man cannot act freely because he is the prisoner of Satan. In further contradiction, man cannot act freely because his nature is corrupted by original sin. In still further contradiction, man *can* act freely in matters not pertaining to his salvation. Beyond this he resorts to an experiential argument: "It is written in the hearts of all men that there is no such thing as free will"[15] — an obvious instance of projection. All these self-contradictory positions are asserted in the "Enslaved Will" with the impassioned assurance of a man who speaks always from profound conviction. A psychiatrist once remarked that only doctrinaire determinists and psychotics who lack the experience of inner freedom deny man's free will. Both parts of this statement evidently apply to Luther. But there is still another angle. In his review of Erasmus' preface, Luther lets slip one of his favorite anti-papal cliches: "The Pope binds and ensnares consciences which the gospel declares to be free." It is this use of such totally incongruous language that baffles so many commentators on Luther.

iii. Luther against Luther

Another of his works Luther thought worthy of preservation for posterity was the "Catechism." There is a certain ambiguity about this designation because in the spring of 1529 he published two catechisms, often distinguished by the names "Large" and "Small." The Weimar editors[16] tell us that in Luther's mind the word "Catechism" stood for the content rather than the format, and therefore he meant both volumes. Accepting this opinion, we shall describe both works.

The Small Catechism, a rather colorless performance, is little more than an outline presentation of (1) the Ten Commandments, (2) the Apostles Creed, (3) the Lord's Prayer, (4) the two sacraments of Baptism and the Eucharist with the non-sacrament of Confession sandwiched between them and (5) daily prayers and grace at meals. There is also a preface instructing his preachers that members of their congregations must memorize the exact language of the text, since any variation in wording would be sure to confuse them. After his charges have acquired the elements of religion set forth in the Small Catechism, the preacher should expatiate on the same topics with material from the Large Catechism. The doctrine of the "Enslaved Will," Luther's other immortal work, is not mentioned and by implication is repudiated.

The Large Catechism, following the same structural pattern as the Small, is about ten times as long and very different in tone and content. In large part it resembles the sermons Luther had preached by way of preparing to write it. The rest of it represents that combination of slanderous attack on adversaries and self-revelation that characterizes so much of his literary production from mid 1520 on. We recall that its author has passed through the horrors of the 1527 depression and note the increasing prominence of the paranoid symptoms. The denial and projection mechanisms are a prominent feature. His favorite polemical targets, the papacy, clerical celibacy and monastic life are given lavish attention. On selected topics, such as baptism, his heterodox opponents are similarly favored. In contrast, the Small Catechism contains only three trifling allusions to the Pope and these are confined to the preface; clerical celibacy and monkery are ignored.

Before looking at a few of the more interesting passages, we may review the circumstances that account for the preparation of the catechisms. Luther had for many years been expressing himself on the basic elements of religious belief and practice. Among his earliest published works (1518) are numbered a short tract and a sermon series on the Decalogue, and an exposition of the Our Father. In 1520 he issued a sort of forerunner of the Catechism entitled a "Short Form of the Ten Commandments, the Creed and the Our Father," intermediate in the scope of its treatment of these topics between the Small and Large Catechisms. Its first and third parts are basically a reproduction of his earlier discussions of the Decalogue and Our Father, to which he added a new section providing a commentary on the Creed.

In the preface to the "Short Form" Luther explains how its three parts relate to his view of the Christian life. From the Decalogue the Christian learns that he is a wicked and helpless sinner, from the

Creed he learns how he may remedy this condition, and from the Our Father how to ask for the help he needs to fulfill the commandments and be saved. This work, produced before Luther's regression, much of it indeed based on his outlook of two or more years prior to that event, is probably his most successful endeavor in catechetical writing. It may be regarded as a misfortune that he did not confine his efforts to such work and the closely related task of preaching, for which he had superior native talent, instead of veering off into speculative theology for which he was not well equipped.

Later on in 1522 Luther reissued the "Short Form" in a new and greatly expanded format entitled the *Betbuchlein* ("Little Prayer Book"). The first part of this volume, essentially a reprint of the "Short Form," included discussions of the Ave Maria, about a dozen Psalms and Paul's Epistle to Titus, instructions on confession, hearing mass and preparing for death, and some devotional exercises. The *Betbuchlein,* popular throughout the 1520s, was expressly intended to replace existing prayer books. It thus served a purpose comparable to the new liturgical services and hymns Luther composed during these years. Toward the end of the decade he apparently felt a different sort of book was demanded for the changing religious situation (see below). Also he wished to remove some of the archaic features of the work such as a favorable reference to prayer for the souls in Purgatory.

During the mid 1520s Luther's attitude toward the Decalogue might be described as one of 'enthusiasm,' as the term is used in Ronald Knox's classic ("Enthusiasm: A Chapter in the History of Religion," 1950), tempered by psychosis. In 1525 he preached an extended series of sermons on Exodus. In one of these (referred to above in Ch. 6 — see note 26) which he delivered in August and printed the following spring, he explained what should be the attitude of the modern Christian to Moses. ('Moses' was often Lutherese for the Ten Commandments.) The law of Moses is no longer binding. Moses is dead. What Moses wrote, even though the word of God, does not apply to us Christians. And Martin hammered away at this theme, communicated to him by the Spirit, in his inimitable fashion from a half-dozen different points of view. He did put in a significant qualification, asserting he obeyed the Decalogue anyway, not because of Moses, but because it is 'implanted in my heart by Nature.' It is to be doubted that this attempt to express a Pauline point of view made much impression on the hearts of the simple folk of Wittenberg. And in the same sermon he declared with regard to a practice followed in the Mosaic dispensation whereby a man could have several wives: 'This was an excellent rule.' Here was a philosophy the common man (and woman) could understand, and emulate in principle, even though Germanic law did not countenance the legalization of multiple unions.

Inevitably there was a deplorable decay of moral standards not only in Wittenberg but elsewhere in Saxony during the 1520s. Consider the unsettling experiences that had befallen the people of Saxony during this decade. The Pope was vilified and the authority of the bishops rejected. The time-honored laws on fast and abstinence were ridiculed and discarded by the Lutherian preachers. The preachers also repudiated the rule of celibacy and took wives, some of them a series of wives. Clerical garb was often abandoned. Hundreds of monks and friars left their monasteries and behaved in an unedifying fashion. The confessional was eliminated and the rule of a minimum annual reception of the Eucharist was abrogated. What had been regarded up till then as the Hussite (heretical) practice of the cup for the laity was installed. Images and sacred pictures were thrown out of the churches, desecrated and destroyed. The churches were degraded from the status of the house of God to that of a lecture hall when the Blessed Sacrament was no longer preserved in the tabernacle. The souls in Purgatory and the saints in Heaven were ignored and forgotten. In the famous tourist attraction of Wittenberg, the castle church, it was forbidden to say mass. The report of Dantiscus (see Ch. 3) testifies to this disruption of religious life in Saxony. Enroute to Wittenberg in August 1523 he found the Elbe in flood, overflowing its banks and destroying crops. He relates that local peasants viewed this disaster as divine retribution visited on Saxony for the Lutherian revolt against traditional religious practice and belief.

The preaching of Luther on the Decalogue was thus only one factor out of many, but it helped. Besides eliminating the Ten Commandments he also insisted, as we saw earlier, that no one — from an early age — could refrain from sexual intercourse. The Wittenberg students were not slow to take advantage of this socio-biological discovery. To implement it, some consorted with the prostitutes who began to invade this inviting field of operation, and others contracted 'secret marriages' with local belles, who found themselves deserted after graduation day. The Rev. Dr. Martin Luther did not take kindly to this practical application of his copulative imperative, and later on erupted like Vesuvius when a housemaid resident in the Black Monastery was found to be pregnant. Attempts were made to drive the prostitutes out of town and a faculty committee was appointed to study the question of how unmarried students could handle the copulative imperative.

It gradually dawned on the chief author of this moral debacle that a new approach was called for. This realization was strengthened when he finally mustered enough courage to resume his travels in Saxony. By March of 1528, nearly three years after the Peasants

Revolt, he felt bold enough to accompany a party as far as Alten-burg, the town he had been afraid to visit in 1525 to attend Spala-tin's wedding. Later in the spring he journeyed all the way to Weimar and Jena. Belatedly he undertook some of the visitation duties. The fruit of these observations was the Catechism, for which he warmed up by preaching a sermon series on the subject matter during 1528. By this effort he hoped, vainly as it would appear, to restore moral decorum to a generation that had lost its moorings under the impact of the Lutheran gospel. As he put it in disgust, these people could understand nothing but 'this rotten carnal liberty.'

In the Catechism as in its predecessor the "Short Form" of a decade earlier, there is none of the boastful disdain of 'Moses' that marked the period of enthusiasm of the earlier 1520s. Luther is now one hundred percent behind the Ten Commandments. The Large Catechism exhibited capacity for growth; in the second edition that appeared later in 1529 it developed a tail in the form of a little essay on the Lutheran style of not-quite-sacramental confession. The following year it grew from the other end with a new preface. This opened with a slashing attack on the clergy of Saxony, including both holdovers from the time of the papacy who had hung onto their jobs by conforming to the Lutheran gospel and more recent gradu-ates of Wittenberg. They appeared to have found to their liking the Lutheran proclamation that the 'work of a Christian is to snore and do nothing.' When Luther said this, he did not of course really mean it; he was merely condemning 'works' in order to push 'faith.' No one worked harder than Martin – or outranked him as a faithful Christian. But who could be surprised at the operation of a sort of Gresham's Law on the lush coinage of Luther's utterances?

And so the Saxon clergy found themselves compared to pigs and dogs and described as lazy-bellies. Somewhat more oddly, they were berated for lapsing into 'security.' It may be remarked that many years earlier when Martin was under the influence of the *Imitatio Christi,* he had likewise denounced 'security.' Then under the relent-less pressure of increasing anxiety, he executed a 180-degree turn and began to extol the nascent *sola fide* program for providing him a 'comforting certainty of salvation,' the while reviling the Pope for 'demanding that I doubt my salvation.' He has not in 1530 returned to the view of the *Imitatio* and still requires assurance that he is saved. But claiming this assurance as a right has quite a different effect on the behavior of individuals with a normal psyche than on one who is continually bedevilled by pathological anxiety. We are observing here, incidentally, the basis of later remarks, even before Luther's death, that no one knows what his doctrine really is.

In the "Enslaved Will", despite its marked intellectual confusion, Luther had unmistakably professed a rigid determinism, denying man's freedom of choice, and giving as the reason — among others — for this conclusion the inescapable consequences of divine predestination. In the Catechism, on the other hand, he presented the traditional point of view that the Christian must strive to obey the Ten Commandments and will be punished for not trying. The determinism of the earlier work is not only not mentioned but it is completely inconsistent with the outlook of the Catechism. If these writings were not both known to be Luther's, being separated by an interval of little over three years, they would have to be assigned to different authors. The problem raised by these facts must be examined carefully in any serious study of Luther though it is regularly ducked by the Luther-cult authors.

The explanation lies partly in the compartmentalization of Luther's mind that impeded his recognizing self-contradictions. More important, however, is the story of how the doctrine of the servile will developed. It first appears as a thesis in the Heidelberg disputation in the spring of 1518. The theses Martin prepared for disputations, while undoubtedly related to his current psychic state, were primarily designed to provoke debate, and in general should not be regarded as firmly held positions. From the published version of the Heidelberg theses the one attacking the freedom of the will found its way into the bull *Exsurge Domine* as article 36. It was in his response to this condemnation that Luther in the Latin "Assertion of All the Articles" insisted on this article being the 'best and most important part of my doctrine.' Also it is here that he first states it is not in man's power to choose good or evil because 'all things happen by absolute necessity.'

Melanchthon's "Theological Commonplaces," issued several months after the "Assertion," gives the first systematic presentation of Luther's doctrinaire determinism. The plan to present the enslaved will as the real foundation of 'my theology' may very well be due to Philip — even though he was later to turn very sour on it — rather than Martin, who was hardly capable of systematizing material this way. His characteristic procedure was to write down a list of propositions for debate. On this assumption, Luther's inordinate praise of the "Theological Commonplaces" would be due in part to his delight in seeing a quasi-systematic order for the first time imposed on his ideas. In the next, and major, presentation of his determinism, the reply to Erasmus in the "Enslaved Will," he is not expounding this position spontaneously, as he did earlier with the *sola fide*. He is reacting to criticism. And Luther's characteristic response to criticism of his ideas was not merely to react but to over-react. It was one of his unlovely traits to strike back sharply at his critics just because they had 'aroused the dog.' In fact in his response to *Exsurge Domine* he remarked that he had not previously held all 41 articles with conviction, some being primarily debating topics. But now that the Pope had condemned them, he was going to reply as if convinced of the absolute truth of all 41.

From these considerations it may be inferred that Luther's determinism was to some extent a pose, engendered in him by his unavoidable urge to give his critics as violent a rebuff as he could. This sort of childish rejoinder was typical behavior in the psychotic Luther. Also his practice, noted in an earlier chapter, of proclaiming his doctrinaire determinism only in Latin writings to be read by academic opponents, while supporting the orthodox view of man's freedom in the tracts written in German for the ordinary citizen, is in accord with this view. After his discharge of hostility in the Latin "Assertion" of late 1520 he was free to deal in the German tract "Defense of All the Articles" published some weeks later with the subject of his real concern in article 36. This was the distinctly traditional view that divine grace is indispensable for salvation. This concern is quite apparent also in the discussion provided in the Heidelberg disputation, where there is no mention of a doctrinaire determinism. In this publication he was interested in attacking academic opponents who had defended an exaggerated view of man's unaided moral capability, and also preoccupied with the consequences of his inability to experience love for God. His discussion of 'free will' is marked by his customarily sloppy use of the term and features one of his favorite misquotations of Augustine who in his "The Spirit and the Letter" wrote: "A man's free will avails for nothing except to sin *unless he knows the way of truth.*" Luther achieved quite a dramatic effect by skipping the italicized words. Modern Luther editors in identifying the source of this passage seem disinclined to point out Luther's trifling omission.

Erasmus' essay criticizing Luther's determinism is based on the truculent defense of article 36 in the "Assertion." When Erasmus composed the essay this was Luther's only published defense of the topic. As we have seen, Luther had threatened to give Erasmus what for if he dared interfere in print in Luther's quarrel with Rome. Luther's long delay in replying to Erasmus indicates the low priority he gave the enslaved will doctrine. If Erasmus had attacked the *sola fide,* one would expect a very prompt reply from Wittenberg. Thereafter Luther did not again see fit to publish an exposition of his determinism. From these considerations we conclude that Luther's theological masterpiece was essentially a polemical publication engendered by his compulsive urge to retaliate, that it was not the expression of any deeply held conviction, and that if Erasmus had not written his essay, Luther's own contribution to this subject would have ended with the 1520 polemics in the "Assertion."

There is abundant support for this conclusion in Luther's utterances. He regularly takes for granted the common sense view that a man does have the power to choose between good and evil and the commonplace N. T. teaching that the faithful must make a personal effort to obey the Ten Commandments. It would be pointless to quote such statements, which abound in his published works. Alongside of this it must be recognized that he takes quite a different point of view when dealing with his anxiety states (*Anfechtungen*) and the *sola fide* defense. This ambiguity became crystallized in the business of the 'two times,' which received perhaps its most graphic presentation in the Lectures on Galatians delivered in 1531. At least during the 'time of grace,' i.e., when Luther had the anxiety under tolerable control, he maintained the attitude toward the Decalogue manifested in the Catechism.

There remains to consider Luther's nomination of the "Enslaved Will" for enshrinement in the Hall of Fame. The background of this decision is as follows. In the later 1530s sentiment developed for bringing out an edition of Luther's writings. Nothing significant had issued from his pen for several years, and the establishment of the schismatic churches to which his literary efforts had been largely devoted was now well advanced. It was in these circumstances that he was led to pronounce an opinion on which of his works were marked for immortality. (He felt that most of them were not.) Given the importance to him of the *sola fide,* one might opine that he would select at least one work from his abundant store giving expression to this, the real heart of 'my theology.' But alas, this professor of Unsystematic Theology had never really composed a treatise specifically devoted to the *sola fide* program. As remarked earlier, the nearest he had ever come to such an exposition was the 1520 tract known as "On Christian Liberty" or the "Freedom of the Christian."

He was thus in the droll situation of having to range side by side as his bequest to posterity his hymn to freedom and his denunciation of it. Whether he actually pondered this dilemma, so eminently characteristic of his peculiar genius, is not recorded. A guess at why he gave the nod to his hymn to human bondage is that on this occasion he was writing to a long-time correspondent in the ranks of the (heterodox) humanists and wanted to recommend a work that might have some appeal to this group. That required a composition in Latin and the *De Servo Arbitrio* was one of Luther's very few substantial treatises in that tongue. Furthermore it was directed against Erasmus, the prince of humanists (recently deceased), over whom Luther claimed to have triumphed.

Finally we turn to another aspect of the enslaved will doctrine — Melanchthon's repudiation of it. Without disturbing his intimate friendship with Luther he had arrived by 1530 at the view given here: "During and after Luther's lifetime I rejected that Stoic and Manichean delusion propagated by Luther and others that all works, whether good or evil, in all men both good and evil, take place by necessity. Now it is evident that this doctrine is opposed to God's word, injurious to all discipline and blasphemous against God."[17] It is doubtful if there is a more bizarre incident in the entire story of the Lutherian revolt than this episode involving the two leaders of the schismatic church of Electoral Saxony. Both emphatically claim their doctrinal positions represent 'pure Scripture,' Luther maintaining all Scripture supports his deterministic view and Philip that this view is both contrary to Scripture and blasphemous. One could hardly find a more satisfactory empirical demonstration of the speciousness of the *sola scriptura* position.

The end result of this controversy has been a large scale coverup by Luther biographers. Luther is honored as a great theologian and prophet while Philip is given the minor role of schoolmaster of Germany. The story of his charging Luther with heresy is suppressed, the "Enslaved Will" is celebrated as a great theological masterpiece in full harmony with Augustine, and its gross contradiction of the Catechism and other Lutherian works is ignored. Finally, the public is allowed to think that John Calvin himself conceived the deterministic doctrine of the enslaved will which actually he took over ready-made from Luther, complete with the provision of the absolute predestination to heaven or hell of all members of the totally depraved human race.

Chapter 8

Activities Of The Early 1530's

i.   The unfilial son; second summer at a fortress

As if to signal the increasing severity of the paranoid symptoms, on New Year's day of 1530 Martin directed his hostility against a new and rather surprising target — the Wittenberg congregation. There were other indications of the worsening of his disorder. As an instance of the increasing grandiosity, six months earlier he complained that he felt as though the entire world was depending on him for (spiritual) support: "I am forced to be Hercules and Atlas."[1] Also as noted earlier, in the preface to the revised Catechism he expressed hostility even toward the clergy of his church of Electoral Saxony. In his New Year's sermon, after an impassioned exposition of the *sola fide,* he cut loose against the Wittenbergers.[2] It was their fault that the automatic performance of good works consequent upon the acquisition of 'faith' had not materialized. Freed from the tyranny of the Pope, the dear burghers should have been making donations to the poor box, now dubbed the 'common chest.' But so far from doing this, they were lax even about their obedience to the civil government, and devoted their spare time merely to counting their money. They were also guilty of false 'security,' the same charge he was now bringing against his fellow members of the clergy.

Undeterred by the failure of his prophecy guaranteeing the automatic appearance of good works among the faithful, he again laid on the line his infallible judgement. Within two years as divine retribution for this hardness of heart, the peasants and burghers of Saxony would find themselves at the mercy of the Turks. They could expect the same fate as had lately befallen the peasants of Austria.

But the real bombshell was reserved until the end of the sermon. Luther had told his audience that their lack of attention made his preaching task most disagreeable to him; he would sooner preach to stupid dogs. Now he told them that he was finished with them. He would never preach to them again, or at least till his passion cooled and he could again feel in his heart a call to preach. This announcement generated a shock wave throughout schismatic Saxony and aroused the Elector, Duke John, to action.

In a letter to Martin dated January 18 he expressed his consternation and demanded to know what had brought about this decision. Using a Lutheran style of argument, he pointed out to Luther what joy the news of his defection would bring to the enemies of the gospel. While offering to take action against members of the congregation if they were at fault, he made it clear that Luther was to preach at least every Sunday or else lose the good will of his sovereign. Luther had in fact stuck to his word and abstained from preaching the first three Sundays of January. But apparently the letter from Duke John softened his heart for the moment and he did preach on the fourth and fifth Sundays of the month. Then the effect of the reprimand wore off and he shunned the pulpit through all of February and on into March.

On March 14 the Elector wrote him again, but this time concerning quite a different matter. The Emperor had sent out official notice to the German principalities and cities about his plans to settle the religious question at the impending diet of Augsburg. The March 14 letter instructed Luther, Melanchthon and Jonas to appear at Torgau (by early April) to join the delegation from Electoral Saxony. Receipt of this letter seems to have reminded Luther that he was in a state of disobedience to the Elector; at any rate he gave a sermon on the following Sunday but skipped the last one of the month. But during April, while in the company of the Elector, who enjoyed listening to Luther's sermons, he rapidly regained his form. During the week before and the week after Easter Sunday, which in 1530 fell on April 17, Luther is reported to have delivered 12 sermons, some of them on the journey to the south and west through the Elector's domains and the rest at the Coburg fortress, the southernmost of his possessions, which was to be Luther's residence for the next half year.

From the viewpoint of present day psychiatry the motivation of Luther's decision to stop preaching is apparent. The state of affairs that led to the decision, namely, the moral decay in Saxony that impelled him to prepare the Catechism, was described in the preceding chapter. Since the Catechism was no more effective in producing Christian behavior in Luther's congregation than had been the preaching, Luther's defensive reaction was automatic. Luther had to be right; therefore the congregation must be wrong. They had now become the swine before whom the pearls of the Lutheran gospel must no longer be scattered. It is to be noted that the Weimar editors of the volume of Luther's sermons for 1530 (vol. 32) speculate on his motive for the decision to stop preaching.[3] After citing the available facts, together with comments by Melanchthon and Luther's scribe George Roerer, the editors feel that in the judgment of his intimates Luther was at this time suffering an attack of mental illness. The editors accept this judgment, which is made more plausible with a bit of folklore psychology: that great men are especially prone to spells of depression. It is of interest that Melanchthon and other associates of Luther had by 1530 come to agree with such observers as Erasmus and Pirckheimer on the state of Luther's mental health. It is of almost equal interest that the same conclusion was reached (in 1906) by the Weimar editors who, unlike some of the biographers, felt obligated to discuss what appeared to them as a radically new behavior pattern.

On the Saturday after Easter the Elector, leaving Luther – still under the imperial ban – at the fortress and accompanied by his other theological advisers, set out from Coburg on the final leg of the journey to Augsburg, around 150 miles farther south. For company at the fortress, which was in a remote situation on a high broad hill overlooking an extensive countryside, Luther had with him two Wittenberg students, one of them being his nephew Cyriac Kaufmann. He remained there until autumn, finally returning to Wittenberg on October 13. The sojourn at Coburg gave rise to a number of developments. One of the most significant was further regression, due partly to the effect of his extended separation from Melanchthon and other close associates for almost a half year, and partly to new anxiety over the threat of imperial action against the continuance of the ecclesiastical schism in Electoral Saxony and Hesse. The anxiety inspired a flurry of pamphlets during the years 1530-33, after which Luther lapsed into comparative silence until toward the end of the decade. It is likely that the impulse to deliver the lecture series on the Epistle to the Galatians (1531) also derives from the Coburg experience. Still another consequence of the stay at Coburg is the large number of letters to close friends he had occasion to write, of which well over a hundred are extant. We have previously quoted one of these, the letter to Jerome Weller on devices for dealing with anxiety.

Almost two months before Martin departed Wittenberg for Coburg he had received a letter from his brother James in Mansfeld notifying him their father Hans was gravely ill and desired a visit from his famous elder son. Not quite a year earlier (April 19, 1529) the father and brother had visited Martin in Wittenberg just before he himself went off for a ten-day visit to the Electoral court in Torgau. This was apparently the last meeting of Hans and Martin. His response to the parental request, dated February 15, 1530, is the only extant letter Martin sent to his father.

The excuse for refusing to visit his dying parent with which Martin begins his reply recalls a similar letter to Spalatin in the autumn of 1525:

> I would gladly have come to visit you but my good friends have advised against it and dissuaded me, and I myself believe I should not tempt God by endangering my person, for you know the feeling lords and peasants have for me. But it would give me great happiness if you and my mother could manage to come here to us. My Katie and all of us with tears beg you to do so.[4]

We pause here to examine this use of the denial mechanism. It was noted earlier that by 1528 Luther had sufficiently recovered from his fear of danger to his person on the road to make journeys in Saxony if accompanied by friends. His most recent trip was one to distant Marburg the preceding autumn (September-October 1529). Going and returning, he had been on the road for some four weeks counting the stopovers to preach and socialize with acquaintances. In view of this experience we cannot accept the statement that he was still afraid to make a two-day trip on which he could certainly have enjoyed the company of his loyal associates. The further statement that these associates had advised him not to visit his father during this illness is indeed preposterous. The real obstacle must be the inhibition which had apparently kept him from crossing the threshold of the parental home since the summer of 1505.

Likewise we do not regard as sincere (or meaningful) the invitation for his parents to move into the Black Monastery. If taken straight, the invitation would have to be regarded as highly inconsiderate, for it would require an old man presumably in his final illness traveling a long distance in an unheated wagon in the midst of winter. What Martin was really saying was "I won't come to see you but you can come to see me, even though the journey will probably be the death of you." Furthermore, his mother would be the last person he would want as a permanent guest in his home. Thus what purported to be an invitation must be regarded as an extension of the alibi.

In the next and longer part of the letter, Luther composes a pious exhortation designed to prepare his father spiritually for death. He brings this section to a close by saying that "the leaving of this life to go to God is much less than going from here to Mansfeld or from Mansfeld to Wittenberg . . . It is like an hour's sleep; then everything will change." Coming from one who has such an abject fear of death as Martin, the statement reflects the spirit of falsification with which the letter opens. But in the next and final paragraph Martin deviates into a vein of sincerity:

> I ask your pardon for my bodily absence which (God knows) saddens my heart. We greet you and pray for you faithfully — my

Katie, little Hans, little Lena, Aunt Lena and our whole household.

Your loving son,
Martin Luther

Hans lived on till the end of May. When Martin, now at the Coburg retreat, learned of his father's death he is said to have expressed appropriate grief. For undoubtedly he had some affection for his father and must have felt greatly ashamed of his unwillingness to attend the old man. If Martin had had any affection for his mother, he would at least have written her a letter of condolence, but there is no hint that he did anything of the kind.

A year later (May 20, 1531) Martin had occasion once more to write a dying parent. The only extant letter to his mother also begins with a falsification: "I have received my brother James' letter about your illness, and it deeply grieves me, especially because I cannot be with you in body as I should like to be. But I do appear bodily with this letter and will be with you in spirit, along with all my family."[5] It is to be observed that on this occasion the son offers no explanation for failing to come to his mother. This probably caused no surprise in Mansfeld, for as the record indicates he had avoided visiting her for more than a quarter of a century.

The next paragraph sounds as though Martin were writing to a stranger toward whom he had incurred an obligation: "I hope that your heart has long since been abundantly instructed without my help . . . . and been adequately provided with preachers and comforters. However, I will do my part too and *acknowledge that, as your child I have a duty to perform to you as my mother* . . . . Therefore I shall add myself to the number of your comforters." Having thus identified himself as a properly qualified member of the circle of her clerical advisers, Martin proceeds to preach a lengthy sermon on redemption and death, pausing once or twice to interject 'dear mother,' although 'my dear brethren' would have been much more in harmony with the context. An interesting feature of the sermon is the inclusion of a rhetorical description of death strongly reminiscent of something that appeared about this time in his academic lectures on Galatians.

The sermon, i.e., letter, concludes with the scantiest of perorations: "All your children and my Katie pray for you. Some weep, some eat and say: 'Grandmother is very sick.' God's grace be with us all. Amen."

Your loving son,
Martin Luther

The least that can be said for this conclusion is that in it Martin avoided the hypocrisy of expressing any personal grief at the prospect of his mother's approaching death. This event occurred about a month after the letter reached Mansfeld and presumably brought him a measure of relief. While Luther's attitude toward his mother would be called inhumane in a person with a normal psyche, with him it was involuntary and well within the emotional range observed in those who suffer from comparable psychotic symptoms. In line with Martin's habit of citing Scripture texts that reflect his current moods and intentions, it seems appropriate here to recall the text most relevant to his refusal to visit either his father or mother during their final illness. It occurs in the 25th chapter of the gospel according to Matthew in the parable of the Last Judgment. Since Luther had already repudiated this gospel in general and the parable in particular, it may be doubted that when writing his parents he recollected the words which so aptly describe his behavior on these occasions: "I was sick and you did not come to me."

About the time of his father's death, there issued from the press Luther's longest composition of the early 1530s, a bitter and scurrilous attack on the bishops and other clergy taking part in the diet, "A Warning to the Clergy Assembled at the Diet of Augsburg." One need only scan this rather tedious harangue to see why the Elector chose not to ask Luther to compose the document later to become famous as the Augsburg Confession. Of more interest for its revelation of the character of the Luther of the 1530s is the much shorter and little noticed piece entitled "Disavowal of Purgatory," written in June. While its date of composition may suggest that it was intended as a going away gift to his departed father, it is rather to be viewed as a blow at the papacy to help make up for the conciliatory stance currently being taken by Melanchthon at Augsburg.

Two years earlier Luther had defended a doctrinal position (the practice of infant baptism) on the basis that it must be accepted even though not supported by Scripture because it was guaranteed by ecclesiastical tradition. In the "Disavowal of Purgatory" in a characteristic self-reversal, he attacks a much better founded tradition on the ground that it is not explicitly set forth in Scripture. According to this tradition the souls of the justified in order to make reparation for sins committed during their earthly sojourn may have to undergo a period of purification before being granted the Beatific Vision. The tradition also holds that while enduring this purgation they can be aided by the prayers of the faithful on earth. This tradition dates back to a period well before the Christian era. Its most explicit witness in the Old Testament occurs in the book of 2 Maccabees, composed during the second century B.C. Witnesses to the tradition in the early Christian centuries include inscriptions in the catacombs and the second century theologian Tertullian, who in his treatise "On Monogamy" argues that it is the duty of a widow to pray for the soul of her departed spouse, the performance of this duty being in his view one of the impediments to a second marriage.

The tradition is given repeated witness in the writings of the Church Fathers. One of the most detailed of these is found in a sermon of Augustine on a text from 1 Thess. 4 concerning "those who have died in Christ":

> It is the tradition of the fathers and the universal practice of the Church to pray for those who are dead in the communion of the body and blood of Jesus Christ and to commemorate them in the place prescribed in the same sacrifice that is offered both for them and for the living. Who can doubt that the works of mercy performed for their intention are any less advantageous than are the prayers so full of fruit offered for them before God.[6]

In passing we might note Augustine's reference to the offering of the sacrifice of the mass for the welfare of the living and the dead. No other teaching had Luther combatted so violently and with so much verbal abuse for the past decade as this one. Reading this sermon of Augustine's we can better understand Luther's motivation in declaring (but only in private) that he was finished with Augustine once "I learned how to read Paul."

At some point in the 1520s he came to reject the tradition because it no longer harmonized with the needs of his psychic constitution. The doctrine requiring the penitent to make satisfaction for his offenses, which was given more stress in the first centuries than in later times, was a perennial target of Luther's hostility. The arguments he develops against the tradition in the tract reflect the heavy reliance on the denial mechanism that characterizes the paranoid phase of his disorder. The most pervasive of the falsifications, repeated from many different angles, is the denial that this most ancient of traditions is an 'article of faith.' Luther avoids so far as possible any direct mention of the content of the tradition, identifying it repeatedly with just the term *Fegfeur* (Purgatory) which by one of his favorite polemical techniques thereby becomes a dirty word. Ignoring the abundant witness to the tradition in the early centuries, he boldly asserts it was the 'lying sophists' who made *Fegfeur* an article of faith by distorting the meaning of a passage in the "Dialogues" of Pope Gregory VI (late sixth century). His assertion that the belief in the efficacy of prayers for the dead dates from a time after Gregory is more likely one of his conscious falsifications rather than an instance of the denial mechanism. As noted in an earlier chapter, he had stated some years previously that he accepted this belief on the authority of Augustine, who lived a couple of centuries before Gregory.

The principal theme of Luther's argument is that the 'sophist lie' about *Fegfeur* being an article of faith is inspired solely by greed. To introduce this slander he quotes the well known text from 2 Maccabees 12 referred to above, which begins "Judas [Maccabeus] took up a collection of 12,000 silver drachmas and sent it to Jerusalem to provide for an expiatory sacrifice for the sins of the dead," and ends "It is a holy and pious thought to pray for the dead that they may be released from their sins." This text had served a liturgical use for centuries, being read in masses offered for the dead. The sermon of Augustine quoted above contains an echo of this text.

After quoting the passage, Luther at once proceeds to deny that 2 Maccabees is Scripture. The argument he employs here is of especial interest inasmuch as the *sola scriptura* slogan contains no criterion for distinguishing Scripture from non-Scripture, this being one of its several inner contradictions. Luther's rationale in this instance is that 2 Maccabees was not received as Scripture by the 'old Fathers.' He is careful not to mention names, for the only distinguished 'Father' of the western Church to question the canonical status of 2 Maccabees was Jerome, who by the 1530s occupied a prominent place on Luther's enemies list. Augustine, on the other hand, not only regarded this book as Scripture but rebuked Jerome for his attitude. Since Luther from time to time during the paranoid years professed publicly to respect Augustine's authority, he had to proceed cautiously here to avoid embarrassment about his authorities. Of still greater import is Luther's direct confrontation with a text of Scripture which he finds unacceptable and must perforce discard from the canon. Such a confrontation naturally exposes one of the grosser inadequacies of the *sola scriptura,* on which Luther relies strongly in this tract. His calling upon the 'traditions of men' to rescue the *sola scriptura* is one of those delightful self-contradictions he so often exhibits in the exercise of his distinctive intellectual qualities.

Along with the charge that *Fegfeur* is a lie of the sophists – in all Luther numbers eight specific lies of this sort in the first two sections of the tract – is the accusation that greed is their sole motivation for the lies. To help render this slander plausible, he finds the 12,000 drachmas mentioned in 2 Maccabees made to order. This monetary sum runs through the tract like a leitmotif, making an appearance in twelve different places, once for each thousand drachmas. In the closing paragraph it shows up in a rather puzzling context:

> If Mammon were my god and I was able to hand over 12,000 drachmas, you would see that I could convert all the sophists and heretics in one day, and bring to an end not just Purgatory but the entire papacy before a month went by. My doctrine lacks nothing but the divinity of the great god Mammon; if it had that, it would be called not heresy or error but the pure truth. But now it is erroneous and heretical. Why? Because it is poor. Poverty is my error and heresy.[7]

With this Master of the Denial Mechanism one can not always be sure what really lies behind the rhetoric. In an age of authoritarian princes who decided what form of worship would be permitted within their boundaries, Luther had long since learned what made 'my theology' prosper. It is quite true that his god was not Mammon, but he knew how to make a very strong pitch to the princes who were not averse to serving this god. On occasion he could lament the widespread plunder of monastic and other Church wealth, but he was not so naive as to be unaware of what more than anything else promoted the triumph of his gospel, though he was naturally averse to acknowledging it in public. In the words of the finale just quoted, so unrelated to the subject of the tract, it would appear that we are witnessing another exhibit from Luther's inexhaustible store of defenses.

By 1530 the revolt against the Church inaugurated by Luther a decade earlier had become thoroughly politicized. This was inevitable in an age when it was widely presumed the exercise of religion should be integrated into the local political and social structure. The status of religious practice in Germany was peculiar in that — at least in theory — the governments of the hundreds of German principalities and free cities were themselves subject to the rule of the Emperor. The significance of the diet of Augsburg of 1530 is that it was the first major confrontation between the imperial government, which supported the papacy, and a group of German states and cities that during the 1520s had set up their own church establishments based on the innovations of Luther and Carlstadt. By casting off the rule of the bishops these German governments had stopped the flow of funds in the form of taxes and other payments to Rome. By expropriating various kinds of ecclesiastical property within their domains they had been able to gain control of additional sources of revenue. Quite apart from the differences on doctrinal questions, these economic benefits acted as a formidable barrier to attempts to induce the dissident governments to return to unity.

To initiate proceedings at the diet, the more influential of these governments were directed to present a statement of their positions on doctrine and practice before the assembled representatives. The discussion of this document (later known as the Augsburg Confession) and a reply to it issued under the auspices of the imperial government occupied a period of some weeks beginning in the latter part of June. In addition, a group of four cities including Strasbourg submitted a statement of their positions, and Zwingli sent in a third. The upshot of the discussions was that a majority of the representatives found the positions taken by the separatist governments unacceptable. There followed several weeks of private discussions among specially appointed committees, who vainly attempted to discover some sort of compromise that would be mutually acceptable.

After all attempts to reach an amicable settlement had failed, an imperial decree was promulgated ordering the dissenting governments to desist from further innovations and to report by the following April on their plans for rejoining the religious community.

Luther, though extremely interested in the actions of the diet, played virtually no role in the proceedings. In fact, had he been suddenly removed from the scene early in 1530, it is doubtful if the subsequent history of religious developments in Germany would have been significantly modified. While effective as an agitator, he had no real political talent, and in consequence of his psychic disorder could only be a source of discord. And that was a commodity by no means in short supply.

An instance of Luther's ineffectiveness in the political sphere was provided before the sessions of the diet began. Philip of Hesse, the most bellicose of the princes who had joined the schism, had by no means given up his ambition to form a military alliance with Zwingli. In Augsburg during the weeks preceding the opening of the sessions of the diet, Melanchthon became alarmed at the progress of Philip's negotiations with the Swiss and appealed to Luther to take a hand. But a few weeks of comparative isolation at Coburg had upset Luther's psychic equilibrium. In a letter to Melanchthon dated May 12, in which he alludes to the request to deal with Hesse, he reports on his anxiety symptoms. "I was alone . . . and Satan overcame me to the point of driving me from my room and forcing me into the company of men. I hardly expected the day I would finally see that spirit so powerful and of clearly divine majesty."[8]

Along with this humiliating inability of the supposed *homo religiosus* to remain in a room by himself in communion with his God, he suffered from a peculiar inhibition with regard to reading and writing. In this same letter he complains of a ringing, or thundering, in his head which prevents him from dealing with the written word. We hear a good deal about this condition in Luther's later years. For example, in a Table Talk item of March 1532 he declares: "I am overcome . . . . I eat, drink and sleep, but I am quite unable to read, write or preach." A week or so later in a letter to Amsdorf (April 2) "the indisposition of my head has for more than a month kept me from the duties of writing, reading and teaching."

It was thus nearly six weeks before Luther felt able to address himself to the Hesse-Zwingli problem in the form of an epistle to the Landgrave. In it he delivered an argument against rejecting the Real Presence in the Eucharist, with no allusions to the political question that was disturbing Melanchthon. He revived the curious declaration made five or six years earlier in an open letter to a Strasbourg group that he would like very much to be able to deny the Real

Presence himself but could find no compelling reason to do so. Another oddity in the letter is that at a time when Melanchthon was trying to persuade the assembly at Augsburg of the antiquity of the Lutherian doctrines, Luther himself proclaims their novelty. "Ah Lord God! it's no joke or jest to teach novelties. One must have not darkness or his own delusions or uncertain arguments but a clear powerful text . . . I have suffered such great trouble and danger over my doctrine I would not want my efforts to be in vain."[9]

It is unknown just what impression the letter made on Philip. It failed to deter him from proceeding with his plans, for shortly thereafter he completed the pact with Zwingli, only to have it unexpectedly nullified the next year when Zwingli fell on the battlefield during the Swiss civil war and his army was defeated.

Another echo from the past occurred later in the summer in a letter to Melanchthon. As noted in an earlier chapter, Luther had proclaimed in August of 1520 that in attacking the papacy "anything is permitted us," – the Lutherine privilege. Now in August of 1530 he repeats his claim to this privilege in new and more interesting language, occasioned by the evasions and equivocations being employed by Melanchthon in the Augsburg negotiations. To simulate a conciliatory approach Melanchthon was offering concessions on various disputed matters the Wittenbergers had no real intention of making. Referring to Melanchthon's apparent willingness to subvert the Lutherian gospel, Luther writes in a characteristically grandiose vein:

> I know you are able to do nothing in this matter save possibly to sin against my person, so that I might be charged with bad faith and instability. But what of that? The matter will easily be straightened out because of the truth and constancy of our cause. I doubt this will happen, but if it should, then as I say there is no need to despair. For if by obtaining a settlement we avoid violence, we can easily be forgiven our tricks, lies and stumblings, because His mercy reigns over us.[10]

Luther's booking in advance the forgiveness of his sins calls to mind another of Samuel Butler's rhymes about Luther's spiritual progeny in England during the following century:

> For they have tricks to cast their sins
> As easy as serpents do their skins.

ii. Response to the Diet of Augsburg

In some of his letters Luther manifests extreme irritation at what was going on at Augsburg. By mid July he evidences at least partial recovery from the indisposition shown in the letter to Melanchthon quoted above. Addressing himself to all four of the Elector's theological advisors, he begins with a comment on the argument from tradition: "Fathers, Fathers, Fathers, Church, Church, Church, usage and custom — this is all you hear." Then after delivering a lecture on what is owing respectively to God and Caesar, and ignoring the fact that his correspondents are in attendance at the diet on orders from Caesar, he forthwith commands them to depart from it. "I absolve you in the name of the Lord from this assembly. Come home at once, come home! Don't hope for agreement or concessions. I never pray to God for that because I know it to be impossible."[11]

The letter closes with a thrust at the papal legate Campeggio, with whom Melanchthon held several parleys: "If Campeggio mentions his powers of dispensation, I reply with the words of Amsdorf: I shit on the legate and his master with their dispensations; we can find our own dispensations. When the Lord teaches, disregard the dispensations of his servant, especially when the servant is such a brigand and usurper of power. Home, home!" There is a comparable outburst in a letter dated September 20 to Jonas. After damning up and down the attempts at compromise, he writes: "I am almost bursting with anger and indignation. I pray you, break off your negotiations with them and come back here." Earlier in the summer he had taken a different line, threatening to descend on Augsburg in person, into the 'terrible teeth of Satan,' but had found it possible to restrain himself from this adventure.[12]

Writing to a clerical friend in Zwickau toward the end of September, he complains again of his enforced idleness at Coburg occasioned by the ringing or buzzing in his head which is "like the whirling of the winds." "Lest I be altogether idle I am reduced to writing commentaries. But now the buzzing is starting to let up and I have an occasional respite from it."[13] (In a letter written some weeks earlier to Katie on August 14, he had announced that he had been in excellent health, with no buzzing in his head since August 10.) Luther appears to have exaggerated the extent of his inactivity at Coburg, for he turned out a rather considerable batch of material for the printers in addition to well over a hundred letters during his five and a half months there. Without particularizing on the quality of the work, there are more than a half dozen tracts of varying length and commentaries on a number of psalms, some of them quite extensive. All told there was more than enough to fill up one of the large volumes of the Weimar edition.

The decisions reached by the diet of Augsburg were published during the following winter in an official document copies of which did not reach Wittenberg till along in March of 1531. Luther had become acquainted with the substance of these decisions before his departure from Coburg at the conclusion of the sessions of the diet and began promptly to compose a response to them. But he held up publication of his tract, which was entitled "Warning to his Dear Germans," until the Recess, or imperial edict, was in his hands. He reacted to a reading of this document in his usual style by composing a specific reply to it, in addition to the other tract just mentioned. This reply took his favored form of a running commentary on selected topics from the Recess and he chose to give it the quasi-academic title of "Gloss on the Alleged Imperial Edict."

The outcome of the diet as embodied in the official Recess created a serious image problem for Martin. He had been presenting himself as a law and order man (even though outlawed by the imperial government a decade earlier), and emphasized this role for himself especially since his encounter with Muentzer. To preserve this image while urging his fellow Germans to disobey the imperial edict presented a real challenge to his rhetorical powers. An examination of the above mentioned tracts, which were in print by late March or early April, shows that as usual he was equal to such a challenge.

It should perhaps be noted that in advocating armed resistance to the Emperor in the "Warning" Luther was making one of his many reversals of doctrine. Just a year earlier in a letter to the Elector he had come out strong for a policy of complete non-resistance as dictated by Scripture. If the Emperor attacks us on account of our religious beliefs, we have no right to strike back even in self-defense. The Elector, of course, would not buy this argument and in March of 1531 was active in completing the formation of a military alliance — the Smalkald League — with other schismatic states to wage war if necessary against the Emperor. In view of this action by his sovereign Luther may be said to have adjusted his reading of Scripture to conform to the new status quo. Such considerations underlay all his exegetical shifts whether prompted by external developments as here or by inner psychic changes. One recalls the dictum of the medieval schoolmen, "Authority has a nose of wax," although for them the authority referred to was that of a human author rather than Scripture as with Luther.

The "Warning to his Dear Germans" provides evidence of the progress of Luther's psychic disorder, particularly of his further loss of contact with reality. In contrast with earlier writings which exhibit occasional or even frequent use of the denial mechanism, the "Warning" shows Luther to have retreated into a fantasy world from which he seldom emerges. In substance the "Warning" is largely an exercise in mendacious slander of members of the hated and despised Church. Its expressed intent is to advise his fellow Saxons to resist the imperial decree issued at Augsburg which aimed to arrest and contain the schism. Luther's unconscious purpose was to defend against the anxiety aroused in him by his new posture as a manifest rebel against the imperial government.

His extreme agitation at the time of composition is shown, for example, by his emotional remarks on the possibility of losing his life in the armed conflict he anticipated between the schismatic states and those loyal to Church and empire. At one point he speaks like the villain in a Grade B Western film: "If I am murdered in the rebellion [caused by the papists] I will take a crowd of the papal clergy with me." He looks with complacency on this gruesome event as a stupendous triumph for himself. "They will go to hell with the devils and I to heaven with God." The survivors of this holocaust would look with awe upon the great doctor who surpassed all the bishops, priests and monks as a Christian teacher. He repeats a variation of the grandiose challenge which became a favorite boast during the paranoid years: "Living I will be your plague, dying I will be your death." His adversaries are in no respect a match for him; in the event of a butting match they will find even that his head is harder than theirs.[14]

Elsewhere there is a hint of the preoccupation with human excrement which marks his declining years: "Dear sirs, step away from the wall, do it in your breeches, and hang it around your neck." This adjuration is followed by more pathological boasting: "Let them rage in the name of all the devils while I laugh in the name of God."

Of interest is Luther's attempt to dissociate the Emperor from the villains in the papacy who are causing all the trouble. He pauses in the midst of the attack on his opponents to devote three or four pages to praise of Emperor. A similar element of fantasy is to be observed in the tract issued contemporaneously with the "Warning," the "Gloss on the Alleged Imperial Edict." Here the falsification expressed in the title is restated at length in the opening paragraph:

> I, Martin Luther, teacher of the holy Scriptures and preacher to the Christians of Wittenberg, state the following condition in this public letter, that everything I write in this little book against the alleged imperial edict should not be understood as written against the imperial majesty or public authority whether ecclesiastical or secular . . . . I am not opposing the pious Emperor or the pious lords but the traitors and rascals (whether princes or bishops) who under cover of the Emperor's name . . . have undertaken to carry out their desperate and malicious designs.[15]

The public fact which Martin here is forced pathologically to deny is that it was Charles himself who directed the diet to take decisive action in checking the ecclesiastical schism in Germany. When his purpose was thwarted by the refusal of the schismatic principalities to make any meaningful settlement of the religious differences, he was in favor of bringing them to heel by military action. What kept him from prompt recourse to this policy was his lack of suitable armed forces in Germany at the time. What with one problem or another confronting him, the most serious being the perennial threat of a Turkish invasion of Europe, Charles did not resort to military force against Electoral Saxony, Hesse and their allies until many more years had passed, in fact, until shortly after Luther's death. Thus the great doctor of Wittenberg was denied the distinction of giving his life to the cause and taking with him to the grave a sizable batch of his hated opponents.

It is worth inquiring as to who were the dear Germans Luther appealed to in these anti-imperial tracts of early 1531. In recent years he had repudiated not only the hopelessly ungodly German peasants but also townspeople and the ruling classes in general. Somewhat more than a year earlier (cf. Sec. i above) he had foretold that Germany would soon be overwhelmed by the Turkish armies as divine retribution for their recalcitrance over accepting the Lutherian gospel, his own Wittenberg congregation being the vessels chosen to receive this proclamation. In other writings he lets it be known that the group of the Elect is indeed tiny. But since the primary object of the "Warning" is to persuade as many Germans as possible to join in battle against the Emperor in the event of armed conflict over religious differences, these particularist considerations are shelved. Doubtless mindful of them, however, Luther at first is more than a little vague about the identity of his audience. But after warming up to his new vocation, he then proudly announces his new title, 'Prophet of the Germans,' rather than prophet merely of the Elect.

It is in the latter half of the "Warning" that Martin makes clear, if only by implication, which Germans he is addressing. They are the Germans who have not renounced their allegiance to the Church. Such Germans, by supporting the Emperor, will be guilty of all the crimes of the papacy. What these crimes are is not left in doubt, for Luther provides quite a long list, which he runs through with great gusto, bearing down hard first of all on such crimes as the 'whoring, adultery and fornication' in the cathedral chapters and monasteries and the 'sodomy of the Roman court.' Luther maintains a curious double standard with regard to the sins of the flesh. Here he puts them at the head of the list, presumably because on this occasion he regards them as best calculated to destroy the good name of his sacerdotal enemies. On other occasions when he is glorifying his own status as a doctor and theologian, and explaining how he attained this eminence with the help of his dreadful temptations and sins against the 'first table,' i.e., his blasphemy and hatred of God, the sins of the flesh are dismissed as trivial. When following this other game plan, he ridicules the 'sophists' for their despicable inferiority to him, accusing them of harping on nothing but sins of the flesh. They do this because they are ignorant of the really serious sins of which Luther has had such a vast first hand experience.

About half way through his catalog, specifically just after excoriating the twin abominations of Purgatory and the mass, Martin pauses as if to catch his breath and wonder out loud if he has perhaps been too free with his name calling and vituperation. Not a bit of it. He then starts off on a different kind of list — a list of reasons why his abusiveness is right and proper — and then gradually works his way back into his colorful enumeration of the sins of the papacy.

The "Warning" closes with a characteristic Lutherian touch. It is a special form of the denial mechanism observed in paranoid individuals who are prone to claim their innocence of any wrong-doing. In this instance Luther is at pains to declare that so far is he from inciting his dear Germans to rebellion that he is urging nothing but peace, not even armed action in self defense. If war comes, the entire blame for it lies elsewhere, none of it on him. "I am innocent."

iii. The paranoid paternoster

Not long after the two tracts, the "Warning" and the "Gloss," had gone on sale, a letter of protest about them from Duke George was received at the Electoral court. It might be noted by way of background that this was not the first occasion on which the Duke had complained to his cousin about Luther's scurrilous compositions. In a letter of June 1528 to his one-time monastic brother Wenzel Link, now a preacher at Nuremberg, Luther had included a number of insulting and libelous comments on Duke George. As was then the fashion, copies of the letter were circulated, one of them finally reaching the Duke. (A similar occurrence in 1522 was described in an earlier chapter.) Among the letters and published tracts that resulted from the libelous epistle to Link, the best known is Martin's "On Secret and Stolen Letters." In an admonitory letter to Luther dated January 18, 1529 Elector John instructed him to print nothing more about Duke George or other persons of princely rank without first submitting a copy to the Elector for approval. Likewise he reminded Luther of the order issued early in the 1520s by Frederick that before publishing anything concerned with doctrine he have it checked by the university authorities. It may be remarked that these rules restricting Luther's freedom of publication, while they appear to have had little practical effect, are a good indication that he was regarded by his sovereigns as not altogether responsible.

In the new protest of April 1531 George pointed out that Luther's two tracts were in open defiance of the imperial edict, which forbade the printing of abusive books, and they tended to incite the citizenry to rebellion. As for their abusive language, which was directed against men of all estates both high and low, no one had ever heard

the like before. The Elector relayed this complaint to Chancellor
Brueck, then stationed in Wittenberg, with instructions to discuss
the matter with the offender. Brueck replied promptly, reporting
that he had had a discussion with Luther, that as the Elector knew
Luther was a conscientious and upright soul, and expressing the wish
that all might have heard the beautiful and powerful sermon Luther
had delivered that very day (Palm Sunday). The Elector then sent a
rather non-committal reply to Duke George, saying that he himself
was at times the target of harsh criticism, and that he had instructed
Luther to be moderate.

Realizing that it was useless to expect any action against Luther
from his noble cousin, Duke George tried a different approach. He
composed and had printed a short tract by way of answer to the
"Warning" in which he advised the German people to ignore Luther
and obey the imperial government. This provided Luther with an excuse for returning to the fray with another tract which he called the
"Assassin (*Meuchler*) of Dresden." (As usual he paid no attention to
the Elector's order about obtaining permission to print such pamphlets.) While the new tract adds nothing to Luther's stature as a
writer, being largely an exercise in name-calling, there are in it at
least two matters of interest.

In the "Warning to his Dear Germans" as a means of identifying
his followers he had made use of the term 'Lutherian' (*Lutherischen*),
which had achieved currency at the diet of Augsburg. He did this
very gingerly, like a man testing the swimming pool temperature with
his toe and finding it too uncomfortable to proceed any farther. Elsewhere in that tract he preferred for the purpose a term translatable
as 'my side' (*Meinen*), and in previous years he was prone to refer to
his supporters as 'Christians.' But since Luther maintained there
were hardly any real Christians, just himself and a few others, this
latter term was not suitable either. Now in the spring of 1531 with
the further development of his paranoid symptoms, he lapsed into
the bitterly partisan, hopelessly unchristian spirit that he was to refer
to as his bequest to posterity. The term 'Lutherian' is the most frequently used epithet in the "Assassin," appearing almost 50 times. It
serves as an effective counter to his own earlier innovation 'papist,'
which likewise turns up repeatedly in the tract, alternating with
'blood-hounds,' to designate his hated opponents. This hammering
away at his adversaries with the epithet 'Lutherian' is not to be interpreted as a sign of Luther's pride in the public recognition that he
is the author of a set of heterodox teachings. Rather it is the expression of his pathological defiance — the defiance of the immature ego,
as observable, say, in a small boy shouting the same derisive epithet
over and over at an opponent.

For the student of Luther's character the most significant portion of the tract is found shortly before the end. Recurring to his commitment to permanent separation — the refusal to be reconciled — he had first announced in July of 1520, he writes:

> My glory and honor shall be this, and this is what I want: that henceforth it will be told of me that I have nothing but evil words, reviling and curses for the papists . . . I will curse and revile the scoundrels till I am in my grave and they shall never hear a civil word from me. [Consider Luther's apparent self-condemnation in a contemporary sermon: "Since a Christian bears no hatred or hostility toward anyone, his response to the hate, envy, slander or persecution of others should not be hate, persecution, slander or cursing, but instead love, assistance, blessing and prayers."][16] I will toll them to the grave with my thunder and lightning. For *I cannot pray unless I curse.* If I should say: 'Hallowed be thy name,' I am compelled likewise to say: 'Cursed, damned, dishonored be the name of papists and all who blaspheme thy name.' If I should say: 'Thy kingdom come,. then I must add: 'Cursed, damned, destroyed must be the papacy together with all earthly kingdoms that oppose thy kingdom.' If I should say: 'Thy will be done,' I am compelled likewise to say: 'Cursed, damned, dishonored and brought to nought be all the aims and purposes of the papists and of all who strive against thy will and judgement.'
>
> In truth, *I pray this way orally every day and in my heart at all times,* and with me all those pray who believe in Christ, and I feel confident that my prayer will be heard . . . . Nevertheless, I maintain a good, friendly, peaceful and Christian heart toward everyone; even my worst enemy knows that.[17]

This passage is of signal importance for assessing the claims of the Luther-cult writers that Luther possessed an extraordinary insight into the Christian gospel, that he was an exceptionally endowed religious personage notable for a rich inner life with God, and that he enjoyed excellent mental health. The subterfuge sometimes employed in the coverup of the real Luther — that in his writings there can be found only an occasional statement difficult to square with the legendary image — can hardly be advanced to explain away the self-revelation gratuitously provided in the "Assassin of Dresden." For here is revealed a scandalously unchristian inner life which Martin himself tells us is his habitual state. Furthermore it is for such grossly uncharitable demeanor that he wants to be remembered and honored by future generations.

It is of interest to observe what Luther was saying from the pulpit on the subject of refusing to be reconciled with others during the same period he was boasting in print that he would never be reconciled with the members of the Church that excommunicated him. In his current sermon series on the gospel according to Matthew (in which he was substituting for the absent Bugenhagen) he ran head on into the teaching that anyone who refuses to be reconciled with his brother is not acceptable to God (Matt. 5:23-26). Much of Luther's discourse on the Matthew parable of the man who is advised to leave his gift at the altar and make peace with the person with whom he is at odds may be described as evasive. Luther asserts, for example, that the parable applies mainly to the rich and powerful, thereby seeking to exonerate himself. He then switches abruptly to an irrelevant personal reference: only the dear Emperor, who has of course been misinformed, opposes me for a reason other than sheer malice. The parable ends with the threat of eternal retribution for the one who refuses to be reconciled. About this Luther is silent, perhaps because of the danger that such considerations might stir up his anxiety. But there is one paragraph in the middle of the sermon in which Martin provides an admirably precise description of his own paranoid behavior. He speaks of respectable and educated people who are filled with hatred and anger toward others, who remain unaware of their condition, entertain a firm belief in their righteousness and even expect to be praised for their hypocritical behavior. This section of the sermon reads like a spirited condemnation of the author of the "Assassin of Dresden."

The reader may be puzzled by the final sentence in the passage quoted above, in which Luther, after one of the most appalling displays of venmous hostility toward his fellow men to be found in his writings, proclaims that his heart is 'friendly, peaceful and Christian' toward all. This proclamation exemplifies the pathological defense mechanism known to psychiatrists as 'isolation.' One of the well established clinical observations of paranoid characters is their real lack of awareness of their own attitudes or inner states. The way such individuals look upon themselves is nevertheless of interest. About the same time Luther was writing the "Assassin" and preaching the sermon on Matthew 5 just reviewed, in one of his letters he made a comment on what he conceived the condition of his heart to be. The letter, dated in mid May, was addressed to his disciple John Brenz, converted to the Lutherian gospel back in 1518 but still uncertain in 1531 about the meaning of Lutherian faith. To help clarify this elusive concept, Martin offered his own experience by way of explanation: "There is in my heart nothing that could be called faith or love, but I put Jesus Christ in place of those and say: 'There is my righteousness.'"[18]

This declaration suggests that while the paranoid is unaware of what is really in his heart, he may very well have knowledge of what is *not* there. Luther's unembarrassed acknowledgement that there is no love of Jesus in his heart does not of course come as a surprise to the student of his writings, but it provides useful corroboration of the many other indications of this condition. The twin disclosure that Luther's heart is also empty of 'faith' must have been something of a surprise to Brenz and it may be suspected that he would have welcomed an explanation of Luther's explanation. To round off the present discussion of Luther on Luther as a man of prayer, we quote the following self-appraisal written the next year: "When I was a monk I never truly prayed even one paternoster."[19]

Continuing the story of Luther's encounters with Duke George, we next look at an episode of 1533 when Luther involved himself in a controversy between the Duke and a group of his subjects in Leipzig who wanted to introduce Lutherian innovations in their parish. As he had done two years earlier, the Duke lodged a complaint with Luther's sovereign, the new Elector of Saxony, who was now the youthful John Frederick, son and heir of the recently deceased Duke John. To stigmatize Luther for his unlawful interference in the affairs of another state Duke George proposed that the Elector regard him as an "untruthful, perjured and renegade monk." When the Elector turned down this appeal more brusquely than his father had done on a similar occasion two years earlier, Duke George and his staff issued a series of tracts attacking Luther. These publications provoked him into writing what proved to be his final pamphlet in their prolonged verbal duel — "A Short Answer to Duke George's Latest Book."

Belying its title, the "Short Answer" does not actually deal with the Duke's published tract save for a few pages at the end. Instead it is a response to George's private denunciation of Luther as an "untruthful, perjured and renegade monk." Since Luther was typically unruffled by personal criticism, the vehemence of his reaction on this occasion suggests he had been hit at a vulnerable spot. Indeed the "Short Answer" is one of his most revealing compositions and in particular provides a key to the understanding of the stories Martin often recited in the 1530s about the privations and penances he inflicted on himself in the monastery, fabrications that have long puzzled objective students of Luther and enthralled his devotees.

The 1521 tract "Judgment of Monastic Vows," described in an earlier chapter, presents a dazzling array of sophistical arguments to prove that the monastic vows are invalid and hence that the monk who renounces his profession performs an act pleasing in the sight of God. In the "Short Answer" there is an attack on the monastic ideal based primarily on a theme not featured in the "Judgment," the 'monastic baptism.' As pointed out above (Ch. 3 ii) this name refers to a saying current in the early days of the monastic movement (fourth century) that the taking of his vows has an effect on the newly professed monk comparable to the reception of the sacrament of baptism. About half of the "Short Answer" is devoted to this theme; so obsessed does Luther become with it that he refers to it more than 50 times in the course of a dozen pages.

Also in this tract Luther exerts his most strenuous effort to identify with Bernard, asserting that Bernard was "like me a real apostate, perjured and renegade monk. Although he did not put off the cowl, leave the cloister or take a wife, he spoke his heart in these words ['I have wasted my time, etc.']. He did not want to be saved by his monkery but only through Christ's merits and righteousness. Now it is well known that God judges not according to the outer man but by the heart. Because St. Bernard abandoned monkery in his heart and despaired of it, he became in God's sight a real apostate, perjured and renegade monk."[20] Martin next invents the sermon Bernard would have preached had he really depended on his monastic baptism:

> 'Dear God, I must now die; here I come with my monastic baptism and my order's holiness. I am pure and innocent. Open wide the gates of heaven, for I have indeed merited to enter.' . . . But St. Bernard would have none of this. He withdrew, let go of his monkery and grasped the suffering and blood of Jesus Christ. In the end all monks must apostasize in this way, abandon their monastic baptism and become perjured, or else they will all go to the devil with their cowls and tonsures.

Despite Luther's emphasis on the fantasy of monastic baptism, a different fantasy about monastic life, inspired by his stories of the formidable austerities to which he subjected himself in the monastery, has become enshrined in the Luther legend. While this theme plays a lesser role in the "Short Answer," where it is represented by such a remark as "I tortured myself to death with watching, prayer, study and other works," Martin clearly signals the motivation underlying it. He declares that if "any monk could gain heaven through his monkery I could have gotten in. And all my monastic brothers who know me can testify as to that."[21] In the Table Talk and the later sermons the fantasy of self-martyization in the cloister achieves fuller bloom. This fantasy, like the ones about Bernard and the monastic baptism, helps defend against the painful recollection of his repudiation of vows he once held sacred. He had in a sense foretold his agony over his defection in a passage in the 1521 "Judgment" about monks who quit the convent without a deep enough conviction of how abominable the vows are in God's sight: "Satan will arouse their consciences and torment them with the thought of their apostasy and broken vows."[22] The vehemence of the "Short Answer," together with the irrelevance of its principal content to the presumed purpose of the tract, bears eloquent witness to the anxiety he suffered from his own 'apostasy.'

iv. In defense of clerical privilege

In keeping with his egocentric character, Luther typically acted in a high-handed manner toward anyone disinclined to bow before his demands. Even before his regression he showed signs of this trait. On the other hand with those who were willing to be dominated he could be most affable. Not unexpectedly, as his paranoid symptoms grew more severe, his dictatorial tendencies became more pronounced. A notable instance of this development was his conflict with the town council of Zwickau in 1531 over their ejection of a preacher named Lawrence Soranus from his post in St. Catherine's parish.

Soranus appears to have been one of those preachers employed rather for their willingness to proclaim Lutheran doctrine than for a vocation to the Christian ministry. Among the charges brought against him at the time of dismissal were wife beating and adultery. Several months earlier he had described the feelings against him in the parish in a letter (October 18, 1530) to Luther, who suggested accepting this trial in a spirit of Christian resignation or else leaving the parish. Instead Soranus delivered from the pulpit a 'shockingly violent attack' against the burgomasters Muehlpfort and Baerensprung, the town clerk Stephan Roth, and the members of the council.[23] Matters came to a head during February of 1531 and Soranus was given notice of his termination as of May 1.

During the decade of the 1520s the senior preacher in St. Catherine's parish was a close friend of Luther's, Nicholas Hausmann, who had been called there in the spring of 1521 to replace a far more famous clergyman, Thomas Muentzer. When Hausmann learned of the council's action against Soranus, taken without consulting him, he was extremely incensed and threatened to inform Luther. The council told him to go ahead and do so and even provided him a wagon for the trip. He went off in a huff, taking Soranus along as a fellow sufferer, and aroused Luther's ire against the Zwickau officials. Hausmann then proceeded to the Electoral court at Torgau to gain the Elector's support.

This situation throws a good deal of light on the fluidity of 'my theology.' At the start of his propaganda campaign Luther had come out strongly for the 'priesthood of the believer' by which he meant the clergy had no right to the privileged status they had claimed for centuries but were on the same footing as the laity. To give this message a practical basis he had in 1523 published a pamphlet to prove from Scripture that a local congregation had the right to choose and dismiss its preacher. What he failed to do in the early 1530s was to publish a new tract proving the doctrine he had promoted with such zeal in the 1520s was now repudiated and the new clergy who supported the Lutherian gospel had acquired the privileged

status earlier denied the incumbent clergy. There are few examples in
Luther's career of such blatant reversal of his personal teaching for
no other reason than to advance his own interests.

The immediate fruit of Hausmann's visit to Wittenberg appeared
in the form of two very strong letters to the town council and to
Stephan Roth, obviously written when Luther was 'bursting with
rage and indignation,' expelling them from the ranks of the Elect.
The letter to Roth was a particularly brutal display of paranoid
hostility:

> Do you think, my good chaps, you can domineer like this in the
> church, grab and steal the revenues you didn't donate and give
> them to whom you please, as if you were lords in the church? I am
> tempted to make a public show of you and those beasts of Zwickau
> in a pamphlet exposing your shameful acts . . . . I want to blot out
> you and your kind from the fellowship of my Lord Jesus Christ.[24]

An interesting feature of this letter is Luther's resort to the kind
of mendacious slander against some of his partners in the schism that
he normally reserved for members of the papacy. The Zwickau council were not pilfering church revenues but getting rid of one of the
rotten apples in the Lutherian clergy, a matter at which we shall look
presently. The purpose of the mendacious slander in a letter that was
certain to receive abundant public exposure in Zwickau was to divert
attention from the sins of Soranus. To appreciate the piquancy of
this situation, one should recall that Roth as a protégé of Luther's
some years earlier had been properly indoctrinated with the 'priesthood of the believer.' So close was he to the great doctor in those
days that he had sat at his feet and transcribed a large batch of sermons that were thereby preserved for future generations. Furthermore, one of the Zwickau burgomasters, Hermann Muehlpfort, was
none other than the man to whom back in 1520 "The Freedom of
the Christian" was dedicated. Hermann apparently was too slow
witted to keep up with the shifty semantics of the prophet of Wittenberg. Later in the year during a face-to-face confrontation with
Luther at an official hearing in the Electoral court he told the author
of the "Freedom of the Christian" that the men of Zwickau had
learned too much to go back under another pope. To this Luther
could only lamely retort that while making others so learned he
knew nothing himself.[25]

In view of the tension between Hausmann and the Zwickau council, any consultation between them over the selection of a replacement for Soranus was not to be expected. When the news that the
council had made the new appointment reached Luther, he again
reacted violently, dispatching to Hausmann two letters, a week
apart, during the latter half of April. In the meantime he had re-

ceived conciliatory letters from Roth, the mayors and the council, but having resolved to break off relations with the beasts of Zwickau he returned their letters unread via Hausmann. During April Luther was taking the line that Hausmann should stress his rights and duties as pastor and his firm intent of remaining at his post while keeping aloof from the council members lest he become tainted with their sacrilegious behavior. Since Luther had effectively taken over the management of the Zwickau dispute, he even composed a sermon for Hausmann to deliver to his congregation. It reads as follows:

> My dear people, you know I am your pastor and must work for your sake and risk life and limb every day against the devil and all the perils souls must face. Therefore I must and will provide preaching for the city. But now you have thrown out a preacher without a trial and without my consent, even though this was my province. Furthermore, you have installed another [preacher] without consulting me and thereby you have usurped my office. Since I am the pastor here and must continue to be, I will not desert my post or give up preaching. But I will do as Christ teaches, and give my coat to the one who takes away my cloak. I will suffer domination and robbery; that is what I will do. And I tell you that this pastorate is mine and I am obligated to provide for and maintain the preaching office. I will not abandon or give up that office. But now that my authority has been seized and extorted from me, I will suffer these things and allow myself to be robbed and despoiled, and will continue to yield until God restores to me what is mine. In the meantime, we shall see who is impudent enough to venture to put himself into my usurped and stolen pastorate, and what kind of conscience he has who takes over my office.[26]

We shall see presently why Hausmann is to assert repeatedly that he is going to stay on the job. Having suitably oriented the congregation with this sermon, Luther now proceeded to pin back the ears of the new preacher. Though not yet aware of the identity of this interloper, Luther composed for his edification and by way of welcome to the church of Electoral Saxony the following most Christian epistle. He addressed the newcomer, who at the moment was stationed in a parish in Bohemia, as the 'preacher of the Zwickau council':

> I hear, my good man, that you are the preacher of St. Catherine, replacing Lawrence Soranus, who was evilly and foully cast out though neither accused nor found guilty of anything. I am amazed at your assurance, for as you know very well Nicholas, the pastor, is in charge of the church of Zwickau and the believers of that place, for whom he is compelled to answer to Christ. And yet you

have usurped or taken over this ministry without being asked by
him or consulting him. With what sort of conscience can you do
this and persist in doing it? It is true the council called you, but
they did so without asking or consulting the pastor, into whose
charge the city is committed. I write this to you in order both to
warn you and inform you that I do not want to share in or approve this deed of yours or the council's. I stand aloof and pure of
your sin, which Christ will judge. Look out for yourself, for you
will not get me to justify or have fellowship with you. Farewell in
the Lord and take care about your conscience.[27]

Martin Luther

Egged on by Luther's relentless interference, another member of
the Zwickau clergy named Conrad Cordatus added more fuel to the
flames. Soon after the installation of the new preacher on May 1
Cordatus delivered a bitter personal attack on him from the pulpit
with the intent to degrade him in the eyes of the Zwickau congregation and destroy all respect for him. Not to be outdone by his junior
associate in this pious exercise of their Christian ministry, Hausmann
proceeded to unleash an attack against the Zwickau council, using
for ammunition the very phraseology Luther had provided him in a
recent letter. He threatened to expose the whole story before the
congregation on the feast of the Ascension (May 18) unless the council dismissed the new preacher. While carrying out the threat from
his pulpit, Hausmann burst into tears, betraying the neurotic traits
which had originally made him an adherent of the Lutherian gospel.
The congregation were said to have found his performance childish.

A day or two later he received another letter from Luther pressing
him to depart from Zwickau at once and join his mentor in Wittenberg. This letter reveals both Luther's hitherto undisclosed scheme
— to leave the Zwickau congregation without a pastor — and his
duplicity in trying to implement it. Hausmann was to insist on the
rights of his office and his firm resolve to stay on the job; then under
the pretense of a short visit with Luther extend his absence to an
entire year. Hausmann complied with this plot, quietly decamping
from Zwickau on a foggy night and later notifying the council that
he was not abdicating his charge. An interesting bit of Luther's
unconscious humor appears in this letter to Hausmann: "Don't
be concerned about the scandal this business may cause in the towns
round about Zwickau; it isn't your fault. What can we do if sects and
factions spring up against our will?"[28]

Meanwhile the sermons of Cordatus had become so offensive the
congregation petitioned the council to dismiss him as it had done
earlier with Soranus. During the resultant turmoil more instructions
arrived from Wittenberg, and Cordatus, also pretending only a
temporary absence, joined Hausmann there. [To maintain a feeling

for the chronology of events during this busy spring of 1531, we may note that it was early in this same month of May that Luther published the "Assassin of Dresden" which closes with his paranoid paternoster, that in between his final letters to Hausmann on May 19 and Cordatus May 23 he wrote to his dying mother (May 20) and that on July 3 he began his lectures on Galatians.] Luther now continued the combat by correspondence, writing letters both to the congregation and the junior clergy who took over after Hausmann and Cordatus deserted their posts. Prior to the official hearing on the Zwickau affair at the Elector's court, Luther was very guarded in his references to the members of the council, referring to them only very obliquely in his best conspiratorial style as 'enemies of God,' who was of course an enemy to them. Fearing that further disturbances in the town might prejudice the case against Hausmann, he urged his correspondents to carry out the services in the parish with circumspection.

The official hearing at which Luther himself was present so he could glower at his one-time friends Muehlpfort and Roth was held in early August. The Zwickau council's decision to expel Hausmann and Cordatus from the positions they had abandoned at Luther's prompting was ratified and an edict was promulgated that henceforth all such dismissals and new installations must have the prior consent of the Electoral government. For some reason Luther regarded this decision as a victory for him. Writing to the Zwickau junior clergy a fortnight after the hearing, he informed them that 'your pastor' has been freed from the society of 'those beasts.' "The pastor is in the grace and favor of all good men, while those beasts are held in hatred and disgust as their signal pride and ingratitude deserve."[29] Luther relished this epithet so heartily that it rolled off his pen four times in the paragraph expressing this paranoid projection. In passing we might mention an incident recorded about one of the clergy addressed in this letter, Adam Schumann, for some years a deacon in Hausmann's parish. Back in the summer of 1525, just a month after Martin's wedding, Schumann married the rectory cook, who eight weeks later presented him with twin sons. The chronicler of this episode remarks that the births were 'untimely,' a term that might be applied more accurately to the marriage ceremony.[30]

Cordatus remained in Wittenberg with Luther for well over a year and was among the earliest members of his household to record there the conversations later published as the Table Talk. Hausmann continued to squabble with the Zwickau council long after his dismissal, demanding that he be excused from repaying them a debt amounting to more than a fourth of his annual salary on the grounds that he incurred it on his travels to Wittenberg to secure Luther's advice. The next year he obtained the post of court preacher in one of the minor German principalities not far from Wittenberg. Late in the year 1538 he transferred to a parish in southeastern Germany, pausing on his way through Wittenberg for what proved to be a last visit with his old friend. On the occasion of delivering his first sermon in the new pulpit he suffered a fatal stroke. In Luther's time such a death was widely regarded as a sign of divine displeasure with the deceased. Since Luther was always on the lookout for signs that his cause enjoyed divine favor, such a death for an ardent propagator of the Lutherian gospel and on such a special occasion came as a tremendous shock to him. It is of interest to note the report of this event in the Table Talk. Melanchthon and other members of the inner circle were with him when he received the news and stayed with him all through the day as he sat weeping over this rudest possible shock to his complacent faith in the divine approval of 'my movement' (# 4084). Evidently they feared a recurrence of the 1527 depression. But his further regression during the ensuing decade accompanied by the hardening of his delusional system appears to have rendered him immune to further depressions.

It should be recognized that the clergy who followed Luther into schism were by and large not a very admirable lot. We have previously recorded Erasmus' observation on these characters. Perhaps the least undesirable among them were the fellow neurotics who welcomed the *sola fide* for reasons similar to Luther's. More numerous would be the men who were allured by the prospect of taking a wife. Luther himself, as we have seen, complained about such clergy with his characteristic inconsistency. Then there were the really obnoxious preachers who abused their pulpit privilege by venting their rancor against whoever displeased them. Luther himself, of course, set the worst possible example for such preachers, and his gospel with its lack of emphasis on charity and self-restraint provided a favorable climate for promoting this all too human proclivity. In this connection one recalls another of Samuel Butler's sprightly couplets about these ranters who

> Compound for sins they are inclined to
> By damning those they have no mind to.

Of the three Zwickau preachers involved in the episode discussed here, Hausmann and Cordatus, both older than Luther and formerly secular priests, exhibited neurotic symptoms, while Soranus, a one-time Franciscan friar, appears to have been a devotee of the copulative imperative. Both Soranus and Cordatus were guilty of using the pulpit to defame others.

A reading of Luther's correspondence with the schismatic clergy shows him to have been most tolerant of their unseemly conduct, an attitude in marked contrast with what he displayed toward clergy who refused to follow him. He could overlook almost any fault in those who preached his gospel. As an example, we might mention John Guelden, an ex-priest turned Lutheran preacher, who displayed even a sharper tongue and more pronounced sexual irregularities than Lawrence Soranus. In the summer of 1526 Martin wrote Guelden a carefully phrased letter suggesting that he be more gentle about introducing the Lutheran innovations in the small town parish where he was stationed.[31] Coming from the agitator whose campaign to suppress the mass at the Castle church we looked at in an earlier chapter, this letter is one of the choicer bits of Luther's unconscious humor. To provide some relief to Guelden's victims in his parish, the Saxon government finally moved him to another one. Though of course married, he found one woman insufficient for his requirements, and in his solicitations was given to using violence akin to what he practised in the pulpit. He made his servant girl compliant by holding a knife to her throat. On another occasion he was guilty of an even more serious indiscretion, attempting to rape a married woman. But she proved too strong for him and raised such an outcry that he was forced to flee from the region. In Electoral Saxony rape was a capital offense. Some time later, being foolish enough to return to the scene of his crime, Guelden was apprehended, imprisoned, and despite pleas for clemency from Wittenberg was beheaded. While he was in jail Luther wrote him a letter of consolation, advising Guelden to be patient and humble in order to atone for his fault.[32] At the time Luther apparently hoped that Guelden might later be set free and given another preaching assignment. In view of the type of clergyman that Luther backed, his assertions that it is doctrine that really counts, not conduct, take on new meaning. The evidence reviewed in this section is quite consistent with the negative part of the claim that he was promoting doctrinal, not moral, reform.

v. The mature professorial style

The academic lectures on the Epistle to the Galatians delivered during the latter half of 1531 (July 3 to December 12) and published through the editorial efforts of the ever loyal George Roerer during 1535 constitute a document of major interest. As the lectures on the first epistle of John (autumn of 1527) reveal Luther in depression, so this final effort of Luther to deal with an important N. T. writing reveals him in the paranoid stage of his disorder. In a sense it may be regarded as continuing his reaction to the diet of Augsburg of the previous year. In substance it is an extended harangue in support of the *sola fide* defense, and includes a superabundant display of hostility to the papacy, with special attention to monastic life, and also to the new sectarian groups that by 1531 were giving

Luther serious and unwelcome competition. (In his later years Luther proclaimed these lectures, along with a sermon series on John 14-16 delivered in 1537-38, as his best work.) These lectures also provide an interesting counterpart to the lecture course Luther gave on the Epistle to the Romans some 15 years earlier in showing the changes in his use of Scripture texts to cope with the anxiety. Concurrently with the academic lectures, Luther was still preaching the two series of weekly sermons — on Matthew 5-7 Wednesdays and on John Saturdays — that he had begun late in 1530 as substitute for the Wittenberg pastor Bugenhagen. Some echos of the sermon material occur in the lectures.

Since these lectures fill a volume and a half (in the latest English translation), we can in this section look at only a few highlights. We note merely in passing that the lectures are plentifully supplied with expressions of Luther's grandiose and persecutory delusions, and with his attempts to identify with Paul. In particular he gloats over Paul's rebuke to Peter concerning the problem of the Jew eating at table with gentile Christians, seeing in it an obvious foreshadowing of his own attacks on the Pope. (When he has a different axe to grind there is of course no connection between Peter and the Popes, whose first appearance on the stage of history is said to occur many centuries after apostolic times.) One of the more unexpected developments is a qualified renunciation of the *sola scriptura*. As remarked earlier that was a polemical weapon rather than an integral part of Luther's defenses, for as even one with Luther's impaired intellectual powers could understand, it is not the text of Scripture that is decisive but rather what the commentator declares to be the meaning of the text. The occasion for Luther's throwing in the sponge on the *sola scriptura* at this time was the old problem of trying to reconcile the numerous scriptural texts on reward and merit with the *sola fide*. It will be recalled that Melanchthon in his "Theological Commonplaces" a decade earlier had himself given up on this intricate problem. Belatedly in 1531 Luther follows Melanchthon's example — but in his own inimitable fashion. His retreat is accompanied by the standard application of the denial mechanism to this topic — what he calls 'the righteousness of works.' Also instead of frankly recognizing his defeat as Melanchthon did, he arranges to dissociate himself from his repudiation of the *sola scriptura* by formulating a set speech for his followers to recite when countering opponents who bring up the unwelcome passages from Scripture. He implies that he doesn't need this crutch himself.

Setting up his favorite antithetical framework, he says that on one side we have Christ, the ruler over Scripture, and on the other the Scripture texts which seem to invalidate the *sola fide*. Luther doesn't care if there are as many as six hundred of these. I am on the side of

the Lord and Author of Scripture, and am opposed by you hypo-
crites who claim Scripture contradicts itself. "You insist upon Scripture, the servant, and not the whole of it or the best parts, but only
the places concerned with works. I let you have this servant; I insist
upon the Lord, who rules over Scripture. He was made my merit and
the price of my righteousness and salvation. I hold and cling to him
and leave you the works, which you never do anyway."[33]

Elsewhere in dealing with the same part of Ch. 3 of Galatians
which provoked this about face on Scripture, Luther makes a grandiose identification of himself with Christ, who on account of his
preaching was charged with blasphemy and rebellion. Paul was similarly accused and today the same thing is happening to Luther. It is
presumably the development of his grandiose delusions that enables
Luther in the early 1530s to relinquish the *sola scriptura*. Like Jesus,
Luther is now above Scripture. In a number of places in the lectures
Luther refers to the gift of infallibility he enjoys with respect to
judging all laws, doctrines and types of behavior in contrast with the
benighted papists and fanatics, who are incapable of judging anything
correctly. It is this evident infallibility of his that proves the Holy
Spirit resides in him, even though the fact of this indwelling may not
of itself be evident and the ungodly may find it incredible. (His possession of the Spirit will become clear to the world only when in
time of trial he will abandon wife, children, real estate and even life
itself rather than deny his Lord.) Hence all the slings and arrows of
his outrageous antagonists bounce off his armor without effect. Also
in view of his prestigious condition his former habit of sinning has
become much ameliorated, and the only sins he now commits are
indeliberate and occur through ignorance.

Among the numerous passages devoted to the *sola fide* one of the
most interesting concerns his advice to his followers on how to make
it work, i.e., how they can move from uncertainty to certainty about
whether they are pleasing to God. Luther gives an outstanding
account of the operation of the *sola fide* in his commentary on verse
4:6 (cf. LW 26: 374-389). It is in this connection that we learn the
chief duty of theology: to find ways of making us believe we have
found favor with God, one of the signs of which is that we hate the
Pope. The teaching of the Church on this matter, presented in the
usual denial stereotype that the Pope commands us to doubt or dis-
believe we are in such a state, comes in for a hearty lambasting. In
the course of this onslaught, Luther unwittingly reveals that his
own propensity for disbelieving in the likelihood of his salvation is
not something he acquired from the Pope but is rather an integral
component of his anxiety condition. Not content, however, with
blaming the Pope for it, he goes on to project this 'wicked notion'
onto the entire human race, saying it has infected the whole world

and is innate in all of us, an aspect of our total depravity. But this does not exonerate the Pope; on the contrary the papacy is condemned not only as the devil's kingdom but a torture chamber of souls. The very worst of its innumerable crimes is teaching consciences to be in doubt. Although the acquisition of faith is easy, nevertheless we must work hard to benefit from it, i.e., overcome the terrors of the Law and the conscience and the roaring of Satan, and make ourselves confident of our (alien) righteousness. The horrors Luther experiences in his anxiety states frequently intrude into this scriptural commentary and he even projects these feelings on Christ in the garden of Gethsemane.

A probable reason why Luther lectured on the N. T. so infrequently during the last quarter-century of his academic career was the above mentioned contradiction between the *sola fide* and the N. T. teaching on reward and merit. The Epistle to the Galatians contains a good deal of material that such a slick operator on Scripture texts as Luther could readily manipulate into a convincing argument for his most cherished teaching. Its eminent suitability for this purpose was doubtless one of Luther's reasons for choosing to lecture on it at this time. Nevertheless toward the end of the epistle Paul disobligingly lapses into a statement about a man reaping what he has sowed that is as antagonistic to the *sola fide* as some of the worst parts of the gospel according to Matthew. A little earlier in the epistle comes the well known enumeration of the fruits of the Holy Spirit, and in his comment on the list Luther demonstrates how adroitly he could react with the denial mechanism when anything the least bit inimical to 'faith' reared its ugly head.

In this enumeration, it will be recalled, Paul leads off with the chief Christian virtue of love (*agape*) and doesn't insert faith (*pistis*) till toward the end, in the seventh place. To counteract this denigration of faith Luther might have claimed the arrangement was due to a scribal error, but instead he uses quite a different technique. The word faith (*pistis*) which elsewhere in the epistle Luther saluted with enthusiasm is in this verse not be understood as meaning faith at all. Instead, here (being only in seventh place) it obviously denotes the lesser virtue of honesty or fidelity by which one man keeps faith with his fellow man in the affairs of this world. And Martin provides a touching little sketch of the simple honest man who, endowed with this trait, believes what he is told and is never suspicious. Luther then indulges his fondness for the antithetical with a picture of the man who trusts no one, yields to no one, is forever insulting others and distorting what they say, in short the kind of person who makes peace and concord impossible. While this sounds like an authentic description of Martin Luther, its author shows no awareness that this is so. Alas, he exclaims, what kind of a world would this be if one man couldn't believe another man?

The enumeration of the gifts of the Spirit is found in the last main section of the epistle, which treats of Christian living, specifically of the response demanded by Christian moral standards. In the course of his remarks, apparently as an aside, Paul mentions that those who have been instructed in the Christian revelation must provide for the support of the catechist who instructed them (6:6). He then returns to the main line of his discourse, asserting that a man will reap according as he sows — either in the field of the flesh or that of the spirit — and promising a reward to those who continue to do good. Faced with Paul's deplorable backsliding into the ranks of the works-righteous, Martin does not assail him with the kind of language dedicated to the description of the papistical monks or even the lesser obloquy reserved for the author of the Epistle of James. Nor does he find it necessary to come to the rescue of the Apostle of the gentiles, as he did for St. Bernard, with a story of deathbed repentance. Displaying a sleight-of-hand artistry perfected by years of practice, Luther saves both Paul and the *sola fide* with material right at hand. He has already worked up the adjuration about the faithful providing for the material needs of their teacher into one of his oft repeated sermons on how stingily his fellow Saxons recompense the Lutherian preachers. He never seems to tire of contrasting the niggardly habits of those who now bask in the great light of the gospel with the unflagging generosity displayed by the benighted souls who formerly languished in the darkness of the papacy.

He carries this theme over into his exposition of the subsequent verses of the epistle. When Paul speaks about a man reaping what he sowed, this has nothing to do with the state of being righteous but applies only to the duty of supporting ministers of the gospel. That there may be no danger of confusing these verses on sowing and reaping with righteousness by faith alone, Luther repeats this highly personal interpretation six times in rapid succession. At the beginning he is becomingly demure about broaching this delicate subject. It may seem immodest in one who himself gives instruction in the gospel message to expatiate on a text which speaks so highly of the members of his profession. Yet there it is, plain as print. In his usual rambling approach Luther even digresses into a defense of the rather questionable practice of expropriating revenues donated in former years by papists to their church and turning them over to a ministry dedicated to the destruction of that church. But since God has commanded this, we can in good conscience help ourselves to these funds. And so he runs on through page after page (of the printed text of the lectures) so that the attention of his audience is effectively distracted from the actual meaning of the scriptural passage he is bent on concealing. It is not unlikely that the stu-

dents who made up Luther's original audience were so beguiled by
his performance as to be quite unaware they were being hocussed
by one of the most expert con men in ecclesiastical history.

The lectures contain an abundance of material on the Law-Gospel
antithesis appropriately related to the two times of Luther, namely
the periods during and after an anxiety attack, and to the application of 'faith' to control it. We hear the familiar confession that
during the periods of anxiety Satan is likely to win the first round by
causing Martin to forget all the comforting scriptural texts and then
is in a position to overwhelm him with the threatening (ungospel)
ones. Lecturing before a group of students, Luther prefers to use the
third person in describing the hatred of God he experiences during
the anxiety attack. It is the Law that, by revealing to a man his sin
and the wrath of God, causes him to hate and blaspheme his
Creator. This of course is the 'use' of the Law, without which one
might remain a hardened, smug, unrepentant sinner. After a certain
duration of feeling terrified and crushed by the Law, and driven to
despair, the sinner 'takes hold' of Christ and thus makes his escape,
though the details of this transition are left unsatisfyingly vague.

It is likely that Luther himself didn't understand what led to the
termination of these states. From an analysis of the various accounts,
it would appear that a key factor was his ability to transfer the
hostility from God to Moses, the personification of the Law which
was 'biting' him. With the hostility directed away from God the
Father, Luther was then able to excite the feeling that he was going
to be saved by the Son. This feeling is what the *sola fide* is all about;
when Luther is able to excite it, he can 'take hold' of Christ and
when it eludes him he 'loses' Christ. This hypothesis makes understandable his remarks about the 'doctrine of faith' being hard to
grasp, or difficult to apply, and why Luther is so often afraid that he
will lose this faith. It also explains the otherwise inexplicable hostility
to Moses, who is described at one point in the lectures as worse than
an excommunicated heretic, the Pope or the devil, the number one
targets of Luther's hostility. But the Law is not always represented
by Moses. In another place it is regarded as female: 'Lady Law, the
Empress' who engages Christ in a duel for the souls of men. Luther
fancies that he discovered this figure in Paul but it stems more appropriately from his own pathological psyche, and the gender of the
personified Law is more usually neuter. Luther ingeniously turns
his image of the duel into an argument for the *sola fide:* since Christ
is the only combatant fighting against the Law in the duel, there can
be no question of any human effort in one's salvation.

This approach also provides Luther with ammunition for attacking theoretically the charity or love which he is unable to experience
in practice. Early in the lecture course (on verse 2:4) he had insisted

that the faith which makes one righteous is a faith without love. He relates this argument to the anxiety states, asserting that in the agony of conscience, the victim takes hold of Christ by faith alone — without love. The text that really gave him trouble in preaching faith without love comes toward the end of the epistle (5:6), 'In Christ Jesus neither circumcision nor the lack of it counts for anything; only faith, which expresses itself through love.' We have noted earlier Luther's radical departure from Paul on the greatest of the virtues, in particular with regard to his denial of the tribute to love in 1 Cor. 13. Luther's approach to 'faith working through love,' is basically the same as in the passage mentioned above about a man reaping what he sowed; he denies flatly that this expression has anything to do with justification. His discussion of the verse is a typical exercise of Lutherian sophistry with a strong admixture of slander for those who disagree with him.

While Luther engages in repeated attacks on monastic life in the lectures he seldom descends to the level found in others of his works. The reason for this is in a sense supplied by Luther himself when he says his movement is directed against not the sinfulness of the clergy but their teaching on the way to lead a holy life. He was treading on rather delicate ground here, for the Lutherian clergy as we have seen did not set a shining example of moral conduct. At any rate the attacks in the lectures are aimed primarily at the sincere monks, particularly the Carthusians, who are reputed to be the only religious order that has never fallen away from the ideal of the founder to an extent that a reform has been needed. Nevertheless, toward the close of the lectures Luther stoops to uttering one of the nastiest slurs of his entire career, on no less a person than Francis of Asissi. He has been discussing Paul's statement that he bears the brand marks of Jesus in his body (6:17). This verse is commonly interpreted to refer to the welts and bruises he sustained from being often scourged, beaten with rods, and stoned during his missionary work.

As noted earlier, in these lectures Martin repeatedly attempts to identify with Paul and time after time he finds that what happened to Paul many centuries before is now happening to him. To cite only one example of this, the schismatic tendencies among the Galatians that provided the occasion for Paul composing this epistle Luther with evident relish finds reflected in the contemporary sects known as Sacramentarians and Anabaptists. But Paul's reference to the marks of the whip on his flesh fills Luther with shame at the recollection of how cravenly he has avoided any danger to his own person. (In the concurrent sermon series on John, and presumably with Paul's missionary journeys in mind, Luther offers an excuse for never going outside Saxony to preach. It is not because I am afraid to go, he tells the congregation but because I don't have a call from God to do this.) The thought of Paul's brand marks may well have stirred up recollections of Muentzer's taunts about the soft-living flesh of Wittenberg. Some such painful emotion must be predicated to account for Luther's astonishing comment on the verse. Francis is conjured up for the occasion because of his well known reception of the stigmata. The thought of a friar celebrated for his Christlike character and the founder of a religious order as well being given this extraordinary mark of recognition by Jesus was extremely mortifying to the contriver of the *sola fide*. In his most spiteful vein he declared that the stigmata of Francis were fraudulent, something that Francis faked for himself out of vainglory.[34]

Having delivered himself of this venomous though childish slander, Luther then thoughtfully provides posterity with an unmistakable display of his megalomania. First he declares that the marks on Paul's body result from his physical sufferings, i.e., illnesses, the assaults of Satan, and the mental anguish to which he has been subject because of the persecution consequent upon his preaching of the gospel. I too, says Martin, bear such marks on my body, and the reason I bear them is that Satan terrifies me and the world persecutes me merely because I teach that Christ is our righteousness. I did not inflict these marks on myself, as Francis did, but I glory with Paul that both of us bear them on our bodies.

Chapter 9

Self-Revelation In The Later Years

i. Table Talk

Luther's Table Talk, like the sermons and academic lectures of the 1530s and 1540s, consists of utterances taken down by admiring auditors with the Doctor's acquiesence and subsequently edited by them (or their associates) for publication. The earliest of these editions, prepared by one of the note takers, appeared a score of years after Luther's death. The most authoritative, including the notes of well over a dozen scribes and representing an enormous editorial effort, fills six large volumes (1912-1920) of the Weimar edition of the complete works. The Table Talk may be described as an unorganized conglomeration of thousands of impromptu remarks running in length from a sentence to a few pages but typically about a paragraph long, delivered for the most part at Luther's dinner table. This appears to have been a well attended affair, including in addition to his family various members of the academic community and miscellaneous visitors. From this immense collection which contains much that is useful to the student of Luther's personality we shall examine a group of entries that amplify or corroborate information provided by other sources.

As is to be expected, allusions to recurrences of his anxiety states abound in the Table Talk. Among those most frequently touched on is the fear he experienced especially during the 1520s that if his gospel is not really from God, then he is guilty of the destruction of countless souls. Here for comparison is a very early account of this self-reproach written in the summer of 1521 at the Wartburg hide-out: "How often has my quaking heart trembled and rebuked me with the strongest and sole argument [of the papists] : Are you alone wise? Is everyone else in error? Is the whole world uninstructed? If you are wrong, how many have you seduced by your errors into eternal damnation?"[1] A decade later we hear the echo of this theme in one of its many variations in the Table Talk:

> I have suffered no greater or heavier temptation about my
> teaching than this thought: this means you alone are right; if you
> are wrong, you are responsible for leading many souls to hell.
> I have often gone into hell on account of this temptation till God
> called me back and encouraged me that my teaching is God's
> word and true. But it cost me a great deal until comfort came.
> (# 141)

It seems likely that the motivation of Luther's never ending claims
to speak with the voice of God is to help cope with anxiety arising
from this source. The habit of making these assertions would be a
factor in the formation of the grandiose delusions.

The anxiety states are usually represented as bouts with Satan and
often have a strongly academic tone. Once when his table companions were praising his great learning he noted that they paid too
little attention to his skill as a debater, i.e., his mastery of dialectic
and rhetoric.

> God indeed works through me. Dialectic is an art that is applied
> to other disciplines. I learned it thoroughly in my youth. Satan
> knew me well and saw at once that I was a highly gifted lad who
> would love Scripture; therefore he hated me. He has often tried
> to overcome me but failed. (# 143)

To illustrate his accomplishments he provides the following demonstration:

> The worst of Satan's temptations is when he says: 'God hates
> sinners; you are a sinner; therefore God also hates you.' Other
> people experience this temptation in a different way. Satan
> doesn't remind me of my evil deeds, such as that I have celebrated
> mass, or did this or that when I was young, as he does with other
> folk. Now in this syllogism the major premise is merely to be
> denied: it is untrue that God hates sinners. (# 141)

On other occasions the battle is waged with scriptural texts.
Martin admits that Satan is a master at quoting Scripture, especially
it would seem the gospel according to Matthew, and when the
anxiety state is at its peak he himself can recall none of the 'comforting texts' to hurl back at his adversary. These are the occasions when
he almost 'loses Christ.' In the next example we see Luther after he
has emerged from an attack and is arming himself for another:

> When Satan argues with me about whether I am in God's favor,
> I cannot quote the text: 'Whoever loves God will possess the king-
> dom of God' [John 8:23], because he will at once respond: 'You
> have not loved God.' Neither can I argue that I am a conscientious
> lecturer or preacher. That horseshoe [a hex to ward off the devil]
> doesn't hang right. Instead I say that Jesus Christ died for me or
> recite the article on remission of sins. (# 352)

Satan's favorite time for the 'spiritual assaults' is during the night hours. And he is a constant visitor, always ready to tackle Luther on the Law versus the Gospel:

Almost every night when I awake the devil is there and wants to argue with me. This is how I handle it: if the argument that the Christian is outside the Law and above the Law doesn't work, right off I chase him away with a fart. (# 469)

While to the modern reader the discharge of flatulence to spite the devil may not appear particularly effective and certainly not dangerous, Luther informs us in another conversation that to do this is a very risky business, definitely not for the faint-hearted but only for bold skirmishers like himself. On some occasions the combats assume an even more markedly non-academic tone:

When the devil comes at night to torment me, I give him this answer: 'Devil, I must now sleep for that is God's command, to work by day and sleep at night.' Then when he keeps on bothering me by bringing up my sins I say: 'Dear Devil, I have heard the list, but there is still another that has been left out. Write down that I have shit in my breeches; hang them around your neck and wipe your mouth in it.' Thirdly, if he won't stop upbraiding me with my sins, I say in contempt: 'Holy Satan, pray for me! For you have done no evil and you alone are holy. Go to God, get yourself some grace, and if you want to make me virtuous, then I say to you: Physician, heal yourself.' The devil is an arrant knave who has inflicted on me such great evils as celebrating mass, despising God, etc. From such things may God protect me. (# 1557)

The devil seeks me out when at home in bed and there are one or two devils who lie in wait for me and are persistent devils. If they can't overcome my heart, they grab me by the head and torment me that way. When that no longer works, I turn my ass to them, which is where they belong. (# 491)

The devil does not always wait until Luther is awake to begin tormenting him. He seems to have read his frequent experience of night sweats into the ejaculation of the psalmist: 'Every night I flood my bed with weeping' (Ps. 6), replacing the psalmist's tears (which he himself seldom experiences) with floods of perspiration:

Satan never gives up disturbing and worrying people so that even at night while we are asleep he troubles us with restless dreams and anguish until sweat pours from our whole body because of our mental distress. (# 802)

In the bouts with Satan Katie often proves to be of little assistance: "The best battles I have with him are in bed beside my Katie." (# 508) "Often I lie beside my Katie, and although she is a woman worth loving the sweat pours from me because of my anxiety." (# 476)

Among the new sources of anxiety that came to plague Luther after his excommunication and repudiation of his vows were the slaughter of the peasants in 1525 and the proliferation of heretical teachings and sects in the regions exposed to his propaganda. His display of unrelenting hostility to the other innovators, discussed earlier, is to be explained in large measure as an attempt to escape from the guilt feelings aroused by recognition of his responsibility for the disruption of the unity of Christendom. This situation would likewise contribute to the forming of his grandiose delusions, since one way to 'refute' these undesirable competitors is to assert that Luther is the only man sent by God to restore the Christian faith, while all the others are emissaries of the devil. Not surprisingly, the persecutory delusions are also associated with the guilt feeling as when he laments that as a result of his preaching the gospel "I must bear up against the whole world, Emperor and Pope . . . . The devil also tortures me with this argument: 'You were not called,' as if I weren't a doctor." (# 453) At times he tried to stifle this anxiety by the favorite device of identifying with Paul, as in the following entry of early 1533:

> Scandals have arisen from my doctrine, but I console myself as Paul did with Titus, that his doctrine is spread abroad for the faith of the Elect . . . . I wouldn't waste a word over the others . . . . Zwingli and Erasmus are like hollow nuts, just dung in your mouth. (# 452)

As for the slaughter of the peasants in 1525, Luther projects the sense of guilt aroused by that catastrophe first on all other preachers and then on God to help him share the blame:

> Preachers are the greatest murderers because they exhort the magistrate to perform his duty, i.e., punish criminals. I, Martin Luther, killed all the peasants in the revolution, for I bade them to be killed. All their blood is on my head. But I refer this to our Lord God, who commanded me to say this. The devil and the unrighteous kill, but they haven't the right to. (# 2911b)

After the revolt was put down the peasants came to occupy a position not far from the top of his enemies list, a compilation it need hardly be said of prodigious length. [In the *Gesamtregister,* an analytical guide to the volumes of the Weimar edition, 7 or 8 pages are devoted to a selection of passages under the heading 'Enemies.' (WA 58, 114-121)] Beginning with the two pamphlets against the peasants in June-July of 1525, Luther could never again say a good word about the social class from which he originated. One of his milder comments on them recorded like the three preceding entries in early 1533 was evoked when the excellence of the glass of wine he was drinking at the moment reminded him of the good wine God gives the peasants to drink as well as all kinds of food and other benefits. He then proceeds to contrast their impiety with his own elevated status: "But there is one thing he does not grant them, namely, himself. By considering all the good things he gives to these wicked blasphemers, we can better realize how much more he will bestow on us."

An illustration of the interlocking or systematic character of his delusions is provided by the following entry recorded in mid June of 1540. The particular conversation started with the question of whether Satan can perceive the thoughts of men; this prompted Luther to assert that Satan not only knows about but causes

> the frightful thoughts in our hearts: hatred of God, blasphemy and despair. These are the 'fiery darts' [Ephesians 6:16]. St. Paul understood this when he felt these darts in his flesh. These are the greatest temptations, which no papist understands. These stupid asses don't know of any other temptations than lust . . . . For they and their saints write of no other kind of temptation. Once when Benedict was tempted with lustful thoughts he threw himself naked into a bramble bush and scratched his ass properly. But the devil laughs at all this and thinks: 'Hee-hee, how they dispute about these matters, neglecting the word of God, about which they can never learn what it is or means.' # 5097

Here the mention of Satan evokes Luther's memory of the blasphemous thoughts during anxiety attacks. This experience he projects into other men in general and St. Paul in particular, with whom he grandiosely identifies. The grandiosity is then asserted with respect to the papists over whom Luther towers in his incomparable superiority concerning (a) the diabolical horror of his sins (against the 'first table') (b) his knowledge and understanding of Scripture and (c) his rejection of monastic life here objectified in the anecdote of the sixth century St. Benedict, the most revered proponent of monastic life in the West. While hardly any of this material relates to the topic under discussion, the various components have become so intertwined in Luther's psyche that the entire sequence pops out like a jack-in-the-box when the release button is touched.

It is of interest to observe that Luther made some attempt to control his famous irascibility. Here he describes his efforts in that direction; they border on the heroic:

> I must have patience with the Pope, the fanatics, the nobility, my relatives, Catherine von Bora. And so much patience must I have that my whole life is nothing else but just patience. (# 2173b)

Seeing Catherine bringing up the end of a list headed by the Pope, one may raise the question of how Luther viewed their relationship.

That he was of at least two minds on this matter is apparent from the Table Talk. On one occasion he tells her: "Katie, you have a pious husband who loves you; you are an empress. Take note of this and thank God." (# 1110) But at another time he could say: "I never loved my wife for I always suspected her of being proud (as she is). But God so willed that I show mercy to the abandoned girl [Catherine had been jilted by her first suitor]. And by the grace of God it turned out for me a very happy marriage."

While Luther speaks of his attempts at self-restraint with distaste, he takes evident pleasure at blowing off steam. The discharge of hostility serves as a form of therapy: "Prayer, preaching, writing never go along better for me than when I am angry. An outburst of anger refreshes my blood, sharpens my wit, and drives away the temptations." (# 2410)

As we have seen, Luther required almost constant companionship to help manage the anxiety. In a number of places of the Table Talk there is mention of his fear of being by himself; if no human being is at hand he will seek the society of even a pig. This is of course an unseemly condition for one proclaiming himself to be so super-eminently pious, for the truly devout spend considerable time in communion with God. But Luther was cut off from such communion, what theologians call interior prayer, not only by his need to be constantly with others but also by his singular relationship with his Creator. One of the many indications he lacked the capability for genuine prayer is the disclosure in the Table Talk entry just quoted that what he called prayer went best for him when he was angry. When wakeful during the night hours instead of praying he argues with the devil, his most constant companion. And he often tells his auditors that his conception of prayer is to recite the Decalogue.

That Luther was embarrassed by his incapacity for private devotion is apparent from disclosures such as occur in a Table Talk entry of early 1532 (# 1329). Here he attacks the papists for teaching: "If you wish to know Christ, try to be alone . . . . Away with those who say: 'Remain by yourself and your heart will become pure.'" His language in this entry suggests he is recalling with displeasure a passage from Bk. I, Ch. 20 of the "Imitation of Christ": "Whoever resolves to attain to an inward and spiritual life must with Jesus turn away from the crowd." In his early sermons and lectures on Scripture Luther spoke frequently of the 'inner man' after the fashion of the "Imitation of Christ" and other works on the spiritual life. His denunciation of such material in later years reflects one of the more unhappy effects of his emotional disorder.

ii. Remembrance of things past

The recorded reminiscences of Luther's early years are few and deal mainly with unpleasant incidents. The unhappy childhood suggested by these facts is hardly surprising in a person with such a severe emotional disturbance as Luther's. There are, for example, the well known stories of harsh beatings by both his father and his mother. One may suspect a certain exaggeration in these accounts, for example, the one about his mother whipping him till the blood ran for a mere nothing – just the theft of a nut. Then there is the more lurid tale that a schoolmaster beat him 15 times of a morning because of his slowness in acquiring the elements of Latin grammar. This story possibly reflects the practice in medieval and post-medieval schools of compiling a list of offences throughout the week and then administering the entire catalog of penalties to the unfortunate culprit at one time. If Luther is exaggerating, his motive is evident, since it was the very strict parental discipline that he held accountable for the cowardice of which he was ashamed: "By their severe discipline my parents turned me into a coward." (Table Talk # 3566)

But of the severity of some of the punishments inflicted on the boy there can be no doubt. It is a well established clinical observation that individuals who exhibit sadistic behavior, such as Luther manifested toward Carlstadt and Agricola, themselves suffered sadistic treatment during childhood. Since it is likely that as a boy Martin was endowed with the stubborn, unyielding character of his adult years, it may be presumed he absorbed a great deal of corporal punishment. Another source of unhappiness in childhood would be his learning problems, attested to by the need of four additional years of preparatory schooling after completion of the standard school program in Mansfeld. Inasmuch as his recorded recollections stem from a period of his career marked by defensive boasting about his superior intellectual gifts, there is naturally little direct testimony about this aspect of his childhood.

A favorite period of reminiscence was his early life in the monastery. Such memories were likely to be evoked not by the taste of a bit of a *madeleine* in a cup of tea or (to Teutonize the setting) of a pretzel in a stein of beer but rather by a scriptural passage that reminded him of his hostility toward his God. Since his failure at the monastic vocation and his repudiation of the vows he had held as sacred were among the great sorrows of his later life, one expects a very large element of fiction in these recollections. For example, the stories of the extreme mortification he practised in the monastery, referred to in the preceding chapter, are invented to help prove that even though he tried much harder than his fellow monks to win assurance of salvation, his failure to achieve it stems not from personal shortcomings but from the evil institution. His scorn for the practice of mortification during his monastic years is evident in his taking sides against the 'Observants' of his order, those who wanted to follow a strict rather than relaxed form of the rule. Note the names he calls these 'work-saint' brothers in a 1515 (pre-*sola fide*) sermon [WA 1:52]: "Poisonous serpents, traitors, cowards, murderers, thieves, rogues, tyrants, devils in flesh and blood."

Against the mortification fantasies must be balanced the opposite falsification about the extreme laxity in the monasteries: "Throughout all my years in the papacy I never saw even one genuine fast. Instead there was only feasting and gluttony, hypocritically feigned to deceive God and the people."[2] Martin does not of course explain how either God or the people could be deceived into regarding this gluttony as a fast, but then he rarely makes an attempt to impart a touch of versimilitude to such bald and unconvincing narratives. The evident purpose of this type of fiction is to help justify his withdrawal from so abandoned a community; the part about the gluttony also may defend against his own practice of stuffing himself at table as a device for controlling anxiety.

By far the most famous of these remembrances are concerned with the so-called 'Tower experience,' a topic which received a vast amount of attention from Luther specialists during the earlier decades of the present century. This subject is one of the more complicated in Luther biography, mainly because of the contradictory features in the numerous reminiscences found in the Luther record. The fact that these accounts of Luther's earlier life all date from the 1530s and 1540s helps explain his imperfect recollection of them apart from the other fact that they lie in the area of his psychic disturbance. The material in question is concerned with two distinct episodes in Luther's monastic career separated by roughly a decade. To clarify the subject, I will present the results of an analysis of a dozen or so items in the record involving these two episodes and an interpretation of Luther's experience of sudden illumination.

The first episode concerns Luther's early misunderstanding of an important scriptural phrase, the 'righteousness' or 'justice' of God, or *justitia Dei* in the Vulgate text used by Luther. We do not deal here with the complexities of the concept of righteousness as elucidated by modern Scripture scholars but merely with what might be called Luther's simplistic understanding of the term. As we shall see presently, when he first encountered this phrase in one of the Psalms he took it to refer to the divine attribute whereby God judges and punishes sinners. Later he came to realize that instead it means the righteousness by which God justifies sinners. This is, of course, the traditional interpretation of the phrase. The points of interest in this episode include the date when Luther's misreading occurred, the reason for the misunderstanding and its effect on him, how he later became aware of the traditional understanding, and the date of this awareness.

From various indications it would appear that Luther ran afoul of the 'righteousness of God' not long after his entrance into the monastery, for he began to read the Bible almost immediately. In Ch. 1 we described the circumstances of his joining the Augustinian order. The following Table Talk item (# 5346; summer of 1540) describes how he began to read Scripture: "As a youth at Erfurt I saw a Bible in the university library and read part of Kings .... When I entered the monastery and left all things, despairing of myself, I asked again for a Bible. The brothers gave me one." This recital has the ring of truth; it lacks defensive elements and the description of his psychic state at the time accords with our other information. From another reminiscence it appears that the Bible constituted his principal reading matter during his first or novitiate year.

Next we consider what is perhaps the most satisfactory account of the experience of the misreading and subsequent clarification. It is fairly low-keyed and free of defensive falsifications.

> When I first began to read the Psalms and sang 'In your righteousness deliver me' [from Ps. 31 or Ps. 71] I was frightened every time and hated the words 'righteousness of God,' 'judgment of God,' 'work of God,' for I knew nothing other than that the righteousness of God meant his severe judgment. But would he save me from his severe judgment? Thus I was eternally damned! But the 'mercy of God,' the 'help of God,' this phrase was very pleasant to me. May God be praised, I came to understand this matter and realized that God's righteousness means the righteousness given us by Christ Jesus. Thus I understood the expression and *for the first time found the Psalter pleasing.* (# 5247)

Luther had a comparable experience with the second Psalm (verse 11): 'Serve the Lord with fear . . . lest he be angry.' In the 1531 lectures on Galatians he tells his audience: "Formerly I hated this verse because of those words."[3]

With no background in scriptural exegesis in the early years and given his prevailing anxiety, the error about the 'righteousness of God' is understandable. The reference to the liturgical chanting of a verse found in both Ps. 31 and Ps. 71 provides further support for an early date of this event as does his reference to a time when he did not enjoy reading the Psalter. The above account fails to specify how and when Luther acquired a correct understanding of the phrase. In the next excerpt the source of his illumination is suggested:

> I could understand nothing about what the words meant until as time went on I read 'The righteous man lives by faith.' (Rom.

1:17) This verse explains the righteousness of God. When I discovered this, I was delighted and more joyful than ever before. And thereby was opened to me what I had read in the Psalms: 'In your righteousness deliver me.' (Ps. 31:27). Before, I had trembled all over and hated the psalms and scriptures that spoke of the righteousness of God, because he was just and judged according to our sins, not one who received and justified us. All Scripture stood like a wall before me until I understood the expression: 'The righteous man lives by faith.' (# 5553)

This account adds two more elements to the previous one: that Luther gained his new understanding by reflecting on a verse from Paul, and that thereby he experienced tremendous relief. His experience of relief at reaching an understanding of a scriptural passage seems to have been a fairly common occurrence in the earlier years. In a sermon of the 1540s he recalls that "when I began to understand a verse I felt as though I was born anew."[4] In later years when he could not conceive a comforting interpretation of an unpleasant text, Luther would resort to the denial mechanism. A striking example of this is with the "Whatsoever you bind on earth . . .' of Matt. 18, dealt with above in Ch. 5. In 1520 Luther says of this verse that it "tormented my soul for a long time." For him it meant the "Pope can do with us what he will."

We now quote another Table Talk account of the discovery:

The expression 'righteousness of God' was like a thunderclap in my heart for when I was in the papacy I read 'In your righteousness deliver me' and elsewhere 'in your truth.' I thought at once that this meant the fury of vindictive justice, i.e., the divine wrath. I hated Paul in my heart when I read: 'The righteousness of God is revealed in the gospel.' [Rom. 1:17] But later on, when I saw what was written after this: 'The righteous man lives by faith,' and moreover consulted Augustine, I became joyful. (# 4007)

If this account is to be credited, Luther is saying that the first half of Rom. 1:17 (here quoted inaccurately) made him hate Paul as he already hated parts of the Psalter, and that after a time of unspecified duration the second half of this verse — with an assist from Augustine — served to clarify the real meaning of righteousness for him. Merely reading Augustine's exposition of this phrase could have set him right, and it is not unlikely that it was Augustine who provided him with the key. Perhaps the main interest of this reminiscence is the disclosure that at one time Luther felt hostile to Paul, and this suggests an early date (before 1510) for his new understanding.

The earliest contemporary indication showing his knowledge of the traditional understanding consists of marginal notes Martin wrote in a copy of the "Sentences" of Peter Lombard about 1510. A few years later in his first academic lectures on the Psalter (1513-1515) he refers repeatedly to the concept of God's righteousness and its traditional interpretation in such a casual way that one would never guess the phrase had formerly been a problem for him. To summarize this part of the analysis, it seems probable that Luther's misunderstanding of the scriptural phrase occurred during his first year in the monastery 1505-06, that it contributed appreciably to his anxiety, and that at some point during the next few years he was greatly relieved upon discovering his mistake, with Augustine as the most likely source of his clarification.

The second episode included in the 'Tower experience' figures in the development of the *sola fide* program. This is, as we have seen, a well documented affair. We quote here a brief but illuminating comment on it found in the Table Talk (autumn of 1532): "I did not learn my theology all at one time. I had to meditate on it more deeply, and my temptations [anxiety states] helped me along, for one can learn nothing without practice." (# 352) This candid statement is in line with one of the conclusions of this study, that for Luther theology is not a speculative or theoretical discipline as ordinarily conceived, but a psychological technique for controlling pathological anxiety. Since, as shown in an earlier chapter, the development of the *sola fide* defense required a number of years, we can readily understand what Luther means by 'not all at one time.'

With this background we are now in a position to examine the reminiscences that gave rise to the modern concept of the 'Tower experience.' Unlike the reminiscences dealt with above, the next group will be found burdened with defensive material, that is, falsifications that shield Luther from painful experience. Early in June of 1532 he began to deliver a course of lectures on the fourth penitential psalm, Ps. 51. In this, the most famous of the penitential psalms, the phrase 'the righteousness of God' does not occur till toward the end. This psalm is a highly emotional lament of the sinner before God and Luther's commentary reveals that he has claimed it, anachronistically, as a support for his heterodox views on original sin, a concept that was unknown to the psalmist. The psalm opens with the phrase 'Have mercy on me, O God.' At the sound of these words Luther goes haring off in his own direction, for they have, like a magic formula, summoned up memories from the murky depths of his unconscious.

He begins his commentary on this verse with one of his major falsifications and almost at once repeats it; to this use of the denial mechanism we shall return presently:

Nearly all the holy Fathers (*sancti patres*) who have written on the psalm interpret the phrase 'God is righteous' as referring to his avenging righteousness, rather than to his making us righteous. Thus it befell me in my youth (*iuveni*) that I hated this name for God, and because of this former habit I still shudder today when I hear God called righteous. Such is the force of impious teaching when impressed on the mind early in life (*prima aetate*), yet nearly all the old teachers (*veteres Doctores*) interpret it this way. But if God is thus righteous so that he righteously punishes according as one deserves, who can stand in the sight of this righteous God? . . . . Away with this kind of righteousness and righteous God![5]

And so he goes on for page after page (in the printed form of the lectures) as is his habit when reacting to such a stimulus, his discourse having little or no bearing on its nominal subject. But in this torrent of words he tells his auditors nothing about how he subsequently learned of the error of these ancient teachers and how he himself discovered the truth. It seems plausible to infer that one or another of the students later asked the great doctor to finish his story. For the date of delivery of the lectures (unfortunately the precise chronology is lacking) falls within the time period assigned to the Table Talk account of what later came to be called the Tower experience. It seems preferable to regard this recital as the answer to a question arising from the incomplete anecdote of the lecture rather than attributing its appearance at this time to sheer coincidence: (# 3232b)

These words 'righteous' and the 'righteousness of God' were like lightning in my conscience. I listened to them with a beating heart: He is righteous, therefore, he punishes. But once when reflecting in this tower on the words: 'The righteous man lives by faith' and the 'righteousness of God,' and thinking that we are to live righteously by faith, and the righteousness of God makes for the salvation of all who believe, I was suddenly cheered by this thought: It is the righteousness of God which saves and makes us righteous. And these words now made me rejoice. This knowledge came to me from the Holy Spirit in the privy (*cloaca*) of this tower.

In his remark about the 'holy Fathers' in the psalm lecture quoted above, Luther intends to except Augustine. When back around 1900 the Dominican scholar Denifle came across this falsification he grew so incensed that to expose it he looked through some sixty early commentators on the scriptural phrase and reported that they all agreed with Augustine. We do not ask with Denifle whether Luther is thereby shown up as either an ignoramus or a liar but instead inquire as to what psychic benefit Luther derived from the falsification. The unpalatable fact he is presumably trying to blot out here is that he, Martin Luther, the greatest of all interpreters of Scripture, committed an elementary error on a topic that was well understood by everyone else. This lecture series abounds in similar falsifications of well established teaching and as may be expected there occurs in it a reference to Luther's excommunication as a heretic. It would appear that having appropriated this psalm to validate the truth of his heterodox positions on sin and total depravity, he is reminded of his conflict with the papacy and this awareness releases a spate of defensive material.

The Table Talk item quoted above appears to be the only place in the record where Luther claims direct inspiration from the Holy Spirit on the meaning of righteousness and locates this sublime event in the privy of the monastic tower. The Table Talk item # 1681, which essentially duplicates the information of # 3232b quoted here, seems to be a record of the same conversation by different scribes. The falsification about how all the 'holy Fathers' save Augustine shared his own former error is, however, repeated elsewhere. The most celebrated of all these reminiscences is found in the autobiographic Preface to the 1545 edition of the Latin works. This deals mainly with other topics but toward the end Martin adverts to his old problem. Now an elderly paranoid with few remaining inhibitions, he tells his readers openly that he hated not only the scriptural phrase but also the righteous God who punishes sinners. The earlier commentators (save for Augustine) are castigated for leading poor Martin astray on the meaning of the righteousness of God. In this account he does not mention any problem with the Psalter but lays great stress on his long and soul-searing quest in the Epistle to the Romans for a true understanding, to which he attained after prolonged anguish. Only then did he discover that Augustine had also achieved some grasp of the same truth, albeit inferior in clarity and precision to his own. A source of confusion in this reminiscence is the way Luther artfully assimilated his early difficulty with the scriptural phrase in the Psalter with his much later illumination in the monastery tower.

An important feature of the account in the Preface is that it provides an approximate date for the experience, namely, the period when Luther was starting his second course of lectures on the Psalms. It will be recalled that his journey to Augsburg for the session with Cardinal Cajetan took him away from Wittenberg from late September to the end of October of 1518. In the latter part of March 1519 he delivered to the printer a batch of material developed for the lecture course covering the first five Psalms. It may be surmised that his illumination in the tower occurred during the weeks preceding or following the Augsburg journey when he was planning or preparing these lectures.

This lecture material (published as "Operationes in Psalmos") might be expected to contain a clue to the actual subject of his illumination. In the commentary on the last verse of Ps. 4, "You, O Lord, have wonderfully established me in hope," Luther executes a startling about-face from a previous attitude. In his earlier lectures on the Psalms and on Romans he had, following the pattern of the *Imitatio Christi,* recommended a willing acceptance of a state of uncertainty about his prospects of salvation as part of the larger theme of patiently enduring tribulations – the 'road of the cross' or 'theology of the cross.' In developing this theme he had attacked those who lapse into a state of presumptuous security about their spiritual condition. Now, reversing himself, he assailed monks and theologians who advocate the state of doubt or uncertainty, and asserted the Psalm verse means the Christian must feel secure and confident about his salvation.[6] In terms of the defensive programs described in Ch. 1, it is clear that Luther is in process of abandoning the second or 'road of the cross' program for the *sola fide.* That he is perturbed about this defection from a long cherished ideal may be inferred from his interjecting in the commentary on Ps. 3 a sentence in praise of the road of the cross that might almost have been lifted from the *Imitatio,* and especially from a resounding affirmation in the commentary on Ps. 5 that the "cross alone [*CRUX sola*] is my theology." But this seems to be the last substantive defense of the road of the cross in his writings. That the break is definite can be seen in the commentary on Ps. 13 (14) written some months later in which he presents a stirring exposition of the *sola fide* and is silent about the cross.[7]

Commentators on Luther's reminiscence in the Preface have had a problem with his assertion that not until 1518-19 did he understand the phrase 'righteousness of God' although the record shows he had been aware of its meaning for something like a decade previously. In view of the analysis given here, it appears that what suddenly became clear to Luther in the tower was not the meaning of God's righteousness itself but a happy *consequence* of it – the consequence that through it he could be relieved of his intolerable anxiety about his salvation if he had faith. It was the joyous prospect of this desperately sought relief that helped propel him out of the road of the cross program into the *sola fide.* The significance of his reversal on 'security' in the early 1519 Psalm lectures is that it provides something like contemporary verification that the event in the tower did occur during the period in question.

It is of interest to compare Luther's illumination with a similar experience of Nietzsche at Sils Maria in August 1881. One day he suddenly realized that if the doctrine of eternal recurrence of all happenings were true, he could be set free of his anxiety about his fate after death. In 1881 he had known about 'eternal recurrence' at least as long as Luther had understood the meaning of the right-eousness of God in 1519. His illumination consisted of the sudden realization of how he himself could benefit from this ancient con-cept. His report of the tremendous exhiliration he experienced on this occasion matches Luther's own reaction as described in his reminiscences. The anxiety-ridden egocentric has his own way of relating to the world beyond the boundary of the psyche; in the area of his disturbance especially he perceives objects not as neutral but as potential or actual threats or benefits to himself. When something formerly recognized as a threat capable of arousing his anxiety is suddenly perceived anew as a benefit instead, he momentarily ex-periences unbounded elation. As Luther testified, "the gates of Para-dise have opened" for him. This is the basis of what modern writers on Luther with a defective understanding of his psychic problems and his prior mental history have celebrated as the 'evangelical break-through.' What follows the exhiliration? With Nietzsche, for whom we have reliable evidence contemporary with the emotional swings, there was shortly afterward a plunge into the depths; as he puts it in a letter on that occasion: "Five times did I call for Doctor Death." While information like this for Luther is not available, we know his illumination was followed roughly a year later by one of his most severe anxiety attacks to date and some months after that by psy-chotic regression. Whether he experienced further illuminations thereafter the record does not reveal.

From these reminiscences of Luther's inner life we shall turn for a brief look at some remarks about his bodily health. For one with his emotional problems, particularly his anxiety and his suspicious outlook, symptoms of hypochondria would hardly be unexpected. Of the many allusions to his physical illnesses and disabilities we shall consider a Table Talk account (summer of 1540) of an experience which evidently occured in the early 1520s — the period of the Dantiscus report (Ch. 3):

> I very often believed I had been given poison to drink, but this one time I was positive I had drunk some. I had been out to a drinking party, and when I came home I went to bed feeling very ill though I was not drunk. Soon afterward I vomited profusely three times. After vomiting, I had three very large bowel move-ments and three other smaller ones. At the same time there was a great liquid discharge from my nose, and then I began to sweat as never before, and the sweat stank fearfully. Also I had a most shocking emission. There was no opening in my whole body from which something didn't flow. I believe God thought: 'They wanted to give him poison, so I will purge him.' And indeed the next day

I was quite well again. (# 5370)

The absence of an estimate on the quantity of urine passed – after a drinking party – suggests Martin withheld this information to lend credence to the view he had really been poisoned and was not merely drunk, with the 'shocking emission' provided as a substitute to complete the tale of discharging orifices. What he could not be expected to know was that the sudden onset of symptoms of nausea, diarrhea and chills, followed by rapid recovery, indicates he was suffering from ordinary food poisoning rather than from the kind of draught said to be so popular in those days among the Borgias.

That in his later fifties he could retain so vivid a recollection of an experience that occurred 15 years or more in the past can be accounted for by the integration of the memory of the event into his strong persecutory feelings. During the later years we hear a good deal about such complaints as dizzy spells, roaring of the ears and the near brushes with death during attacks of the stone. But these many indications of the delicate state of Luther's health must be tempered by the evident delight in his undiminished capacity for consuming food and drink, as well as by the three uncalled for journeys to his homeland during the final months of his life – in marked contrast with his refusal to make the same trip 20 years earlier to visit his dying parents.

iii. The tyrant of Wittenberg

The unique relation between Melanchthon and Luther is a matter of perennial interest. During Luther's later years Melanchthon was the only man of intellectual distinction in Germany who continued an early attachment for him. The desertion of the Wittenberg prophet by nearly all those above a certain level of education (apart from the circle of Wittenberg intimates) is symbolized in the story of a one-time Luther enthusiast named George Witzel. A few years Melanchthon's junior and with similar native gifts, Witzel entered the University of Erfurt at the age of 14 or 15 and somewhat later transferred to Wittenberg. He was ordained to the priesthood when only 20 (in 1521) and began his clerical career in his natal village. Two years later he applied to his ecclesiastical superior for permission to take a wife. This being refused, he married anyhow and was presently ejected from his living.

After some wandering about, he was installed through Luther's intervention in the small parish of Nimegk not far from Wittenberg. Here he remained from 1525 to 1531, and in the latter year there was a cordial letter from Luther to Witzel and a fellow cleric replying to their application for an official release from their parish assignments. Luther was soon to learn the reason for this request and to alter his tone from cordiality to hostility. Witzel had devoted his rustic leisure to the study of the works of the early Church fathers and through this educative process had discovered they were not the theological ciphers Luther had claimed. His eyes had also been opened to the essential hollowness of 'my theology.' As he himself remarked, he had originally embraced Luther's teaching when in a state of theological ignorance.

A modern commentator on Witzel has observed that he had not become a follower of Luther through wanting to learn how to feel that his sins were forgiven or to acquire a sense of security about his salvation.[8] Instead, like many others, his original enthusiasm for Luther was based on the expectation that what Luther called 'my movement' would lead to a reform of abuses in the Church and a renewal of religious life. It might be said that Witzel's attachment to Luther was primarily ideological whereas Melanchthon's was primarily personal. That explains why Witzel could cease to be a Luther partisan once he had acquired a fairly considerable background in the theology of the Fathers. His disenchantment with Luther's program was complete when he witnessed the decay of morality in Germany consequent upon the Lutheran revolt.

We are not concerned here with the story of Witzel's extensive efforts over the next 40 years (he lived until 1573) to promote reform by his writings. His literary attack on the Lutherian teaching commenced shortly before the time Luther himself suffered that peculiar inhibition with regard to writing pamphlets mentioned elsewhere in this book. Two of Witzel's earlier tracts were entitled "The Gospel of Martin Luther" and "Lutherianism Unmasked" (*Retectio Lutherismi*). He also pointed out errors in the famous Wittenberg translation of Scripture. But despite this intense provocation, perhaps the most galling of his entire career because it came from a well informed critic and former disciple, Luther remained silent. Whether discouraged by Witzel's expert criticism or unwilling to give more publicity to this distressing defection or prevented from writing by his inhibition of the mid 1530s is not known. Instead, the reply to Witzel was delegated to one of the underlings of Luther's circle. To this tract Luther contributed only a brief foreword from which we quote a sample to display the personal abuse he substituted for intellectual discourse when referring to critics of his gospel: "Witzel's shameless and lying mouth and heart openly tell such lies against his own conscience in his blasphemous book they should be apparent to his papist self even if he were blind. Therefore I don't think it worthwhile replying to the lies of this no good scoundrel."[9]

By the mid 1530s doctrinal differences between Luther and Melanchthon had reached the point that an open quarrel between the two seemed not unlikely. Luther himself mentioned the scandalous possibility of a public controversy with Melanchthon such as he had carried on against Carlstadt and Zwingli in the 1520s. This situation persisted on into the following decade. When Luther announced in the spring of 1544 that he was preparing a new statement of his views on the Eucharist, one of the topics on which they had diverged, it was feared in Wittenberg that this tract would finally reveal the long anticipated break. By this time Luther was also at odds with quite a number of heterodox tractarians who like him believed only in the absolute authority of their own personal interpretations of Scripture. Owing to the flagging of his literary powers it took him all summer to complete this not very long tract. The Wittenbergers sighed in relief to discover that while Luther had vented his hostility against a variety of the other exponents of the *sola scriptura* he had spared Melanchthon. An indication that he had not entirely lost his polemical skill was his artful coinage of the epithet 'Stenckfeld' to designate one of his theological opponents named Schwenkfeld. (While such verbal shenanigans may seem ill suited to the dignity of the subject of the tract, the device harmonized with the general tone and incidentally provides a fair sample of the literary artistry of the mature Luther.)

To account for Luther's willingness to exempt Philip from the vituperation that was plainly his due for departing from the Lutherian party line, we must invoke their unique personal relation. We noted earlier that Staupitz remained in good odor even though after retiring to Salzburg he became further immeshed in monkery and even included a mild criticism of the Lutherian doctrine in his final epistle to Martin. As Staupitz' successor in the role of maternal substitute, Melanchthon enjoyed the same immunity from attack. Unlike Staupitz he did not depart from Luther's side though he had a number of attractive offers from other universities. For the neurotic Melanchthon needed Luther as much as the psychotic Luther needed him. A most striking bit of evidence for this conclusion is provided by Melanchthon's well known reaction to his role in the bigamy of Philip of Hesse (described in the next section). While away from Wittenberg attending a theological colloquy in the summer of 1540 he became so smitten with remorse over his part in the affair that he was stricken with what would be diagnosed today as neurotic depression. He retired to bed, refused nourishment and looked forward to death. Alarmed, his associates sent for Luther, whose presence and consoling words soon restored Philip to normal health. Luther was quite proud of his accomplishments as therapist.

Additional evidence for his dependence on Luther is provided by his willingness to endure the older man's tyrannical demeanor. At the time of Luther's death Philip delivered the funeral oration, a rhetorical exercise with lavish praise for his departed mentor. Philip, it must be acknowledged, whether through his long association with Luther or from some other cause, was a man inclined to adapt his statements to the needs of the occasion rather than basing them solidly on fact. In the oration Luther is described as one marked by outstanding affability toward friends and not the least quarrelsome or contentious. Furthermore he was said to display a dignity of demeanor appropriate to one of his exalted state. It may be supposed a good many knowing smiles were exchanged among members of the audience in the Castle church upon the recital of these two whoppers. One must look at Melanchthon's private correspondence to discover his real opinion of Luther's character.

The occasion for one of his candid revelations is as follows. When Duke George died in 1539 he was succeeded by his younger brother Henry, who promptly converted Ducal Saxony to the Lutherian gospel. A few years later Henry was succeeded in turn by his son Maurice, who proved to be a staunch devotee of *realpolitik*. Presently Maurice fell out with his cousin John Frederick, Elector of Saxony, over the dividing of the spoils of some ecclesiastical property to which they had conflicting claims. Maurice then allied himself with the Emperor Charles and they jointly attacked the Smalkaldic League, the military alliance of schismatic states. Maurice, showing considerable talent for warfare, helped Charles defeat their opponents. For this service he was made Elector of Saxony, and John Frederick was cast into durance vile for five years. Also Maurice was given dominion over a large chunk of what had been John Frederick's domains including the city of Wittenberg.

Fearing that the Emperor in conjunction with Maurice might take repressive action against the state church of Saxony, a number of prominent citizens hurriedly left town. Philip was among those who elected to stay, and during the initial period of uncertainty about the degree of toleration that would be extended to the adherents of the Lutherian schism he chanced to unburden himself in a private letter on the tyrannical character of its perpetrator.

In April of 1548 writing to Carlowitz, an official in the government of the new Elector Maurice, on how he would conduct himself in the face of the anticipated repression of the Lutheran gospel, Melanchthon stated he knew how to keep silent, having had considerable practice in that art. To shelter himself from the effects of Luther's extremely contentious disposition, "I had to endure a servitude that was little short of degrading."[10] This was not the first of his complaints about Luther's tyranny. In 1538 in a letter to Viet Dietrich, one of the earlier Table Talk scribes, he wrote: "You knew about our state of bondage when you were here. Well, it has become still more harsh. To avoid giving any occasion for the storms, I take refuge in Pythagorean silence."[11] And six years later when Luther was preparing his new statement on the Eucharist he let it be known that if Luther wanted to drive him out of Wittenberg he would gladly quit that prison.

From the mutual forbearance Luther and Melanchthon practised toward one another it seems fair to conclude that each man had such a strong need for the other as to make him endure provocations that would otherwise have led to a permanent rupture. We now look at two episodes of the later 1530s that exhibit Luther exercising his domineering habits on the local scene.

On Pentecost Sunday (June 9) of 1538 there was on sale outside the parish church of Wittenberg a slender volume of Latin verses by a member of the student body named Simon Lemnius. About the time copy No. 50 had found a buyer, the Rev. Dr. Martin Luther happened along, glanced through the book, and, in the words of the Weimar editor, became 'inflamed with violent anger.' At once he demanded that Lemnius be summoned to a hearing before the university rector, who happened to be Philip Melanchthon. Lemnius had no difficulty persuading Philip of the harmlessness of his verses lampooning certain local dignitaries. Nevertheless, on the grounds that Lemnius had published politically offensive material without permission, Luther had him put under house arrest and the printer thrown into the town jail. The unsold copies of the volume of poems were impounded.

If the reader is surprised at these indications of a police state, it should be recalled that Germany was then passing through a sociopolitical revolution instigated in part by Luther himself. The literary activities of a paranoid psychotic with exceptional talents as an agitator performing in the guise of a religious prophet had caused special problems for Electoral Saxony as well as other states exposed to his propaganda. There is a certain irony in the fact that the statute Luther invoked against Lemnius and the printer had been promulgated earlier as a means of controlling Luther himself. He was regarded as far too valuable a property for the Saxon government to suppress outright, and it had instituted the censorship rule with a view to avoiding embarrassment from such of his libellous utterances as were felt to be contrary to Saxon interests.

Lemnius had no intention of remaining in Wittenberg to discover what was in store for him. Early the next morning he made his escape when a farmhand opened the town gates to drive in a herd of cows pastured outside during the night. (As mentioned below, earlier that year another student had suffered a month's imprisonment for making derogatory remarks about Luther in a personal letter.) The following day official action was taken against Lemnius by the university senate. His belongings were confiscated, the books seized on Sunday were burned, and procedures were instituted leading to his official expulsion from the student body.

The cause of Luther's tremendous outburst of anger or, as we would call it today, paranoid hostility, was not the covert satire in the verses some of which was directed against him. What aroused him was the dedication of the book to Albert, Cardinal Archbishop of Mainz, the ecclesiastical dignitary of the Hohenzollern family to whom Luther had sent the famous 95 Indulgence Theses more than 20 years ago. Unaware that Albert was one of the prime targets of Luther's hostility, ranking only a notch or two below the Pope and Satan, Lemnius had blundered into a hornet's nest. Albert, with the easing of his financial problems following the costly purchase of the archbishopric of Mainz, had blossomed into a patron of the arts, the sort of personage a hopeful litterateur such as Lemnius would praise in print. To exhibit the fierceness of Luther's hostility toward the primate of the Church in Germany, we shall present a translation of a statement that Luther read to the congregation in the parish church of Wittenberg the Sunday following the arrest of Lemnius, entitled "Declaration against Simon Lemnius."[12] The reader will readily sense why this item has not graced the anthologies.

Dr. Martin Luther to all the brothers and sisters of our church in Wittenberg, grace and peace in Christ, our dear Lord and Savior. Just this past Pentecost Sunday, an infamous rascal named Simon Lemnius put out some verses without the knowledge or consent of those whose office it is to approve such writings. It is a downright brazen, disgraceful and lying book which injures the image of many honorable men and women of the town and church.

For this, according to all justice (if the rascal could be captured and brought back here) he deserves to lose his head. Consequently, in the absence of our dear pastor Dr. John Bugenhagen (for without doubt he would not endure this as we all know perfectly well) I as substitute pastor cannot tolerate this slanderous, knavish roguery. Loaded as I am with my own sins, I cannot be burdened with the many sins of another (especially of such a shameful scoundrel who has been taught and has witnessed far better things among us and who repays us with such shameful ingratitude).

I ask and admonish all pious and true Christians who hold and love the same belief and teaching as we do, that they will cast out such slanderous poetry and burn it in honor of our holy gospel. In this way our adversaries in other lands may not boast in their writings, as they are inclined to do, that we do not punish scoundrels even though they well know we punish more severely than they do in their states, especially as they use their holy clerical celibacy as a standard.

Because this same rascally poetaster has praised Bishop Albert, that miserable town clerk (if I may be permitted to speak thus) and made a saint of the devil, I will not tolerate the publication of this kind of stuff in our church, school and town. This same shit-bishop is a false, lying character and has the habit of calling us Lutherans rascals although he will hear from St. Maurice and St. Stephen that he is the worst rascal of all on the [last] day, as he knows very well, but consoles himself that he doesn't believe so. And if God gives me life and time, I will some day make a fine example of him.

Now once more, may all of our people and especially the poets or their adherents never again publicly praise or brag about the shit-parson in this church, school or town. Otherwise let them await their own lord and I will await mine. And know that I will not permit anyone here in Wittenberg to praise that self-condemned unholy parson who would like to see us all dead. More on this before long.

A perusal of this little composition is rewarding for its revelation of the personality of the mature Luther. Of note is his favorite alibi for character defamation — he would be adding to his own sins if he failed to expose the sins of another. A matter that is bugging Luther at the moment is the remnant of the 50 copies of the poems that he had been unable during the past week to track down and persuade their owners to destroy. The depth of his animosity toward Albert is apparent in the gutter level of the name calling. In view of the example he set for his fellow preachers in this display of hostility, the tone of the pulpit oratory in the churches of Electoral Saxony, commented on elsewhere in this study, is hardly surprising.

Luther's appetite for retaliation was far from sated by the pulpit performance. With his characteristic scorn for any laws that would restrain his own freedom of action and himself committing the offense with which he had wantonly charged the poet, he had had a printer run off a batch of copies of the libelous "Declaration." As if anticipating the legendary account of the nailing of the 95 Indulgence Theses to the Castle church door, a story that was not to be invented until after his death, he affixed a copy to the parish church door after the service. The printed copies of the broadside were then disseminated throughout Germany. By this action Luther had published a gross and unprovoked insult against a member of the powerful Hohenzollern family. Albert himself remained silent in face of this calumnious assault but his nephew Joachim of Brandenburg demanded that punitive action be taken against this most scurrilous of prophets. The Elector of Saxony, following the example of his father and his uncle in the past, rebuffed Joachim and the prophet was free to go ahead with a new attack on the Hohenzollern.

Luther had been pursuing his vendetta against Albert for nearly two decades. His displeasure had stemmed originally from Albert's promotion of indulgences and his ignoring Luther's famous protest against this policy. It was subsequently refueled by the archbishop's decision not to join the schism. Albert had indeed considered this option, what was known euphemistically as secularizing his archbishopric. But in taking this step he would have encountered legal difficulties that might well have deprived him of some of his extensive holdings, and he would certainly have had to give up his titles of Archbishop and Cardinal. So he took what appeared to him the better deal and stayed within the Church. His official position brought him into conflict with the aggressive proselytizing of the Lutherian party. His administration of the episcopal city of Halle proved to be a major source of friction. In the crazy-quilt map of late medieval Germany, Halle was an enclave in Electoral Saxony hardly a day's journey from the propaganda center of Wittenberg.

While in hiding at the Wartburg, Luther had written his first attack on Albert, "The Idol of Halle." Spalatin intercepted this manic production and forestalled its publication. Thereafter Luther contented himself with an occasional threatening letter. Albert evinced no desire to retaliate and in 1525 even sent the Luthers some cash as a wedding gift which Catherine insisted on keeping over Martin's objections. In the mid 1530s a new focus of controversy developed when Albert had one of his servitors, John von Plaenitz, executed on grounds of malfeasance in office in what was widely regarded as a judicial murder. During a visit to Luther the victim's brother aroused him anew against Albert. In Luther's correspondence at this time there appears a new note; three times, as remarked by the Weimar editors, he compares himself to Elias as one divinely commissioned to rebuke publicly an evil monarch.[13]

But at this period Luther's writing career, as we have seen, was in a state of eclipse. All he could do was issue threats. Even after the emotional peak he experienced during the Lemnius incident, it was around six months before the long promised tract against Albert appeared, late in 1538, signalling the rebirth of his literary powers. Not that it was worth waiting for, since it ranks among his dullest compositions. Even the title: "Against the Bishop of Magdeburg, Cardinal Albert" was stodgy as well as uninformative. The work is a rather pointless review of the Plaenitz case, now three or four years old, rather than the expected gut attack on Albert. To see how Luther's wit has deteriorated one need only compare this tract with the sparkling manic production called "Against the Hyperspiritual, etc., Goat Emser" of 1521. Nor does it have any of the earthiness of the blast against Albert Luther read from the pulpit in his "Declaration."

In contrast with the dullness of the tract against the Cardinal

(which is rarely exhumed for comment) is Luther's equally un-
noticed riposte against Lemnius. After his escape from Wittenberg
the poet composed and published some new verses about the great
doctor in which he made playful allusion to a bout with diarrhea that
Luther had recently sustained. To show his facility as a versifier and
his contempt for Lemnius, Luther composed ten lines in his best
classical style. These verses, known as the "Merd Song," are in
modern times printed only in complete editions of the Table Talk.
(# 4032) The key term *merda,* i.e., excrement, is repeated a dozen
times in a variety of grammatical forms to express sentiments about
Lemnius in perfect harmony with the level of the diction.

The second cataclysm which shook Wittenberg in the late 1530s
arose from Luther's attack on an old friend John Agricola. It is of
interest as showing how he dealt with subordinates who would not
stay in line. Agricola, about ten years Luther's junior, had received
his theological formation at the feet of the master and was a long-
time Luther enthusiast. A resident of Luther's birthplace, Eisleben,
he was also a personal friend; when a new Latin school was established
at Eisleben in 1525 Agricola was put in charge. Two years later when
his wife evidenced symptoms of depression, Luther invited her to his
Wittenberg home for therapy. Agricola cherished the ambition of
joining the Wittenberg theological faculty but did not go to the
trouble of taking a doctorate. From time to time he accompanied
the Elector to colloquies as a theological consultant. Though a layman he had attained popularity as a preacher in his home town.

In 1536, still looking for a position on the faculty, he returned to
Wittenberg, and early the next year Luther chose him as substitute
for both lecturing and preaching during his absence at Smalkald. By
summer, Luther had heard rumors that Agricola was preaching erroneous doctrine, to wit, that he was misleading his auditors about the
current status of the Decalogue in Wittenberg theology. In an earlier
chapter we remarked about the shift in Luther's attitude toward
'Moses' during the 1520s. As late as 1525 he was asserting that
'Moses' was only for the Israelites, but thereafter had reversed himself upon becoming aware of the moral decay in Saxony. Agricola
had imbibed the heady doctrine of 'down with Moses' in the early
days, and it was his misfortune, isolated as he was from party head-
quarters, to have missed the change in the party line. As happens in
revolutionary movements, he had unwittingly become a counter-
revolutionary.

To make matters worse, the party leader was manifesting the
suspicious traits of the paranoid, and Agricola had previously made
enemies in the party who rejoiced at the opportunity of denouncing
him to the chief. In particular there was one of Martin's
ex-Augustinian brothers, Caspar Guettel, preaching in competition

with Agricola at Eisleben, who gladly acted as informer. The situation that now developed was more than a little like that involving the Zwickau town council, with Guettel filling the role of Hausmann. Agricola was apparently not too alert, for not only had he failed to detect an important shift in the party line but it took him the better part of three years to realize he was doomed. Also he was so imprudent as to quote the Luther of the earlier years against the Luther of the 1530s.

Luther's first step, in July of 1537, was to preach a sermon at Wittenberg warning against Agricola's error. Thereupon Agricola wrote Luther a letter of apology asserting he was conscious of no wrong doing. But he was so ill advised as to attempt next the publication of a volume of gospel commentary without clearing it with Luther. Using his authority as dean of the theological faculty, Luther had the printing stopped and confiscated the unbound sheets. He then ordered an academic disputation, at which Agricola failed to show. Instead he sent Luther the following obsequious letter:

> I have always felt and now feel and will feel as long as I live that you are the source and instrument of the most genuine and evangelic truth which enlightens the world in these latter days. Therefore, God willing, I shall always stand and fall on your judgment. For I know you to be my father, one who will always be of profit to me in body and soul.[14]

After further exchanges during the autumn and early winter, Luther sent the following letter in January to his one-time friend:

> At my request and desire you undertook to give lectures on theology lest you be idle and others disappointed. I have now given formal notice to the rector that, again at my desire, your lecturing will stop and that you should withdraw entirely from theology. I inform you of this matter now so that you may know you will have to be granted authority elsewhere to give lectures, namely, by the university senate.
>
> If you speak against me privately, I will not of course try to stop you, but you had better be on your guard. Farewell and submit your understanding to God's mighty hand.[15]

Later in January there was a second disputation that helped bring about a temporary reconcilation after Agricola had publicly confessed his error, and he was once more permitted to lecture and preach in Wittenberg. But the suspicions of a paranoid, once aroused and directed against a target, can not easily be quenched. And Agricola's antagonists were glad to keep feeding the flames. The point at issue was not actually a question of basic doctrine but rather of how to present the Lutherian gospel. Should the preacher try to arouse sinners to repentance (1) by urging them to regard their sins as responsible for the passion of Jesus Christ, or (2) by frightening them with thoughts of punishment for violations of the Decalogue?

When Agricola became aware of Luther's renewed antagonism he wrote him another letter in August of 1538 which later he declared set the Rhine on fire. In this he referred to a sermon ["Meditation on Christ's Passion"] Luther had printed back in 1519 (when Agricola was a student of Luther's) in which the method of meditating on Christ's sufferings is described in highly affective language and nothing at all is said about the Ten Commandments. (This sermon is of interest as revealing Luther in the state of heightened neurotic anxiety that preceded his regression.) Agricola proposed that the Wittenbergers choose a method of preaching repentance on the basis of what was most consonant with apostolic tradition.

Almost at once Luther scheduled a third disputation. In this he made an attempt to excuse his reversal regarding 'Moses.' As noted earlier, since the *sola fide* was designed to help control neurotic anxiety, it had proved very ineffective among parishioners who enjoyed normal emotional health. In consequence, Luther had come to insist that the proper way to generate anxiety in the hearts of the unterrified was by method 2. When excited to an appropriate level of terror, they would be happy to accept the consolations of the *sola fide.* To tie in this approach with his earlier scorn of 'Moses' he projected his own anxiety on to his congregation, saying that when 'under the Pope' and unblessed with the *sola fide* we were so terrified there was no need of the Law to make us grasp the 'promises.' But now that we have escaped from the dominion of Antichrist we have grown unfeeling and secure and need the preaching of the Law to induce a state of terror at the consequences of our sins that is indispensable for accepting the *sola fide.*

Alarmed at the vehemence of Luther's insistence on preaching the Law, Agricola now proposed that Luther himself compose a new public recantation by which would be demonstrated beyond any doubt his loyalty to Wittenberg theology. Luther's next step in this merciless harassment of Agricola was to attack him in a tract which contained the public recantation. Using the well established technique of suppressing the name of his opponent in the title, he called the tract "Against the Antinomians" as he had, for example, many years earlier attacked Carlstadt in "Against the Heavenly Prophets." There is of course no reference in the tract to any person but Agricola, who is named once near the beginning and thereafter designated variously as 'Master Eisleben,' the 'devil,' 'these spirits' or simply 'they.' (Agricola like Carlstadt had the chameleon-like property of assuming the plural number when so required.) Luther scrupulously avoided use of the name 'antinomians' (those opposed to law) in the tract, perhaps because it might cause readers to wonder who the other ones were. With characteristic sadism he addressed the tract as an open letter to Agricola's enemy Caspar Guettel, asking that good and learned doctor to give it all the public exposure he could so that no one would miss the recantation contained in the text. Luther so phrased this as to imply that Agricola would later repudiate it, and when he did so the reader could see by the public recantation that his pernicious teaching was worthless, being recanted in advance. Luther's apparent reason for calling Agricola 'the devil' was that in his writings "he always gives an untrue picture of me and my teachings," that is, quotes from the Luther of earlier years, who was evidently not the Luther of the 1530s. An interesting feature of the tract is the display of Luther's persecutory delusions. On more than a score of occasions he has suffered the assaults of Satan in the area of theology, and he rehearses some five or six of these beginning with the papacy and continuing with Carlstadt. In this way he represents himself as the long suffering victim of Agricola's persecution.

Meanwhile back in Wittenberg the harassment proceeded. Following the third disputation against Agricola — designated as 'the Antinomians' — Luther set up a fourth, and after that a fifth and finally a sixth, each equipped with a set of theses, a product for which Luther was justly famous. During this barrage the arts faculty of Wittenberg, who were in a rebellious mood under the Lutherian dictatorship, proposed to elect the infamous Agricola to be their dean. Learning of this, Martin declared he would much rather have the man from Eisleben excommunicated.

In desperation Agricola at last decided to take the offensive. In January of 1540 he submitted a formal complaint about Luther's mistreatment of him to clergy and public officials in Eisleben and Mansfeld. When this action proved fruitless, he filed a similar complaint with the Elector two months later. To this there was a response; John Frederick was displeased and directed that Agricola remain in Wittenberg until an official decision could be rendered on the controversy. Agricola was unhappy at this outcome, and his fear of losing not only any opportunity for promotion at Wittenberg but even his means of livelihood, a fear which had dogged him since Luther began the harassment in 1537, was intensified. He recalled what had happened to Carlstadt under similar circumstances in the previous decade. Conditions in Saxony were even more repressive by this time.

An illustration of this is provided by an episode involving a Wittenberg student named George Karg, a religious enthusiast with very modest intellectual endowment who had been turned against Luther by a theological opponent. While so minded he had averred in a private letter that even if offered salvation by the Lord himself on condition that he accept Luther's theology he would reject the offer.

This letter came into the hands of the Elector, who sent a directive to Wittenberg officialdom that for this crime Karg be jailed.[16] Luther interviewed the lad and though arriving at the opinion he was a harmless eccentric found it well to incarcerate him so as not to make light of this latest assault of Satan. Accordingly the unfortunate youth was manacled and locked up for a month. During this interval he received instruction from Luther and others on certain articles of faith about which he had difficulties. There is extant his petition to the Elector humbly requesting his release from jail. He acknowledges that he had been misled by others on the aforesaid articles but now that he has received the correct doctrine his difficulties are solved and he promises to abide forevermore in Wittenberg truth.

Agricola, deciding that to remain in Saxony was no longer likely to promote his health or happiness, followed the example of Carlstadt and went into exile. He accepted an offer from Elector Joachim of Brandenburg as court preacher in Berlin. As he had been forced to promise to remain in Wittenberg to stand trial for heresy, Luther took this opportunity to blacken his reputation further. During the spring of 1540 Luther had obtained a copy of Agricola's formal complaint about him. This inspired another tract entitled "Against the [Man from] Eisleben." Of this work the Weimar editor remarks that Luther here speaks little to the point and repeatedly lapses into personal invective.[17] Some excerpts will illustrate the typical suspicions of the paranoid that he is the victim of a conspiracy:

> Eisleben is our enemy, has slandered our teaching and dishonored our theology. The sect he founded at Eisleben proves that and he can't deny it . . . . After establishing and poisoning his Eisleben sect he comes on to Wittenberg, and again behind my back treacherously seeks to poison and alienate the school and church. . . . With his book of sermons [suppressed by Luther] he would lay the cornerstone against us and our teaching – that our doctrine is false and impure and that he alone must be honored as the teacher of pure doctrine.

> [The Elector is then invited to] chastise his lying mouth publicly and restore our teaching and theology to the position of honor he has foully and shamefully stolen and deprived it of.

In May of 1545 Agricola during a brief visit to Wittenberg tried to meet with Luther, who refused to see or speak with him. Alongside his innumerable shifts and inconsistencies is to be noted his unshakable constancy in refusing to be reconciled with theological opponents. His sturdy disdain for putting into practice the fifth petition of the Paternoster is as strong in the last year of his life as it was right after his regression in the summer of 1520. In letters to John Frederick and George Buchholzer of Berlin written at this period he announces with pride his resolve to continue to shun the conniving heretic from Eisleben.[18]

iv. Bigamy for the non-patriarch

Luther's involvement in the bigamy of the Landgrave Philip of Hesse has commonly been treated by the Luther-cult biographers as a deplorable and perhaps inexplicable deviation of the greatest of all religious leaders from the path of moral rectitude. References to it appear in all the standard biographies because it is too well known to be suppressed, but attempts are made to excuse it on the grounds of its uniqueness in Luther's career. It is considered here because of the light it throws on Luther's personality. A brief account of the events and the relevant background is followed by an analysis of Luther's motivation. As will appear, there is nothing exceptional about Luther's decision in the affair; he would have authorized other such marriages had comparable circumstances arisen. Perhaps the most illuminating comment on his attitude is one made by Luther himself shortly after the scandal had broken: " 'Our sins are forgivable but the papists' are not . . . . They put men to death while we promote life and take several wives.' This he said with a merry countenance and loud laughter." (# 5096)

Philip was married at the age of 19 to Christina, daughter of Duke George, and had several children by her. Concurrently, as was not unusual among European sovereigns, he enjoyed a good deal of extramarital sex. This practice started a few weeks after his wedding and continued for upwards of 15 years. There are no accurate figures on the extent of his sexual activity but it may be presumed to have fallen short of the record set by a Saxon swinger of this period, immortalized in the Table Talk, of begetting 43 children in one year. (# 4073) In a book published toward the end of the sixteenth century it was reported that a post mortem examination of Philip revealed he possessed three testicles, though writers seldom utilize the story of this interesting malformation to condone one of the commoner forms of princely misbehavior.

Early in 1539 two events conspired to persuade Philip that a change in the pattern of his sex life was indicated. The first and more serious was his contracting venereal disease from one of his sex partners. A form of medical treatment was available even in that remote age, and while Philip was convalescing there occurred the second event which was to help liberate him from the bondage of casual sexual encounters. This was the death (April 19, 1539) of his father-in-law, Duke George, which gave him a free hand to deal with his wife in any way he saw fit without a threat of reprisal from his noble relative. It might be noted in passing that Luther himself took credit for this happening. In a Table Talk entry of May 1542 he revealed that he had prayed Duke George to death. While this long-time enemy was nearly 68 when he died, Martin made no allowance for old age as a contributory factor. In the same sentence of the Table Talk report Luther announced that he was preparing a like fate for two former members of George's government named Pistorius and Carlowitz. (# 5428) Although Luther predicted he would pray both of them into their graves within the year, his influence in the heavenly courts appears to have waned after his success with Duke George, for Pistorius lived another 20 years after the announcement and Carlowitz 35.

The timely death of Duke George set the stage for Philip to establish an arrangement that would provide him sex without syphillis. At the home of his sister, the Duchess Elizabeth of Rochlitz, whither he had retired till his health was restored, he found just what he was seeking in the person of Margaret von der Saal, the seventeen year old daughter of a family of the lesser nobility. The girl's mother welcomed the prospect of the enhancement of her social position that would accrue from her daughter's union with the Landgrave of Hesse, but felt that instead of allowing her child to assume the status of mistress or concubine to the Landgrave, it would be desirable in the interests of propriety for Philip and Margaret first to go through the motions of a wedding ceremony. In the way of this plan there was, however, an obstacle, for in the Holy Roman Empire bigamy was a capital offense. There was also the lesser problem of squaring the bigamous marriage with church doctrine, not really a formidable difficulty because Philip was not only the head of the schismatic church of Hesse but himself a fount of doctrine as attested by his signing, a decade earlier, the document later known as the Augsburg Confession. Nevertheless, he wanted the support of the professionals in this area and he would settle for nothing less than the approbation of the intellectual leaders of the schism, Luther and Melanchthon.

The process by which Philip obtained their approval is one of the seldom explored aspects of the tale of the bigamous marriage. The matter was far too delicate to entrust to correspondence, and Philip decided to avoid any suggestion of collusion that might arise from inviting the Wittenbergers to visit him at his court. Instead he chose an intermediary, an ex-Dominican friar named Martin Bucer, principally resident in the city of Strasbourg, who in consonance with his geographical location entertained theological positions intermediate between those of Wittenberg and Zurich. Bucer was provided with instructions from Philip and at once set out for Wittenberg, where he arrived in early December of 1539. It is a matter of regret that one or two of the more nimble-fingered Table Talk scribes were not invited to the conference, as a passable substitute for the modern practice of electronic recording of conversations of heads of state and their principal advisers. Without attempting to determine which of the participants in the ensuing negotiations was responsible for which detail of the final solution, we note that it went as follows.

Philip, it was reported by Bucer, suffered from severe scruples of conscience about his inability to overcome his immoderate sexual cravings. His wife of 15 years, whom he had been required to marry for reasons of state rather than affection, was extremely distasteful to him (though he managed to surmount this feeling and continued to produce children from her long after consummating his second marriage. After his union with Margaret, who bore him 8 children, he sired 3 more by the abominable Christina, apparently in exemplification of the French proverb: "Dans la nuit tous chats sont gris.") Since he had no grounds for divorcing her even if divorce were permitted and marrying some more suitable woman, there would be no other way for him to cope with his sexual urge than to resort to immoral relations with another woman, in short, commit adultery. Unless, that is, the theological bureau of Wittenberg judged it permissible for him to take a second wife. This approach was particularly designed to win the sympathy of Luther who, as we saw earlier, in his copulative imperative underlined the need of every man to have available a woman to preserve him from adulterous relations. As for the legitimacy of having two or more wives at once, Luther's stance was not nearly so clear since at various times during the preceding twenty years he had spoken his mind vigorously on both sides of the question. However, Philip, having failed back in 1526 (cf. Ch. 6) to gain Luther's approval of taking a second wife (his request came a year too late), was not depending this time merely on an appeal to Luther's sympathies. As part of his instructions, Bucer was authorized to state that if Luther couldn't see things Philip's way, as had happened in 1529 and 1530 with regard to Zwingli, then the Landgrave would solve his problem by withdrawing his support of the Lutherian schism and seeking marital relief from the Emperor and Pope.

This double-barrelled approach proved highly effective; the day after Bucer arrived he obtained a lengthy statement from the Wittenbergians, bearing the signatures of the two-man board, and giving Philip the green light on a marriage ceremony with Margaret. A perusal of what Preserved Smith calls 'this remarkable document,' which took the form of an epistle to the Landgrave, largely the work of Melanchthon but provided with a spirited conclusion by Luther, shows which of the two barrels carried the larger fire power.[19] For the first of many points made in the epistle, after an expression of thanks that God had cured the Landgrave of his bout with syphillis, was this: "We pray that God will strengthen and preserve Your

Grace in body and soul to his honor, for as Your Grace can see, the poor wretched church of Christ is small and abandoned and truly needs pious lords and protectors. We do not doubt that God will provide them even though all kinds of trials may occur."[20]

In an epistle studded with scriptural quotations one is disappointed at the absence of a text demonstrating the divine will about pious princes like Philip stepping forward to protect the church. The position of prominence given this topic recalls Melanchthon's anxiety at the diet of Augsburg a decade earlier that the pious Landgrave would shift his protection from the church of Wittenberg to that of Zurich. Luther's personal contribution to the epistle concentrates on the same topic, being highlighted by a series of slurs on the Emperor and the Emperor's shocking (to pious Germans) view that adultery is a trivial sin. His appeal for the Landgrave's political and military support is another in the unending series of his doctrinal self-reversals. In 1529 he had asserted that his church "must not take Emperor or king as defender" for the eminently sound reason that those worthies are commonly the worst enemies of the faith, and to give them such a role stirs up the divine wrath.[21]

Sandwiched in between these two appeals to Philip not to desert the ship there are a great many words and a certain amount of matter. Melanchthon briefly reviews monogamy and bigamy in the O. T., points out the distinction between a law and a dispensation, and gives five or six reasons why the proposed bigamy should be kept secret. The reasons for secrecy are all related to the scandal that would result if the fact should become known. One of the sorest points was that the Saxon and Hessian churches by authorizing bigamy would be tarred with the same brush as the infamous Anabaptist community of Muenster which prior to its liquidation a few years back had flaunted polygamy as the preferred way of life for the Elect. After extended moralizing about the need to avoid 'whoremongering and adultery,' an expression of sympathy for the Landgrave's longstanding problems in this area, and an acknowledgement that many princes maintain concubines, Melanchthon finally edges his way down to the principle that applies in this situation: "What is permitted with regard to marriage in the law of Moses is not forbidden in the gospel." Again one notes that these stalwart champions of the *sola scriptura* neglect to provide a N. T. quote validating this most useful conclusion.

After further delays, the marriage of Philip and Margaret was celebrated before a number of witnesses including Melanchthon and Bucer early the following March. The clergyman engaged to perform the ceremony, an ex-Dominican named Melander, was carefully selected for the task. While he had undoubtedly enjoyed less exposure to the fair sex than the lecherous Landgrave, Melander was none-the-less one up on his liege lord in the matter of wives for he was now cohabiting with his third consort since being wafted into a state of evangelical liberty by the winds of Wittenberg. The affair did not long remain a secret. Enraged at the discovery of her brother's perfidy in entering into a state of bigamy with the daughter of one of her attendants whose acquaintance he made in her own house, the Duchess Elizabeth unveiled the secret to both the Elector and his cousin Duke Henry (successor to the recently deceased Duke George.) Thereupon Duke Henry arrested the bride's mother and forced her to divulge some incriminating documents. Space does not permit a review of the extensive correspondence generated among the interested parties by the unraveling of the amateurish coverup planned by Luther and Melanchthon. In the preceding section we described Melanchthon's consequent fall into depression and Luther's successful therapy. Here we shall discuss Luther's own reaction.

Since Luther engaged in a good deal of deliberate prevarication about the Hesse bigamy, it is instructive at this point to consider his views on lying. The following theoretical summary comes to us from a Table Talk entry recorded during the earlier 1530s:

> There are four types of lie. First there is the jocose lie, a good laughable jest by which men are diverted . . . . Second, the obligatory (*officiosum*) lie, which assists the neighbor, a good necessary lie motivated by charity, one by which the neighbor may be protected . . . . Third is the lie pernicious, lying as the worldly do, that is to deceive or to injure. Fourth is the impious lie by which God is blasphemed.
>
> The first two are praiseworthy because they do no harm; the other two are not to be suffered because they offend both men and God. There is also another type of lie, namely the unavoidable (*necessarium*) lie, though it differs little from the second type, the obligatory. This can be engaged in without sin if not supported by an oath, such as 'verily,' 'truly,' 'by God,' etc. (# 1044)

It may be surmised that Luther added the last type, which might be numbered 2a, to cover those of his lies which he felt did not quite fit into class 2. While by far the greater part of the many thousands of falsifications to be found in the volumes of his collected works belong to class 3 insofar as their effect is to deceive and injure others, in general these are unconscious, being instances of a pathological defense mechanism. Some of the lies he concocted in the Hesse case may be classified as a blend of classes 2 and 2a, their obvious purpose being to protect from scandal the church which it was a chief object of his career to promote. Luther's explicit self-justification for telling such lies, as noted earlier, was stated in the summer of 1540. "It is praiseworthy to tell a good round lie in defense of the church."

In fact this is a natural extension of the Lutherine privilege first announced in the summer of 1520. It was then a purely personal affair since in 1520 he had no church to defend by this praiseworthy endeavor but only one to attack. With the broadening of his theater of operations in subsequent years, it was incumbent upon him to restate the Lutherine privilege, adapting it to the changed circumstances.

Luther's desire to keep the Hesse affair secret was so strong that when, a month after the ceremony, the exuberant bridegroom sent him a thank-you note for his help in making possible that joyous event Luther burned the letter. To an inquiry from his loyal friend and former Table Talk scribe Anthony Lauterbach (who had taken over one of the parishes in Ducal Saxony after the demise of Duke George) regarding the rumors that were floating about in his part of Germany, Luther replied with a noncommittal statement suggesting he had no real knowledge of the affair. Perhaps the most revealing of his numerous utterances on the bigamy was a long letter to the Elector dated June 10 responding to a request from his sovereign for Luther's inside information.[22] When this letter is checked against the December document granting the dispensation for bigamy, it is seen to be a curious mixture of falsehood and truth, featuring lies of both types 2 and 2a, as well as of a third type not specified in the theoretical summary quoted above. This is the type singled out by Carlstadt (cf. Ch 5, iii) in which Luther preserves his own reputation by putting the blame elsewhere. For present purposes we designate this as a type 5 lie.

Despite the indication in the grant of dispensation that the Wittenbergers were well aware of Philip's long continued enjoyment of extra-marital sex, Luther asserts in his reply to the Elector that he had only recently learned of such goings-on. Had I only known of them beforehand, he writes, I would never have consented to the dispensation. Another example of the type 5 lie in the letter is his citation of the authority of his 'preceptor' in the Erfurt monastery for sanctioning the bigamy. This man, Luther says, taught me that whether we like it or not we have to put up with this kind of unsavory behavior among our rulers (elsewhere he calls it Philip's 'monster'). And so I was simply acting in accordance with this good man's counsel. Without inquiring into whether this purported episode of the early monastic years is a fantasy invented for this occasion, we do know (a) that the man in question, being a monk, would ordinarily be denounced as a 'lousy, scurvy work-saint' who blasphemously sought to gain heaven by his cowl and tonsure; and (b) that the supposition of Martin Luther, the restorer of the Christian faith, permitting himself to be guided in any matter at all, let alone a matter of such great moment as this, by one of those aforesaid vermin, is so ludicrous that it would test the credulity of even his more gullible admirers.

The most interesting of the falsehoods in the June 10 letter is that Philip's appeal for authorization to commit bigamy is a 'matter of the confessional' and therefore had to be kept secret. (We moderns accustomed to hearing public officials adduce the plea of 'national security' for concealing their misdeeds from the public are most fortunately situated for appreciating this sort of duplicity.) The notion that Philip of Hesse in approaching Luther through an agent armed with a threat to withdraw military support from Luther's church unless given authorization to remain permanently in a modified form of the state of adultery, which has become second nature to him, bears any relation to the state of a penitent seeking forgiveness of sin in sacramental confession is one of the most bizarre that Luther ever hatched. Yet as the event showed, it was planned to be the kingpin of the coverup scheme.

It might be presumed that Luther, having delivered himself of three good round lies would have brought his letter to an end. Instead he temporarily deviated into truth and disclosed to John Frederick the threat by Philip to desert the gospel for the Roman Antichrist. We may take this as a witness to how effectively the Landgrave had got Luther (as well as Melanchthon) over a barrel the preceding December. To the anxiety-ridden chiefs of the Wittenberg politbureau the prospect of their principal non-Saxon ally deserting to the Pope must have ranked as a catastrophe second in magnitude only to the defection of the Elector himself.

The Elector, not satisfied with having only Luther's story of the bigamy, lost no time in obtaining an account from the Landgrave. This came to him in a letter dated June 20, longer than Martin's and fortified with two enclosures.[23] One of these was a copy of sermon material on the O. T. Luther had published during his period of enthusiasm in the 1520s when he was an ardent advocate of a man having multiple wives. The other was a copy of the dispensation. Regarding this, the Landgrave called the Elector's attention to that most useful theological principle about what is not forbidden in the law of Moses being permitted in the gospel, as well as the three signatures of Luther, Melanchthon and Bucer authenticating the dispensation. Philip's lengthy epistle rambles back and forth between two themes. One of these is that it was not he but the women — his sister and his new mother-in-law — who revealed the secret. The other is that his having two wives is not unacceptable in God's sight. To demonstrate this, he cites the statements of the three advisors along with Luther's published sermons, and develops arguments from Scripture. One of the arguments, which reveals him as an apt pupil of Luther, is that Paul's statement about a bishop being the husband of only one wife doesn't forbid an ordinary citizen to have two. Therefore his conscience is clear and he is certain that when he dies God won't close the heavenly gates to him. Then follows the alibi which sets him apart from the Anabaptists: I am not trying to start a new custom or encourage other men to imitate my example.

Once the secret bigamy had become public knowledge, Philip sought to restore his reputation and Margaret's by persuading Luther to acknowledge the dispensation publicly. Luther's lengthy reply (nearly four pages in the Weimar edition) makes as fascinating reading as the text of the dispensation.[24] He absolutely refuses to lend his support to any kind of public statement and threatens to leave Philip stuck in his own mess if a battle of pens should develop, while extricating himself, 'which I know well how to do.' The letter makes clear his low opinion of the state of matrimony which twenty years before he had downgraded from a sacrament, a source of divine grace, to a mere civil agreement, the while concealing the force of this innovation by continuing the celebration of weddings in a church before a clergyman. Toward Margaret he is heartlessly blunt, referring to her several times in the letter not by her name but as a strumpet (*Metze*). "Why are you concerned that people regard your strumpet as a whore? She has had to pass for a whore before all the world thus far – while the dispensation remains unpublished – although in the sight of us three [Luther, Melanchthon and Bucer], that is, God, she is regarded as a married concubine." One must pause in admiration at the matchless gift of phrase that can put into the same sentence two such gems as 'us three, that is, God,' and 'married concubine.' Late in the summer Luther was still insisting on secrecy. In a letter to Philip of September 17 he takes the legalistic view that even if copies of the dispensation are in circulation, being only copies they prove nothing. Just keep the original document under wraps and deny its existence.[25]

To follow the ramifications of the bigamy further would take us beyond the limits of this study, for we are concerned with it only as it illuminates Martin's character. As a closing comment we note the ambiguity of his present situation: whereas two decades earlier in the guise of a reformer he had been pillorying indulgences as a license to commit sin, now as a pillar of the church he struggles to cover his embarrassment at having granted such a license himself.

Chapter 10

Last Will And Testament

i. Drift into antisemitism

With the increasing prominence of Luther's paranoid symptoms it was only a matter of time before the Jewish people found a position on his enemies list. What was exceptional about his lapse into antisemitism is not that it occurred but that it was so slow in developing. The process took place in two stages. At first his late-blooming hostility was directed primarily at Hebrew scholars for misleading their people on the position of Jesus as the Messiah promised in Scripture. It was not until about three years before his death that he exhibited violent pathological hostility toward the Jews as a whole. A roughly parallel situation can be observed in his attitude toward the Turks for their military threat to Germany, and to Mohammed for his refusal to accept the divinity of Jesus. In 1542 Luther published a German translation of the Koran with a preface of his own composition 'refuting' it.

In earlier years Luther had been able to regard the Jewish rejection of Jesus as Messiah without personal animosity. For example, in a tract of 1523 entitled "That Jesus Christ Was Born a Jew" Luther expressed friendly feelings toward the Jewish community in Germany and urged his countrymen to accept Jews as fellow citizens and fraternize with them. This expression, it is true, took place during his proselytizing era, but while he expected some of them to accept the teachings of the N. T. he did not at the time propose that such a response be made a condition for toleration. At this period his hostility was directed principally against his former co-religionists; it would appear that in no way did he then feel the Jews as a threat to him. And he published nothing more on this topic for 15 years.

Luther's first polemic against the Jews in 1538 "Against the Sabbatarians" was little more than a theological disquisition, far milder and less offensive in tone than much that he had written in his battles with the papists or with the other innovators. He is concerned to show that the long exile of the Jews from Jerusalem, having endured for going on 15 centuries, is proof that they are no longer the chosen people. It also proves that their Law has terminated as Scripture foretold it would when the Messiah came. The purported aim of this rather academic sounding tract was to provide arguments for dissuading gentiles from becoming Jewish converts and it appears to have been written on request from others rather than being his own spontaneous expression.

The vicious propaganda in "The Jews and Their Lies" of January 1543, while in striking contrast to the 1538 tract, is by no means out of line with other paranoid productions of the 1540s. It represents what might be called the negative component of Luther's basic drive to find emotional security, namely the impulse to destroy whatever he perceived as a threat to the attainment of that unattainable goal. (The positive component is best exemplified by his quest for 'comforting texts' in the Bible.) It is not clear that a particular incident inspired this outburst of hostility. In any event, one should not make the mistake of looking for a significant provocation on the part of individual Jews inasmuch as the radical disproportion of emotional response to external stimulus is a characteristic behavior pattern of those afflicted with a psychopathology like Luther's.

It is from this point of view that Luther's 8-point program for dealing with the German Jews should be regarded: 1) burn down their synagogues and schools; 2) likewise destroy their homes, forcing them to live in barns; 3) take from them their devotional and Talmudic writings; 4) forbid the rabbis to teach (make teaching a capital offense); 5) refuse them safe-conduct when traveling; 6) forbid them to lend money at interest (and make them pay a sizable bonus to each Jew who accepts Luther's gospel); 7) force the able-bodied to become manual workers; 8) drive them out of Germany if they threaten our families or livestock. In addition, 'we poor preachers' must warn our flocks against associating with these reprobates and urge our government officials to carry out the above program. Luther's fellow Germans, upon beholding a Jew, are to form a mental image of a blasphemer of Christ who would stab us to death if given the opportunity. "The Jews and Their Lies" is far too long for analysis here, being one of the most extended compositions of Luther's declining years; for interested readers an English translation is available.

It is enlightening to recall here what the Luther of 1520 had to say about this aspect of the mature Luther:

> There is a damnable *madness* in some Christians (if they should be called Christians) who think they show in this their obedience to God and do him service when they persecute the Jews with

utter hatred, think every evil of them, and insult their deplorable
misfortunes with the extremity of pride and contempt . . . . If
hatred of Jews, heretics and Turks makes Christians, we *madmen*
are the most Christian of all. But if the love of Christ makes
Christians, without doubt we are worse than Jews, heretics and
Turks, for no one loves Christ less than we do. The *insanity* of
those fools and children is similar, who make drawings on walls
depicting the eyes of Jews being gouged out.[1]

The three references to antisemites as persons who are mentally ill
in this passage written by Luther near the time of his regression
provide a remarkable foreshadowing of his own subsequent history.

We look next at what is perhaps the most picturesque self revelation in all of Luther's late writings. To bring out the tremendous
difference between the Jewish Messiah, an earthly king who is to
restore the worldly sovereignty of the Jewish nation, and his own
Savior, Luther introduces the figure of his favorite animal, the sow.
If he could have in prospect no other Messiah than the Jewish one,
he would sooner be a sow than a man. For the sow, unlike Luther,
is never plagued by thought of death. Here is doubtless one of the
most artistic projections ever penned by a psychotic:

> A sow reclines on her feather bed or manure pile, rests in safety,
> snores softly, sleeps sweetly, fears no king or lord, no death or
> hell, no devil or wrath of God. She lives so free from care she need
> not even wonder where her bran comes from . . . . She has no
> thought of dying; her life is pleasant and secure.
>
> When the butcher comes for her, she thinks a piece of wood or
> stone is squeezing her. The thought of death does not occur to her
> even at the moment she dies; neither before dying, nor after, nor
> at any moment does she feel death. She feels only life – without
> end . . . . She has not eaten the apple that in Paradise taught us
> miserable men the difference between good and evil.[2]

We might pause here to note an interesting point about Luther's
childhood. Unless he is falsifying, he never witnessed a butchering.
For a pig does not go to be slaughtered peacefully, but struggles
desperately – and vociferously – to escape. The folk saying: "He
squealed like a stuck pig" is drawn accurately from life. If a second
pig follows the first to the scaffold, once it smells the blood of its
predecessor the squealing is ear piercing. (Although it is well over a
half-century since as a boy I first attended a hog butchering, I retain
a vivid recollection of the heart rending cries of the victim.) The
implication of this account is that even as a boy in Mansfeld, where
such sights would be commonplace, Luther was so repelled by the
sight of blood which gushes from the animal's throat he shunned the
butcherings. We continue with the projection, which presents a

matchless picture of Luther's pathological fear of dying. The promise of the Jewish Messiah would be of no help:

> I would still rather be a sow. Death, the frightful burden and curse of all mankind, would remain for me. I could have no security; every moment I would be in fear. I would tremble and quake at thoughts of hell and the wrath of God. And there would be no end to this; I would have to expect it forever . . . . And I know that whoever has been pressed down by the terror of death would rather be a sow than endure such a thing for ever and ever.

Faced with a choice between human and animal existence under these conditions Luther would say: "Dear Lord God . . . make me a sow, for it is better to be a sow than to be a man . . . who is forever dying."

Also in this passage written in Luther's richest rhetorical vein there is a reference to the joy he could on occasion experience when the burden of his anxiety was momentarily lifted: "When I need no longer tremble before the wrath of God, my heart would leap in joy and be drunk with sheer pleasure. The fire of love for God would be kindled in me, praise and thanksgiving would never end."

Before the end of 1543 Luther had issued two more substantial tracts commonly classified as antisemitic. Neither of them, however, is nearly as sensational as "The Jews and Their Lies." The later of these tracts, "The Last Words of David," is essentially a scriptural commentary based on a passage in 2 Sam. (23:1-7). Here Luther demonstrates how he interprets the O. T. exclusively in terms of the N. T. intending thereby to set it free from the false interpretations of the rabbis. One lesson he gives the world is that the O. T. cannot be in error as long as it is in harmony with the N. T. In an interesting example of projection he declares that Adam and Eve found great consolation in the promise of a Redeemer (Gen. 3:15) without which they would have fallen into despair. However, Eve was a bit hasty in taking for granted, merely because she was the only woman on earth, that it was to be her own child who would overcome sin and death.

The primary aim of the other tract, "Schem Hamphoras and the Generation of Christ," is to demonstrate that the genealogy of Joseph given at the beginning of Matthew's gospel applies also to Mary and therefore to Jesus. Luther thereby refutes the rabbinical claim that if Jesus was not the son of Joseph he couldn't be a descendant of David. This tract abounds in the sort of vituperation Luther has been heaping on the papists these past twenty years and more; only the names have changed. A point of interest is that there has come down to us the opinion of some of Luther's contemporaries on a feature of the tract commonly called Luther's coarseness. Continuing the barnyard rhetoric of the earlier tract, Martin writes:

Here at Wittenberg outside the parish church there is a stone statue of a sow. Under her lie young piglets and Jews, sucking. Behind the sow stands a rabbi who lifts the sow's hind leg with his right hand and her tail with his left. He stoops down and looks with great interest at the Talmud under the sow's tail as if he would read and learn something subtle and unusual . . . . For there is a German saying about a would-be wise man, 'Where did he read that? (To speak coarsely) in a sow's hind end.'[3]

Another of these gamy morsels, that follows shortly after the Lutherian quip that the Holy Ghost must allow himself to be circumcised, is a sort of fable Luther invents to explain how the rabbis can interpret a certain text of Isaiah in a manner quite incomprehensible to him:

I can't understand how they have such exalted learning unless I consider how Judas Iscariot hanged himself, that his bowels ruptured, and as happens to one who is hanged, his bladder burst. Then perhaps the Jews sent their servants with golden cans and silver bowls to catch the Judas-piss (as it is called) along with other holy things. Whereupon altogether they swilled down this mess and thereby acquired such keen eyes they can see this gloss and others like it in Scripture which neither Matthew, nor Isaiah himself, nor all the angels can see, let alone such accursed *goyim* as we are . . . . Or they have peered into the hind-end of their god . . . and in this venthole have found such things written.[4]

Having hit upon the happy term 'Judas-piss,' and occasionally giving it a partner *Juden-Schweiss* (Jew-sweat) for reasons of alliteration and assonance, Luther repeats it at intervals as is his habit seven or eight times until he reaches the end of his tract. Some members of the present-day Luther cult attempt to excuse Luther's low language on the grounds that it was characteristic of his times, or as the politicians say, "Everybody does it." But Luther's own contemporaries, even those basking in the full (or nearly full) light of the gospel did not share this view. Upon reading the "Schem Hamphoras" tract, a congregation in Zurich declared it to be 'swinish' and 'dirty'; it was, they felt, a production more appropriate for a swineherd than a renowned shepherd of souls. Bullinger, the ranking Swiss theologian, found it to be a filthy piece of writing.[5]

The basic meaning of these three tracts of 1543 is that the Jews of Germany have finally assumed a position in Luther's consciousness alongside the papists, the various sectarian groups, the peasants, the nobles, the lawyers, a majority of the burghers, the Turks. The abundant wordage of the tracts, more than all he had written, for example, in the five years 1533-1538, is due to the involvement of his occupational interest as professor of Scripture. Their nastiness is a reflection of the increasing severity of his paranoid symptoms.

ii.   Against the papacy at Rome

During his later years the leading source of Luther's anxiety appears to have shifted from the threat of damnation associated with his feeling of hostility toward his God to the similar threat arising from his state of excommunication. His plight is aptly suggested by the saying of Augustine: 'he who does not have the Church for his mother cannot have God for his father.' As he gradually adjusted to his unique relation to the Trinity, what had seemed in 1520 the lesser of two evils, that is, excommunication as the price of hanging on to the *sola fide,* at length turned into the major one. This situation becomes manifest in the renewed polemic against the 'papal church' in the later 1530s after several years of comparative silence. With other targets, once he had discharged his hostility in print, it was his custom to give them little further attention. Thus Carlstadt and Zwingli were disposed of before the end of the 1520s, Erasmus and the Anabaptists in the early 1530s. The Cardinal Archbishop of Mainz was a more persistent target, being the object of a verbal assault as late as 1539. But Pope and Church proved to be hardy perennials in Luther's garden of verbal brickbats and against them his attacks were terminated only by death.

Luther's impulse to publish, temporarily in eclipse during the mid 1530s, seems to have been reawakened by the action of Paul III, who after his election as Pope late in 1534 set about calling the reform council in which his Medici predecessor Clement VII had shown small interest. This undertaking required simultaneous agreements with the two most powerful European sovereigns, the Emperor and the French king Francis I, to permit bishops in their territories to attend the council. Since these two monarchs were at war with one another intermittently from the early 1520s until the peace of Crespy in 1544, during which period Francis, instead of assisting the Emperor against the Turks in their invasion of Europe often acted as their ally, it is not surprising the council did not actually begin its sessions (at Trent, in imperial lands) until 1545. From his observation post in Wittenberg Luther was soon taking pot shots at the proposed council. In 1539 he crowned these efforts with what proved to be the longest composition of the last 18 years of his career, entitled "On Councils and Churches" (*Von den Konziliis und Kirchen*).

As might be anticipated with a topic so centrally located in the area of his disturbance, this is a rambling, diffuse expression of his egocentricity. He was no more capable of anything like an objective treatment of this subject than of addressing Paul III as 'my brother in Christ.' He filled up a good many pages with a discussion of the first four general councils, ignoring not only more than a dozen others of that official rank but the thousands of provincial councils of bishops that had become commonplace in the Church by the end of the second century, a number of which are of signal importance in doctrinal and disciplinary developments. This part of the tract approximates the level of what might be expected from an industrious high school youngster working up material from an encyclopedia into a term paper. Such a juvenile would not, it is true, pause here and there to indulge in protracted denunciations of monastic life or apostrophes to the occupant of the Holy See like "You papal ass, you are a nasty sow!" Nor could he have penned the magnificent peroration in which Luther, teaming up with Peter, Paul and Augustine, invites the world to throw off the Pope's government and trample on his neck.

Of the numerous personal touches in this tract one of special interest is the demand by its author that a council be summoned expressly to validate the *sola fide* program. Several times in the tract, and quite unnecessarily it may be said, Luther warns that a council has no authority to promulgate new articles of faith. (The doctrinal work of councils often involves defining hitherto undefined matters of belief that have come under attack by characters like Luther.) Recalling that some years back in a letter to Philip of Hesse Luther had indulged in self-commiseration over his tribulations in teaching new doctrine, i.e., the *sola fide*, we may single out this passage of "On Councils and Churches" as one of the more characteristic expressions of his genius. Another prominent feature is his disparagement of the Fathers of the Church. One reason for their low rating is said to be their propensity to contradict one another. Augustine is introduced in this context primarily as a prop for the *sola scriptura*, which naturally occupies center stage in a discussion of councils, as well as to support the belittling of the (other) Fathers. He is cited dozens of times and patronized as one of Luther's most distinguished associates.

Two years after "On Councils and Churches" he issued another lengthy pamphlet, "Against Hanswurst," directed at Duke Henry of Brunswick. While the Duke, if his conduct may serve as an indicator, hadn't enough religion in his constitution to show up even on microscopic examination, he was classified as a papist because he refused to join the Lutherian schism. Beyond this he incurred Luther's wrath through an altercation with Elector John Frederick and thereby inspired one of the more scurrilous of Luther's compositions. As a measure of the literary caliber of this effusion, in one section, Luther, like a street urchin shouting insults at an antagonist, fires off the eipthet 'whore' upwards of 50 times. Despite the ostensible subject of this tract, it contains a great deal of defensive material that like its predecessor on councils reveals Luther's worries over the danger to his salvation caused by his expulsion from the Church.

In the tract on councils his line of defense had been nothing less than an attack on the term 'church' itself. It is most instructive to observe the evasive tactics he employs here (as elsewhere) to conceal the fact that he is attacking something in Scripture. First he objects with customary irrelevance that the word church (*Kirche*) is not German. *Kirche* (cf. Scots *kirk*), derived from the late Greek word *kyriakon* (= the Lord's [house]), is ordinarily used to translate the N. T. Greek term *ekklesia* (= Latin *ecclesia*) into German. To divert the reader's attention from his real object he next announces he will limit his discussion to the use of the term in the Apostles creed [*sancta et catholica ecclesia* = holy, catholic church]. Thereupon he proceeds to quote a passage in Acts (19:39 f) where the word *ekklesia* appears in a speech delivered by one of the pagans of Ephesus. In this text, the term is used in the classical Greek sense of a (political) assembly of citizens rather than with the new meaning given it by the Christian community to render a Hebrew concept of a religious assembly. Based on this unique pre-Christian use of the term in Acts 19, Luther, ignoring nearly 20 appearances of *ekklesia* in a N. T. sense elsewhere in Acts, thus concludes that the Greek-Latin term means nothing but a group of people. He then goes on to make the startling observation — twice — that the word *ecclesia* is meaningless.

Taken at face value this argument would have to be described as one of the most blatantly dishonest passages in all his works. For as he knew very well, *ecclesia* is a key scriptural term, appearing well over 100 times in the N. T., more than 60 of the occurrences being in the Pauline epistles. Like other nouns it has a range of meanings, one of the more common uses being to designate the Christian community of a given city such as Ephesus or Antioch, and in this sense it has a plural, e.g., 'the churches of Galatia.' The basic N. T. meaning of *ecclesia* is a special group of people with a commitment to their Lord organized under the direction of officials whose authority derives from the Apostles. Its more developed theological meaning is to be found especially in the Pauline epistles, e.g., in Ephesians, where Paul speaks of the Church as the Body of Christ, who is its Head. It is in a sense akin to this that the word is used in one of the most unpalatable (to Luther) verses in Matthew: "You are Peter and upon this rock I will build my church" (16:19).

But applying the appropriate form-critical principle, instead of describing this passage from "Councils and Churches" as cynically dishonest, we recognize it as a typical psychotic defense. Its appearance in this late work shows that Luther's anxiety over his being outside the Church is a permanent feature of his psychic disarray. As if to corroborate this interpretation, Luther obligingly inserts in the midst of his argument an obvious instance of the projection mechanism: What misery we would have been spared, he laments, if only the author of the Creed had been smart enough to use 'people' in this article instead of 'church.' At the same time we can not but admire Luther's admirable memory for scriptural language. For it was this that guided him unerringly without the aid of a concordance to the one place in the N. T. that could supply him with matter for an exercise in sophistry that ranks among the most elaborate of all his falsifications.

To examine another bit of Luther's inexhaustible store of defensive material we now look at quite a different approach to the same anxiety problem in "Against Hanswurst." It was manifestly impossible for Luther to write such a long work (over 70 pages in English translation) about such a low character as Duke Henry. In his verbal abuse of this flower of the Christian nobility of the German nation Luther soon runs out of fuel, indeed, the anti-Heinz portion of the tract serves largely as a framework for other topics. One of these is a review of his experience subsequent to the publication of the 95 Indulgence Theses, a sort of warmup for the autobiographical sketch in the 1545 Preface to his Latin writings. The major topic — more than half of the total wordage — deals with the question of the identity of the 'true church.' It is now two years since the scriptural term 'church' (*ecclesia*) was pronounced meaningless by this most authoritative of Scripture commentators. To one who inquires, Whence did it suddenly take on meaning? the answer is, as Luther's eminent near-contemporary, Sir John Falstaff, would say: "That is a question not to be asked."

Making a deft transition from the devilish dung of Duke Harry to the problem of What is the true church? and without pausing for breath, Luther rattles off ten good and sufficient reasons why he is no heretic and why the church of Electoral Saxony as well as the one under the protection of the Landgrave of Hesse must be so identified. Having proved to the satisfaction of all that 'we are the true ancient church,' he rapidly comes about and sailing briskly along on his starboard tack zips off twelve reasons demonstrating that Satan's whore and synagogue, otherwise known as the papal church, is the 'false new church.' It is of course to salute this 'false new church' that Martin unreels his fifty-odd repetitions of 'whore' whether as simple noun or in one or another of its numerous compounds. While this passage on the true church constitutes one of the most dazzling displays of dialectical prowess in the entire Lutherian oeuvre, it would seem by the way Luther keeps pegging away at the same argument later on in the tract that he doesn't believe a word of it himself. Indeed if he really could believe he was in the 'true church' he would long since have crossed off the list this major source of his anxiety.

We now look briefly at Luther's next composition in this series, called "Example of How to Consecrate a Christian Bishop." The occasion for this document is as follows. The occupant of the see of Naumburg (in Saxon territory) having died, the members of the cathedral chapter in accordance with their obligation elected a successor. But their choice having fallen on a papist, the Elector asserted the divine right of kings, threw him out and put in his own man. This happened to be no other than Luther's old friend and intimate, Nicholas von Amsdorf, who boasted the virtually unique distinction among the Lutherian clergy of having no wife of his own, though he had been berated (by Melanchthon) for succumbing (adulterously) to the relentless pressures of the copulative imperative. But as an enthusiastic adherent of 'my theology' he was forgiven his unseemly avoidance of wedded bliss. Luther, following his notions of how St. Paul would have proceeded in such a ceremony, consecrated him as the new bishop before a crowd assembled in the Naumburg cathedral. Thereupon, as was his wont, he celebrated his accomplishment by writing the aforementioned tract, which, among other virtues, displays with satisfying explicitness what might be termed the anal orientation of his mature years.

The final installment in the anti-papal crusade — which Martin had promised to continue in still another publication if granted longer life — is in several respects by far the most important of the entire series. In contrast with a Luther-cult biographer who expressed the wish that his hero had died before writing "The Jews and Their Lies" (1543), the student of Luther's psychic development is grateful to have "Against the Papacy at Rome, Founded by the Devil" (1545). The title itself is a notable accomplishment, for in no other of his creations does he so expertly unite the two chief targets of his hostility. As the early 1521 tract "Answer to the Hyperchristian, etc., Goat Emser" is a superb example of a manic production, this new work of nearly a quarter-century later is an even more superb expression of the paranoid psyche. A distinctive feature of the tract is the mass of abuse directed against the person of Paul III in contrast to the earlier verbal attacks on an impersonal Antichrist. In this longest and most violently abusive outpouring of pathological hostility against his number one target, Luther employs this favorite expletive barely a half-dozen times. By way of contrast, in a manic tract of early 1522 replying to the papal bull *Coenae Domine* issued during the preceding spring in which the name of Martin Luther brings up the end of a list of condemned heretics, there is no personal attack on Leo X (recently deceased), although the tone and contents of the pamphlet are highly abusive of ecclesiastical authority.

An echo from the past in "Against the Papacy at Rome" is the rather marked genital element that recalls the 1522 composition "Against the Socalled Spiritual Estate of the Pope and Bishops." The re-appearance of this material may be said to reflect Luther's long-standing inner conflict over breaking his vow of celibacy for by this date he has been freed from the stress of the copulative imperative that helped generate the 1522 tract. The villain here is of course the Pope, who for Luther symbolizes the authority enforcing the state of 'unclean celibacy.' An interesting sidelight on Luther's squeamish-ness about some of this material, which he felt was improper but was unable to repress, is that he presents it in Latin rather than the vernacular, presumably to avoid scandalizing members of the fair sex who were not expected to read the language of learning. One of his favorite devices for insulting the reigning Pope Paul III was to refer to him as a woman, St. Paula, or the 'holy virgin Paula,' though this Farnese Pope while still a layman had demonstrated his virility many years earlier by begetting four children. Lest he bring a blush of shame to maiden cheek, Luther writes the following in Latin: "I call upon the holy Roman see, or more particularly that [seat] where the Popes are examined to see whether they are men or women. If they are men let them show their testicles against us heretics. If they are women I repeat Paul's remark: 'A woman should keep silent in the Church.' "[6] Luther alludes here to the scabrous medieval jest about newly elected Popes inspired by the Pope Joan legend, and makes a pun on *sedis,* which means both (episcopal) see and seat or chair. He then takes advantage of the superiority of the Latin vocabulary over the more limited resources of the Saxon dialect to describe the "kings and queens in the Roman curia" as "hermaphrodites, androgynites, cynodeans, pedicons and such-like unnatural monsters."

But the emphasis in "Against the Papacy at Rome" is rather anal than genital; along with the anatomical particularities, the density of reference to excrement and rectal flatulence is unmatched elsewhere in his writings. As 'whore' is the expletive of choice in "Against Hanswurst," so 'fart' has pride of place in "Against the Papacy." It is likely that the consonance of *Farnese* (Paul III's family name) and *Farzen* (farts) sparked Luther's creative imagination in the later tract. To point up the extent of Luther's regression by 1545, a comparison may be made between the childish preoccupation with flatulence in this late pamphlet and the restrained references to it in the 1522 tract against the papal bull *Coenae Domine* cited above. For example, to exhibit his disgust with canon law regarding fast, abstinence, etc., in the 1522 tract, Luther merely remarks it's a wonder the Pope hasn't enacted an ordinance "forbidding farting in privies."[7] A similar contrast is evident between the lurid anti-papal cartoons exhibited below and the distinctly tame sketches of representatives of the clergy and the monastic orders presented in a 1526 pamphlet called "The Papacy and Its Members Depicted and Described." As a sample of the sprightly style and elevated moral tone of "Against the Papacy" consider this bit of imaginary dialogue:

> *Paul:* Be quiet, you heretic! Whatever issues from our mouth must be obeyed. *Luther:* Which mouth do you mean? The one the farts come from? You can have that one. Or the mouth the wine of Corsica flows into? Let a dog shit in that one. *Paul:* You shameful Luther, you mustn't talk that way to the Pope. *Luther:* Shame on yourself, you blasphemous scoundrel . . . . You are a crude ass, you pope-ass, and you always will be an ass.[8]

"Against the Papacy at Rome" includes material from a number of different periods of Martin's life. Memories of toilet-training days crop up in allusions to the terrific stink that would have escaped into the room when he filled his breeches had they not been so tight-fitting. This image appealed so much to its creator that he proceeds to apply it next to his reader and after that to the Pope. Recollections of schoolboy whippings surface in his wish that someone would flog the Pope's behind till the blood runs and thereby encourage him to learn his Latin grammar. From the neurotic years we hear of the persistent problem of the confessional – the injustice of demanding that he feel compunction for his sins or else be denied forgiveness and be delivered to the devil of uncertainty about his prospects of salvation. There is a particularly detailed instance of the projection of his inability to love Christ. If a shepherd of souls carries out his duty of tending his flock without such love then he is not a true shepherd. Since it is evident the Pope can not prove he loves Christ, it follows that he is not the one appointed to 'feed my sheep' in John 21:15 and therefore his claims to authority are nullified. In another place Luther reminisces at length about his trials during the Indulgence controversy.

While the occasion for his writing this tract was related to the imminent opening of the Council of Trent, the underlying motivation is the same as that of the other tracts reviewed in this section. For "Against the Papacy at Rome" is basically just another in the series of Luther's defensive maneuvres against his anxiety over being out of the Church. After a wandering introduction that makes up the first quarter of the tract comes the main argument that fills most of the remaining pages – that the Pope is not the head of the Church (and thereby Luther's excommunication is null and void). The argument is conducted along two lines.

One of these is the remarkable fiction that recognition of the primacy of the successors of Peter in the Roman see dates only from the seventh century, right after Gregory VI (590-604), who according to Luther rejected the primacy for himself. Inasmuch as Gregory was one of the more notable of the popes in the exercise of his official powers, Luther had to support this invention with more than mere assertion. He created for Gregory an analog of the Bernard fantasy, utilizing material from a letter Gregory wrote the reigning Roman emperor to reject the claim of the archbishop of Constantinople to the title of 'universal bishop.' Luther had a considerable admiration for Gregory and thereby preserved him from the damnation to which he was forced to consign all the popes. He likewise indulges in appropriate falsifications for other leading figures in the early Church such as Ambrose and Augustine. The respect shown for Jerome in this tract is especially diverting because hitherto Jerome had been well up on his enemies list, but was removed for this occasion because Luther had found something in one of Jerome's letters he could twist into a repudiation of the primacy of the bishop of Rome. In one respect Luther is extremely consistent: he cites not even one item from the extensive documentation exhibiting the Roman primacy during the early centuries of the Church. This suppression of the entire body of relevant fact to promote one of the most spectacular falsifications of his career repeats the technique he employed seven years earlier with the term *ecclesia* in his "On Councils and Churches." The two operations were dictated by the same emotional dilemma, being attempts to escape the inexpressibly painful awareness of his state of excommunication. Along with the tracts in which they appear, they admirably represent the guiding principle of Luther's vocation as religious prophet: since one is not sufficiently adult to face reality, deny its existence; the while casting insults and filth at the figure of authority who would restrain such childish behavior — and claim a divine mandate for so doing.

Having disposed so handily of 15 centuries of ecclesiastical history, Martin then addressed himself to his other argument. This dealt with the ever serious threat facing him in the gospel of Matthew — the famous exchange between Jesus and Peter at Caesarea Philippi that culminates in the declaration that Peter is the rock on which the Church will be built and the gift to him of the power of binding and loosing: the Keys. Luther had already referred to this passage in his disquisition on the history of the papal primacy, and its reappearance dozens of times in the tract — after such extensive treatment in other writings over the past quarter-century — reveals it to be the most deep-rooted of all Luther's obsessions. Recalling his attempt in the early 1520s to dispose of the symbol of the Rock by means of the exegesis of the Pointing Finger, we note that here he replaces this device by merely rewriting the offensive verse with a meaning acceptable to himself: "The Lord says: 'I am the rock.'" Since Luther's treatment of the Rock and the Keys in this tract is largely just a restatement of what he had said previously on these matters, we turn now to a novel feature of his final polemic against the papacy.

Everyone has heard of Luther's fondness for music and his activities as a composer of hymns. In contrast, hardly anyone, even professionals in the field of art history, is aware of another outlet of his artistic bent, the design of cartoons ridiculing the Pope. Nearly a dozen of these are extant, executed by his faithful friend and fellow townsman, Lucas Cranach. They have been kept in obscurity not because of the level of their aesthetic quality but because of their subject matter, which reveals better than can a thousand words the pathological condition of their creator. Reproductions of them rarely appear in works for the general public and allusion to them in such works is minimal. Only an occasional scholar ever gets to see them. Evidence that Luther was working on the designs as early as 1538 is revealed in his correspondence with Amsdorf. The cartoons appeared in print in 1545 separately from the tract "Against the Papacy at Rome," in which Luther made comments on them. (See the note at the end of this section.)

We reproduce four of the cartoons that are representative of the whole series and provide translations of the doggerel quatrains Luther composed for each of them. Given first is the cartoon called "Birth and Origin of the Pope." This depicts a nude she-devil with a tail giving birth to the Pope and five Cardinals, and fittingly represents the title of the tract. Smaller sketches depict three Furies, Megara, Alecto and Tisiphone, ministering to the infant Pope, who is identified by the tiara. Luther speaks of his design of this cartoon in a letter to Amsdorf of 8 May 1545. Megara represents envy and hate, Alecto implacable evil and Tisiphone the avenger of murder. "Of the three Furies, what I had in mind insofar as they depict the Pope is that the horror of the papal abomination should be expressed by the most horrible words in the Latin tongue."[9] In a letter Luther had written Amsdorf just the day before this one he spoke of his plans to write another book against the Pope but was impeded by illness in his head and by the multitude of letters he was forced to write. "But I will continue with it, God willing, as soon as I am able." His specific comment on this cartoon in the tract states that the Pope was born from the hind end of the devil — and contains one of his many references to the verse in Matthew 16 about the power of the Keys.

> Here is born the Antichrist.
> Megara suckles him;
> Alecto tends his cradle;
> Tisiphone helps him walk.
>
> Dr. Mart(in) Luth(er).

The next two cartoons reveal even more strikingly than the first one the anal orientation of the mature Luther. Cartoon 2, "The Pope, God of the World, Is Adored," shows a soldier with his breeches lowered defecating into the upturned papal tiara. The prominence given the papal coat of arms, i.e., the Keys, symbolizing the power of binding and loosing, points up the link between excretion and the papal power. A significant feature of the composition of the drawing is that the prodigious stool — a sort of wish fulfillment of the Wartburg constipation period — hangs vertically above the point of intersection of the Keys. The other two soldiers, one letting down his breeches as next in line for the tiara, and the other buttoning up after completing his excretion, reflect the propaganda purpose of the cartoons. The commentary on this cartoon in the tract, which deals largely with the dreaded text in Matthew 16 on the Keys, is the most extensive for any of the group. Luther advises his dear Germans to spit on the papal coat of arms and throw filth at it as if it were an idol, thereby glorifying God. The abundant use of the denial and projection mechanisms in the commentary provides ample corroboration of our interpretation of the psychic state responsible for this coprophilic art work.

> What the Pope has done to my Lord's throne
> The same deed to his crown is shown.
> Pay him back double as the Spirit demands, (Rev. 18:6)
> Pour it in with confidence, for God so commands.
>
> Dr. Mart(in) Luth(er).

The third cartoon "Here Kisses for the Pope's Feet Are Pictured" expresses a principal theme of the tract inasmuch as it makes visible the *Farzen* featured in "Against the Papacy at Rome." The juvenile taunts of the protruding tongues and bare backsides, along with the ballooning anal discharges, constitute graphic evidence of the extent of Luther's regression by his early sixties. Here the Pope seated on his throne holds a bull of excommunication that like a weapon emits flames mixed with rocks (meteorites). He is represented as saying: "Even our unjust judgments are to be feared" (a favorite anti-papal gibe), to which the two men respond: "Look at a bare buttocks, you hellish, raving people. Hey, Pope, here's my free show."

> No, Pope, don't scare us with your ban,
> And don't be such an angry man.
> For we will strike a counter blow
> And let you see our own free show.
>
> Dr. Mart(in) Luth(er).

In cartoon 4 "A Just reward for the Most Satanic Pope and His Cardinals" Luther displays the sadistic aspect of his paranoid hostility in depicting the hangman pulling out the Pope's tongue and nailing it to the gallows. The lofty position Archbishop Albert of Mainz occupied on Luther's enemies list is evidenced by his appearing again here (on the left; he was also shown in 1 and 3). The four small figures above the gallows represent devils carrying off to hell the souls of the enemies Luther hangs in effigy. In his comment on this cartoon in the tract Luther makes specific reference to the nailing of the Pope's tongue. He also indulges in a highly emotional vituperation of the papacy, which features his anti-historical fiction of its founding. The device of the gallows enables him to act out the fantasy that the Church has no earthly head, which is heavily emphasized in this part of the tract.

> Were there temporal punishment here below,
> Pope and cardinals would be treated so.
> His blasphemous tongue right well deserves
> What the painter for us here preserves.

> Dr. Mart(in) Luth(er).

Following the appearance of the tract "Against the Papacy at Rome" nothing more of consequence issued from Luther's pen during the period of somewhat less than a year prior to his death. Against the Paris and Louvain faculties, old opponents of his, he left some unfinished business. His final publication, prepared at the Elector's request, was an argument showing why Duke Henry of Brunswick (Hanswurst) recently captured by the Elector and Philip of Hesse in armed combat should remain in prison.

Note on the anti-papal cartoons: Modern study of the cartoons was promoted by the French scholar Jules Paquier, translator and adapter of Denifle. In the second edition of the Denifle-Paquier *Luther et luthéranisme* (Paris, 1913) he recounts how his requests to photograph copies of the cartoons in Luther collections at Wittenberg, Worms and Halle were rebuffed. Then he discovered a set in the British Museum, which he reproduced in the 1913 edition. The cartoons received a detailed study by H. Grisar and F. Heege in *Luther Studien* IV (Freiburg, 1923) and appeared in the Weimar edition (vol. 54) in 1928. For a typical attitude toward the coverup of the cartoons cf. K. A. Meissinger, *Der katholische Luther* (Munich, 1952) 288: "Thank God, they have had so little circulation"; or the editorial reference in *Luther's Works* (Philadelphia, 1966) 41, 260-61, which, avoiding mention of Luther's verses and design of the cartoons, implies they are solely the work of Cranach.

iii. Mansfeld revisited; unfamous last words

As Luther's legacy to the world was an expression of his paranoid hostility, so his testamentary bequest to his wife bears witness to his paranoid grandiosity. According to the laws of Saxony, a widow could not inherit her husband's real property, which went instead to his children. But she could be left a lifetime income from his estate, administered by the guardians appointed for their offspring. Luther did not approve of these laws and refused to countenance them in a document drawn up at the beginning of 1542 as a substitute for a legal will. He left the real estate as well as his personal effects outright to Catherine. The property included a house and grounds in Wittenberg he had bought for his servant, and a small farm at Zulsdorf, south of Leipzig, earlier a part of the von Bora estate, which he had paid for with funds provided by the Elector. [The Black Monastery, a joint gift to Martin and Catherine from the Elector, he elsewhere directed to be given back to its donor.] As for guardians of his children, he refused to appoint any, declaring their mother to be the most suitable person for this office. Finally, he also refused to have the will validated by a notary as the law prescribed. Everyone must recognize, he says, that although he has not used legal forms or words in this testament, he is a public character, known in heaven, on earth and in hell, and has more authority than any mere notary. The world has received a great deal from him, the teacher of the truth, despite the Pope's ban, etc., and the devil's wrath. His own well known hand and seal prove that he is Dr. Martin Luther, notary of God and witness of his gospel.[10]

This grandiose document, a typical expression of Martin's egocentric character manifesting no real concern for what might be its effect on his wife's future, did not impress the Saxon courts when after his death it was presented as a legal will. All Katie finally received was the Black Monastery, which was hers anyhow by the Elector's gift. Instead of retiring to her little farm as planned, she had to remain in Wittenberg, where she managed to support herself by operating the former monastic building as a boarding house. Five years after Martin's death she too died (in her early fifties) as a result of injuries suffered in a highway accident that occurred while she was fleeing an outbreak of plague in Wittenberg. The children, despite their famous father's objections, were already in the charge of guardians appointed at the direction of the court.

During his final months there is a marked contrast between the repeated complaints of increasing bodily weakness due to illness and (premature) old age and the way he spent his time traveling about Saxony and Thuringia. Apart from his enforced sojourn at the Coburg fortress in 1530, he was on the road and away from home much more during the last half year of his life than for any comparable period since his marriage twenty years before. One implication of this fact is that he still enjoyed fairly good health but was suffering an increasing proportion of bad days, which were the source of the complaints. It is evident that he had inherited a rugged constitution and up till his mid thirties had kept himself in condition by a sensible diet and abundant exercise (recall the hike back and forth across the Alps to Italy in winter during his late twenties). After passing the age of 35 (in late 1518) he made his journeys by wagon instead of on foot and began the immoderate eating and drinking he described as a device for controlling anxiety. It is this radical change in his regimen that brought on the corpulence of his later years. That change together with his emotional excesses helped develop the cardio-vascular condition which suddenly ended his life at 62.

He set out on the first of these journeys of his *wanderjahr* in the latter part of July, when the university sessions were suspended for the 'dog-days' recess. In his academic lectures he was still engaged in expounding the book of Genesis, and after a decade of dwaddling over its 50 chapters was at last approaching the end, which he was finally to reach in mid November. His bodyguard on this occasion consisted of his oldest son Hans, recently turned 19, and a Wittenberg student. Three days out from Wittenberg he drafted a most startling letter to his spouse. I am completely fed up with Wittenberg, he tells her, and I never want to go back. The town has become a Sodom. You too had better clear out, for when I die presently, you will not be tolerated there and will have to leave anyhow. Better do it now while my salary is still coming in. Sell everything and retire to the little farm at Zulsdorf. My hard work [of preaching] is wasted in Wittenberg; let Bugenhagen [pastor of the town church] make my farewells there for I can no longer put up with the hostility.[11]

Recalling his decision 15 years earlier (January 1530) to preach no more sermons to the Wittenberg congregation, we may infer as a possible cause of his running away from his obligations of preaching and lecturing at this time that as before something had touched off his easily aroused feelings of resentment. For his reaction on each occasion is the kind of childish response symptomatic of his disorder. As an indication of his irresponsibility, it should be noted he was proposing that Katie handle all the business of disposing of their excess belongings and moving the remainder to their new home. While this was going on, Martin planned to continue his junket around Saxony. He had emphasized in the letter the bounteous hospitality (i.e., abundance of food and drink) extended him by his first two hosts and he now was preparing to visit another one. His reception in the homes of the lesser aristocracy is easily understandable. In those benighted days before television, the sight of his ample figure at their gates must have been most welcome. After he had been prevailed upon to take some liquid refreshment, his extraordinary gifts as raconteur and jokester would blossom in a fashion that richly repaid his hosts.

But there is involved in the decision to depart from Wittenberg another side of Luther's character which has received little attention perhaps because it might be described as recessive rather than dominant. During the tumultous period that preceded his regression he occasionally remarked that he would prefer to 'retire to a corner' rather than perform as a public character. Because he derived such evident pleasure from playing to the gallery and bedeviling his theological opponents, this alleged preference for a life in obscurity has not been taken seriously. But in such a disordered psyche as Luther's, beset with deep-seated inner conflicts, there is room for such an anomalous tendency as this. Perhaps its most explicit expression is to be found in a Table Talk entry of late spring 1531 (# 1937): "If I were not in God's ministry and married, I would go away where no one could find me. I would do this because of my anger and impatience toward an ungrateful world. I would flee from this world not because of any carnal sin, for I don't give a shit about that, but because it is an evil world, contemptuous of God. It blasphemes him and all things which are truly of God."

We can readily understand the anger and impatience upon recalling that at this time Luther is carrying on his battle with the Zwickau town council, is still reacting to the effects of the diet of Augsburg, having recently exposed to the world his paranoid paternoster, and is embroiled afresh with Duke George. As for his reasons for not fleeing Wittenberg, he has omitted the most important, namely his fear of moving about without a bodyguard. The indispensable presence of such a person would make it impossible for him to vanish from the sight of the whole world. All things considered, it must be said that his (occasional) impulse to run off and hide never became irresistible.

The receipt of his letter in Wittenberg is said to have been a cause of consternation. A delegation including Melanchthon and Bugenhagen, to which the Elector added his personal physician, set out to find the wandering prophet and bring him back home. But their concern was uncalled for, because whatever place Luther found himself in would presently become tedious to him and he would if possible go elsewhere. What actually passed between him and his friends is not recorded; at any rate it was more than a fortnight after their encounter before he turned up again in Wittenberg, following a brief visit with the Elector en route. It is of interest that he suffered an attack of the stone on arriving home.

He remained there upwards of six weeks and then started off on another journey, this time to his home town of Mansfeld. The purported occasion for this expedition was to attempt to bring about a reconciliation between Count Albert of Mansfeld and two of his brothers (also bearing the title of Count) who were at odds with Albert over disputed property rights. In view of the outstandingly bad example Luther set his followers in refusing to be reconciled with anyone against whom he entertained a theological animus, the ostensible purpose of this journey can be described as another of the unending series of contradictions that ornamented his path through life. Since it would appear from the record that this was his first visit to his boyhood home in upwards of 40 years, it is a matter of regret that few details of the event seem to have been preserved. An indication of the degree of Melanchthon's anxiety over the prospect of losing his old friend is that he was willing to interrupt his academic duties in order to accompany Luther on this journey. It was undoubtedly owing to Melanchthon's influence that the pair were back in Wittenberg in less than ten days. While at Mansfeld Luther was able to obtain from Count Albert some sort of expression of interest in a settlement of his differences with his brothers. Also he wrote a letter to the other brothers (October 7) offering his services as mediator.

The following month (November 10) Luther celebrated his 62nd birthday and, having attained this ripe old age, the next day officially terminated his career of some thirty-odd years as lecturer on Scripture. It is likely that his brief visit to Mansfeld in October had aroused in him the desire for a longer one. On December 6 he wrote to Count Albert that he had decided to spend the Christmas holidays there. Also he notified Albert that the other two Mansfeld Counts had at length replied favorably to his offer of early October and proposed he name a day in the new year for starting the negotiations. This situation presented Martin with the opportunity of making two more trips to his home town in the near future. On December 22 he set out again for Mansfeld and as before Melanchthon acted as guardian. From the length of their stay — they were absent from Wittenberg for two and a half weeks — it is evident Luther enjoyed renewing ancient friendships and the wining and dining by appreciative hosts.

From a letter to a friend ten days after his return from Mansfeld one could hardly surmise that the urge to spend his golden retirement years in travel had become irrepressible. He describes himself as "old, decrepit, lazy, exhausted, feeble and now one-eyed." Yet he is also "overwhelmed with writing, speaking, doing, conducting affairs" — the sort of complaint he has been making the past 30 years.[12] A week after the date of the letter, despite the inclement weather, he was ready for the road once more. Melanchthon, on the other hand, had had enough, and pleading illness he allowed someone else to supervise Martin. As though to serve as hostages guaranteeing his return, Martin's three sons went along with him, the Luthers being accompanied by an adult. Leaving Wittenberg on January 23, they stopped at Halle and picked up a second adult, Luther's old retainer Jonas, then headed for Eisleben. Here Luther was accommodated in a house belonging to the city government which on this visit served him as an inn as well as an office for the negotiations. Soon after arrival the Luther boys went on to Mansfeld to stay with their Uncle James. For this journey there is considerable documentation including several letters to his wife and Melanchthon. In these we get an interesting rendition of the jocose manner he affected as a cover for his anxiety, which helped make him such delightful company for those who did not challenge his theological views.

In a candid account to Melanchthon (February 1) of his behavior at one of the early sessions with the negotiators Martin admits he seriously offended one of the lawyers. As the man in question happened to be a member of the Wittenberg faculty, one can see why Luther was not universally popular with his academic colleagues. He also recognized his unfitness for dealing with questions of property rights, that is, the problems responsible for the alienation of the Counts of Mansfeld, as well as his complete lack of interest in such affairs. As the first week of negotiations drew to a close his disgust with the whole business reached a point where he wanted to pack up and leave for Wittenberg. In a letter of February 7 he declared that he was ready to grease the wagon wheels with his wrath and depart but was held back from deserting the proceedings by the distress his defection would have caused his fatherland. While it is apparent he was enacting his familiar role as a source of discord, the lawyers managed to overcome the additional obstacle provided by his presence along with the original problems. The biographers, with their penchant for the legendary, give Luther credit for reconciling the Counts.

But apart from the business which occasioned this visit to his native land, he was enjoying himself, especially at table. He describes with relish the flagon of imported wine the town council provides him with at each meal. Sometimes he drinks it all himself, sometimes he shares it with companions. Also he likes the local wine and especially the Neunburger beer, which both acts as a laxative (producing three stools in three hours) and fills his chest with phlegm. The devil is naturally blamed for this latter effect. By the end of the second week, most of the points at issue had been successfully negotiated. In the last letter he wrote — to Catherine on February 14 — he reports that the boys are still with their uncle and he is eating and drinking like a lord, echoing an earlier letter to her in July 1540 from Weimar: "I eat like a Bohemian and drink like a German, thank God. Amen."[13] Two days later the final treaty was drawn up. During the night of February 17-18 he felt ill; in particular he suffered chest pains and chills. Medical help was summoned and everything possible done for him but in the small hours of the morning he became unconscious and died suddenly from a heart attack or stroke. Of note was the question directed at him by Jonas just before he lost consciousness: Do you still stand by the doctrine you preached? to which Martin is reported to have given a positive answer. A point of interest is that Jonas, who had followed Luther out of the Church a quarter-century earlier, could at this late hour consider this a question worth asking.

The body was carried back to Wittenberg with great pomp and ceremony after memorial services at Eisleben and also at Halle en route, followed by considerable oratory at the Castle church, where by order of the Elector Luther was entombed. Thus the town from which he had run away the preceding summer and avowed he would never return to became his final resting place. A measure of his continued official stature is that on the present-day map of the national railroad system prepared by the West German government the two East German towns of Wittenberg and Eisleben both receive the additional designation of *Lutherstadt* (Luther city). No other town in either Germany is similarly distinguished.

We now turn back to the Monday preceding Luther's death to look at his last public utterance which, appropriately, was a sermon, delivered in the parish church of Eisleben. This discourse, running to about ten pages in the Weimar edition, is in two unequal parts, the major portion being devoted to the gospel read in the liturgy of the day. The remainder, little over a page, may be referred to as a coda to the sermon proper; it has nothing to do with the gospel excerpt, but is primarily an antisemitic outburst that Luther considered it important to leave as his final message to the parishioners of his native village.

The gospel text consists of the last six verses of Matthew 11, and these verses, like so much of the rest of this gospel, contain only the words of Jesus. The passage begins with an apostrophe of the Son to the Father: "I thank you, Father . . . that you have hidden these things from the wise and the clever and revealed them to the childlike." While Luther does not remark that this Johannine-like passage is unique in Matthew he evidently relished it, devoting to it the first half of the sermon. His treatment of it is characteristically Lutherian. The theme he proceeds to develop is that there are too many people in the world who think they are wiser than the rest and attempt to make their views prevail. One might guess that Luther could place himself at the head of the list of the wise and clever who insist on forcing all others to bow down before their superior wisdom. But in keeping with the paranoid's unawareness of his inner motivations and outward behavior, in his last sermon Luther assigns himself not to the class of the wise and clever but to the childlike. Passing from the sermon proper to its conclusion, we consider not the attack on the Jews but rather the remarkable expression of Luther's attitude toward the Father and more particularly the Son. Modern commentators on Luther's 'Christology' present markedly divergent interpretations of it.[14] A major reason for the divergence is that underlying Luther's awareness of Jesus there are at least four distinct referents — to employ a precise but rather ungainly term.

First there is the ordinary designation of Christ as the second Person of the Trinity, a traditional concept that Luther accepted without question and often repeated. Next there is the Christ of Judgment Day, the vindictive judge seated on a rainbow, an image that became implanted in Martin's disordered psyche in childhood. Third, there is Jesus as a man like Luther, into whom on occasion he projects his own pathological feelings. This man, as we have noted elsewhere, is at times a coward like Luther who flees from the threat of danger to his person, or who is unable to distinguish between the Law and the Gospel and has to be rescued from his anxiety states by angelic visitors. But this is the same man who at other times takes on himself all the sins of the world and it is the contemplation of this man suffering that fills Luther with joy.

The fourth of Luther's referents for Jesus Christ is not even human but a blend of a member of the animal kingdom and a lifeless object. As pointed out earlier, Luther particularized the bird figures that appear in a few places in Scripture into a brood hen clucking to its chicks and came to view himself as one of the chicks wriggling under the wings of the hen for protection from a hostile enemy — the wrathful God of his anxiety states. Possibly from the related scriptural figure — under the 'shadow of his wings' — Luther's not very poetic imagination conceived the image of a screen or veil beneath which the sinner could hide from the wrath of God. In one of the more elaborate developments of this topic, contained in a sermon of September 30, 1537, Luther ingeniously weaves his concept of the sinner who is always righteous into the image of the brood hen/screen.

> God will forgive and overlook your shame only while you remain beneath these wings. For as long as you stay under the cloak and screen and don't come out, the sin which is in you will not be sin on account of him who covers you with his righteousness.[15]

To relate this construct to other aspects of 'my theology' it can be said that Luther's anthropomorphic deity lacked a sufficiently keen vision to look through this screen (even though it was of his own manufacture) at the guilty culprit lurking behind it. The culprit was guilty because he had performed actions not of his own choosing but that he was forced to carry out at the dictates of this same vengeful deity, or more precisely at the instigation of his antagonist Satan. But this same deity could also present a merciful countenance to those who were predestined to find shelter behind the screen because of their 'faith.' Through long practice the image of Jesus as brood hen/screen had become so integrated into Luther's speech habits he could interject it smoothly into the antisemitic tirade with which he ended his last sermon. We bring to a close our portrait of Luther with this final public message that expresses in his unique personal style the ultimate solution of the problem which had driven him to enter and then leave a monastery and, in his single-minded quest for relief, set much of Europe by the ears.

> We will exercise Christian love toward them [the Jews] and pray that they may be converted and accept the Lord whom they rightly should honor. There can be no doubt that any one of them who will not do so is a most wicked Jew that will never leave off slandering Christ, and will suck you dry and kill you if he can. I beseech you to have no part of this alien sin. You have God enough to pray to, that he may be gracious to you and support your government. I myself pray every day in this fashion and duck behind the screen of God's son, whom I hold and honor as my Lord. To him I must run and flee when the devil, sin or some other misfortune afflicts me. For he is my screen, as broad as heaven and earth, and my brood hen, under whom I crawl to escape the wrath of God.[16]

NOTES

ABBREVIATIONS

CR   *Corpus Reformatorum.* (Halle, 1834 f.)
WA   *D. Martin Luthers Werke. Kritische Gesamtausgabe.* (Weimar, 1883 –)
WBr   *D. Martin Luthers Werke. Briefe.* (Weimar, 1930-70)
TR   *D. Martin Luthers Werke. Tischreden.* (Weimar, 1912-21)
C1   *Luthers Werke in Auswahl,* 8 vols. ed. O. Clemen et al. 3rd ed. (Berlin, 1966)
Smith   Preserved Smith, *Life and Letters of Martin Luther.* (Boston and New York, 1911)
Smith I, II *Luther's Correspondence and Other Contemporary Letters.* Vol. I ed. Preserved Smith. Vol. II ed. Smith and Charles Jacobs. (Philadelphia, 1913 and 1918)
LW   *Luther's Works.* (Philadelphia and St. Louis, 1955 f.) The largest selection to date of the writings, correspondence, etc., in English.

Bibliographical note: The present study of Luther is derived from the primary sources, which are listed here along with some forty secondary works. For additional background the reader may consult Hubert Jedin, *A History of the Council of Trent,* Vol. I (Edinburgh, 1957) and the Kolb-Noyes *Modern Clinical Psychiatry* (Philadelphia, 8th ed. 1973 or 9th ed. 1977)

Introduction

1. Preserved Smith, *Life and Letters of Martin Luther* (see above) 433
2. Karl Meissinger, *Der katholische Luther* (Munich, 1952) 11
3. Lucien Febvre, *Un destin: Martin Luther* (Paris, 1927; 4th ed. 1968) 22
4. Anna Freud, *The Ego and the Mechanisms of Defense* (London, 1937)
5. H. P. Laughlin, *The Ego and the Defenses* (New York, 1970)
6. Paul J. Reiter, *Luthers Umwelt, Charakter und Psychose* (Copenhagen, 1937-41)
7. Roland H. Bainton, *Here I Stand: A Life of Martin Luther* (Nashville, 1950)
8. Erik H. Erikson, *Young Man Luther* (New York, 1958)
9. Robert L. Fife, *The Revolt of Martin Luther* (New York, 1957)
10. Walter von Loewenich, *Luthers Theologia Crucis* (Munich, 1929; 4th ed. 1964)
11. Heinrich Denifle, *Luther und Luthertum* (Mainz, 1906)
12. Erwin Iserloh, *The Theses Were Not Posted* (Boston, 1968)

Chapter 1

1. "Explanations of the 95 Theses," WA 1, 557
2. WA 5, 209-10
3. CR 6, 158
4. WA 1, 374
5. WA 5, 89; 170
6. WA 40^I, 489
7. Placide Deseille in *Théologie de la vie monastique* (Paris, 1961) 503, f.
8. "Predestination of the Saints," Ch. 10
9. WA 56, 391-92
10. WA 1, 224 f.
11. WA 11, 189
12. WBr 1, 16-7
13. id., 513
14. *Confessions,* Bk. III. *Oeuvres Complètes* (Paris, 1959) I, 106-107
15. WA 6, 458
16. Lucien Febvre, op. cit., 25
17. Jared Wicks, *Man Yearning for Grace* (Washington, 1968) 267
18. TR 1, # 347
19. WBr 1, 35-6
20. WA 45, 513
21. "Luther's Debt to the *Imitatio Christi,*" AUGUSTINIANA, 28 (1978) 91-107
22. "On Marriage and Concupiscence," I, 25, 28
23. WA 56, 273-74
24. WA 9, 75

Chapter 2

1. WA 3, 372
2. Henri Strohl, *Luther Jusqu'en 1520* (Paris, 1962) 193 f.
3. WA 40^{III}, 199
4. WA 56, 299-300
5. id., 401
6. id., 370

7. WA 57, 169
8. WBr 1, 57
9. WA 56, 499
10. WBr 1, 59-60
11. WA 57, 114
12. WA 57, 169
13. Paul Hacker, *The Ego in Faith,* (Chicago, 1970) 9 f.
14. WA 57, 169-71
15. WA 1, 525-27
16. id., 540-41
17. id., 595-96
18. id., 329-34
19. WA 56, 446
20. Erwin Iserloh, op. cit.
21. Jared Wicks, op. cit., 241 f.
22. WBr 1, 193-94
23. id., 209-10
24. id., 172-74
25. *Martin Luthers Saemtliche Schriften,* ed. J. G. Walch (2nd ed. St. Louis, 1880-1910) XV, 605
26. WBr 1, 214-15
27. id., 190-91
28. A. Forest and F. van Steenberghen, *Le mouvement Doctrinal du XIe au XIVe siecle* (Paris, 1956) 404-405, note 1
29. CR 1, 269-70
30. WBr 1, 156
31. id., 344-45
32. id., 415
33. WBr. 2, 48-9
34. WA 2, 80-130
35. id., 99
36. WBr 1, 389
37. John Jortin, *Life of Erasmus* (London, 1808) 3, 58-59
38. id., 58
39. WA 2, 401
40. WBr 1, 503
41. WA 5, 434
42. WBr 1, 594-95
43. WBr 2, 42-5

44. id., 41-2
45. id. 48-9
46. WA 6, 174
47. WBr 2, 76
48. WA 15, 394
49. WA 6, 376-77
50. WBr 2, 72
51. id., 77-8
52. WA 6, 228
53. WBr 2, 85
54. WA 3, 282
55. WA 6, 362

Chapter 3

1. Franz Hipler, *Nikolaus Koper-niker und Martin Luther* (Braunsberg, 1868) 72-74
2. Norman Cameron, *Personality Development and Psychopathology* (Boston, 1963) 463
3. J. J. Rousseau, *Confessions,* op. cit., 36
4. Weimar ed. German Bible 6, 10
5. St. Bernard, *Oeuvres Complètes,* ed. Charpentier (Paris, 1867) III, 565
6. WA 8, 601
7. WA 47, 85
8. WA 14, 262
9. WA 38, 148
10. WA 6, 376-77
11. WA 12, 396
12. WBr 5, 518-20
13. Norman Cameron, op cit., 239
14. WA 7, 311
15. WA 10^{II}, 105
16. id., 107
17. "That a Christian Congregation Has the Right and Power to Judge All Doctrine, etc.," WA 11, 408 f.
18. WA 30^{III}, 521
19. id., 522
20. WA 43, 226

21. WBr 2, 125-26
22. id., 118-19
23. id., 120
24. WA 6, 328, 329
25. id., 347-48
26. WBr 2, 273-74
27. id., 134-36
28. WA 2, 110
29. WBr 2, 167
30. WA 6, 581
31. WA 6, 468-69
32. Christopher Dawson, *Dividing of Christendom* (New York, 1965) 68
33. WBr 2, 144-45
34. WA 3, 445
35. *Dict. de Théol. Cath.,* s. v. Bérenger de Tours, II, 722-740
36. WA 6, 526
37. id., 581
38. WBr 2, 195
39. WA 6, 604
40. WA 6, 621
41. WA 7, 146
42. WBr 2, 361-62
43. WBr 2, 290-91
44. id., 253-55
45. WA 7, 627
46. id., 669
47. id., 636
48. id., 675
49. id., 670
50. id., 671
51. WBr 2, 309
52. id., 333
53. id., 336
54. id., 365
55. id., 372

Chapter 4

1. *Jerome Biblical Commentary,* ed. R. E. Brown et al. (Englewood Cliffs, 1968) 43:115
2. W. F. Albright and C. S. Mann,

Matthew [Anchor Bible]
(Garden City, 1971) 197
3. WA 8, 173
4. id., 161
5. id., 157
6. id., 177
7. WA 7, 146-48
8. WA 8, 153
9. id., 389
10. WBr 2, 422-23
11. id., 506
12. id., 448-49
13. id., 453-57
14. id., 459-62
15. WA 10^{III}, 4
16. WBr 2, 478-79
17. id., 471
18. id., 509
19. id., 488
20. WBr 3, 196
21. Erasmus, *Opus Epistolarum*,
    ed. P. S. Allen (Oxford, 1928)
    VII, 198-201
22. WBr 2, 632-33
23. id., 506
24. WBr 3, 16-7
25. WA 10^{II}, 220
26. WA 18, 8-11
27. WBr 3, 34-35
28. id., 41-2
29. WA 12, 649
30. WBr 3, 376-77
31. WA 10^{II}, 29
32. WBr 9, 355-57
33. WA 11, 117
34. WA 18, 22-36
35. WA 11, 394-400
36. WBr 3, 109-10
37. id., 4-5
38. id., 641-43
39. id., 646-51
40. WBr 4, 3
41. id., 18
42. WBr 3, 148-53
43. Erasmus, op. cit., V, 387-89

44. WBr 2, 596-97
45. WBr 3, 563-64
46. WA 23, 26-37
47. id., 31

Chapter 5

1. Richard Simon, *Histoire Critique
   du Vieux Testament* (Paris,
   1678; 5th ed. Rotterdam, 1685)
   432
2. id., 337
3. WA 30^{II}, 466
4. WA 32, 353
5. WA 33, 106
6. id., 83
7. id., 90
8. id., 86-7
9. TR 2, # 1234
10. WA 47, 208-09
11. TR 2, # 1237
12. WA 25, 330
13. TR 5, # 5601
14. WA 12, 92-142
15. WBr 3, 557-58
16. Smith II, 337
17. WBr 3, 572
18. WBr 4, 131-32
19. WA 15, 339
20. E. W. Gritsch, *Reformer with-
    out a Church* (Philadelphia,
    1967)
21. *Thomas Muentzer, Schriften
    und Briefe,* ed. G. Franz and P.
    Kirn (Guetersloh, 1968) 491
22. E. W. Gritsch, op. cit. 106, 109
23. WA 11, 269
24. WA 15, 211
25. id., 214
26. id., 219
27 id., 215-16
28. WBr 3, 480-82
29. WA 18, 394-95
30. id., 399

31. id., 400
32. J. G. Walch, op. cit., XVII, 1526
33. WA 26, 462
34. WA 32, 506

Chapter 6

1. WA 18, 275-76
2. WA 56, 184
3. id., 185
4. WA 9, 215
5. TR 6, # 6816
6. WBr 2, 356-59
7. id., 396-98
8. id., 402-03
9. WA 1, 489
10. WA 5, 438
11. WA 8, 595-96
12. WA 10^{II}, 156
13. id., 152
14. id., 156
15. id., 118-22
16. id., 156
17. WBr 3, 533
18. id., 536-37
19. id., 541
20. CR 1, 754
21. WBr 3, 548-49
22. WA 16, 510-11
23. WA 40^{II}, 84
24. WA 10^{II}, 301
25. WBr 3, 230-31
26. WA 16, 378
27. WBr 4, 140
28. WBr 3, 616
29. id., 634-35
30. WBr 8, 278
31. WBr 4, 319
32. *Der Briefwechsel des Justus Jonas,* ed. G. Kawerau (Halle, 1884) 107
33. id., 104-07
34. S. Arieti, *American Handbook of Psychiatry* (New York, 2nd ed. 1974), III, 456

35. *Dr. Johann Bugenhagens Brief-wechsel,* ed. Otto Vogt, (Hildesheim, 1966) 69-70
36. WBr 4, 226-27
37. id., 228
38. id., 274
39. id., 263
40. id., 272
41. id., 279
42. id., 282
43. id., 299
44. WA 20, 767

Chapter 7

1. WA 18, 213-14
2. CR 21, 86
3. id., 98 and 100
4. id., 108-09
5. id., 149
6. J. Hastings, *Dictionary of the Bible* (New York, rev. ed. 1963) 582-83
7. WA 18, 646
8. Augustine, *City of God,* Bk. V, Ch. 10
9. Erasmus, op. cit., VI, 306-07
10. Erasmus, op. cit., X, 372
11. WA 26, 514
12. WA 18, 783
13. id., 633
14. id., 635
15. id., 719
16. WA 30^{I}, 426-27
17. CR 9, 766

Chapter 8

1. WBr 5, 68-9
2. WA 32, xxi-xxii
3. id., xvii-xxiii
4. WBr 5, 239-41
5. WBr 6, 103-6
6. Migne, *Patr. Lat.* 38, Serm. #172

7. WA 30^{II}, 390
8. WBr 5, 316-17
9. id., 330-32
10. Cl 6, 380; WBr 5, 584
11. WBr 5, 479-80
12. id., 399-400
13. id., 632-33
14. WA 30^{III}, 279-80
15. id., 331
16. WA 32, 398
17. WA 30^{III}, 471
18. WBr 6, 100-01
19. WA 40^{III}, 24
20. WA 38, 154
21. WA 38, 143
22. WA 8, 669
23. WBr 5, 652, note 4
24. WBr 6, 47-48
25. Smith, 281
26. WBr 6, 76-79
27. id., 82
28. id., 102
29. id., 161-63
30. id., 162-63 note
31. WBr 4, 83
32. WBr 7, 191 (June 15, 1535)
33. WA 40^{I}, 459
34. WA 40^{II}, 181

Chapter 9

1. WA 8, 412
2. WA 32, 431
3. WA 40^{I}, 295
4. WA 22, 307
5. WA 40^{II}, 331
6. WA 5, 123-24
7. id., 394-408
8. *Dict. de Théol. Cath.* 15, 3577-82
9. WA 38, 84
10. CR 5, 462 and 474
11. CR 3, 594
12. WA 50, 348
13. id., 389 f.
14. WBr 8, 121

15. id., 186
16. id., 179-84
17. WA 51, 425 f.
18. WBr 11, 85 and 98
19. WBr 8, 638-44
20. id., 643
21. WA 30^{II}, 130
22. WBr 9, 131-35
23. id., 150-55
24. id., 199-204
25. id., 233-35

Chapter 10

1. WA 5, 429
2. WA 53, 542-43
3. id., 600-01
4. id., 636-37
5. id., 574
6. WA 54, 287
7. WA 8, 715
8. WA 54, 221
9. WBr 11, 94-95
10. WBr 9, 571-74
11. WBr 11, 148
12. id., 263-64
13. WBr 9, 168
14. I. D. K. Siggins, *Martin Luther's Doctrine of Christ* (New Haven, 1970)
15. WA 45, 153
16. WA 51, 195-96